It's volume 13!! Thanks for picking it up! Season 2 of
the anime is starting! I'm ready to be wowed again by
the sight of Deku and Katsuki moving around.

KOHEI HORIKOSHI

13

SHONEN JUMP Manga Edition

STORY & ART **KOHEI HORIKOSHI**

TRANSLATION & ENGLISH ADAPTATION **Caleb Cook**
TOUCH-UP ART & LETTERING **John Hunt**
DESIGNER **Julian [JR] Robinson**
SHONEN JUMP SERIES EDITOR **John Bae**
GRAPHIC NOVEL EDITOR **Mike Montesa**

BOKU NO HERO ACADEMIA © 2014 by Kohei Horikoshi
All rights reserved.
First published in Japan in 2014 by SHUEISHA Inc., Tokyo.
English translation rights arranged by SHUEISHA Inc.

The stories, characters and incidents mentioned in this publication are entirely fictional.

Printed in the U.S.A.

Published by VIZ Media, LLC
P.O. Box 77010
San Francisco, CA 94107

10 9 8 7 6 5 4 3 2 1
First printing, June 2018

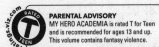

PARENTAL ADVISORY
MY HERO ACADEMIA is rated T for Teen
and is recommended for ages 13 and up.
This volume contains fantasy violence.

MY HERO ACADEMIA

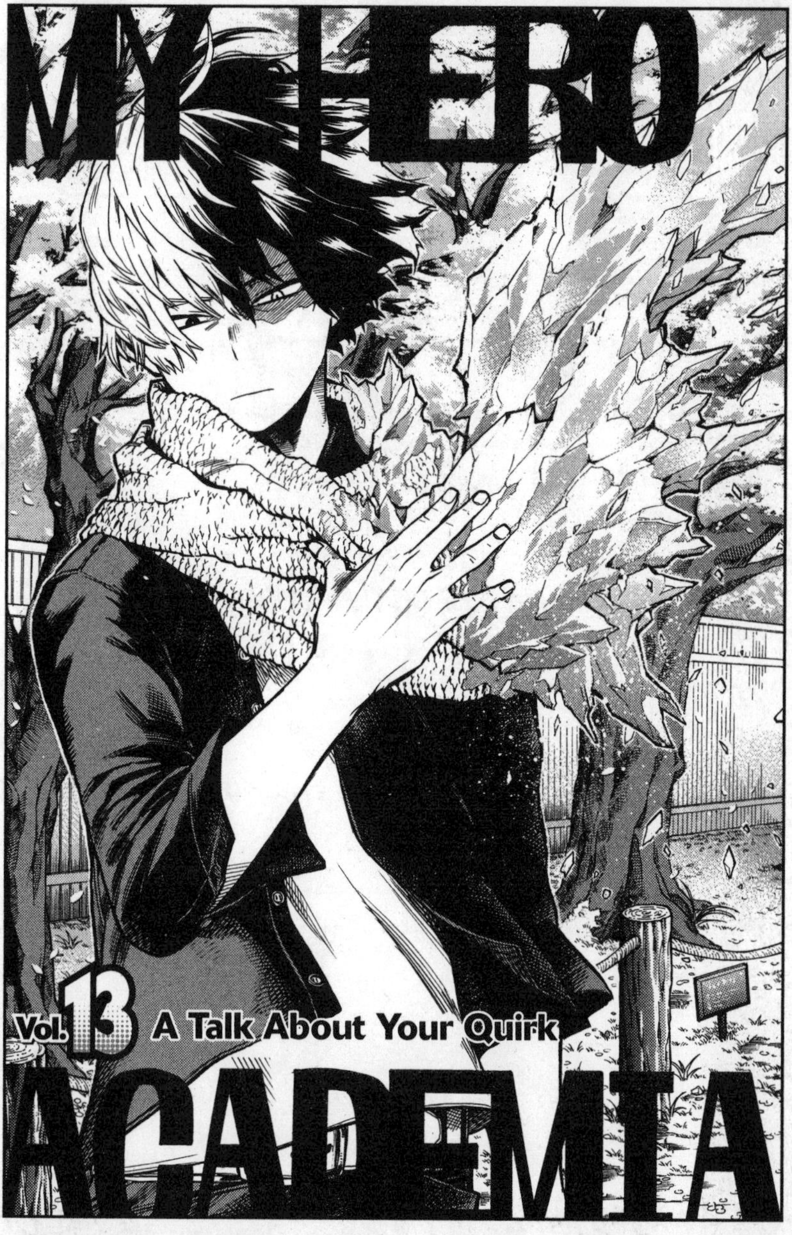
MY HERO
Vol. 13 A Talk About Your Quirk
ACADEMIA

KOHEI HORIKOSHI

SHONEN JUMP MANGA

CHARACTERS

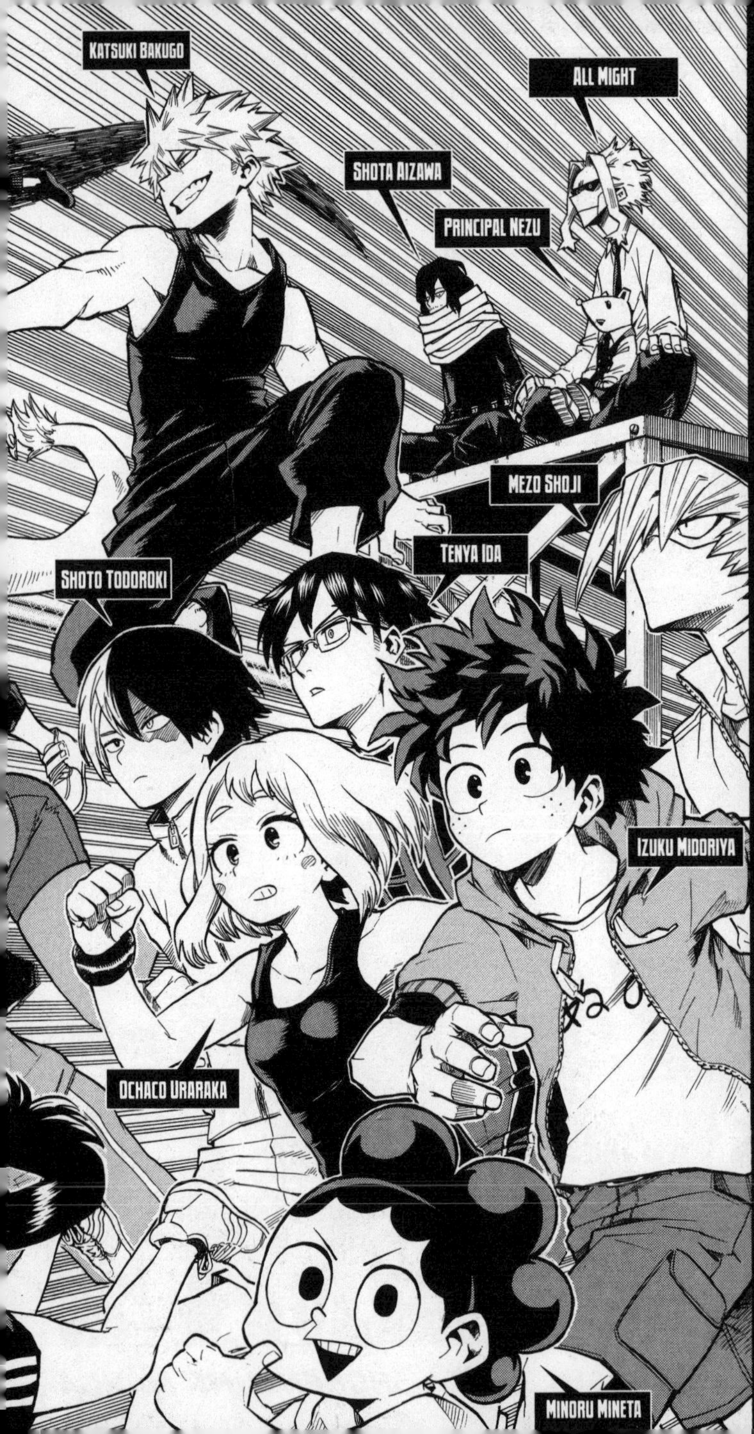
All Might
Katsuki Bakugo
Shota Aizawa
Principal Nezu
Mezo Shoji
Tenya Ida
Shoto Todoroki
Izuku Midoriya
Ochaco Uraraka
Minoru Mineta

One day, people began manifesting special abilities that came to be known as "Quirks," and before long, the world was full of superpowered humans. But with the advent of these exceptional individuals came an increase in crime, and governments alone were unable to deal with the situation. At the same time, others emerged to oppose the spread of evil! As if straight from the comic books, these heroes keep the peace and are even officially authorized to fight crime. Our story begins when a certain Quirkless boy and lifelong hero fan meets the world's number one hero, starting him on his path to becoming the greatest hero ever!

STORY

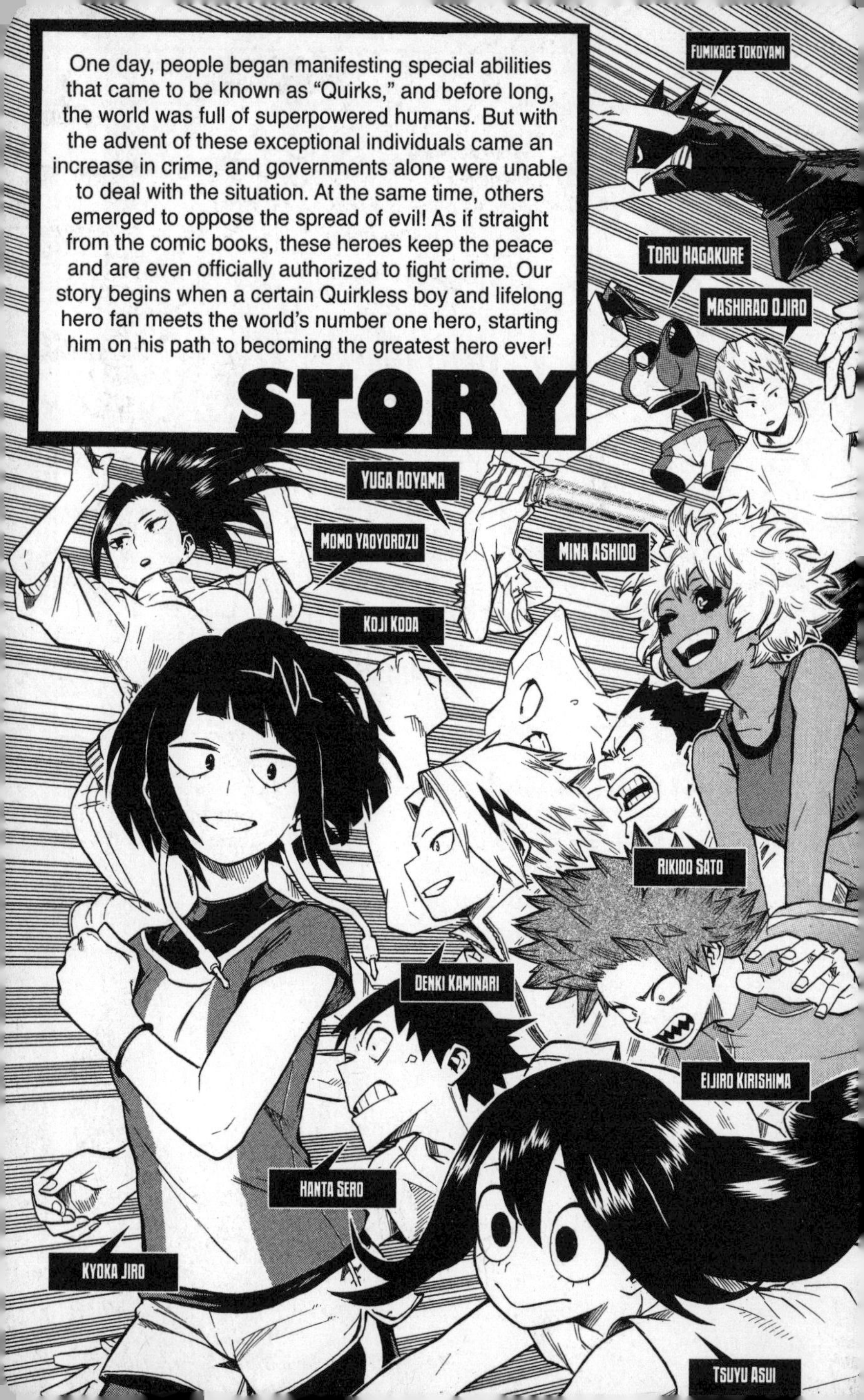

FUMIKAGE TOKOYAMI
TORU HAGAKURE
MASHIRAO OJIRO
YUGA AOYAMA
MINA ASHIDO
MOMO YAOYOROZU
KOJI KODA
RIKIDO SATO
DENKI KAMINARI
EIJIRO KIRISHIMA
HANTA SERO
KYOKA JIRO
TSUYU ASUI

A Talk About Your Quirk

MY HERO ACADEMIA

CONTENTS

Vol. 13

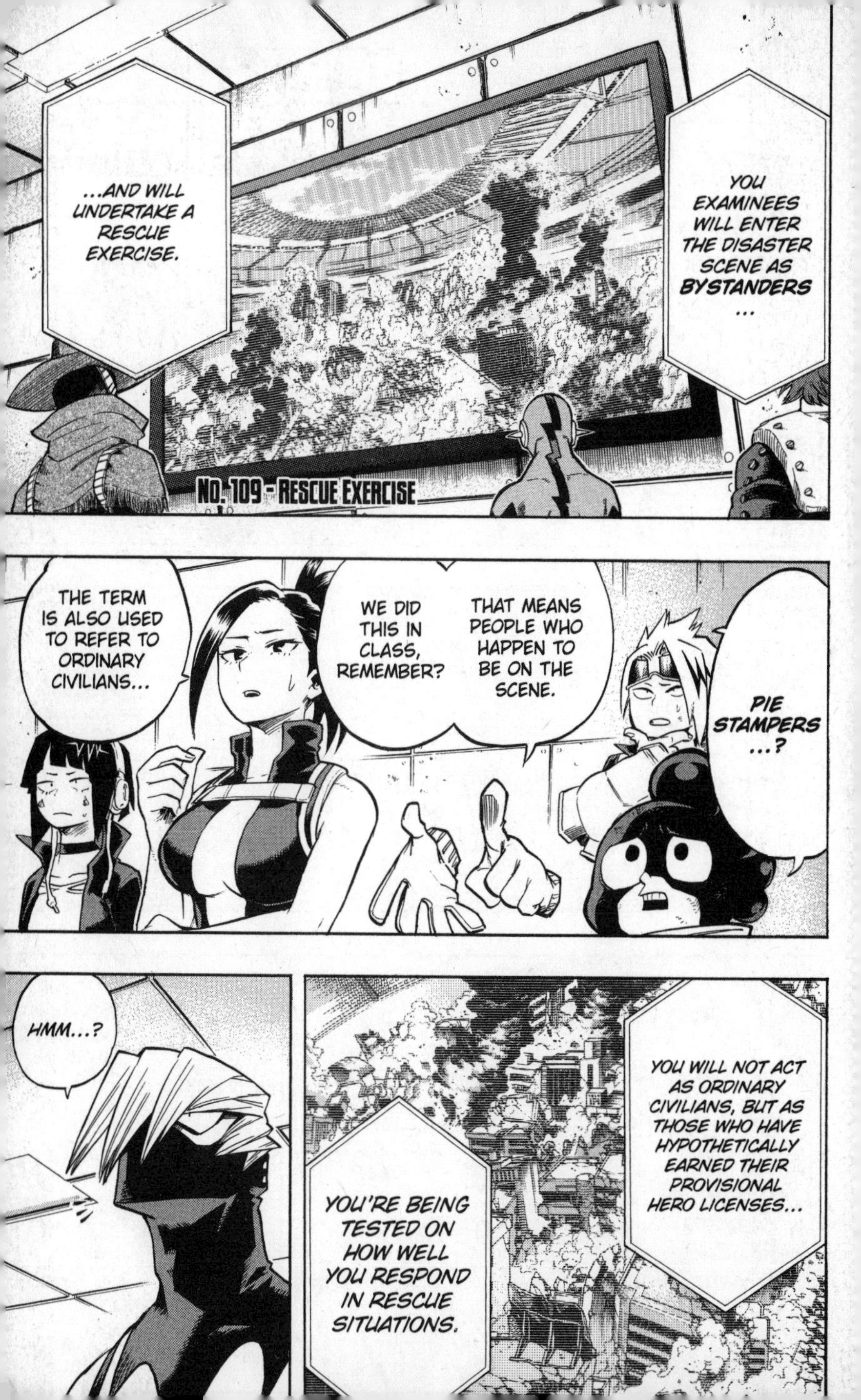
YOU EXAMINEES WILL ENTER THE DISASTER SCENE AS BYSTANDERS ...
...AND WILL UNDERTAKE A RESCUE EXERCISE.
No. 109 - RESCUE EXERCISE
PIE STAMPERS ...?
THAT MEANS PEOPLE WHO HAPPEN TO BE ON THE SCENE.
WE DID THIS IN CLASS, REMEMBER?
THE TERM IS ALSO USED TO REFER TO ORDINARY CIVILIANS...
YOU WILL NOT ACT AS ORDINARY CIVILIANS, BUT AS THOSE WHO HAVE HYPOTHETICALLY EARNED THEIR PROVISIONAL HERO LICENSES...
YOU'RE BEING TESTED ON HOW WELL YOU RESPOND IN RESCUE SITUATIONS.
HMM...?

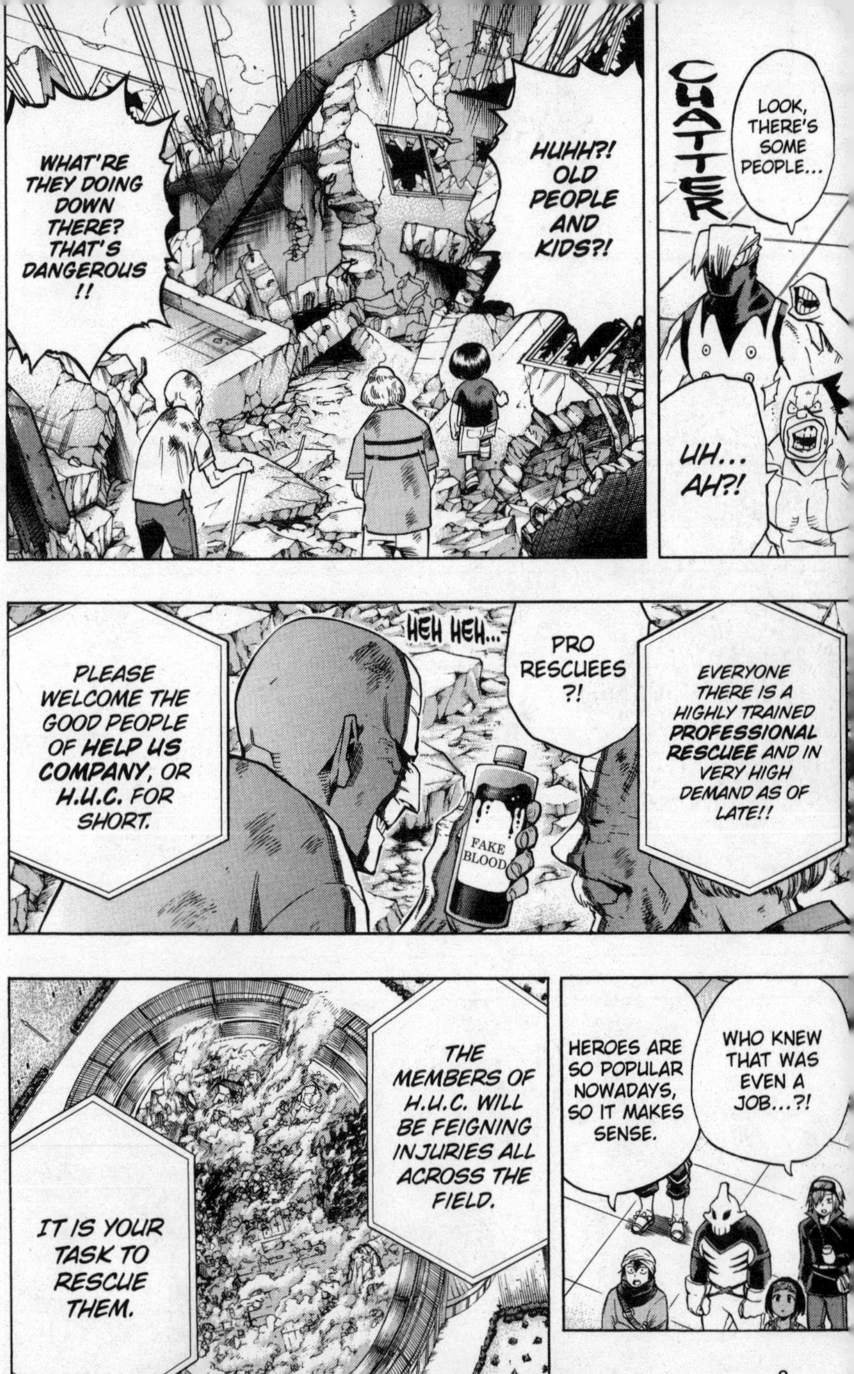

LOOK, THERE'S SOME PEOPLE...
CHATTER
UH... AH?!
HUHH?! OLD PEOPLE AND KIDS?!
WHAT'RE THEY DOING DOWN THERE? THAT'S DANGEROUS!!
EVERYONE THERE IS A HIGHLY TRAINED PROFESSIONAL RESCUEE AND IN VERY HIGH DEMAND AS OF LATE!!
PRO RESCUEES?!
HEH HEH...
PLEASE WELCOME THE GOOD PEOPLE OF HELP US COMPANY, OR H.U.C. FOR SHORT.
FAKE BLOOD
WHO KNEW THAT WAS EVEN A JOB...?!
HEROES ARE SO POPULAR NOWADAYS, SO IT MAKES SENSE.
THE MEMBERS OF H.U.C. WILL BE FEIGNING INJURIES ALL ACROSS THE FIELD.
IT IS YOUR TASK TO RESCUE THEM.

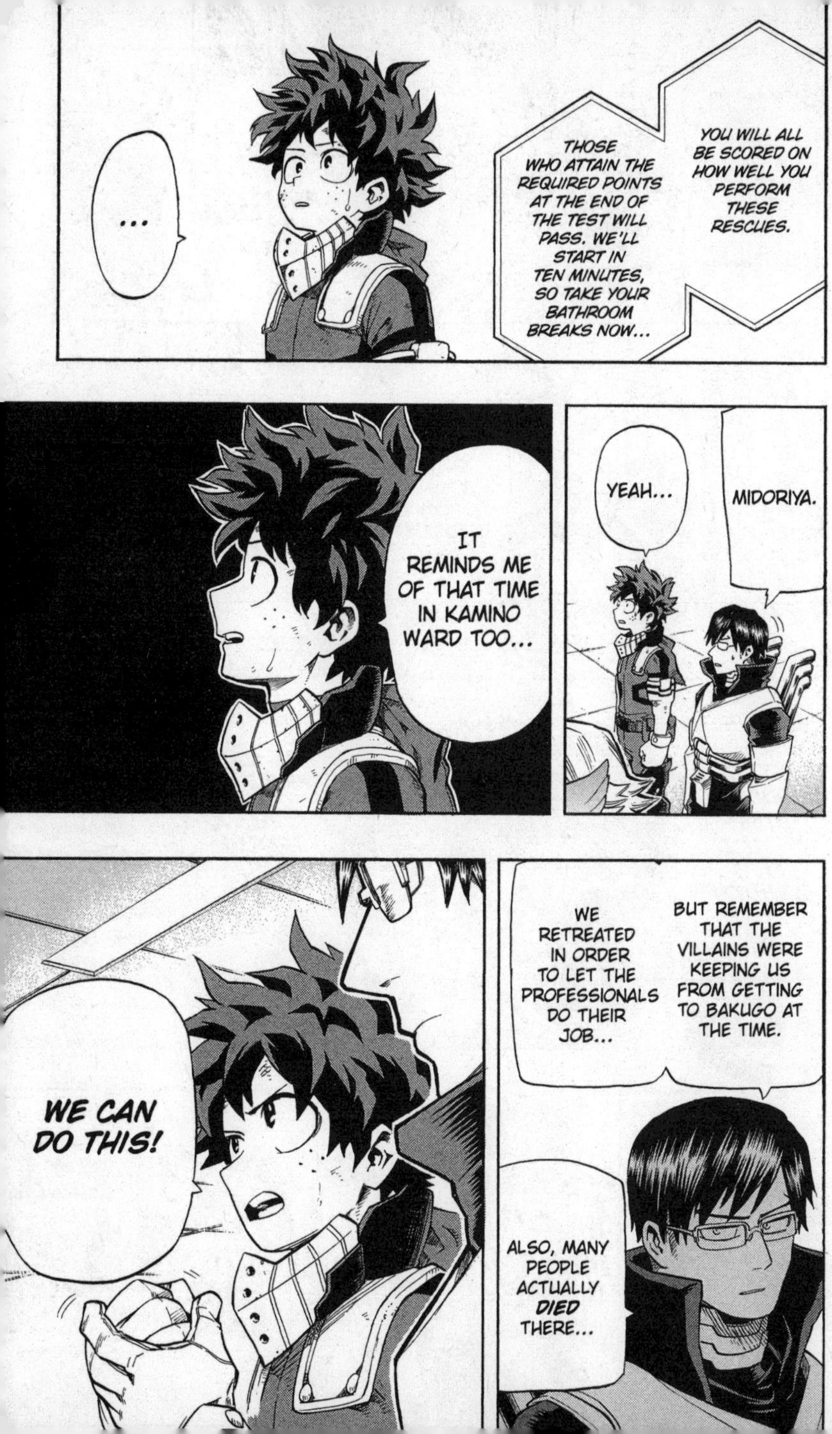
YOU WILL ALL BE SCORED ON HOW WELL YOU PERFORM THESE RESCUES.
THOSE WHO ATTAIN THE REQUIRED POINTS AT THE END OF THE TEST WILL PASS. WE'LL START IN TEN MINUTES, SO TAKE YOUR BATHROOM BREAKS NOW...
...
MIDORIYA.
YEAH...
IT REMINDS ME OF THAT TIME IN KAMINO WARD TOO...
BUT REMEMBER THAT THE VILLAINS WERE KEEPING US FROM GETTING TO BAKUGO AT THE TIME.
WE RETREATED IN ORDER TO LET THE PROFESSIONALS DO THEIR JOB...
ALSO, MANY PEOPLE ACTUALLY DIED THERE...
WE CAN DO THIS!

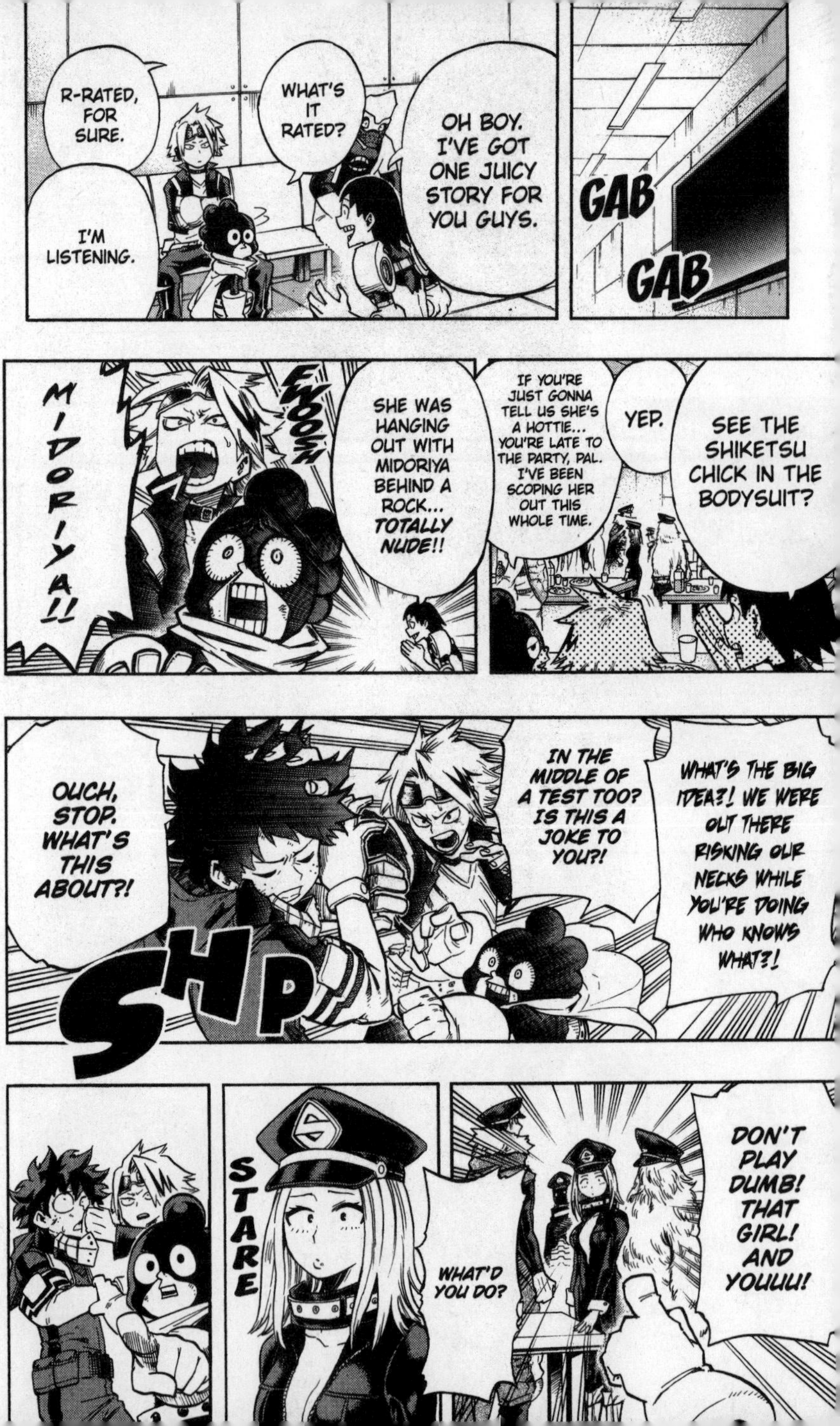
GAB
GAB
OH BOY. I'VE GOT ONE JUICY STORY FOR YOU GUYS.
WHAT'S IT RATED?
R-RATED, FOR SURE.
I'M LISTENING.
SEE THE SHIKETSU CHICK IN THE BODYSUIT?
YEP.
IF YOU'RE JUST GONNA TELL US SHE'S A HOTTIE... YOU'RE LATE TO THE PARTY, PAL. I'VE BEEN SCOPING HER OUT THIS WHOLE TIME.
SHE WAS HANGING OUT WITH MIDORIYA BEHIND A ROCK... *TOTALLY NUDE!!*
FWOOSH
MIDORIYA!!
WHAT'S THE BIG IDEA?! WE WERE OUT THERE RISKING OUR NECKS WHILE YOU'RE DOING WHO KNOWS WHAT?!
IN THE MIDDLE OF A TEST TOO? IS THIS A JOKE TO YOU?!
OUCH, STOP. WHAT'S THIS ABOUT?!
SHP
DON'T PLAY DUMB! THAT GIRL! AND YOUUU!
WHAT'D YOU DO?
STARE

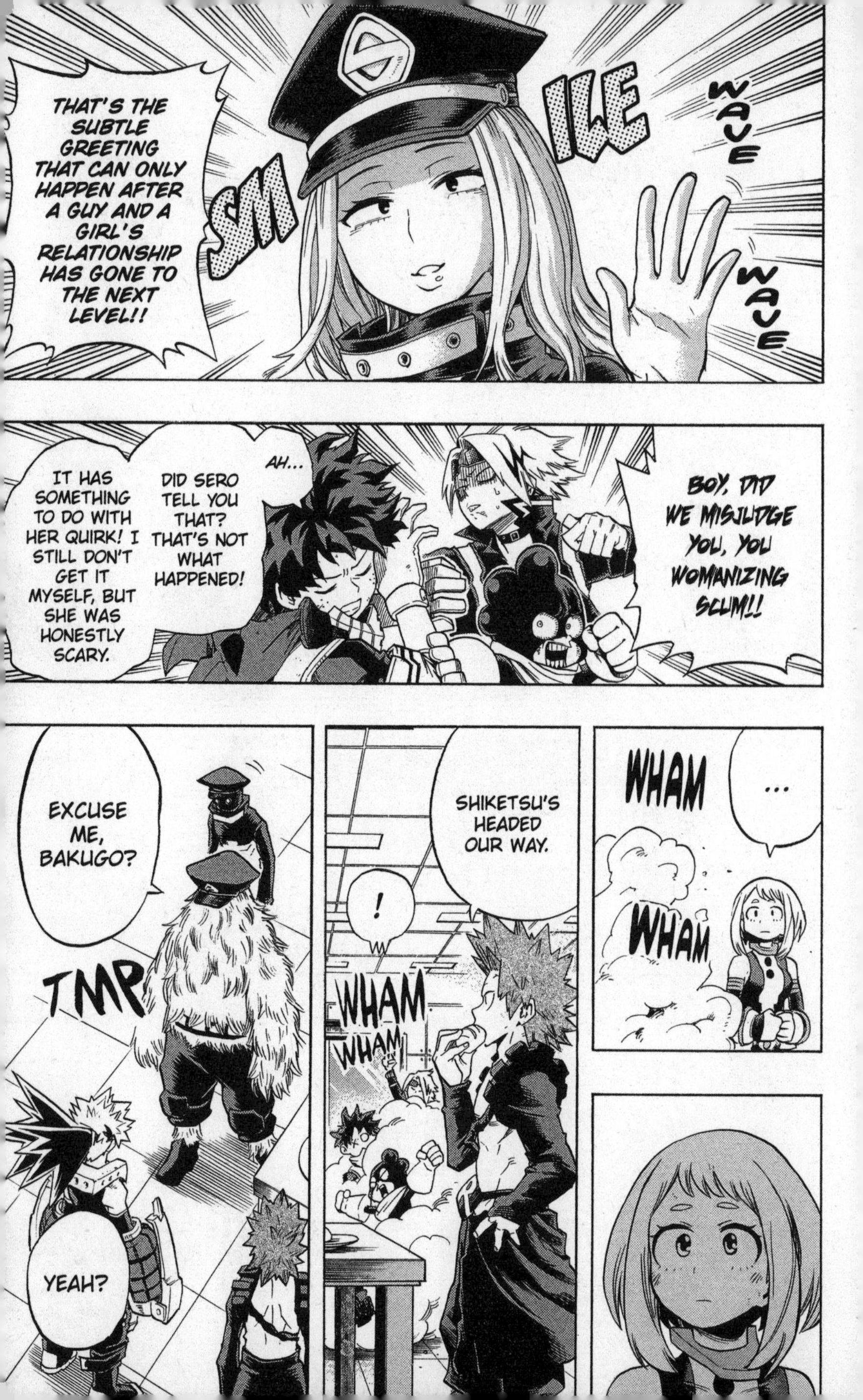
WAVE
WAVE
SMILE
THAT'S THE SUBTLE GREETING THAT CAN ONLY HAPPEN AFTER A GUY AND A GIRL'S RELATIONSHIP HAS GONE TO THE NEXT LEVEL!!
BOY, DID WE MISJUDGE YOU, YOU WOMANIZING SCUM!!
AH...
DID SERO TELL YOU THAT? THAT'S NOT WHAT HAPPENED!
IT HAS SOMETHING TO DO WITH HER QUIRK! I STILL DON'T GET IT MYSELF, BUT SHE WAS HONESTLY SCARY.
...
WHAM
WHAM
SHIKETSU'S HEADED OUR WAY.
!
WHAM
WHAM
EXCUSE ME, BAKUGO?
TMP
YEAH?

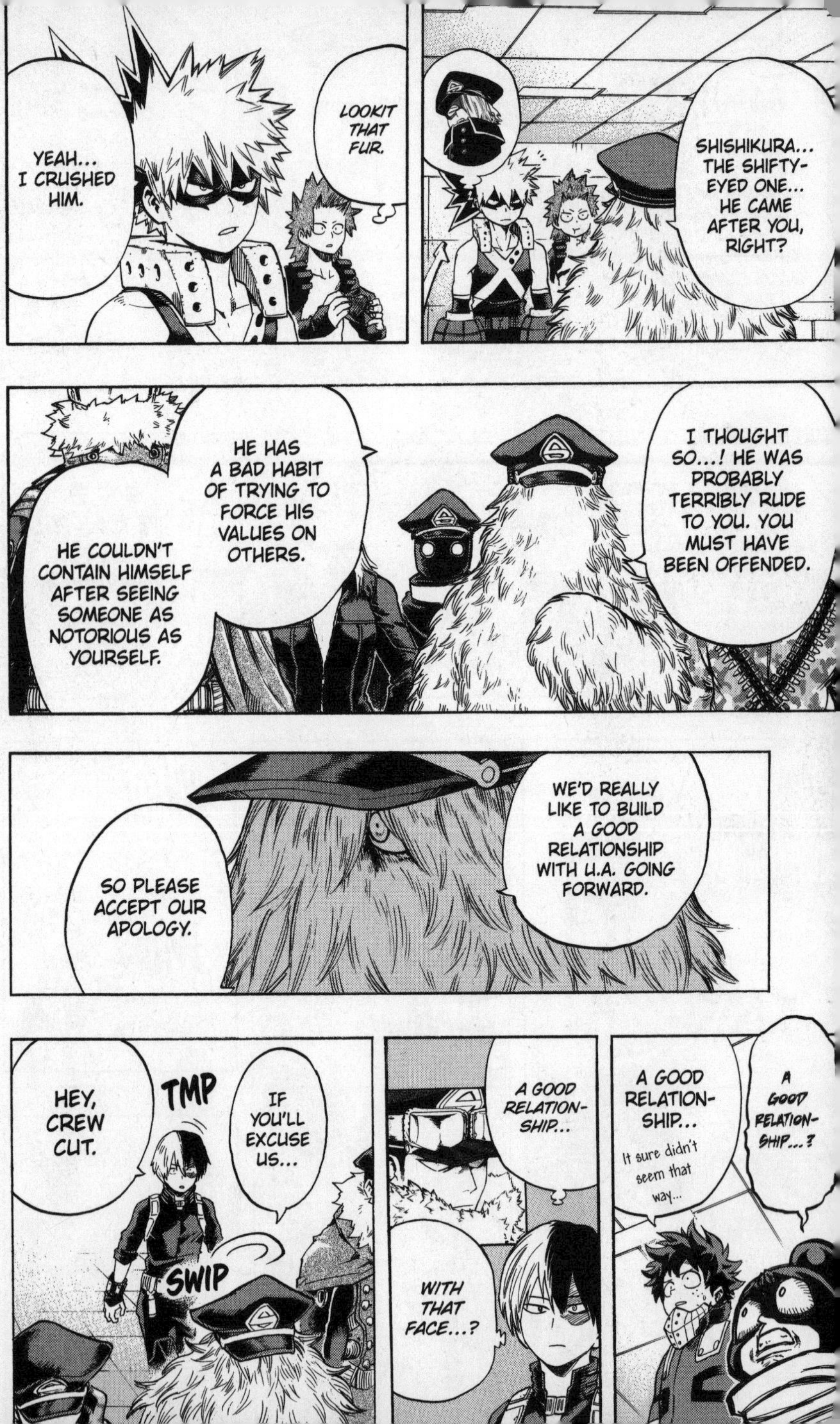
SHISHIKURA... THE SHIFTY-EYED ONE... HE CAME AFTER YOU, RIGHT?
LOOKIT THAT FUR.
YEAH... I CRUSHED HIM.
I THOUGHT SO...! HE WAS PROBABLY TERRIBLY RUDE TO YOU. YOU MUST HAVE BEEN OFFENDED.
HE HAS A BAD HABIT OF TRYING TO FORCE HIS VALUES ON OTHERS.
HE COULDN'T CONTAIN HIMSELF AFTER SEEING SOMEONE AS NOTORIOUS AS YOURSELF.
WE'D REALLY LIKE TO BUILD A GOOD RELATIONSHIP WITH U.A. GOING FORWARD.
SO PLEASE ACCEPT OUR APOLOGY.
A GOOD RELATIONSHIP...?
A GOOD RELATIONSHIP...
It sure didn't seem that way...
A GOOD RELATIONSHIP...
WITH THAT FACE...?
IF YOU'LL EXCUSE US...
TMP
HEY, CREW CUT.
SWIP

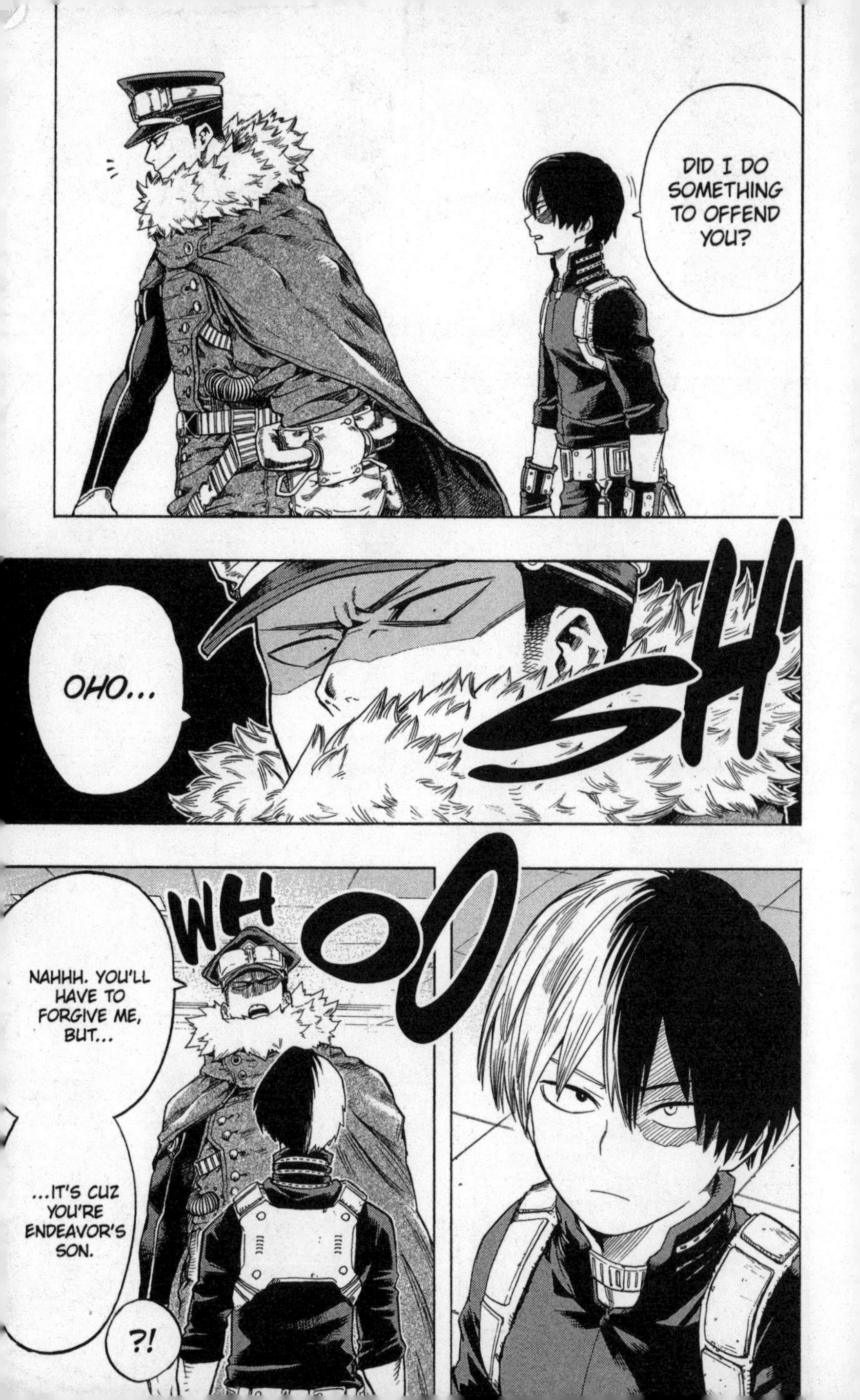
DID I DO SOMETHING TO OFFEND YOU?
SH
OHO...
WHOO
NAHHH. YOU'LL HAVE TO FORGIVE ME, BUT...
...IT'S CUZ YOU'RE ENDEAVOR'S SON.
?!

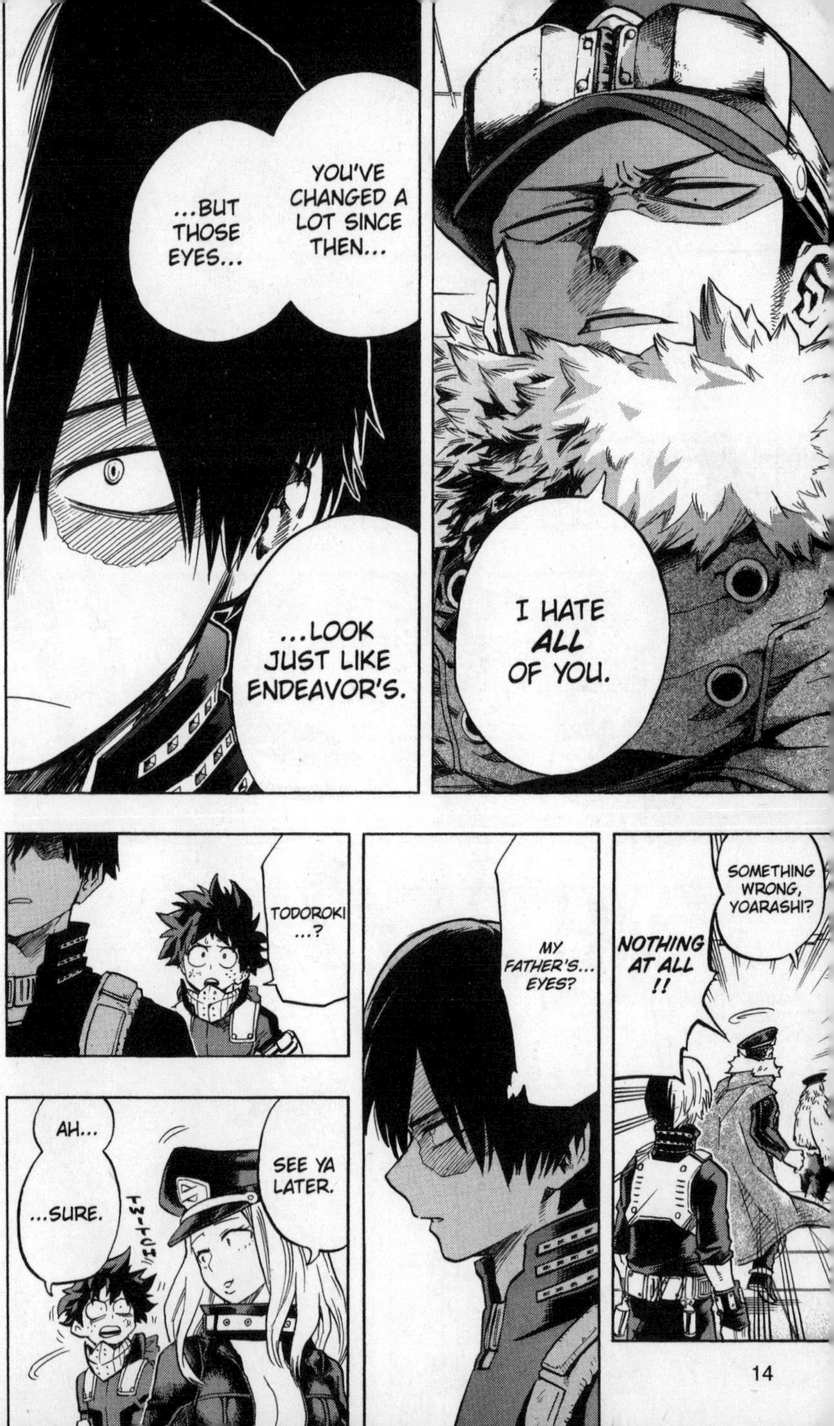
I HATE ALL OF YOU.
YOU'VE CHANGED A LOT SINCE THEN...
...BUT THOSE EYES...
...LOOK JUST LIKE ENDEAVOR'S.
SOMETHING WRONG, YOARASHI?
NOTHING AT ALL !!
MY FATHER'S... EYES?
TODOROKI ...?
SEE YA LATER.
AH...
...SURE.
TWITCH

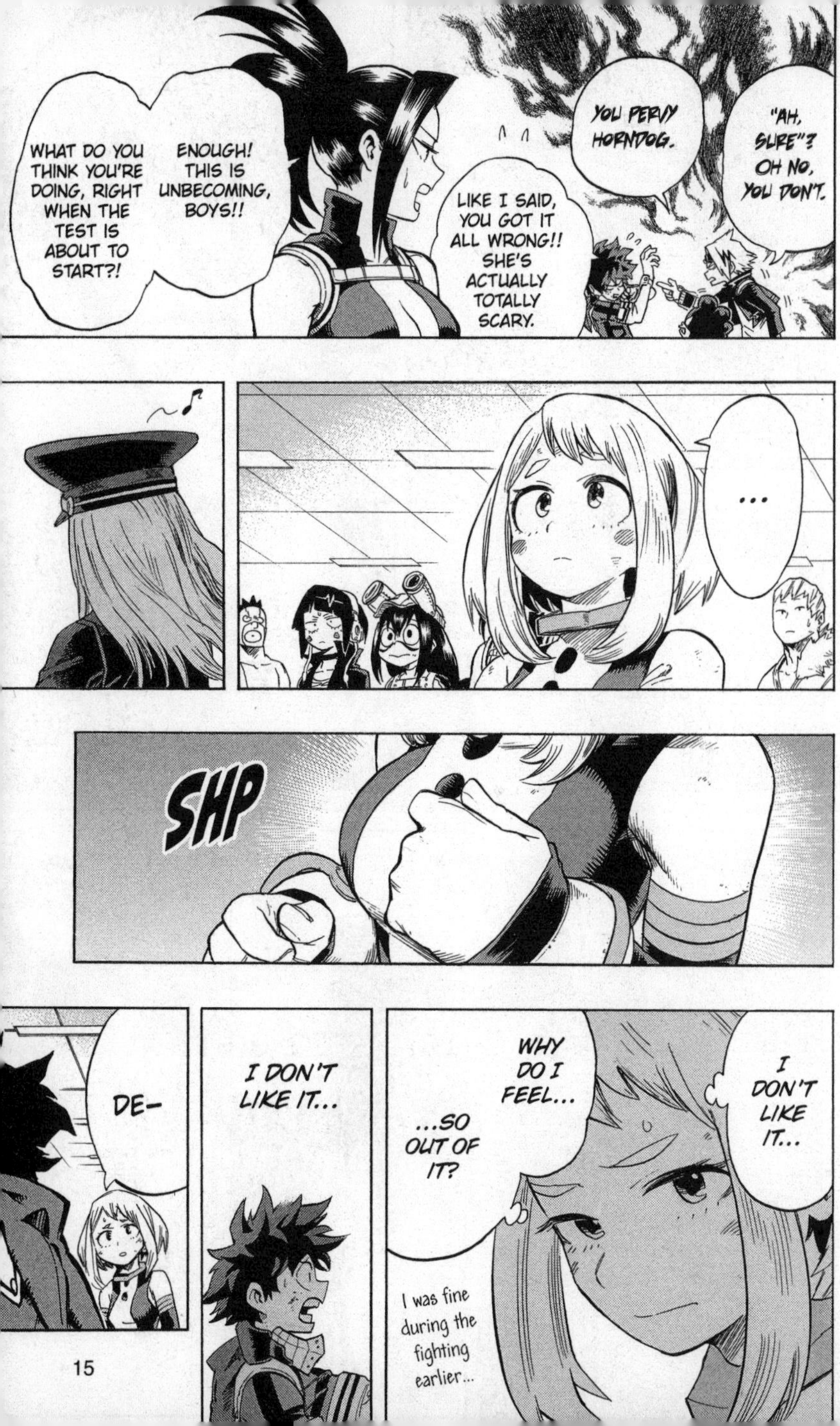
"AH, SURE"? OH NO, YOU DON'T.
YOU PERVY HORNDOG.
LIKE I SAID, YOU GOT IT ALL WRONG!! SHE'S ACTUALLY TOTALLY SCARY.
ENOUGH! THIS IS UNBECOMING, BOYS!!
WHAT DO YOU THINK YOU'RE DOING, RIGHT WHEN THE TEST IS ABOUT TO START?!
...
SHP
I DON'T LIKE IT...
WHY DO I FEEL...
...SO OUT OF IT?
I was fine during the fighting earlier...
I DON'T LIKE IT...
DE-

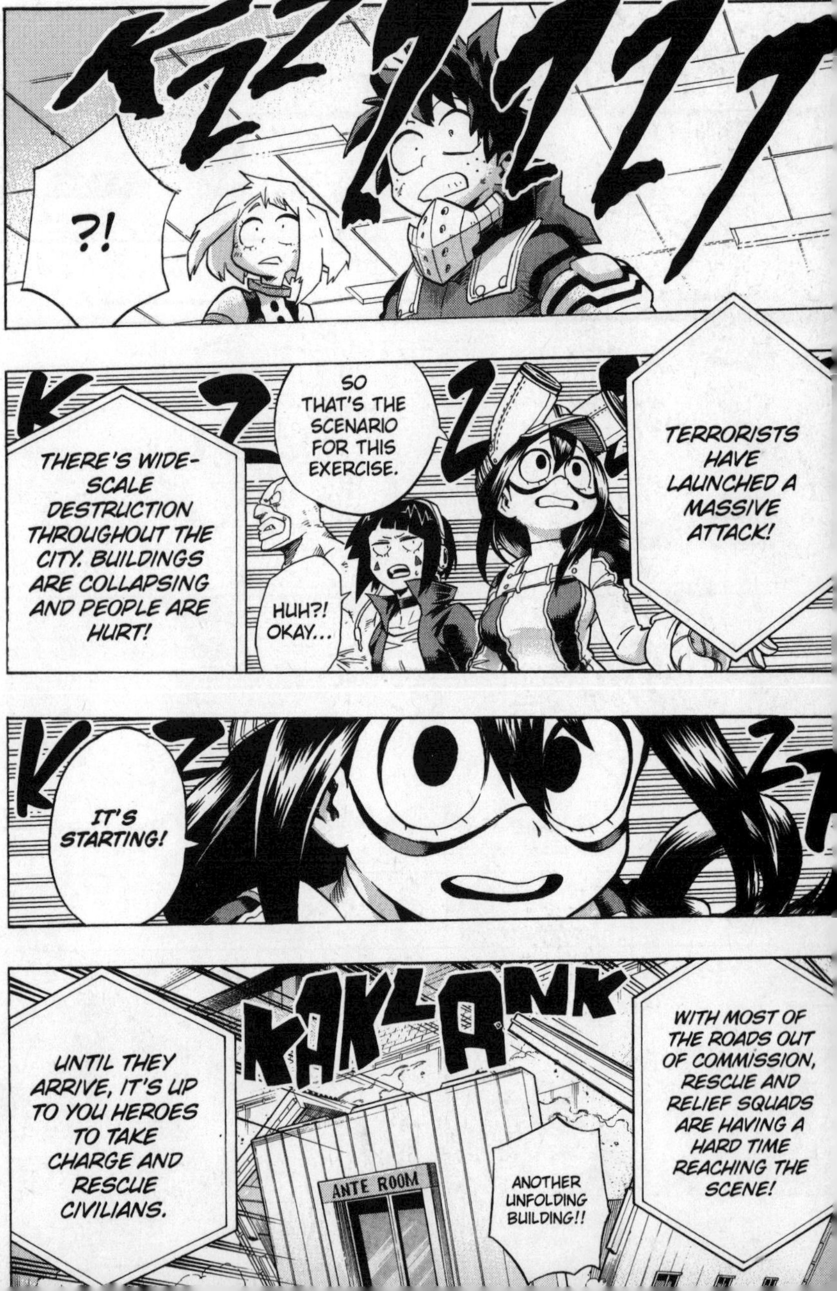
KZZZZZZZ
?!
TERRORISTS HAVE LAUNCHED A MASSIVE ATTACK!
SO THAT'S THE SCENARIO FOR THIS EXERCISE.
THERE'S WIDE-SCALE DESTRUCTION THROUGHOUT THE CITY. BUILDINGS ARE COLLAPSING AND PEOPLE ARE HURT!
HUH?! OKAY...
IT'S STARTING!
WITH MOST OF THE ROADS OUT OF COMMISSION, RESCUE AND RELIEF SQUADS ARE HAVING A HARD TIME REACHING THE SCENE!
KAKLANK
ANOTHER UNFOLDING BUILDING!!
ANTE ROOM
UNTIL THEY ARRIVE, IT'S UP TO YOU HEROES TO TAKE CHARGE AND RESCUE CIVILIANS.

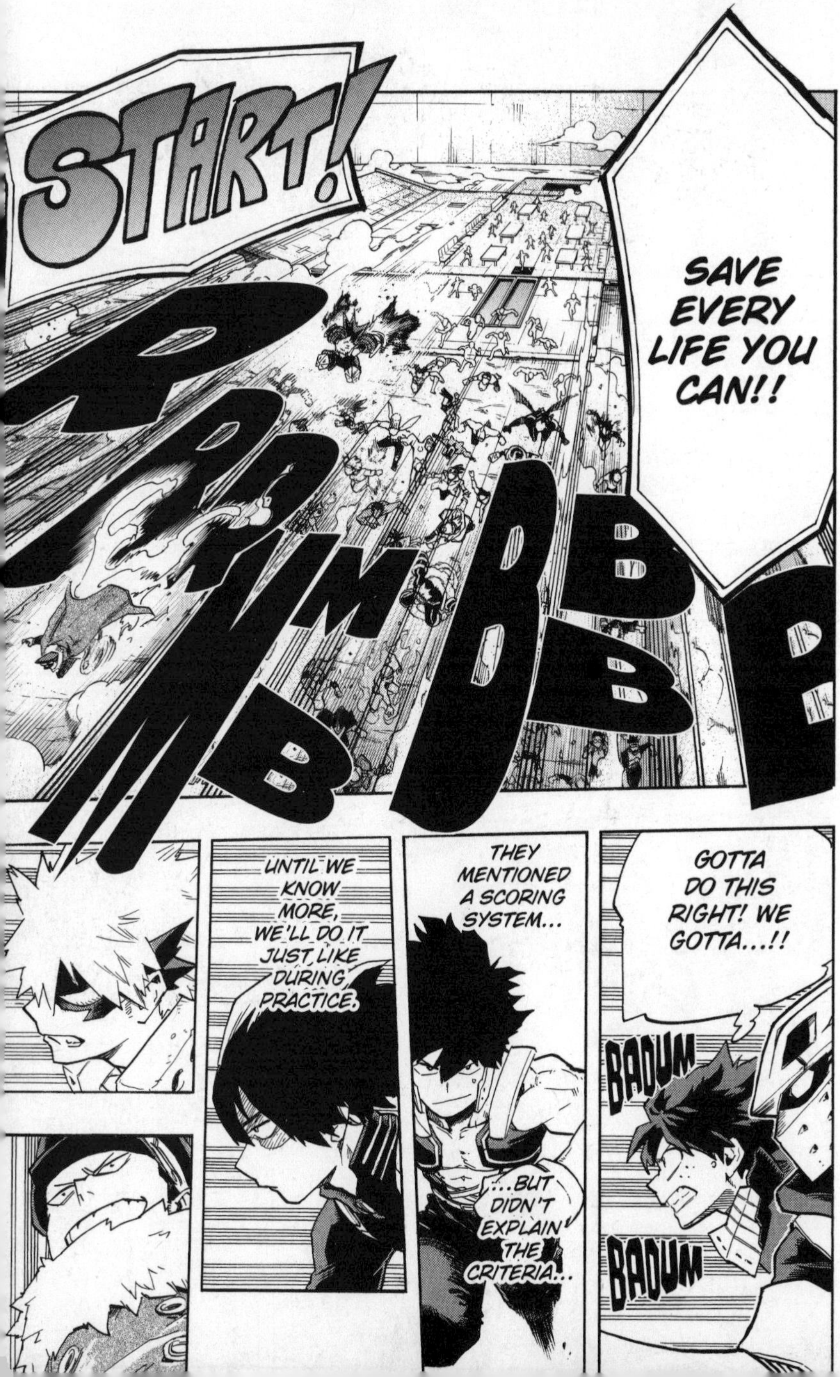
SAVE EVERY LIFE YOU CAN!!
START!
GOTTA DO THIS RIGHT! WE GOTTA...!!
BADUM
BADUM
THEY MENTIONED A SCORING SYSTEM...
...BUT DIDN'T EXPLAIN THE CRITERIA...
UNTIL WE KNOW MORE, WE'LL DO IT JUST LIKE DURING PRACTICE.

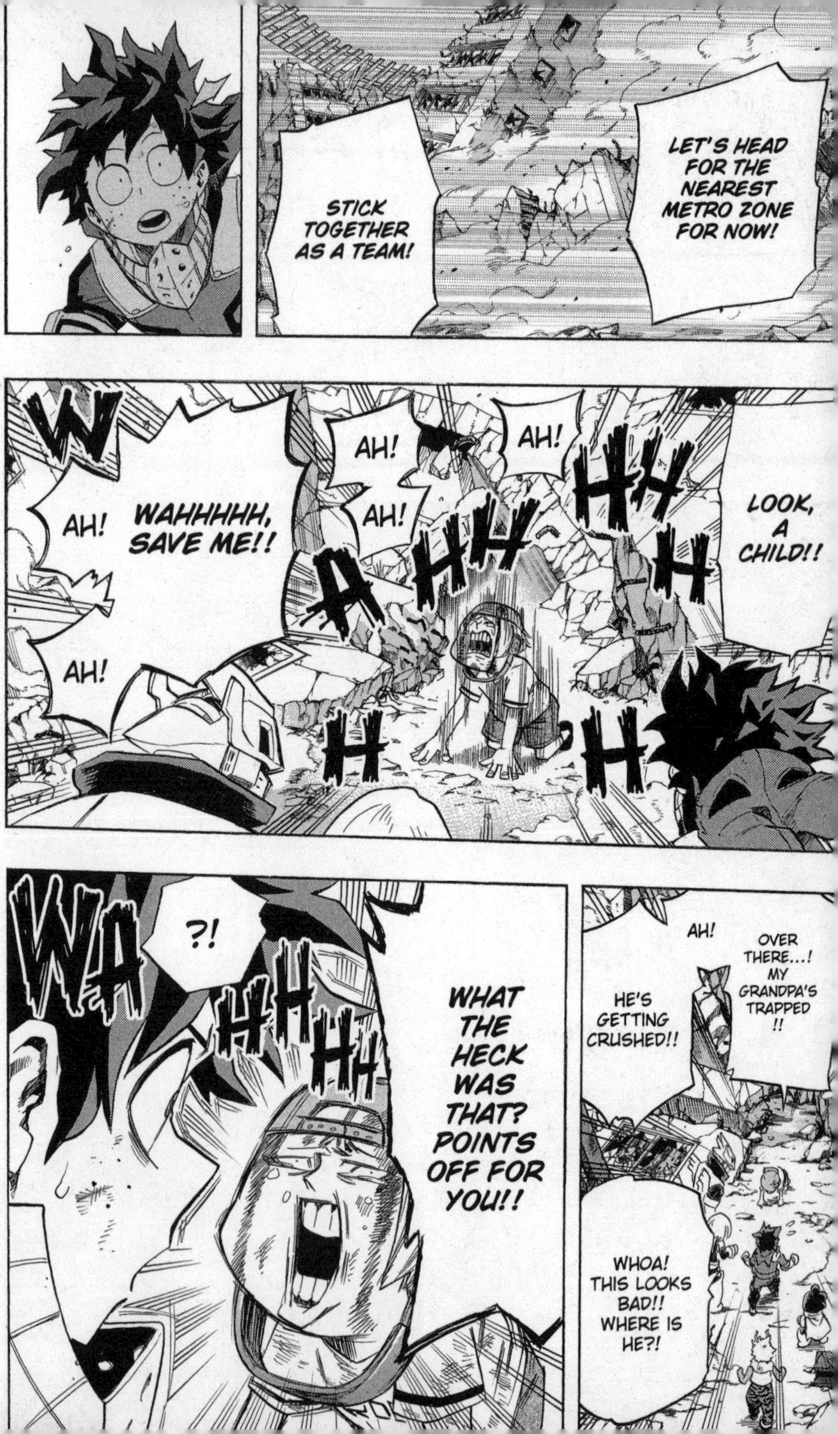
LET'S HEAD FOR THE NEAREST METRO ZONE FOR NOW!
STICK TOGETHER AS A TEAM!
LOOK, A CHILD!!
AH!
AH!
AH!
WAHHHHH, SAVE ME!!
AH!
AH!
OVER THERE...! MY GRANDPA'S TRAPPED!!
AH!
HE'S GETTING CRUSHED!!
WHOA! THIS LOOKS BAD!! WHERE IS HE?!
WHAT THE HECK WAS THAT? POINTS OFF FOR YOU!!
?!
WAHHHH

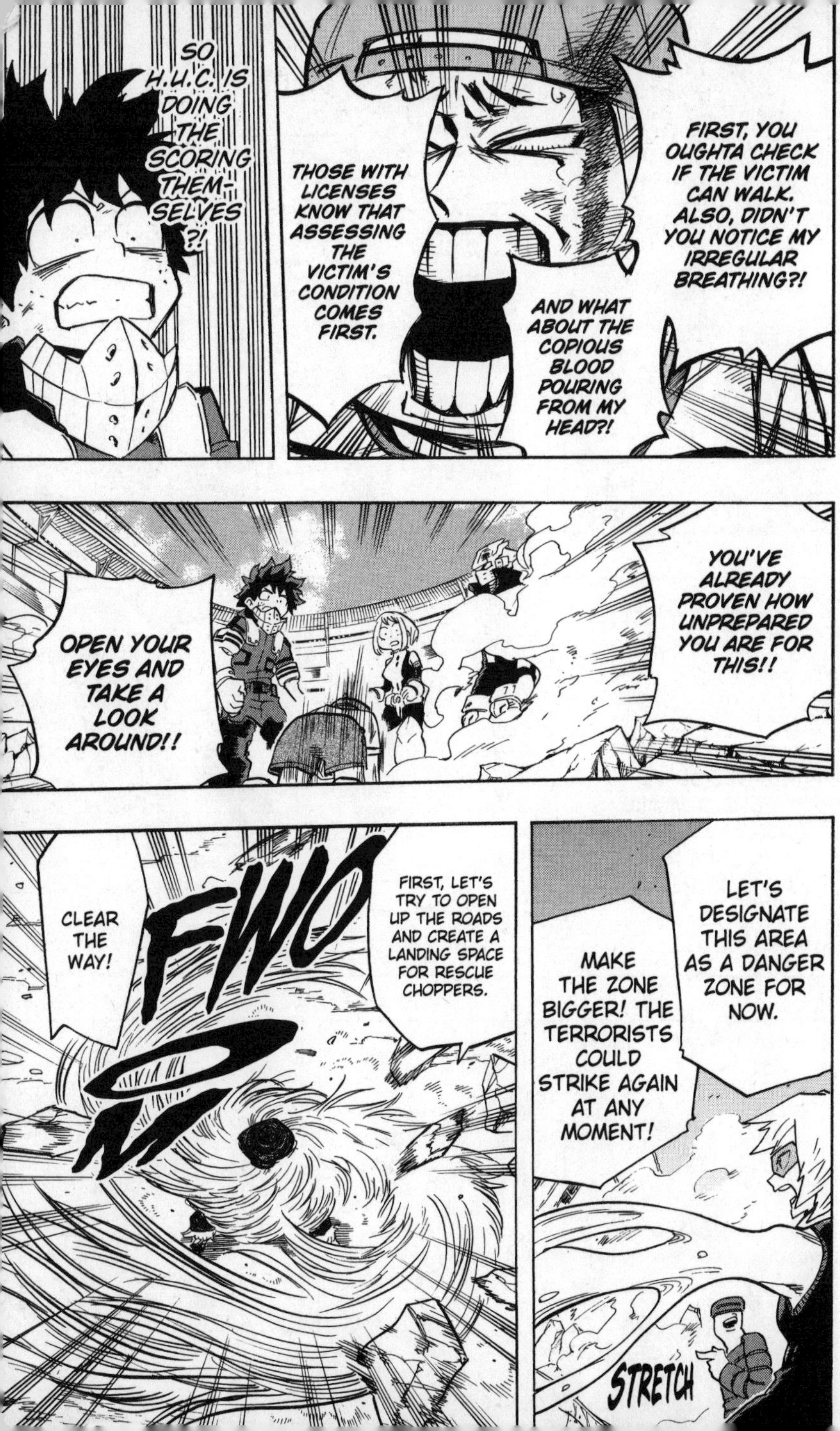
FIRST, YOU OUGHTA CHECK IF THE VICTIM CAN WALK. ALSO, DIDN'T YOU NOTICE MY IRREGULAR BREATHING?!
AND WHAT ABOUT THE COPIOUS BLOOD POURING FROM MY HEAD?!
THOSE WITH LICENSES KNOW THAT ASSESSING THE VICTIM'S CONDITION COMES FIRST.
SO H.U.C. IS DOING THE SCORING THEMSELVES?!
YOU'VE ALREADY PROVEN HOW UNPREPARED YOU ARE FOR THIS!!
OPEN YOUR EYES AND TAKE A LOOK AROUND!!
LET'S DESIGNATE THIS AREA AS A DANGER ZONE FOR NOW.
MAKE THE ZONE BIGGER! THE TERRORISTS COULD STRIKE AGAIN AT ANY MOMENT!
STRETCH
FIRST, LET'S TRY TO OPEN UP THE ROADS AND CREATE A LANDING SPACE FOR RESCUE CHOPPERS.
FWOSH
CLEAR THE WAY!

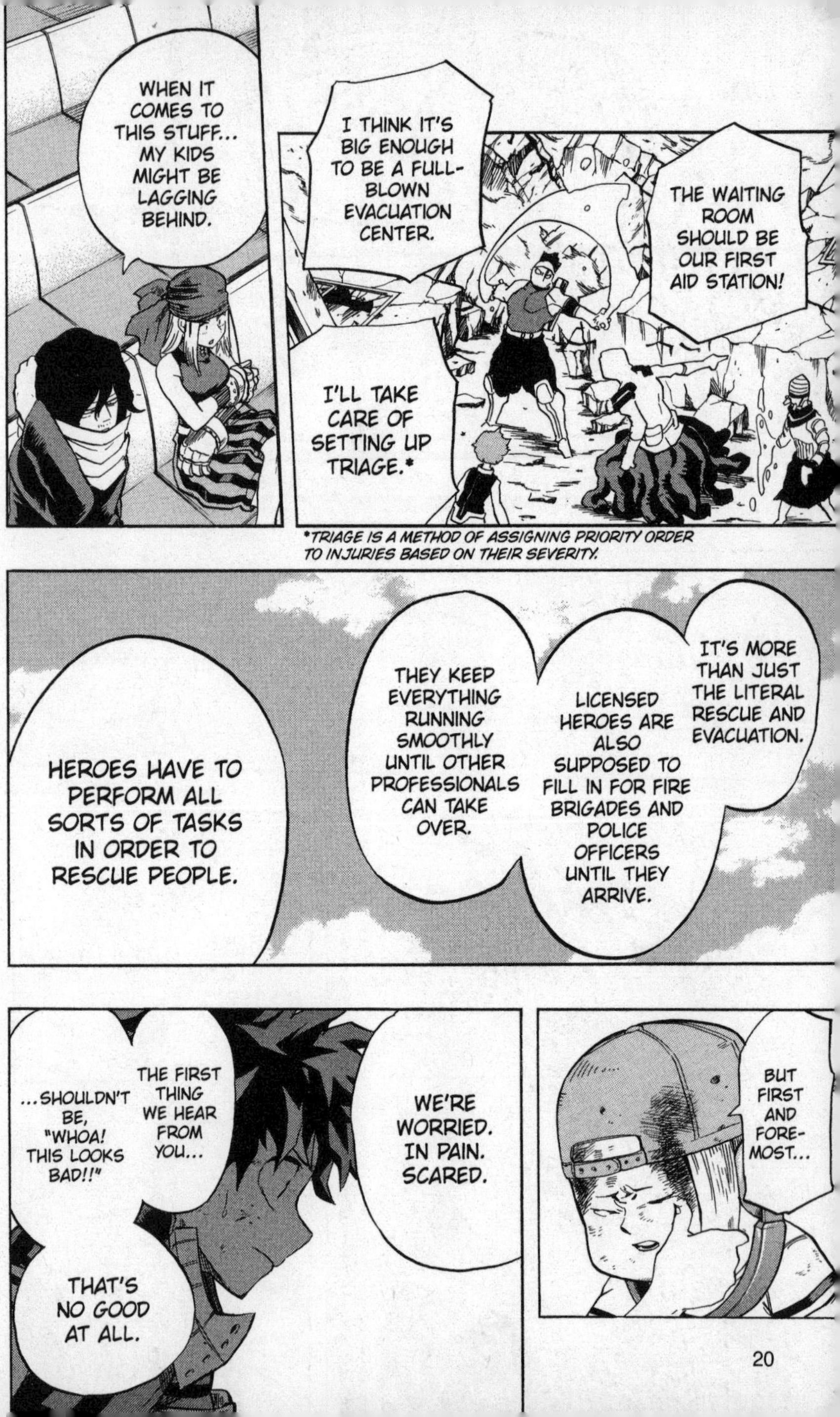
THE WAITING ROOM SHOULD BE OUR FIRST AID STATION!
I THINK IT'S BIG ENOUGH TO BE A FULL-BLOWN EVACUATION CENTER.
I'LL TAKE CARE OF SETTING UP TRIAGE.*
WHEN IT COMES TO THIS STUFF... MY KIDS MIGHT BE LAGGING BEHIND.
IT'S MORE THAN JUST THE LITERAL RESCUE AND EVACUATION.
LICENSED HEROES ARE ALSO SUPPOSED TO FILL IN FOR FIRE BRIGADES AND POLICE OFFICERS UNTIL THEY ARRIVE.
THEY KEEP EVERYTHING RUNNING SMOOTHLY UNTIL OTHER PROFESSIONALS CAN TAKE OVER.
HEROES HAVE TO PERFORM ALL SORTS OF TASKS IN ORDER TO RESCUE PEOPLE.
BUT FIRST AND FOREMOST...
WE'RE WORRIED. IN PAIN. SCARED.
THE FIRST THING WE HEAR FROM YOU...
...SHOULDN'T BE, "WHOA! THIS LOOKS BAD!!"
THAT'S NO GOOD AT ALL.

*TRIAGE IS A METHOD OF ASSIGNING PRIORITY ORDER TO INJURIES BASED ON THEIR SEVERITY.

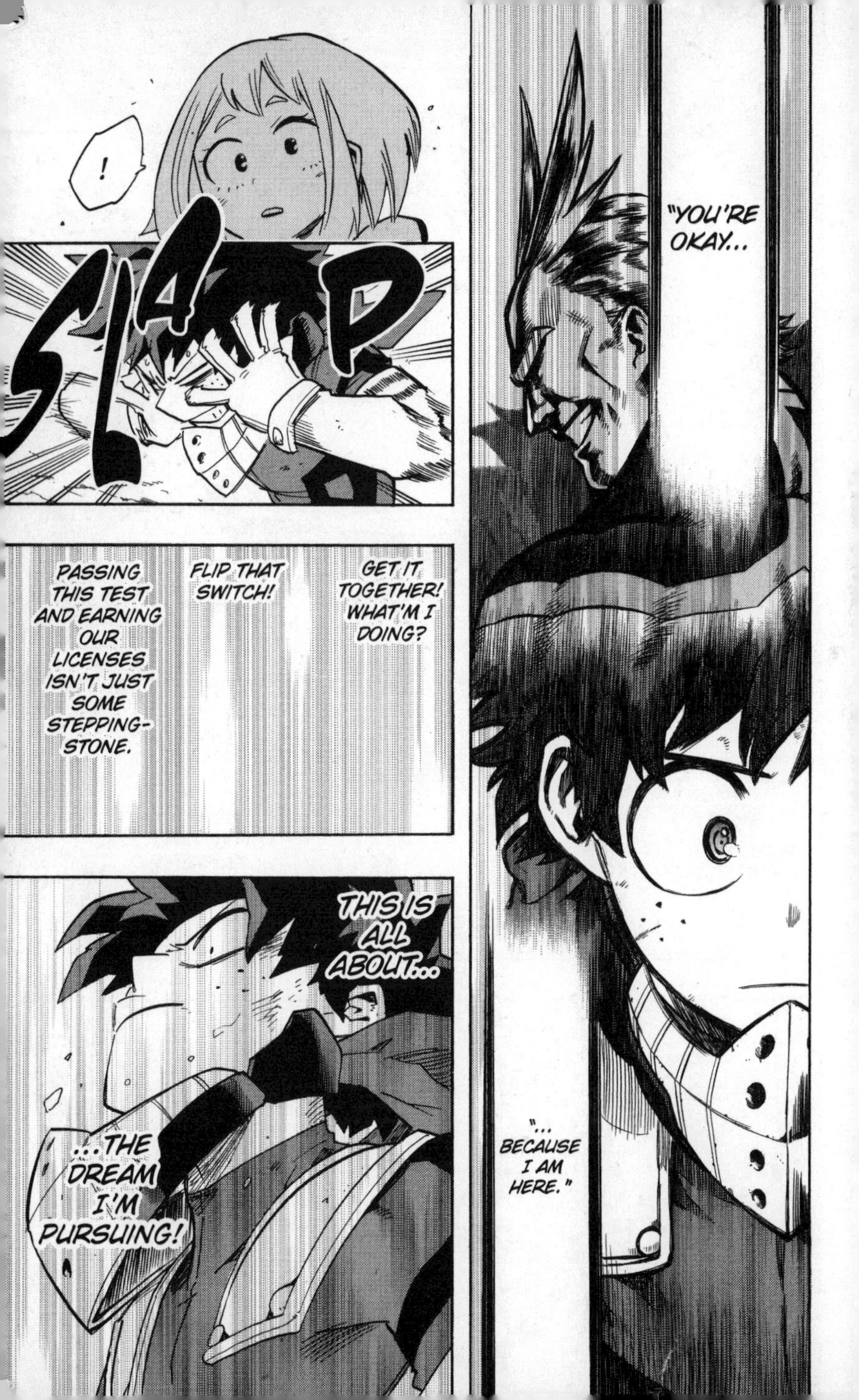
"YOU'RE OKAY...
"... BECAUSE I AM HERE."
!
SLAP
GET IT TOGETHER! WHAT'M I DOING?
FLIP THAT SWITCH!
PASSING THIS TEST AND EARNING OUR LICENSES ISN'T JUST SOME STEPPING-STONE.
THIS IS ALL ABOUT...
...THE DREAM I'M PURSUING!

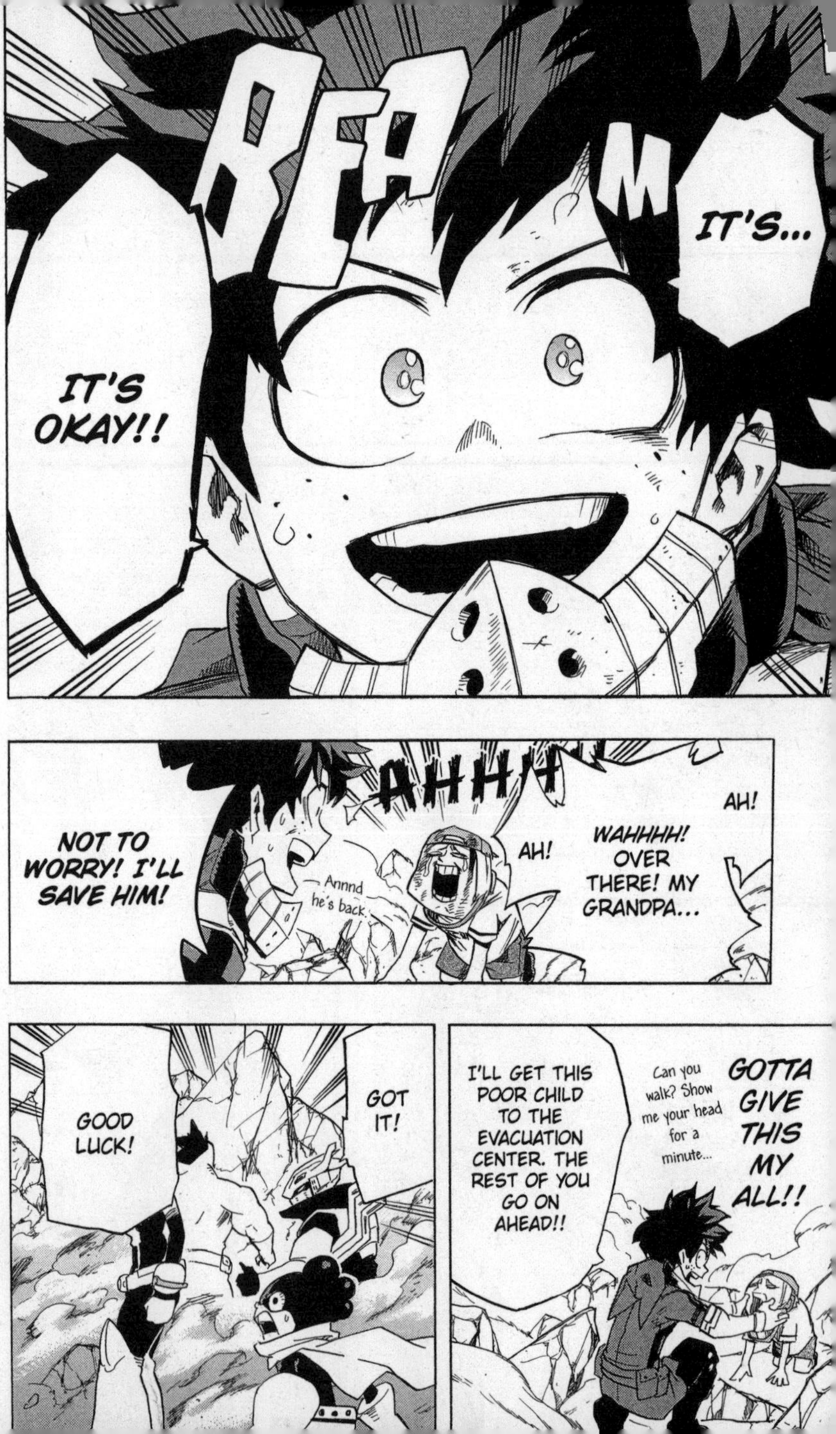
IT'S...
BEAM
IT'S OKAY!!
AH!
WAHHHH! OVER THERE! MY GRANDPA...
AH!
AHHH
Annnd he's back.
NOT TO WORRY! I'LL SAVE HIM!
GOTTA GIVE THIS MY ALL!!
Can you walk? Show me your head for a minute...
I'LL GET THIS POOR CHILD TO THE EVACUATION CENTER. THE REST OF YOU GO ON AHEAD!!
GOT IT!
GOOD LUCK!

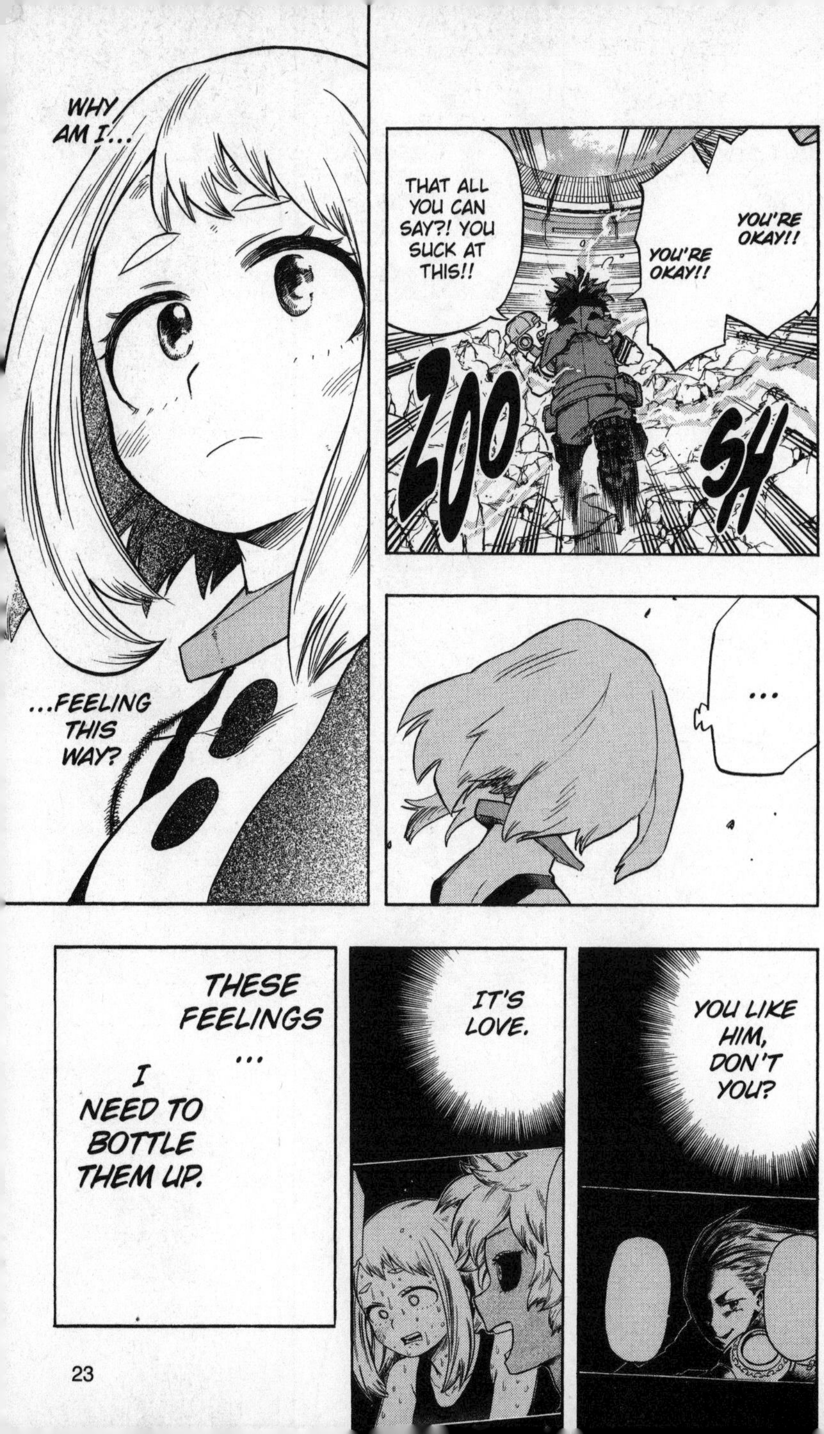
YOU'RE OKAY!!
YOU'RE OKAY!!
THAT ALL YOU CAN SAY?! YOU SUCK AT THIS!!
ZOOSH
...
WHY AM I...
...FEELING THIS WAY?
YOU LIKE HIM, DON'T YOU?
IT'S LOVE.
THESE FEELINGS...
I NEED TO BOTTLE THEM UP.

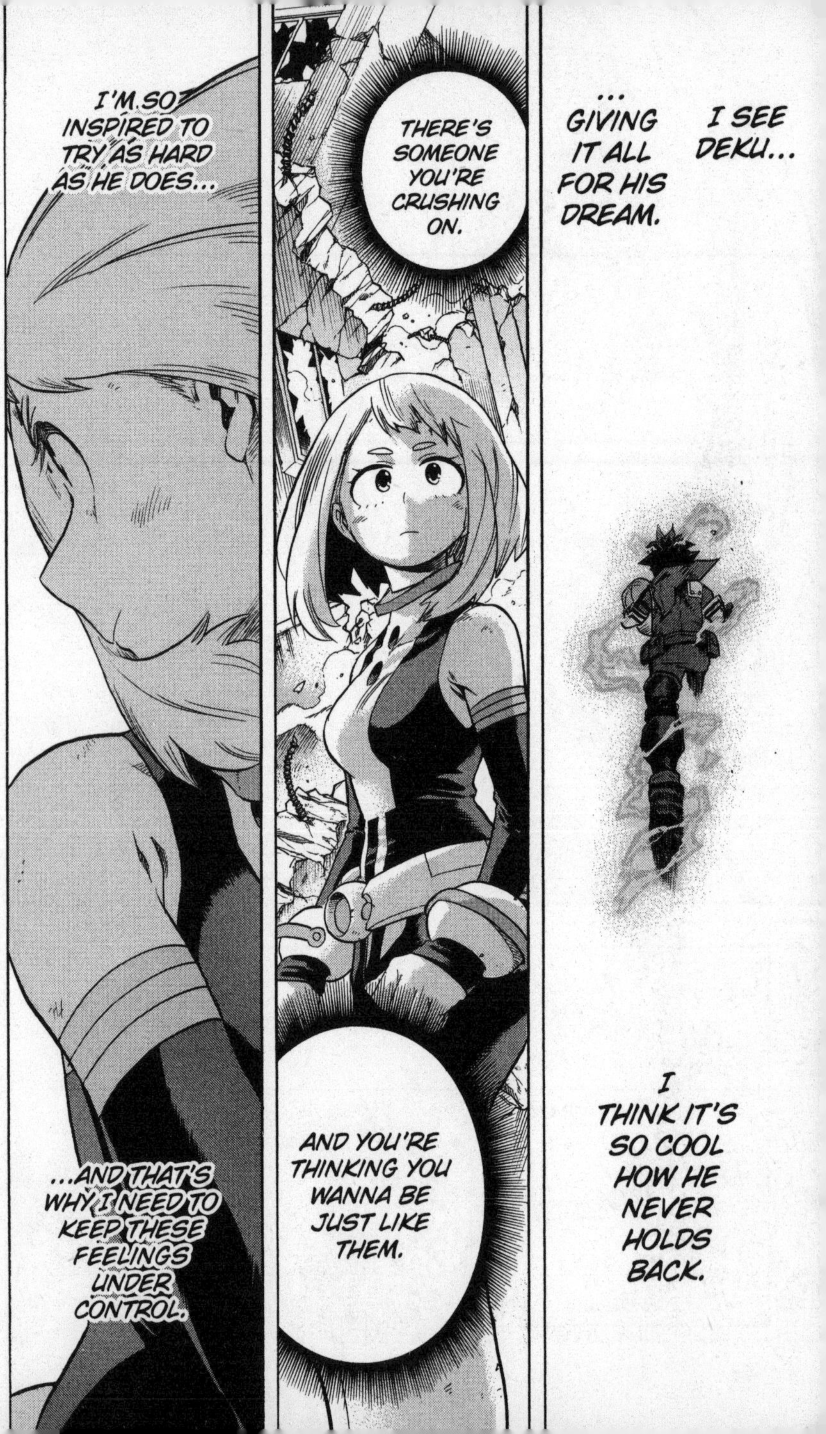
I SEE DEKU...
...GIVING IT ALL FOR HIS DREAM.
I THINK IT'S SO COOL HOW HE NEVER HOLDS BACK.
THERE'S SOMEONE YOU'RE CRUSHING ON.
AND YOU'RE THINKING YOU WANNA BE JUST LIKE THEM.
I'M SO INSPIRED TO TRY AS HARD AS HE DOES...
...AND THAT'S WHY I NEED TO KEEP THESE FEELINGS UNDER CONTROL.

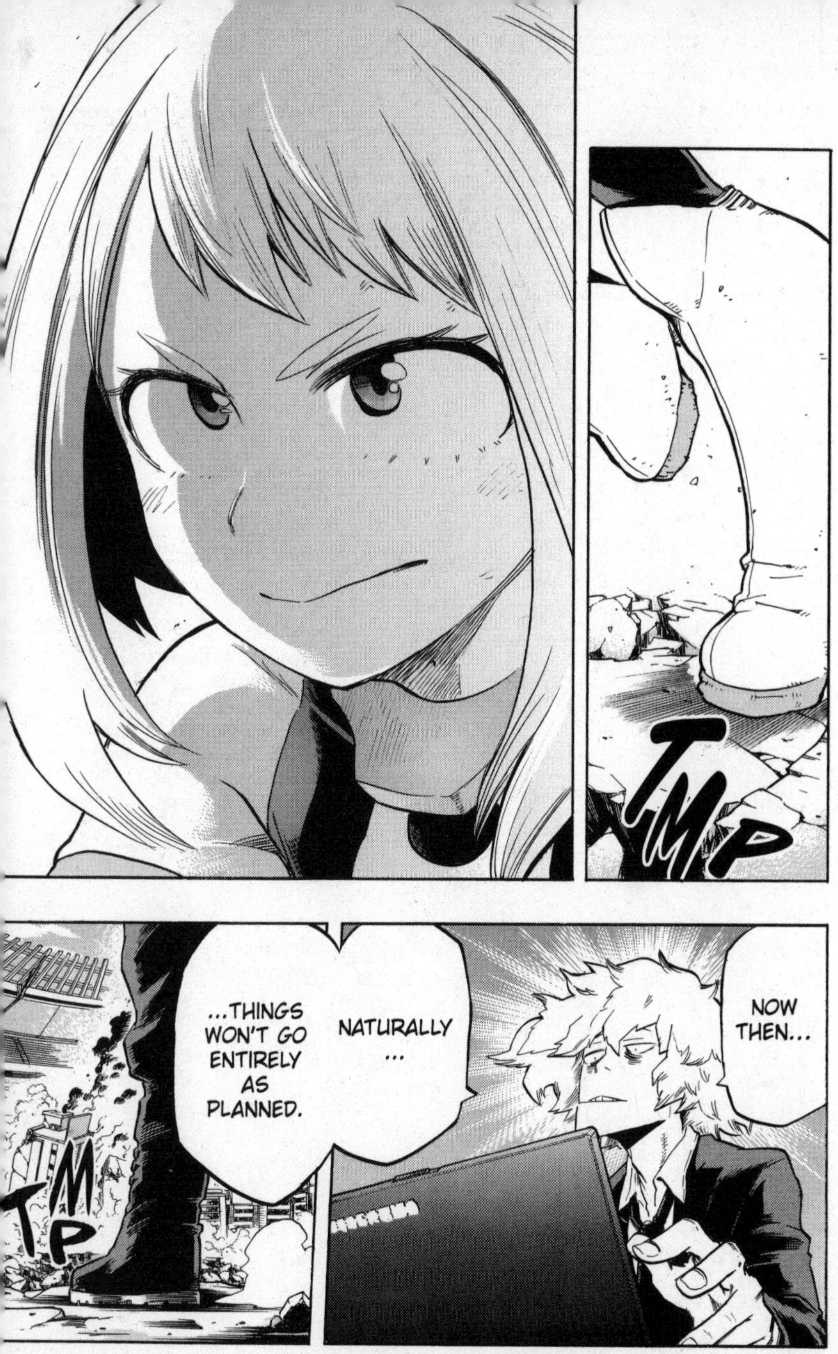
TMP
NOW THEN...
NATURALLY...
...THINGS WON'T GO ENTIRELY AS PLANNED.
TMP

NAGAMASA MORA (16)

STREET CLOTHES

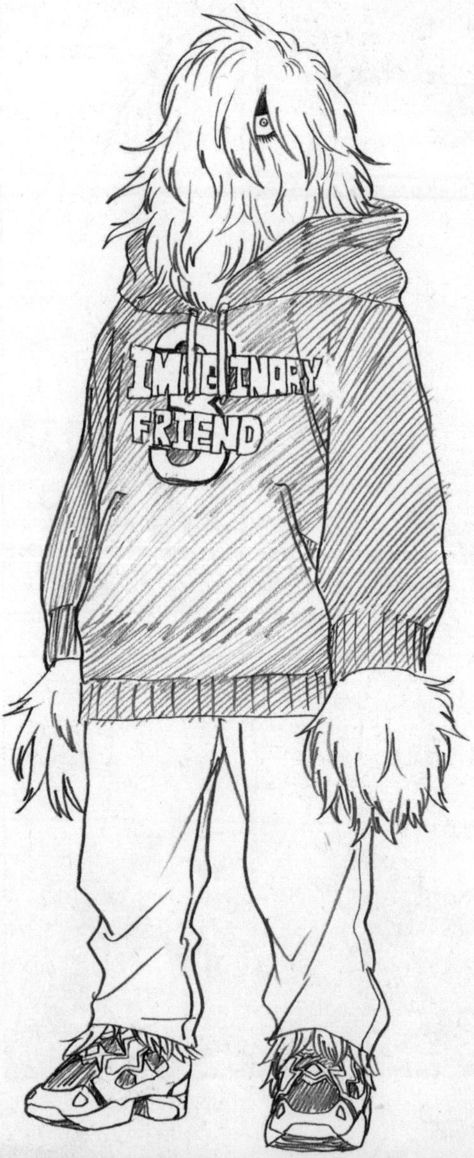
FRIEND

Birthday: 11/13
Height: 180 cm
Favorite Thing: Haircuts

THE SUPPLEMENT

President of Class 2-1 at Shiketsu High. Unlike at U.A., teachers at Shiketsu choose their class presidents based on grades and overall conduct. In other words, this guy was recognized by adults for the outstanding specimen he is. Being a leader is tough, though.

His Quirk is Extend-o-Hair. He can stretch out his hair and control it at will! It's always getting tangled, though, which makes life hard.

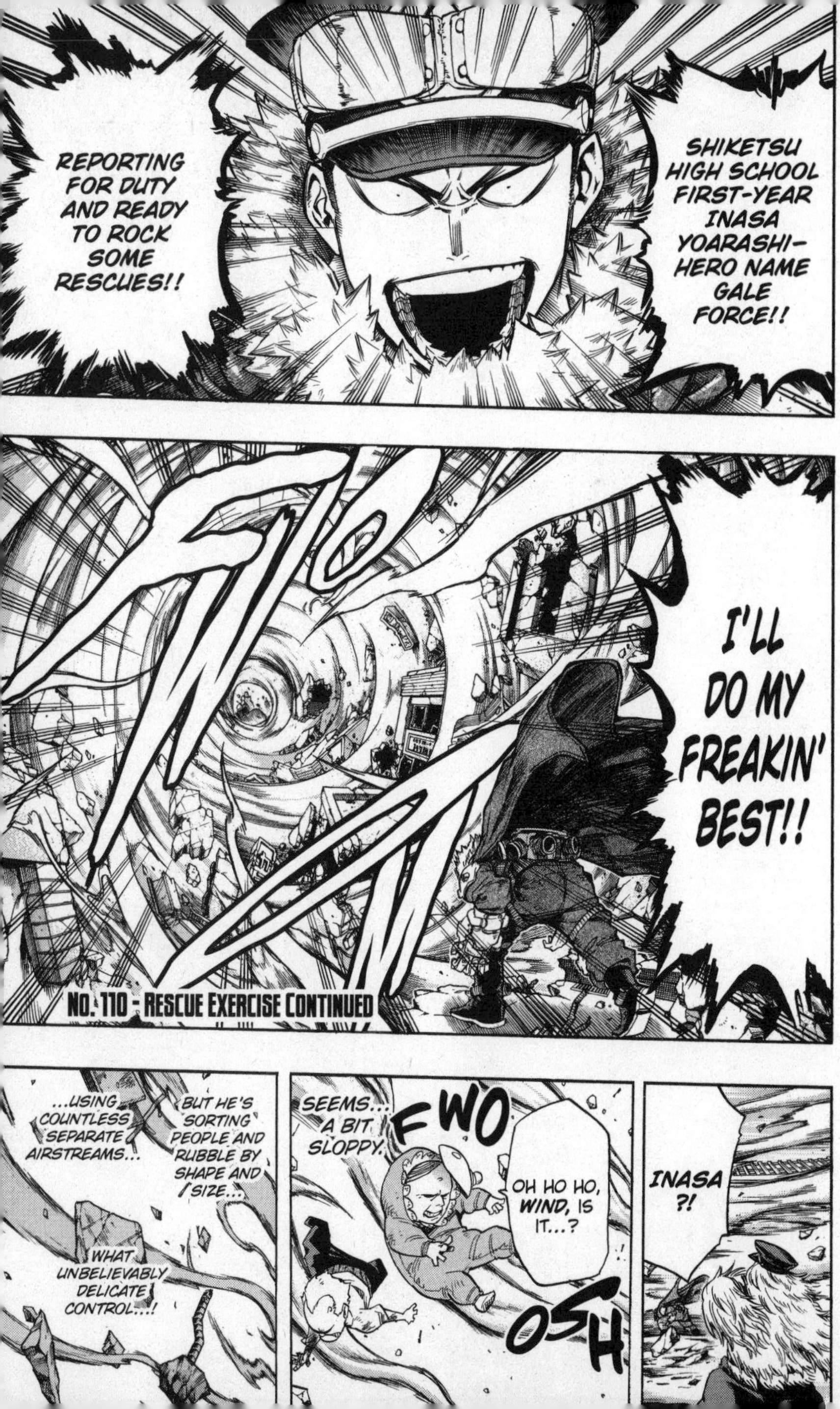
SHIKETSU HIGH SCHOOL FIRST-YEAR INASA YOARASHI-HERO NAME GALE FORCE!!
REPORTING FOR DUTY AND READY TO ROCK SOME RESCUES!!
I'LL DO MY FREAKIN' BEST!!
No. 110 - Rescue Exercise Continued
INASA ?!
OH HO HO, WIND, IS IT...?
SEEMS... A BIT SLOPPY.
FWOOSH
BUT HE'S SORTING PEOPLE AND RUBBLE BY SHAPE AND SIZE...
...USING COUNTLESS SEPARATE AIRSTREAMS...
WHAT UNBELIEVABLY DELICATE CONTROL...!

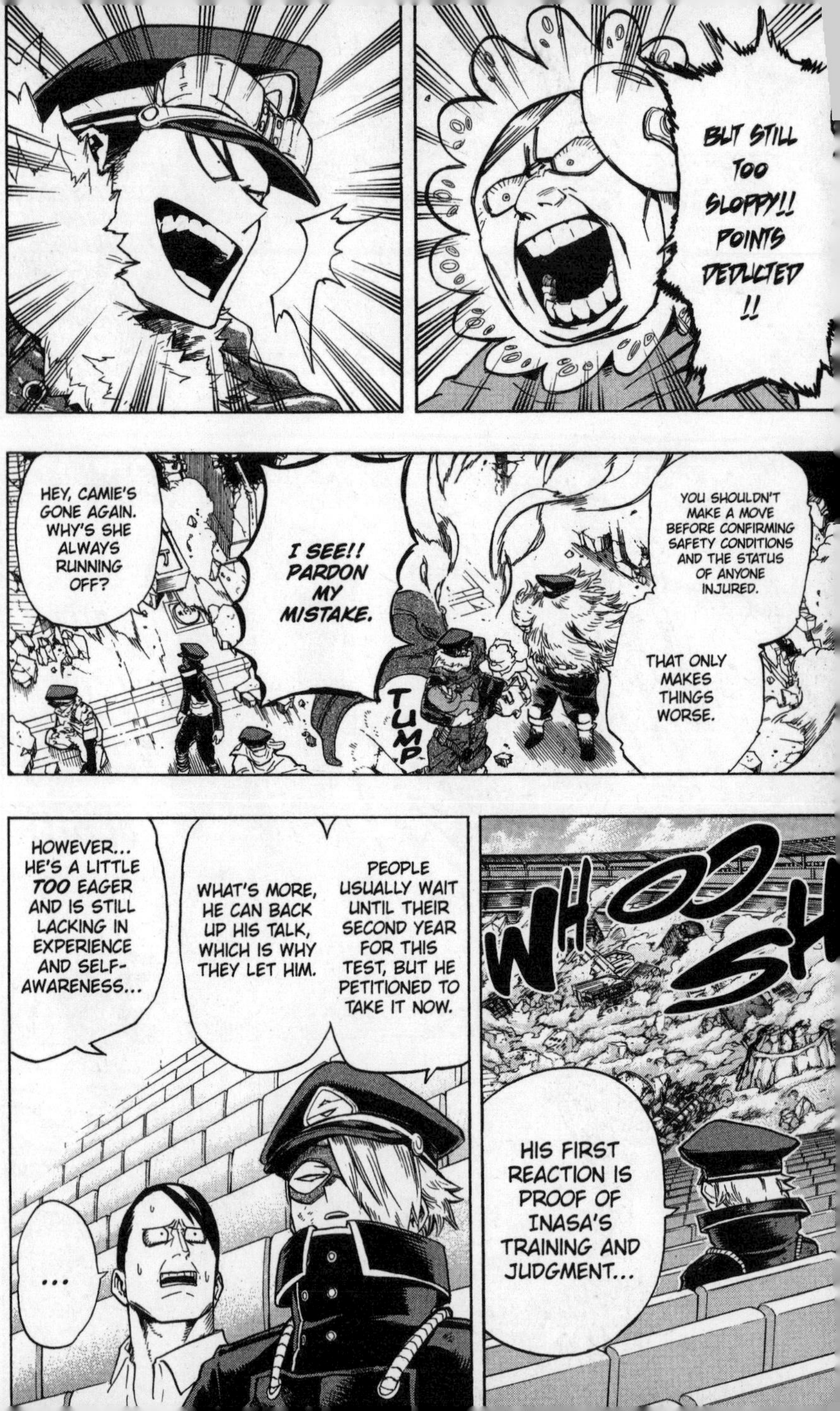
BUT STILL TOO SLOPPY!! POINTS DEDUCTED!!
YOU SHOULDN'T MAKE A MOVE BEFORE CONFIRMING SAFETY CONDITIONS AND THE STATUS OF ANYONE INJURED.
THAT ONLY MAKES THINGS WORSE.
TUMP
I SEE!! PARDON MY MISTAKE.
HEY, CAMIE'S GONE AGAIN. WHY'S SHE ALWAYS RUNNING OFF?
WHOOSH
HIS FIRST REACTION IS PROOF OF INASA'S TRAINING AND JUDGMENT...
PEOPLE USUALLY WAIT UNTIL THEIR SECOND YEAR FOR THIS TEST, BUT HE PETITIONED TO TAKE IT NOW.
WHAT'S MORE, HE CAN BACK UP HIS TALK, WHICH IS WHY THEY LET HIM.
HOWEVER... HE'S A LITTLE TOO EAGER AND IS STILL LACKING IN EXPERIENCE AND SELF-AWARENESS...
...

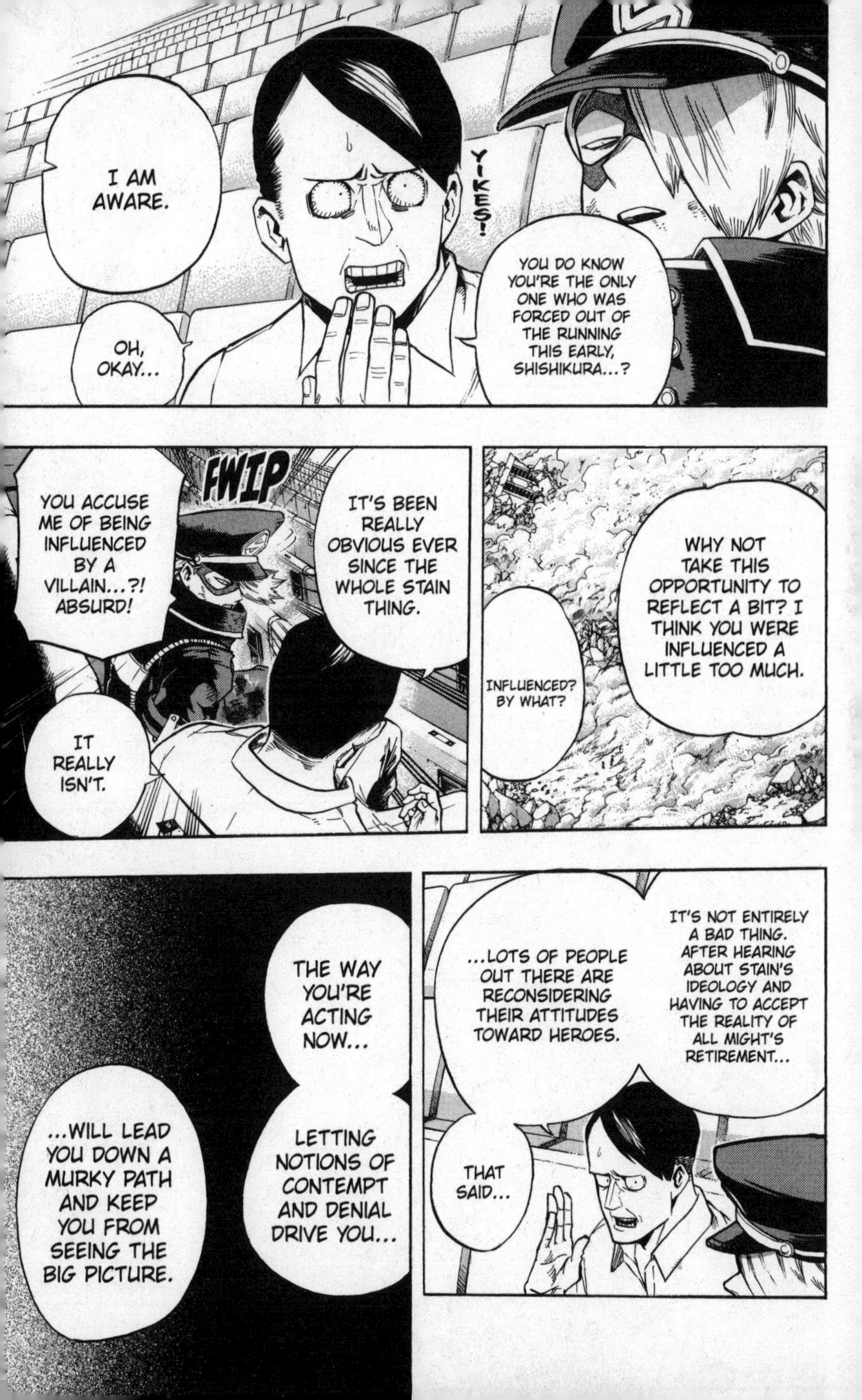
YOU DO KNOW YOU'RE THE ONLY ONE WHO WAS FORCED OUT OF THE RUNNING THIS EARLY, SHISHIKURA...?
YIKES!
I AM AWARE.
OH, OKAY...
WHY NOT TAKE THIS OPPORTUNITY TO REFLECT A BIT? I THINK YOU WERE INFLUENCED A LITTLE TOO MUCH.
INFLUENCED? BY WHAT?
IT'S BEEN REALLY OBVIOUS EVER SINCE THE WHOLE STAIN THING.
FWIP
YOU ACCUSE ME OF BEING INFLUENCED BY A VILLAIN...?! ABSURD!
IT REALLY ISN'T.
IT'S NOT ENTIRELY A BAD THING. AFTER HEARING ABOUT STAIN'S IDEOLOGY AND HAVING TO ACCEPT THE REALITY OF ALL MIGHT'S RETIREMENT...
...LOTS OF PEOPLE OUT THERE ARE RECONSIDERING THEIR ATTITUDES TOWARD HEROES.
THAT SAID...
THE WAY YOU'RE ACTING NOW...
LETTING NOTIONS OF CONTEMPT AND DENIAL DRIVE YOU...
...WILL LEAD YOU DOWN A MURKY PATH AND KEEP YOU FROM SEEING THE BIG PICTURE.

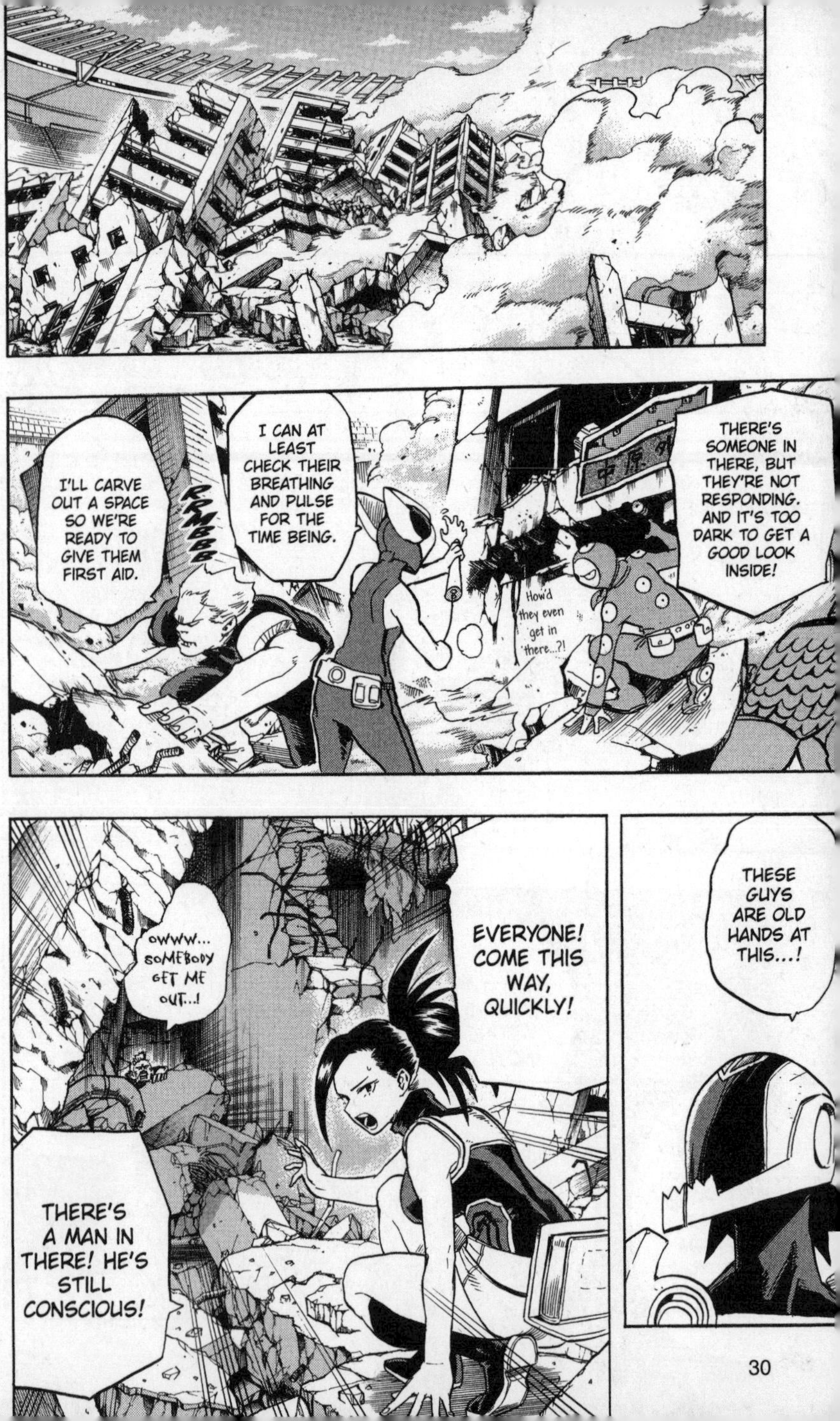
THERE'S SOMEONE IN THERE, BUT THEY'RE NOT RESPONDING. AND IT'S TOO DARK TO GET A GOOD LOOK INSIDE!
How'd they even get in there...?!
I CAN AT LEAST CHECK THEIR BREATHING AND PULSE FOR THE TIME BEING.
RRMBBB
I'LL CARVE OUT A SPACE SO WE'RE READY TO GIVE THEM FIRST AID.
THESE GUYS ARE OLD HANDS AT THIS...!
EVERYONE! COME THIS WAY, QUICKLY!
OWWW... SOMEBODY GET ME OUT...!
THERE'S A MAN IN THERE! HE'S STILL CONSCIOUS!

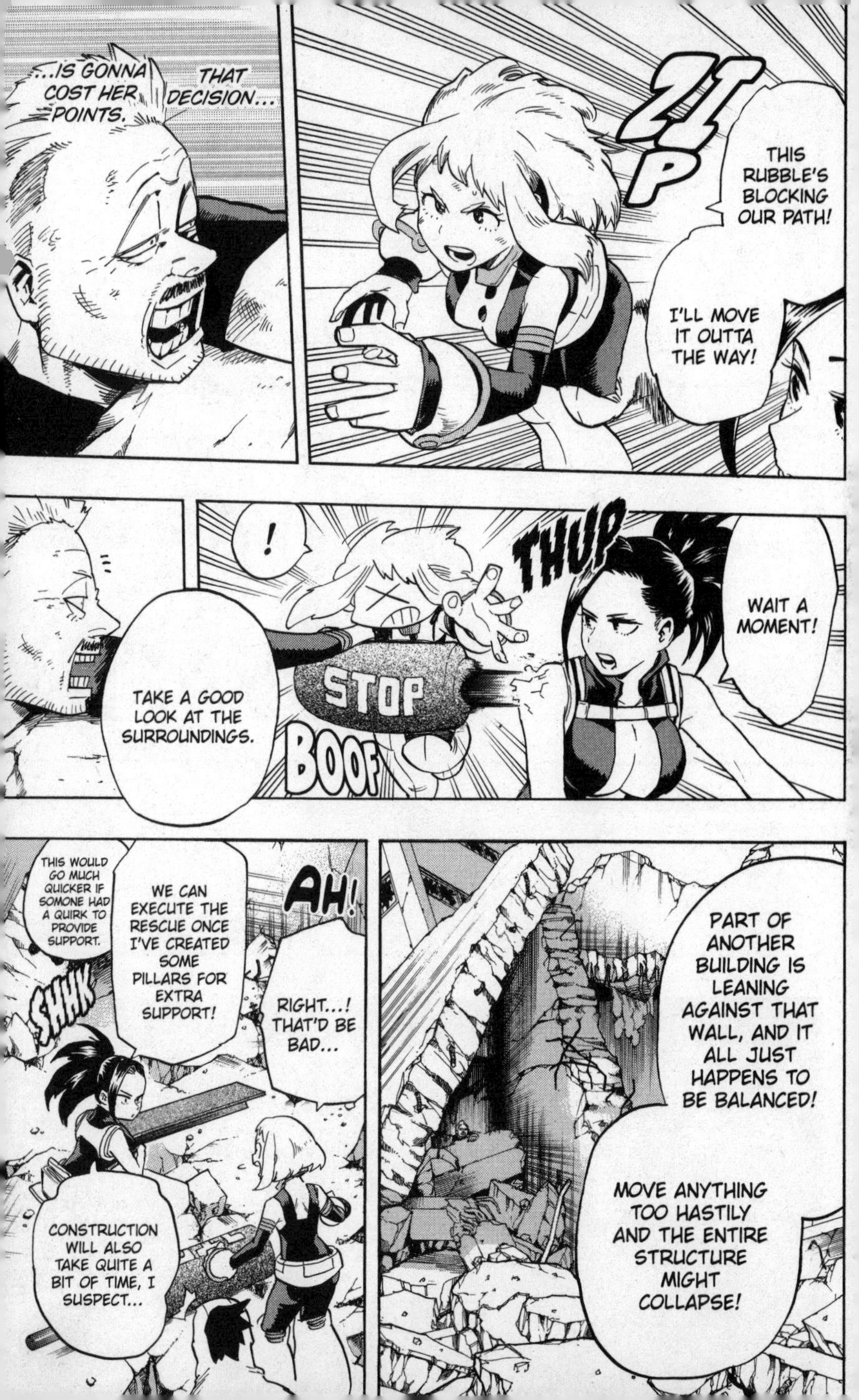
ZIP
THIS RUBBLE'S BLOCKING OUR PATH!
I'LL MOVE IT OUTTA THE WAY!
THAT DECISION...
...IS GONNA COST HER POINTS.
THUP
WAIT A MOMENT!
!
STOP
BOOF
TAKE A GOOD LOOK AT THE SURROUNDINGS.
PART OF ANOTHER BUILDING IS LEANING AGAINST THAT WALL, AND IT ALL JUST HAPPENS TO BE BALANCED!
MOVE ANYTHING TOO HASTILY AND THE ENTIRE STRUCTURE MIGHT COLLAPSE!
AH!
RIGHT...! THAT'D BE BAD...
WE CAN EXECUTE THE RESCUE ONCE I'VE CREATED SOME PILLARS FOR EXTRA SUPPORT!
THIS WOULD GO MUCH QUICKER IF SOMONE HAD A QUIRK TO PROVIDE SUPPORT.
SHHK
CONSTRUCTION WILL ALSO TAKE QUITE A BIT OF TIME, I SUSPECT...

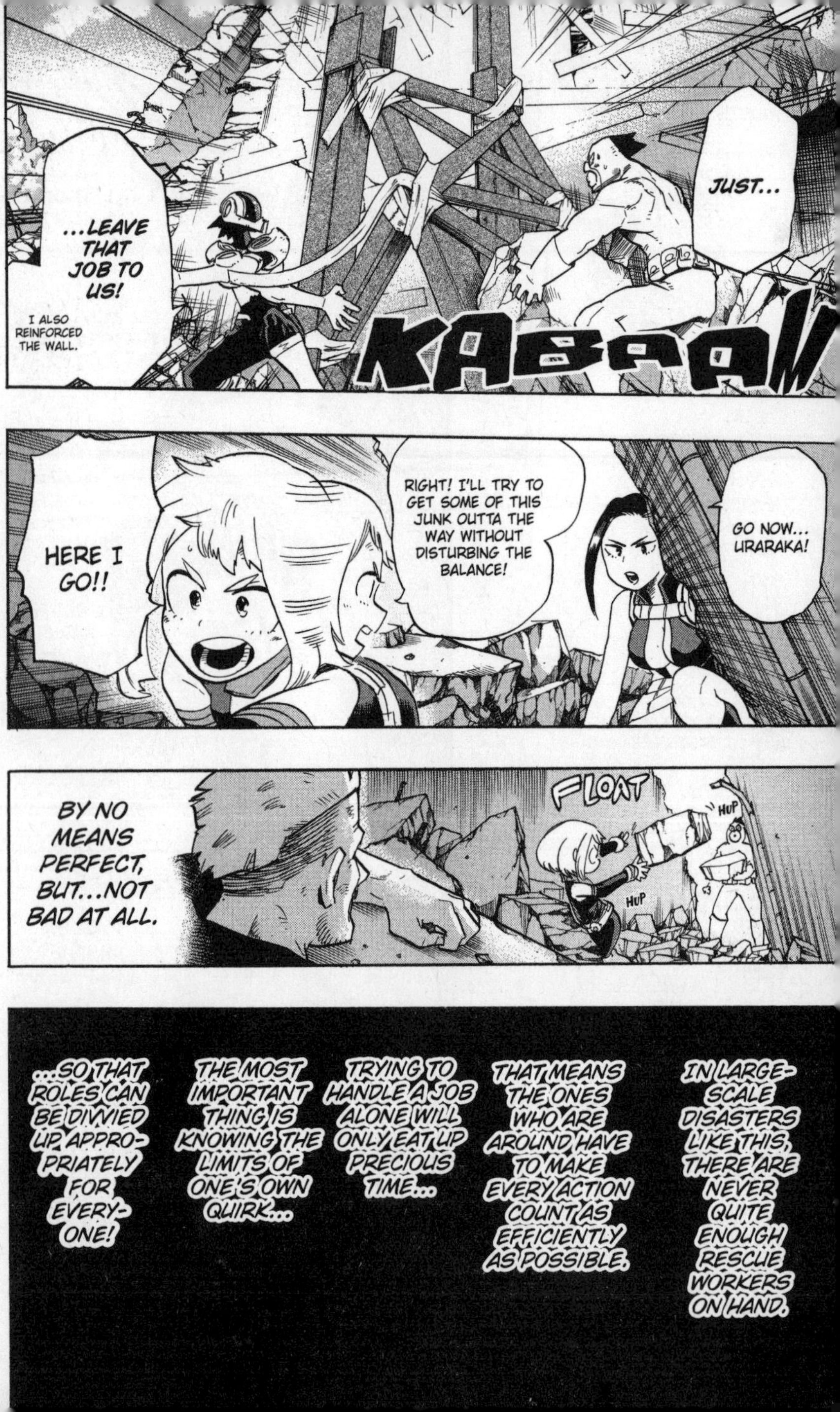
JUST...
...LEAVE THAT JOB TO US!
I ALSO REINFORCED THE WALL.
KABAAM
GO NOW... URARAKA!
RIGHT! I'LL TRY TO GET SOME OF THIS JUNK OUTTA THE WAY WITHOUT DISTURBING THE BALANCE!
HERE I GO!!
FLOAT
HUP
HUP
BY NO MEANS PERFECT, BUT...NOT BAD AT ALL.
IN LARGE-SCALE DISASTERS LIKE THIS, THERE ARE NEVER QUITE ENOUGH RESCUE WORKERS ON HAND.
THAT MEANS THE ONES WHO ARE AROUND HAVE TO MAKE EVERY ACTION COUNT AS EFFICIENTLY AS POSSIBLE.
TRYING TO HANDLE A JOB ALONE WILL ONLY EAT UP PRECIOUS TIME...
THE MOST IMPORTANT THING IS KNOWING THE LIMITS OF ONE'S OWN QUIRK...
...SO THAT ROLES CAN BE DIVVIED UP APPRO-PRIATELY FOR EVERY-ONE!

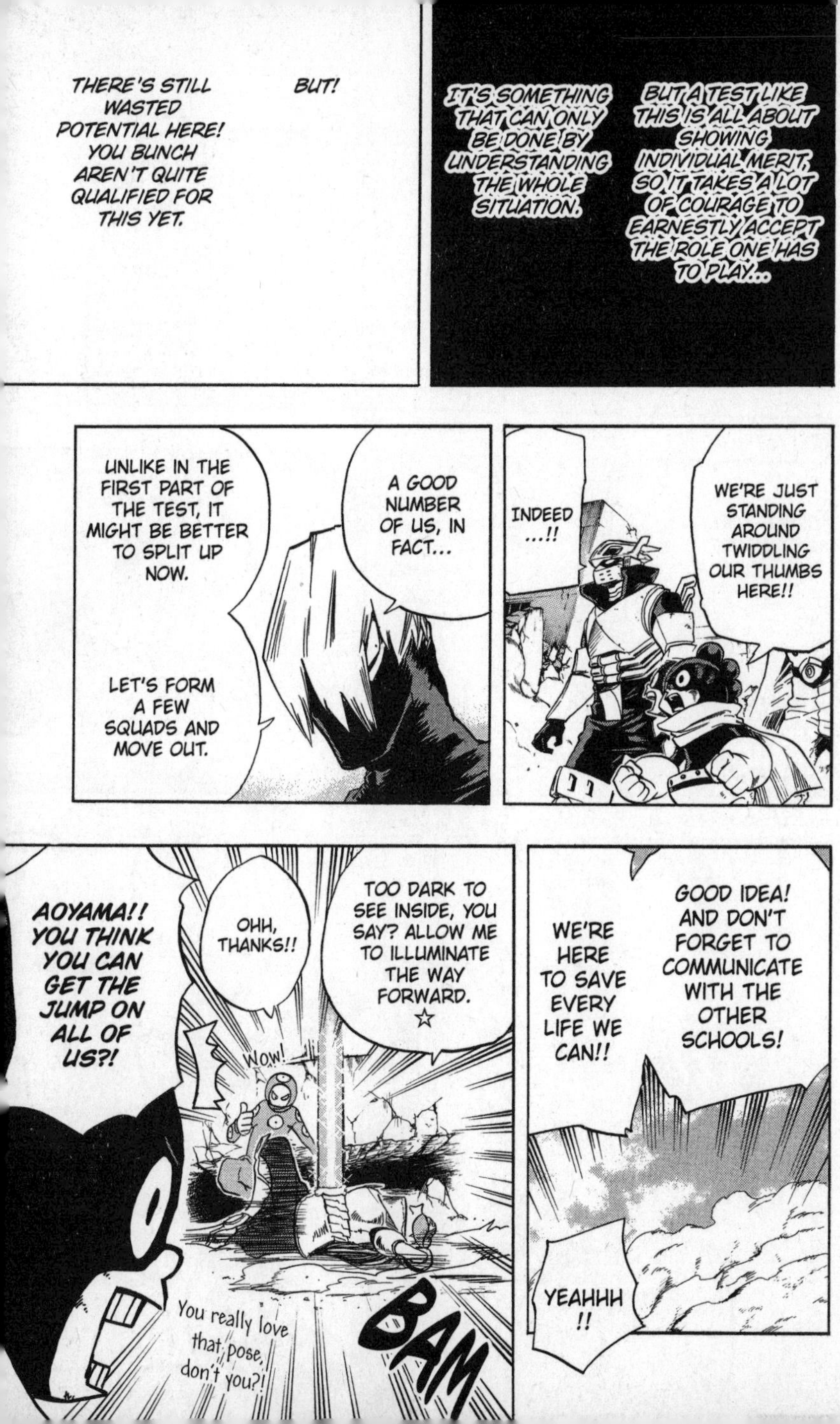
BUT A TEST LIKE THIS IS ALL ABOUT SHOWING INDIVIDUAL MERIT, SO IT TAKES A LOT OF COURAGE TO EARNESTLY ACCEPT THE ROLE ONE HAS TO PLAY...
IT'S SOMETHING THAT CAN ONLY BE DONE BY UNDERSTANDING THE WHOLE SITUATION.
BUT!
THERE'S STILL WASTED POTENTIAL HERE! YOU BUNCH AREN'T QUITE QUALIFIED FOR THIS YET.
WE'RE JUST STANDING AROUND TWIDDLING OUR THUMBS HERE!!
INDEED ...!!
A GOOD NUMBER OF US, IN FACT...
UNLIKE IN THE FIRST PART OF THE TEST, IT MIGHT BE BETTER TO SPLIT UP NOW.
LET'S FORM A FEW SQUADS AND MOVE OUT.
GOOD IDEA! AND DON'T FORGET TO COMMUNICATE WITH THE OTHER SCHOOLS!
WE'RE HERE TO SAVE EVERY LIFE WE CAN!!
YEAHHH !!
TOO DARK TO SEE INSIDE, YOU SAY? ALLOW ME TO ILLUMINATE THE WAY FORWARD. ☆
OHH, THANKS!!
WOW!
AOYAMA!! YOU THINK YOU CAN GET THE JUMP ON ALL OF US?!
BAM
You really love that pose, don't you?!

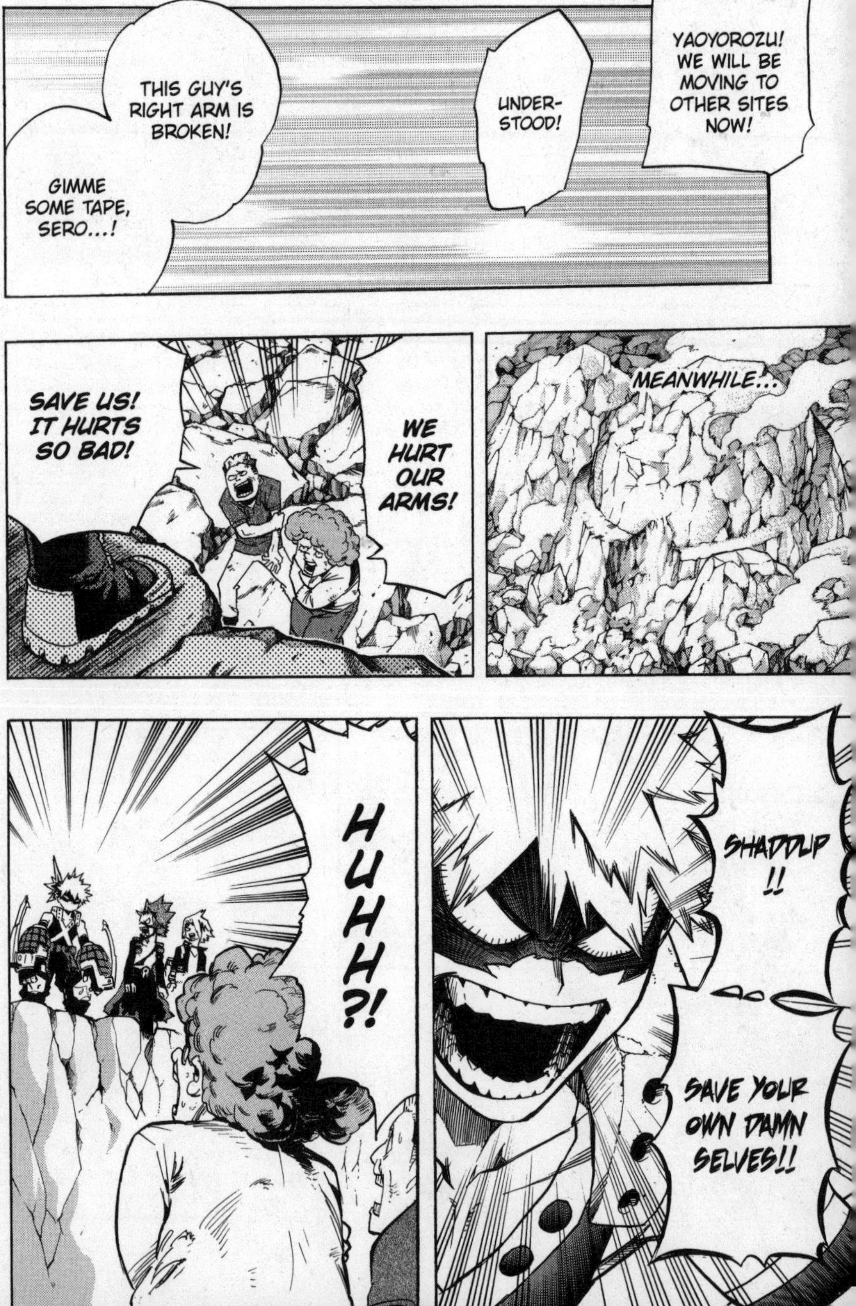
YAOYOROZU! WE WILL BE MOVING TO OTHER SITES NOW!
UNDER-STOOD!
THIS GUY'S RIGHT ARM IS BROKEN!
GIMME SOME TAPE, SERO...!
MEANWHILE...
WE HURT OUR ARMS!
SAVE US! IT HURTS SO BAD!
SHADDUP!!
SAVE YOUR OWN DAMN SELVES!!
HUHH?!

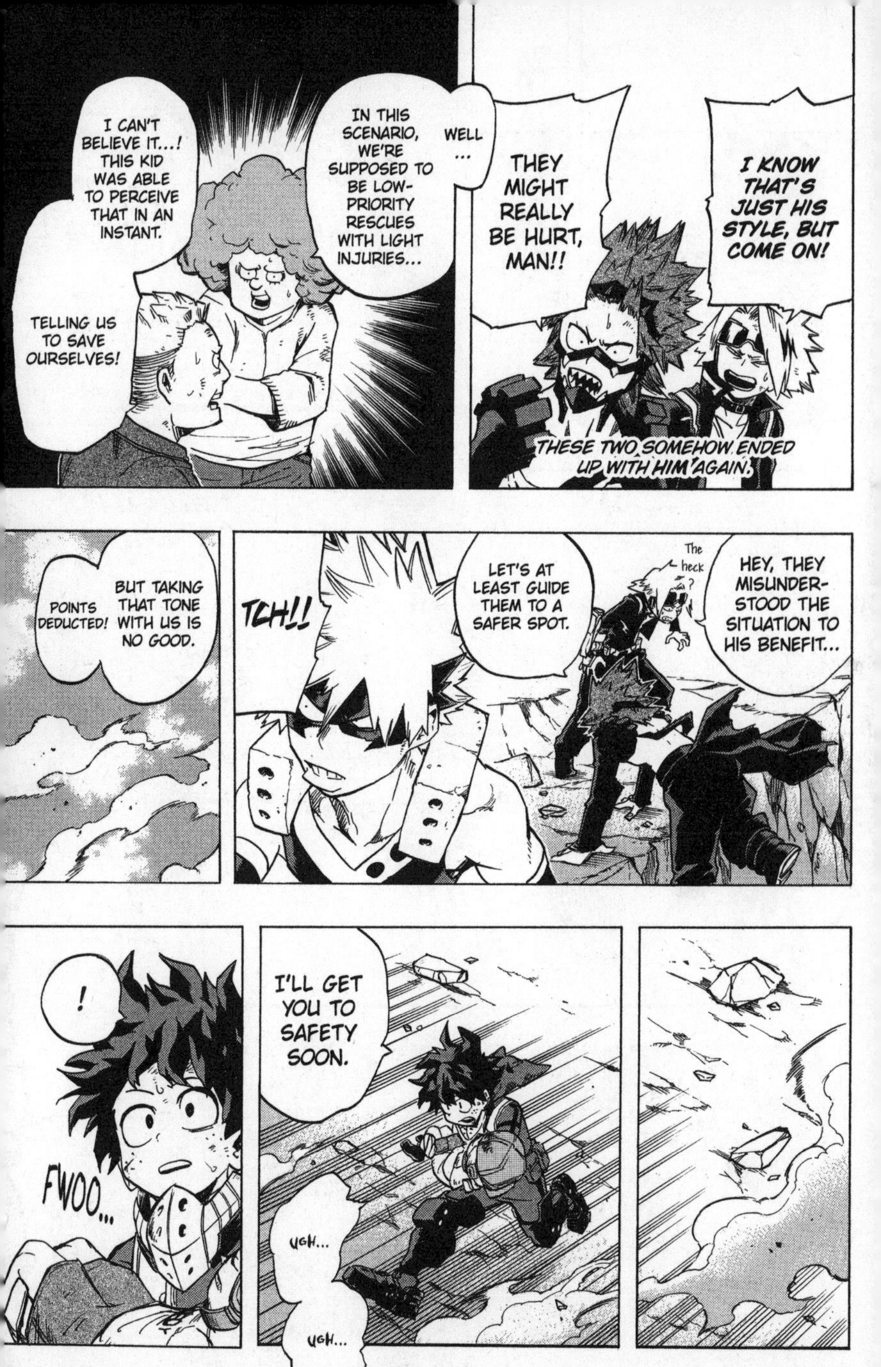
I KNOW THAT'S JUST HIS STYLE, BUT COME ON!
THEY MIGHT REALLY BE HURT, MAN!!
THESE TWO SOMEHOW ENDED UP WITH HIM AGAIN.
WELL ...
IN THIS SCENARIO, WE'RE SUPPOSED TO BE LOW-PRIORITY RESCUES WITH LIGHT INJURIES...
I CAN'T BELIEVE IT...! THIS KID WAS ABLE TO PERCEIVE THAT IN AN INSTANT.
TELLING US TO SAVE OURSELVES!
HEY, THEY MISUNDERSTOOD THE SITUATION TO HIS BENEFIT...
The heck?
LET'S AT LEAST GUIDE THEM TO A SAFER SPOT.
TCH!!
BUT TAKING THAT TONE WITH US IS NO GOOD.
POINTS DEDUCTED!
I'LL GET YOU TO SAFETY SOON.
UGH...
UGH...
!
FWOO...

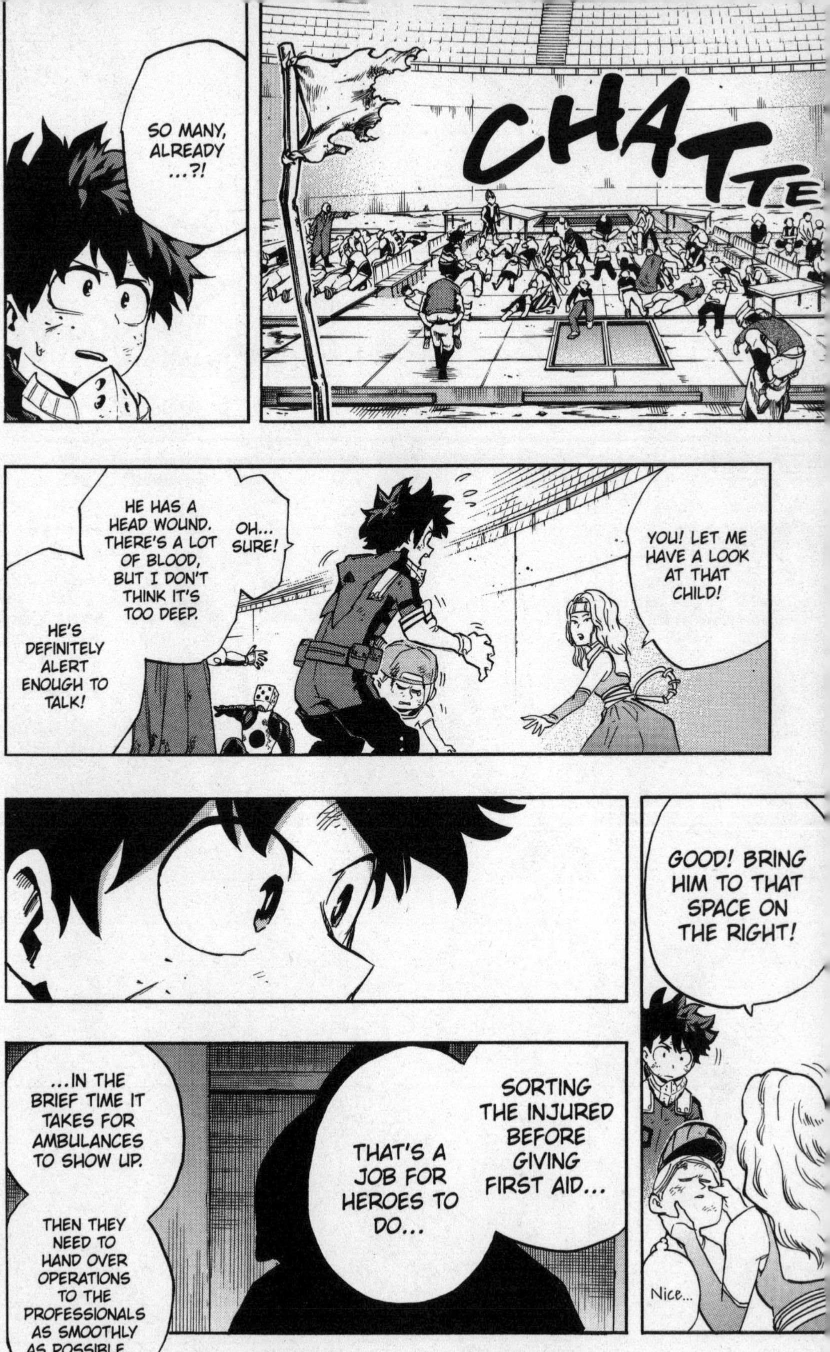
CHATTE
SO MANY, ALREADY ...?!
YOU! LET ME HAVE A LOOK AT THAT CHILD!
OH... SURE!
HE HAS A HEAD WOUND. THERE'S A LOT OF BLOOD, BUT I DON'T THINK IT'S TOO DEEP.
HE'S DEFINITELY ALERT ENOUGH TO TALK!
GOOD! BRING HIM TO THAT SPACE ON THE RIGHT!
Nice...
SORTING THE INJURED BEFORE GIVING FIRST AID...
THAT'S A JOB FOR HEROES TO DO...
...IN THE BRIEF TIME IT TAKES FOR AMBULANCES TO SHOW UP.
THEN THEY NEED TO HAND OVER OPERATIONS TO THE PROFESSIONALS AS SMOOTHLY AS POSSIBLE...

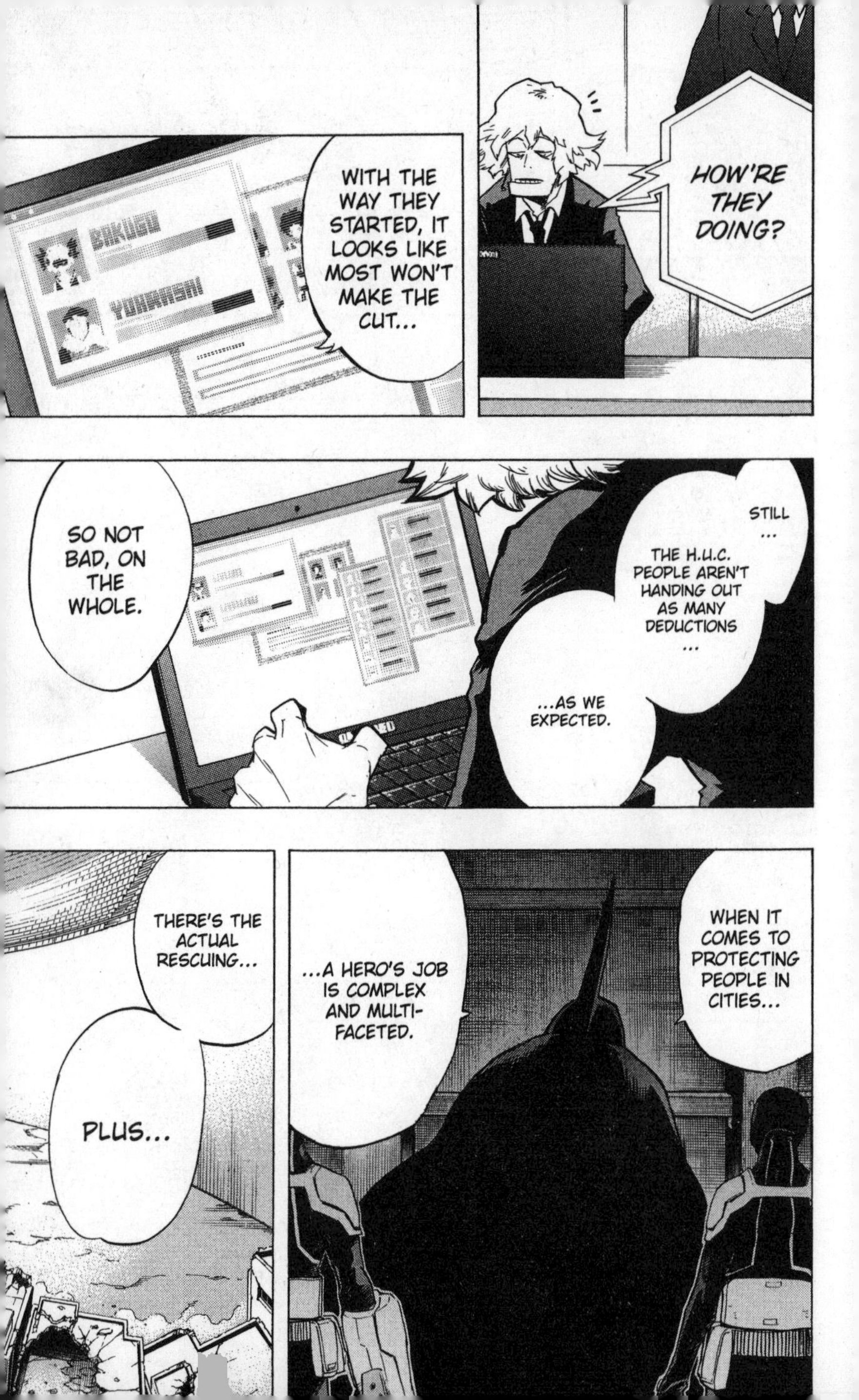
HOW'RE THEY DOING?
WITH THE WAY THEY STARTED, IT LOOKS LIKE MOST WON'T MAKE THE CUT...
STILL...
THE H.U.C. PEOPLE AREN'T HANDING OUT AS MANY DEDUCTIONS...
...AS WE EXPECTED.
SO NOT BAD, ON THE WHOLE.
WHEN IT COMES TO PROTECTING PEOPLE IN CITIES...
...A HERO'S JOB IS COMPLEX AND MULTI-FACETED.
THERE'S THE ACTUAL RESCUING...
PLUS...

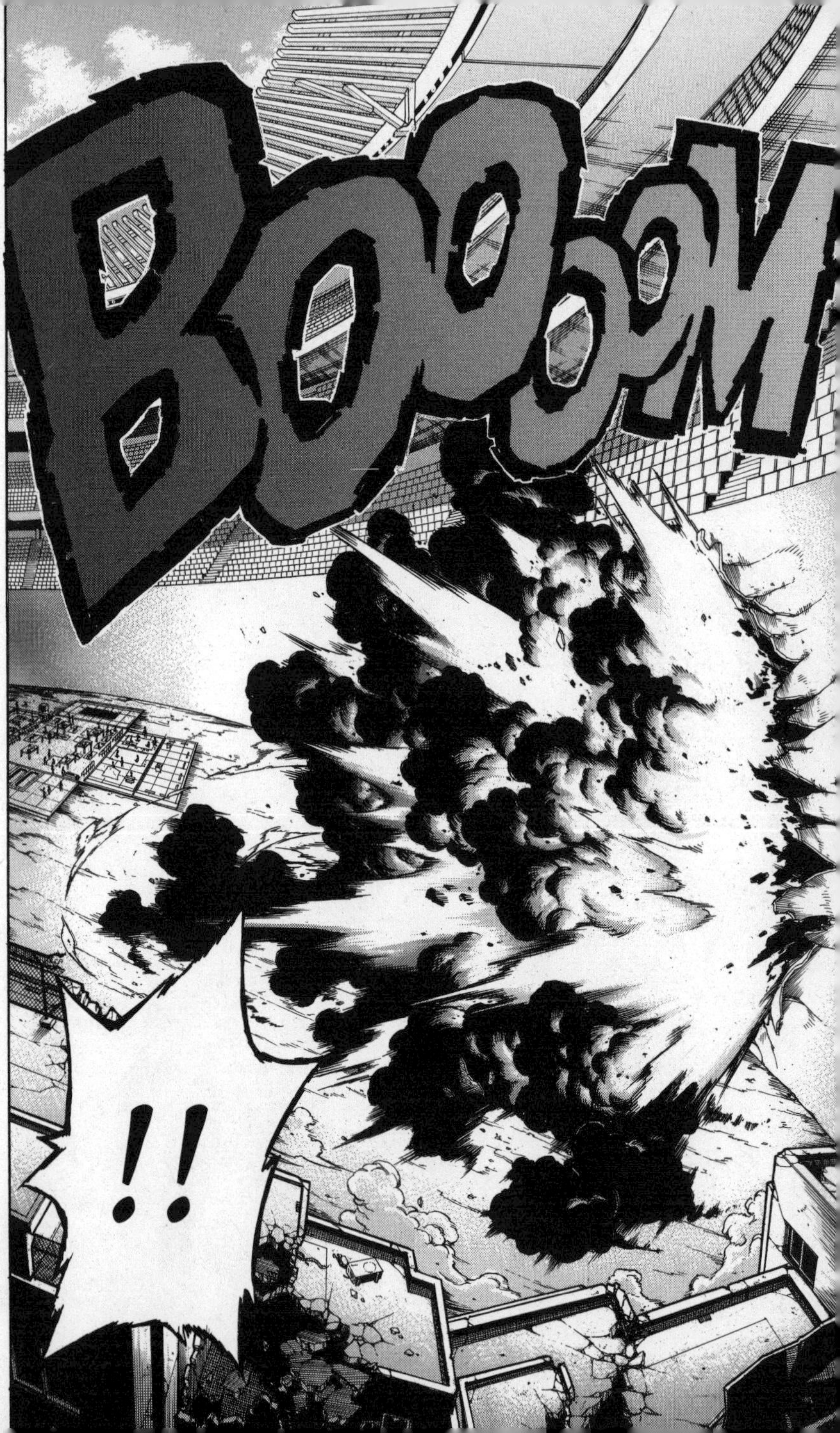
BOOOOM
!!

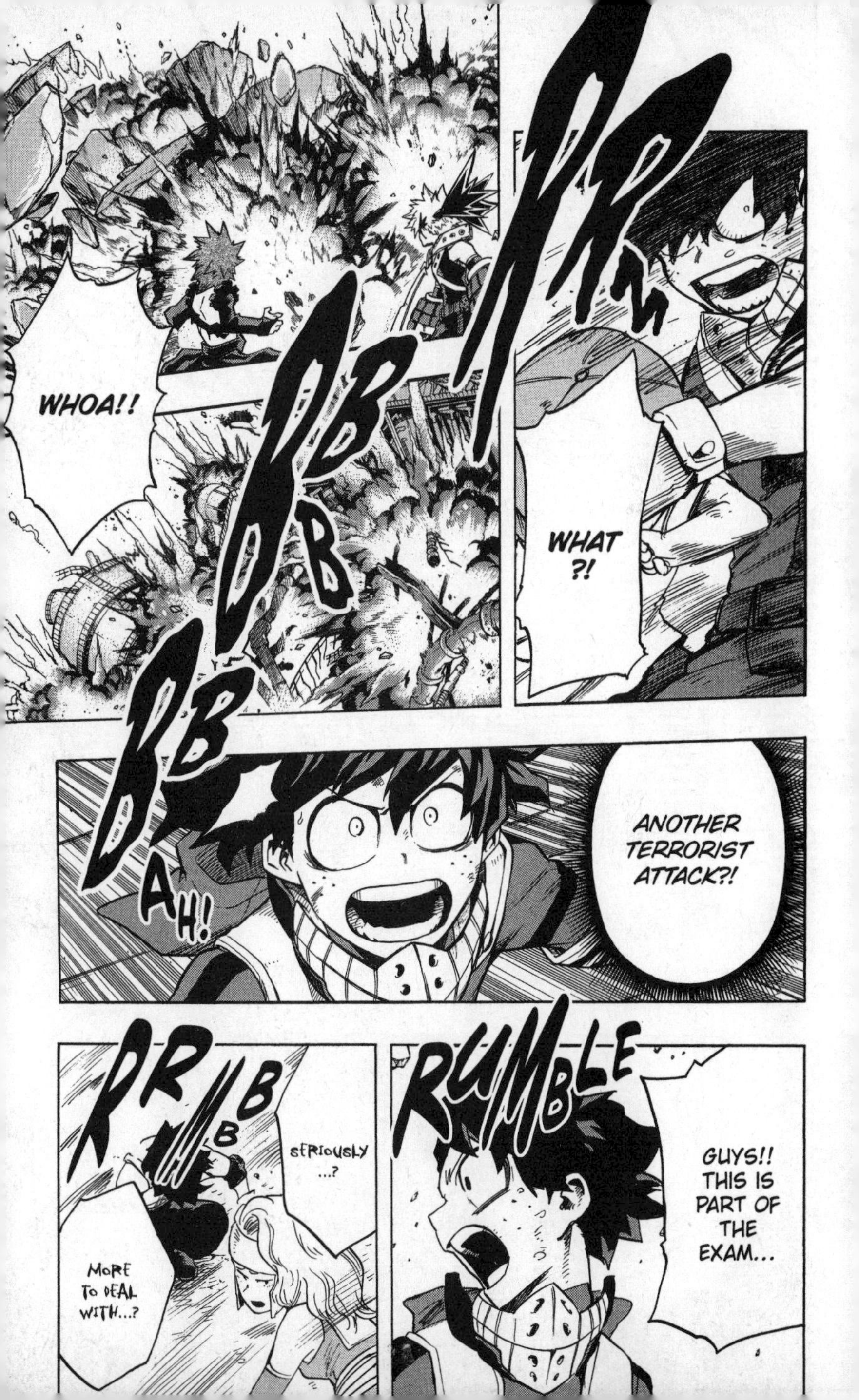

WHAT ?!
WHOA!!
ANOTHER TERRORIST ATTACK?!
AH!
RUMBLE
GUYS!! THIS IS PART OF THE EXAM...
SERIOUSLY ...?
MORE TO DEAL WITH...?

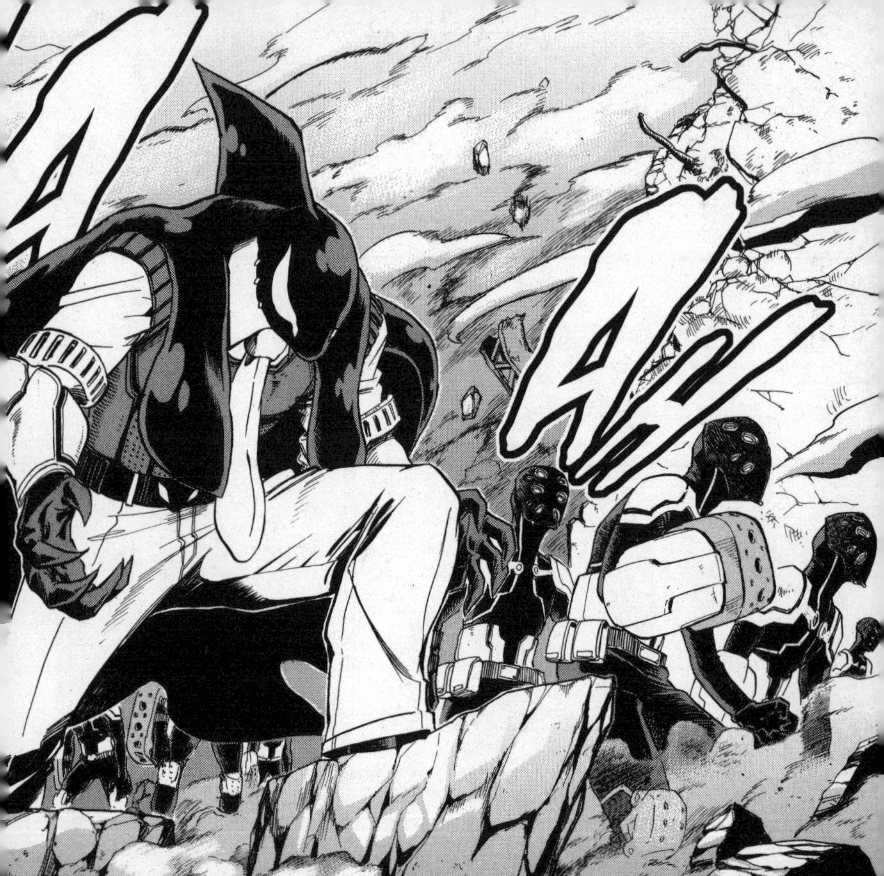

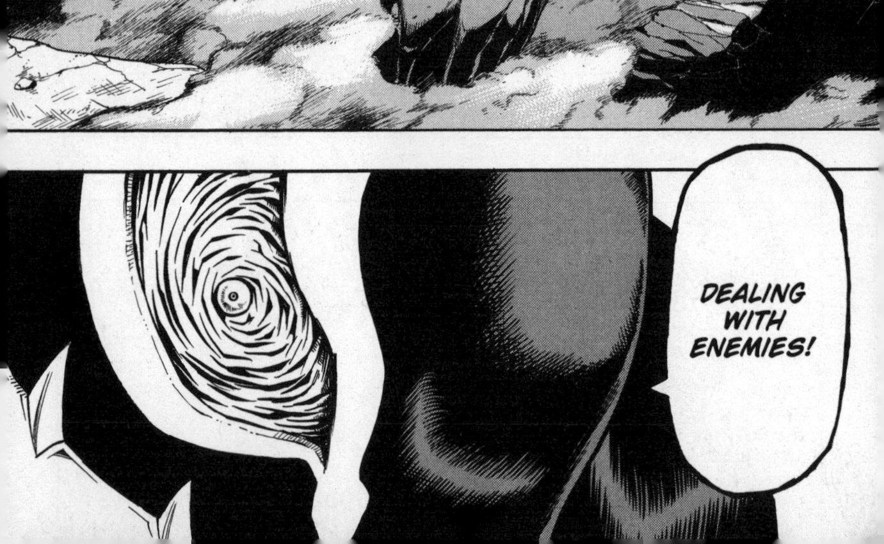
DEALING WITH ENEMIES!

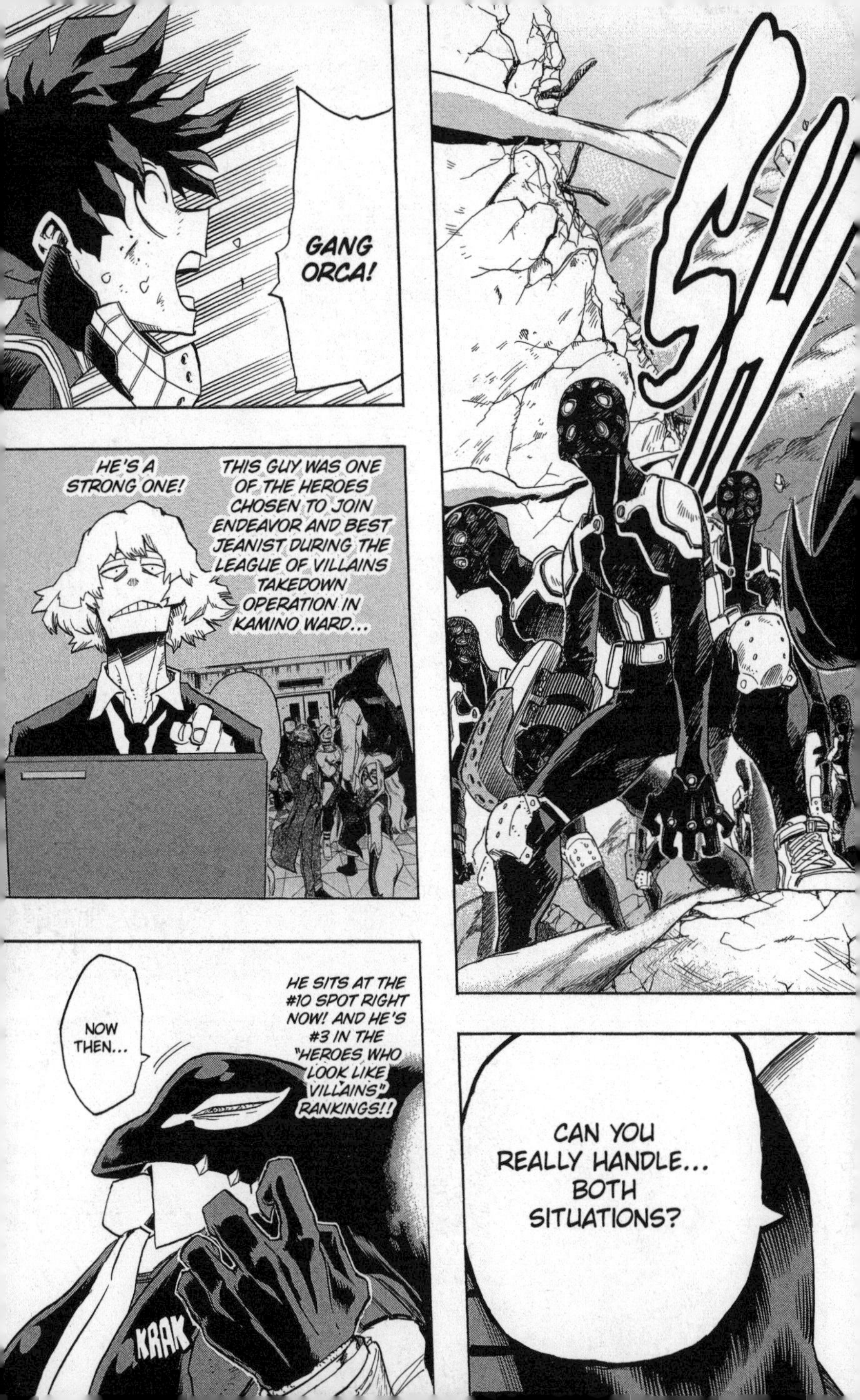
SH
GANG ORCA!
THIS GUY WAS ONE OF THE HEROES CHOSEN TO JOIN ENDEAVOR AND BEST JEANIST DURING THE LEAGUE OF VILLAINS TAKEDOWN OPERATION IN KAMINO WARD...
HE'S A STRONG ONE!
CAN YOU REALLY HANDLE... BOTH SITUATIONS?
HE SITS AT THE #10 SPOT RIGHT NOW! AND HE'S #3 IN THE "HEROES WHO LOOK LIKE VILLAINS" RANKINGS!!
NOW THEN...
KRAK

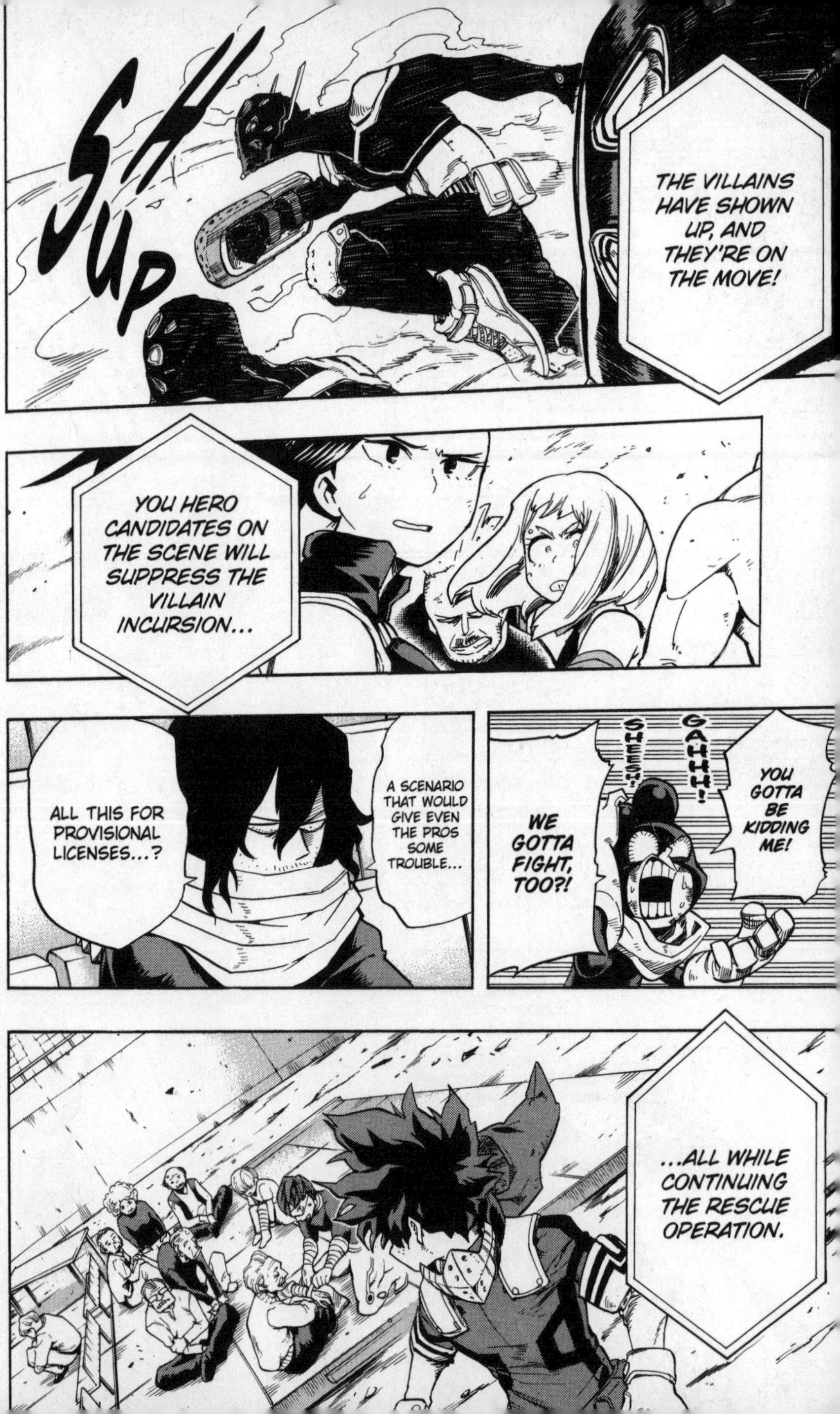
SHHUP
THE VILLAINS HAVE SHOWN UP, AND THEY'RE ON THE MOVE!
YOU HERO CANDIDATES ON THE SCENE WILL SUPPRESS THE VILLAIN INCURSION...
GAHHH!
SHEESH!
YOU GOTTA BE KIDDING ME!
WE GOTTA FIGHT, TOO?!
A SCENARIO THAT WOULD GIVE EVEN THE PROS SOME TROUBLE...
ALL THIS FOR PROVISIONAL LICENSES...?
...ALL WHILE CONTINUING THE RESCUE OPERATION.

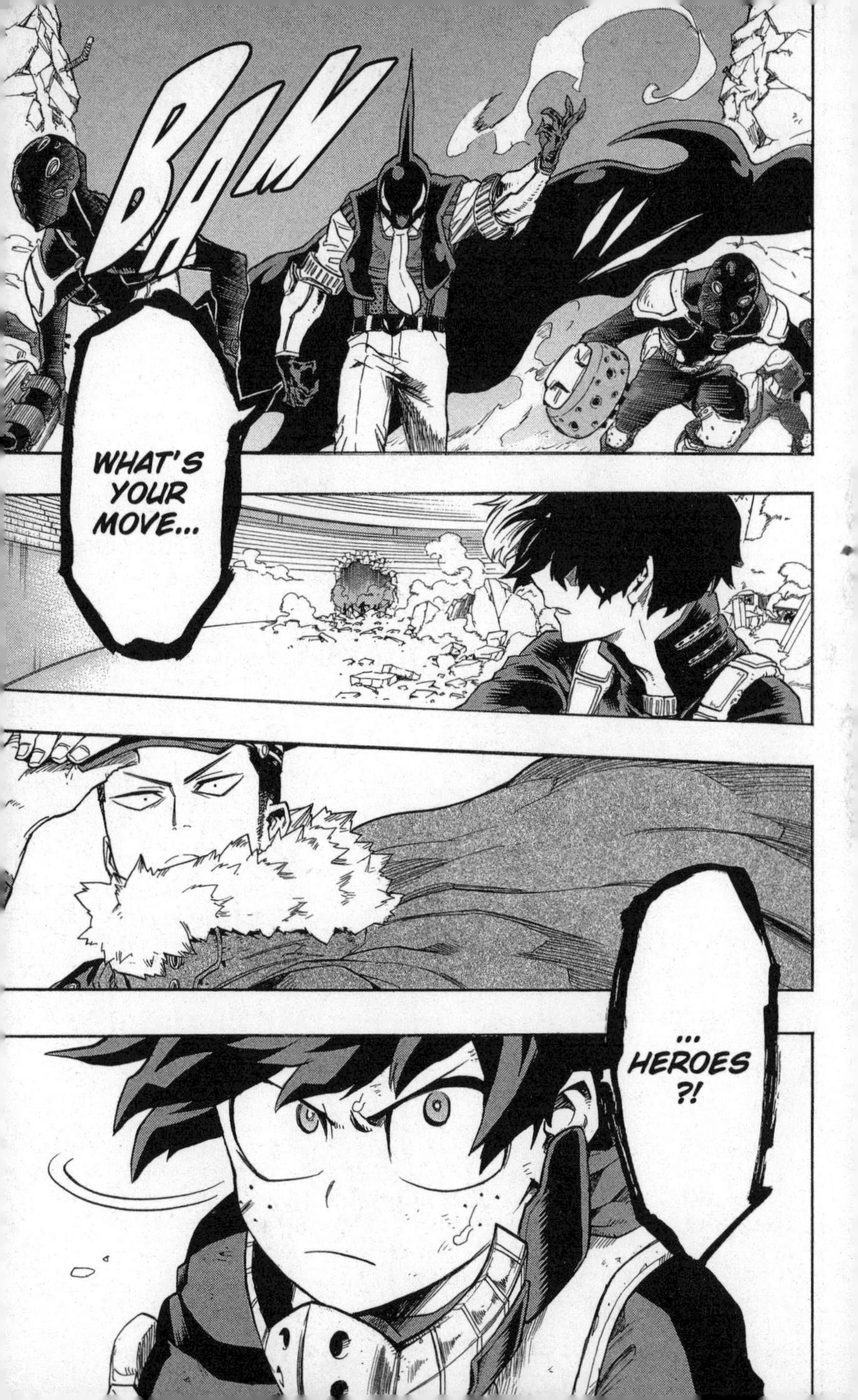
BAM
WHAT'S YOUR MOVE...
...HEROES?!

HERO

GANG ORCA (34) (KUGO SAKAMATA)

STREET CLOTHES

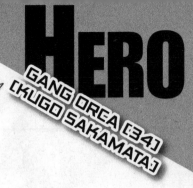

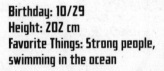

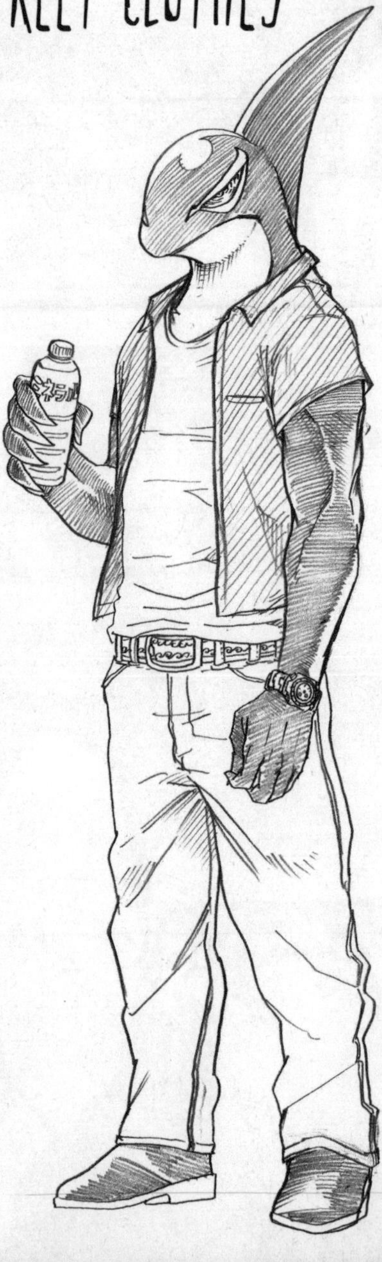

Birthday: 10/29
Height: 202 cm
Favorite Things: Strong people, swimming in the ocean

THE SUPPLEMENT

One of the incredibly capable heroes who took part in the League of Villains takedown.

Every aquarium in the country is constantly asking him to perform shows and give lectures.

However, his stony personality and intimidating face always result in more than a few crying children.

He has some angst about that, secretly.

Lots of angst.

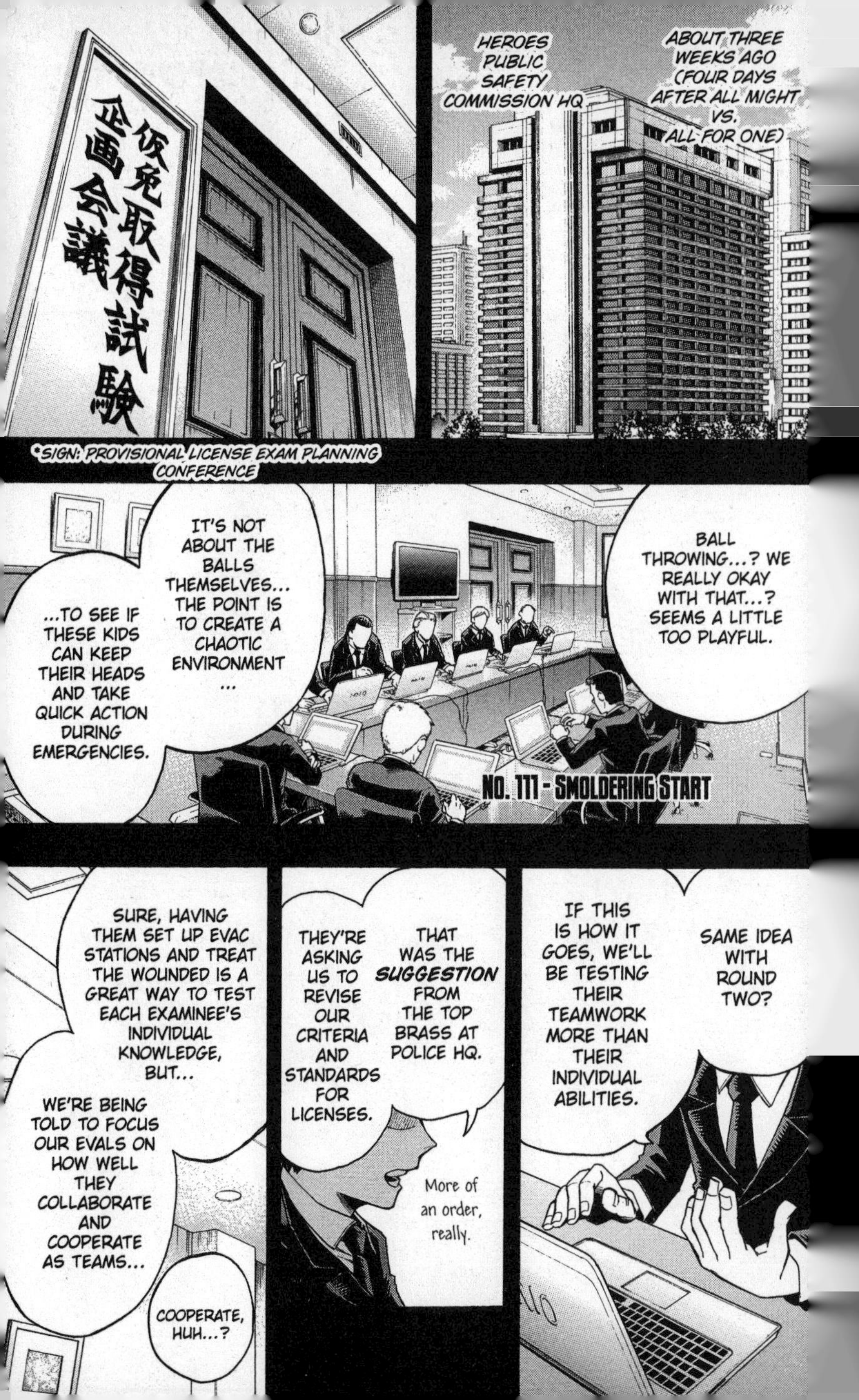
ABOUT THREE WEEKS AGO (FOUR DAYS AFTER ALL MIGHT VS. ALL FOR ONE)
HEROES PUBLIC SAFETY COMMISSION HQ
仮免取得試験
企画会議
*SIGN: PROVISIONAL LICENSE EXAM PLANNING CONFERENCE
BALL THROWING...? WE REALLY OKAY WITH THAT...? SEEMS A LITTLE TOO PLAYFUL.
IT'S NOT ABOUT THE BALLS THEMSELVES... THE POINT IS TO CREATE A CHAOTIC ENVIRONMENT...
...TO SEE IF THESE KIDS CAN KEEP THEIR HEADS AND TAKE QUICK ACTION DURING EMERGENCIES.
No. 111 - Smoldering Start
SAME IDEA WITH ROUND TWO?
IF THIS IS HOW IT GOES, WE'LL BE TESTING THEIR TEAMWORK MORE THAN THEIR INDIVIDUAL ABILITIES.
THAT WAS THE *SUGGESTION* FROM THE TOP BRASS AT POLICE HQ.
THEY'RE ASKING US TO REVISE OUR CRITERIA AND STANDARDS FOR LICENSES.
More of an order, really.
SURE, HAVING THEM SET UP EVAC STATIONS AND TREAT THE WOUNDED IS A GREAT WAY TO TEST EACH EXAMINEE'S INDIVIDUAL KNOWLEDGE, BUT...
WE'RE BEING TOLD TO FOCUS OUR EVALS ON HOW WELL THEY COLLABORATE AND COOPERATE AS TEAMS...
COOPERATE, HUH...?

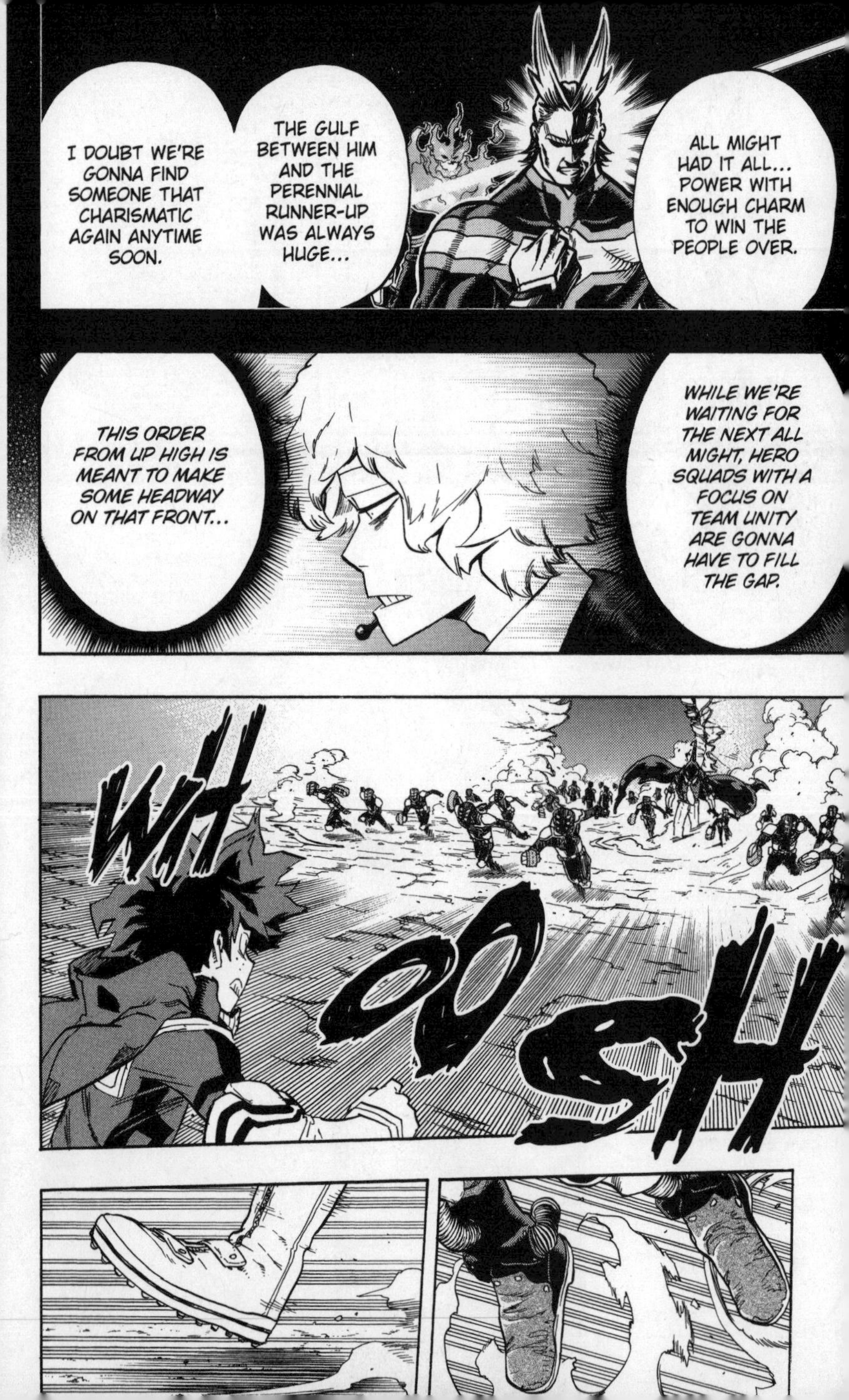
ALL MIGHT HAD IT ALL... POWER WITH ENOUGH CHARM TO WIN THE PEOPLE OVER.
THE GULF BETWEEN HIM AND THE PERENNIAL RUNNER-UP WAS ALWAYS HUGE...
I DOUBT WE'RE GONNA FIND SOMEONE THAT CHARISMATIC AGAIN ANYTIME SOON.
WHILE WE'RE WAITING FOR THE NEXT ALL MIGHT, HERO SQUADS WITH A FOCUS ON TEAM UNITY ARE GONNA HAVE TO FILL THE GAP.
THIS ORDER FROM UP HIGH IS MEANT TO MAKE SOME HEADWAY ON THAT FRONT...
WHOOSH

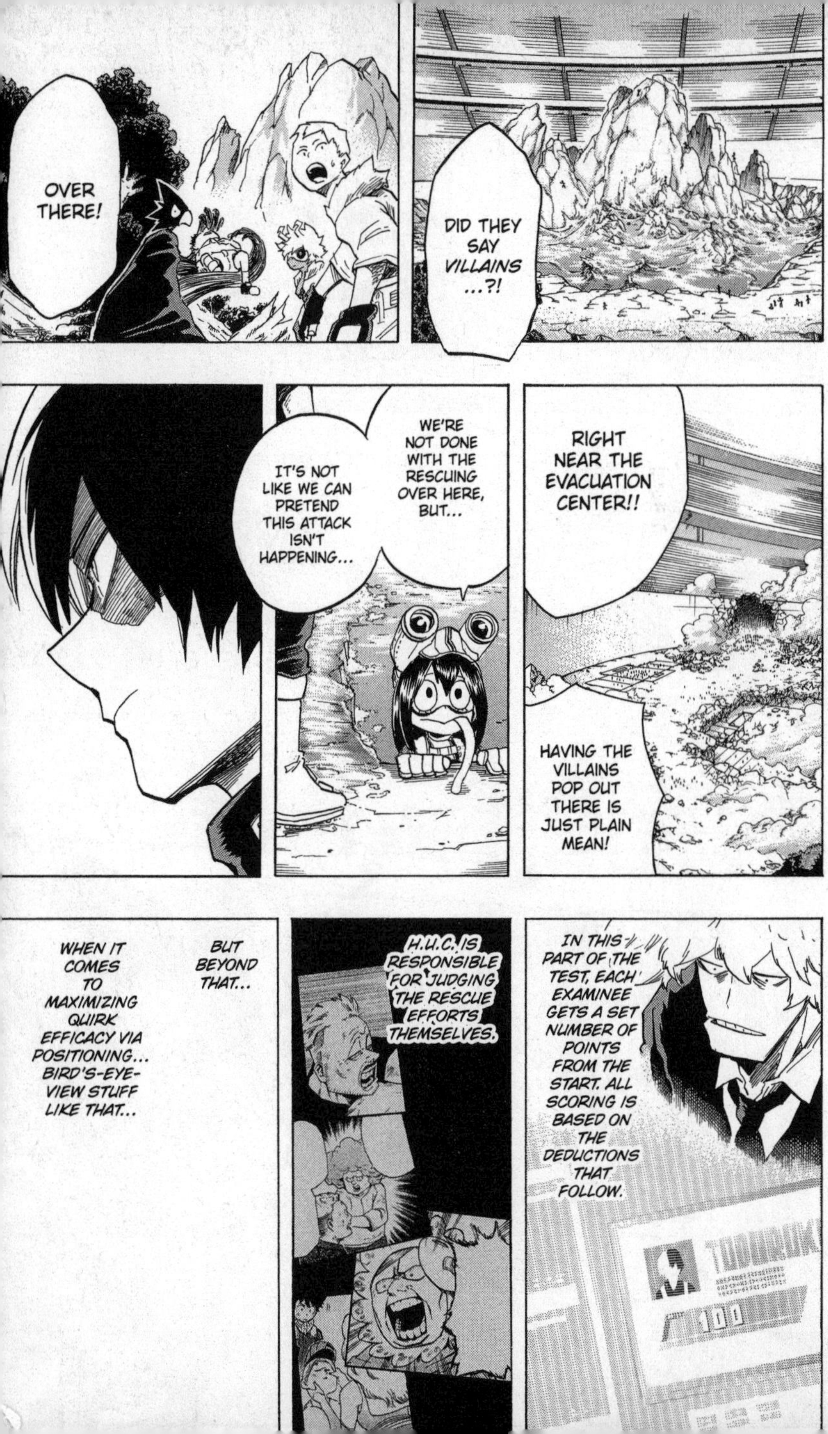
DID THEY SAY VILLAINS ...?!
OVER THERE!
RIGHT NEAR THE EVACUATION CENTER!!
HAVING THE VILLAINS POP OUT THERE IS JUST PLAIN MEAN!
WE'RE NOT DONE WITH THE RESCUING OVER HERE, BUT...
IT'S NOT LIKE WE CAN PRETEND THIS ATTACK ISN'T HAPPENING...
IN THIS PART OF THE TEST, EACH EXAMINEE GETS A SET NUMBER OF POINTS FROM THE START. ALL SCORING IS BASED ON THE DEDUCTIONS THAT FOLLOW.
100
H.U.C. IS RESPONSIBLE FOR JUDGING THE RESCUE EFFORTS THEMSELVES.
BUT BEYOND THAT...
WHEN IT COMES TO MAXIMIZING QUIRK EFFICACY VIA POSITIONING... BIRD'S-EYE-VIEW STUFF LIKE THAT...

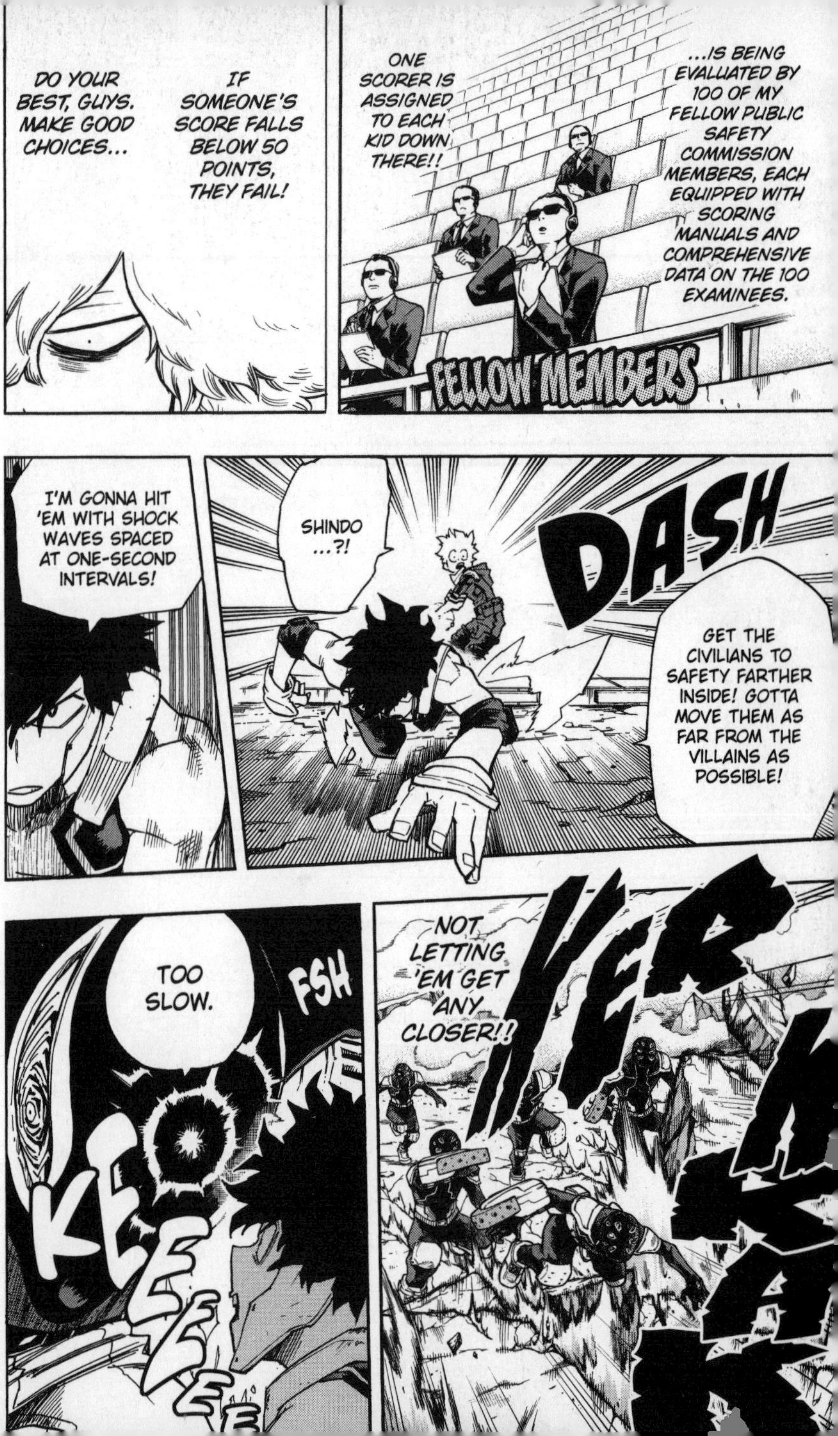
...IS BEING EVALUATED BY 100 OF MY FELLOW PUBLIC SAFETY COMMISSION MEMBERS, EACH EQUIPPED WITH SCORING MANUALS AND COMPREHENSIVE DATA ON THE 100 EXAMINEES.
ONE SCORER IS ASSIGNED TO EACH KID DOWN THERE!!
FELLOW MEMBERS
IF SOMEONE'S SCORE FALLS BELOW 50 POINTS, THEY FAIL!
DO YOUR BEST, GUYS. MAKE GOOD CHOICES...
DASH
GET THE CIVILIANS TO SAFETY FARTHER INSIDE! GOTTA MOVE THEM AS FAR FROM THE VILLAINS AS POSSIBLE!
SHINDO ...?!
I'M GONNA HIT 'EM WITH SHOCK WAVES SPACED AT ONE-SECOND INTERVALS!
NOT LETTING 'EM GET ANY CLOSER!!
TOO SLOW.
FSH
KEEEEE

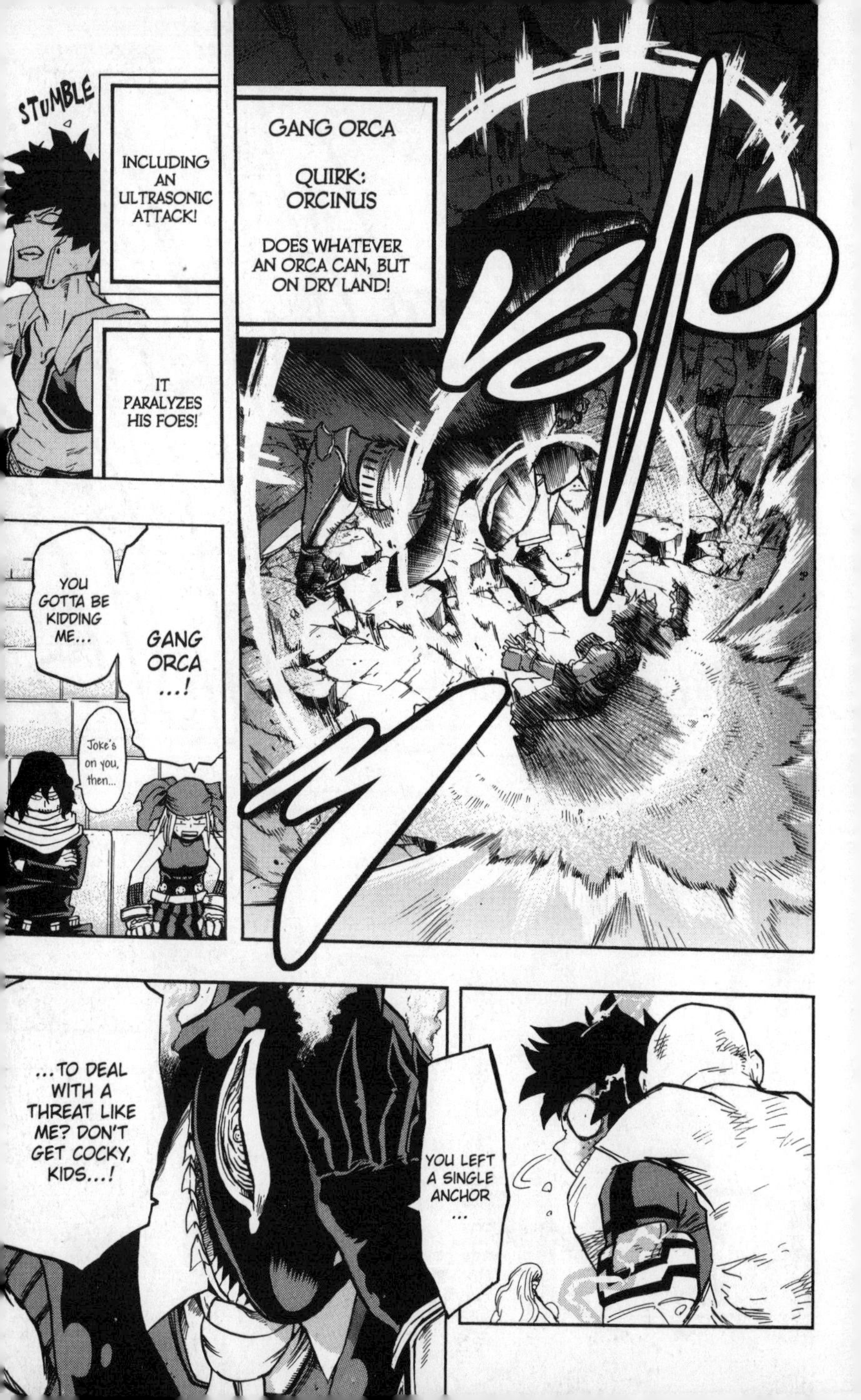

GANG ORCA
QUIRK: ORCINUS
DOES WHATEVER AN ORCA CAN, BUT ON DRY LAND!
STUMBLE
INCLUDING AN ULTRASONIC ATTACK!
IT PARALYZES HIS FOES!
YOU GOTTA BE KIDDING ME...
GANG ORCA ...!
Joke's on you, then...
YOU LEFT A SINGLE ANCHOR ...
...TO DEAL WITH A THREAT LIKE ME? DON'T GET COCKY, KIDS...!

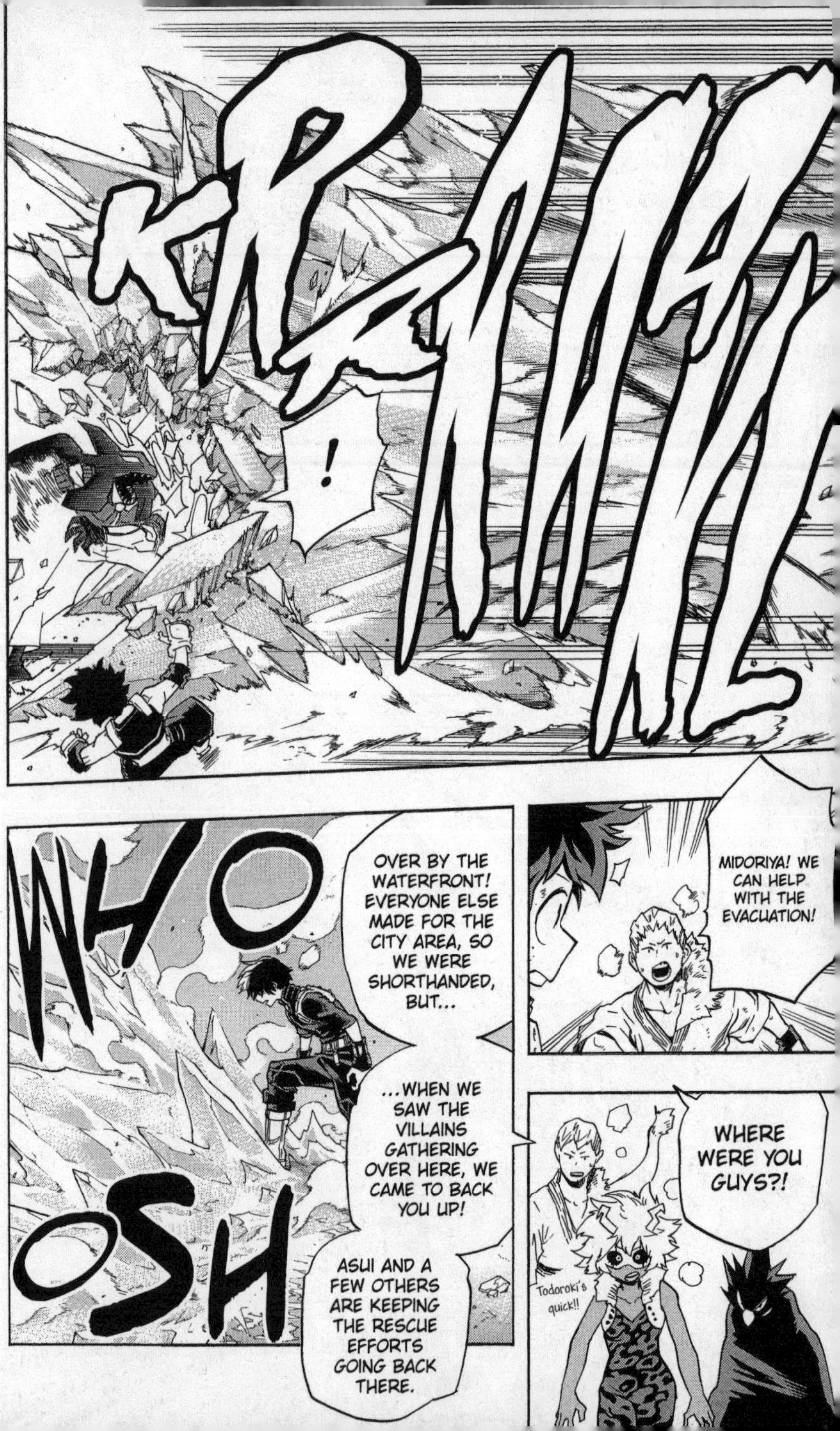
!
MIDORIYA! WE CAN HELP WITH THE EVACUATION!
WHERE WERE YOU GUYS?!
Todoroki's quick!!
WHOOSH
OVER BY THE WATERFRONT! EVERYONE ELSE MADE FOR THE CITY AREA, SO WE WERE SHORTHANDED, BUT...
...WHEN WE SAW THE VILLAINS GATHERING OVER HERE, WE CAME TO BACK YOU UP!
ASUI AND A FEW OTHERS ARE KEEPING THE RESCUE EFFORTS GOING BACK THERE.

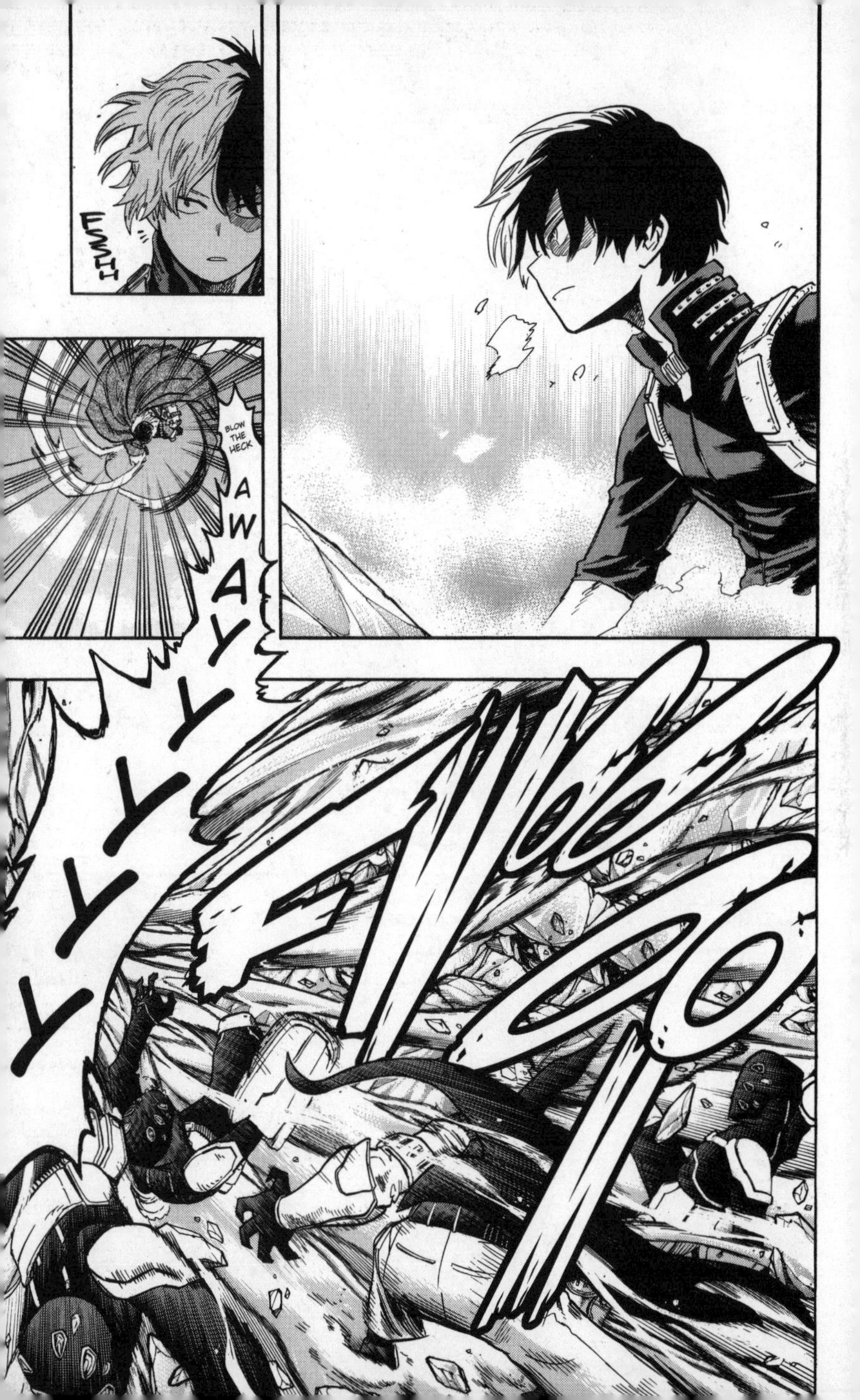
FSSHH
BLOW THE HECK
AWAYYYYY

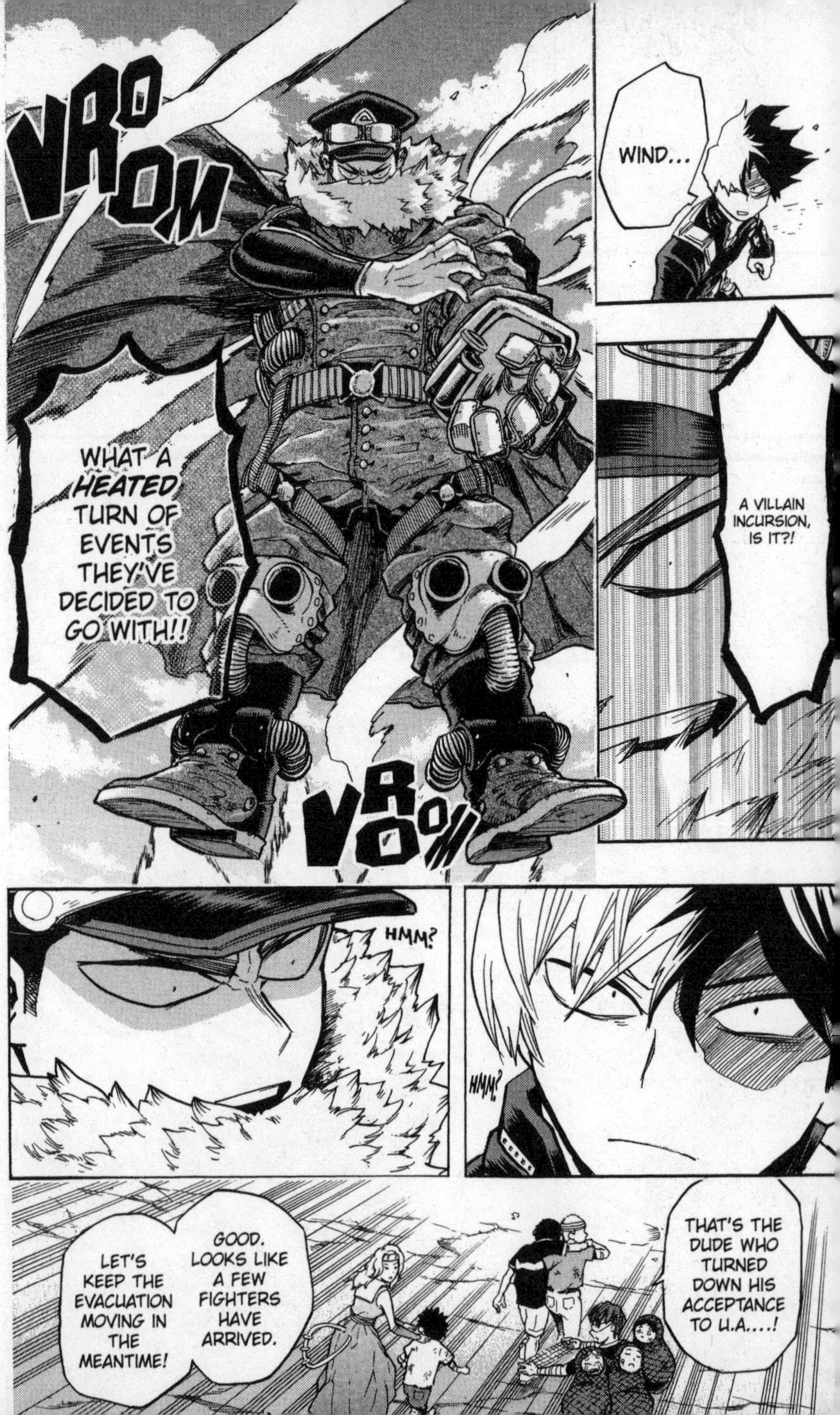
WIND...
A VILLAIN INCURSION, IS IT?!
VROOM
WHAT A HEATED TURN OF EVENTS THEY'VE DECIDED TO GO WITH!!
VROOM
HMM?
HMM?
THAT'S THE DUDE WHO TURNED DOWN HIS ACCEPTANCE TO U.A....!
GOOD. LOOKS LIKE A FEW FIGHTERS HAVE ARRIVED.
LET'S KEEP THE EVACUATION MOVING IN THE MEANTIME!

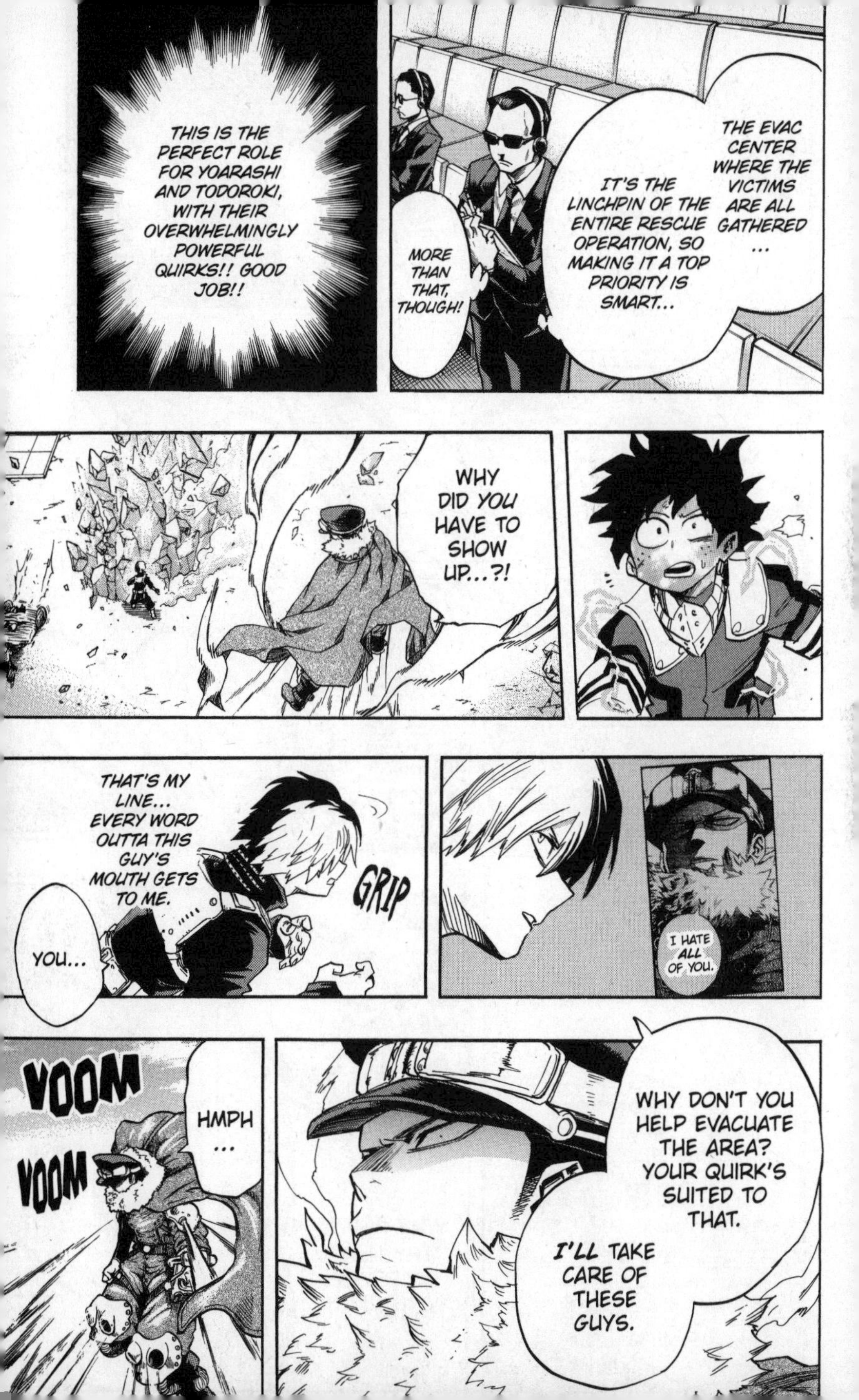
THE EVAC CENTER WHERE THE VICTIMS ARE ALL GATHERED ...
IT'S THE LINCHPIN OF THE ENTIRE RESCUE OPERATION, SO MAKING IT A TOP PRIORITY IS SMART...
MORE THAN THAT, THOUGH!
THIS IS THE PERFECT ROLE FOR YOARASHI AND TODOROKI, WITH THEIR OVERWHELMINGLY POWERFUL QUIRKS!! GOOD JOB!!
WHY DID YOU HAVE TO SHOW UP...?!
I HATE ALL OF YOU.
THAT'S MY LINE... EVERY WORD OUTTA THIS GUY'S MOUTH GETS TO ME.
GRIP
YOU...
WHY DON'T YOU HELP EVACUATE THE AREA? YOUR QUIRK'S SUITED TO THAT.
I'LL TAKE CARE OF THESE GUYS.
HMPH ...
VOOM
VOOM

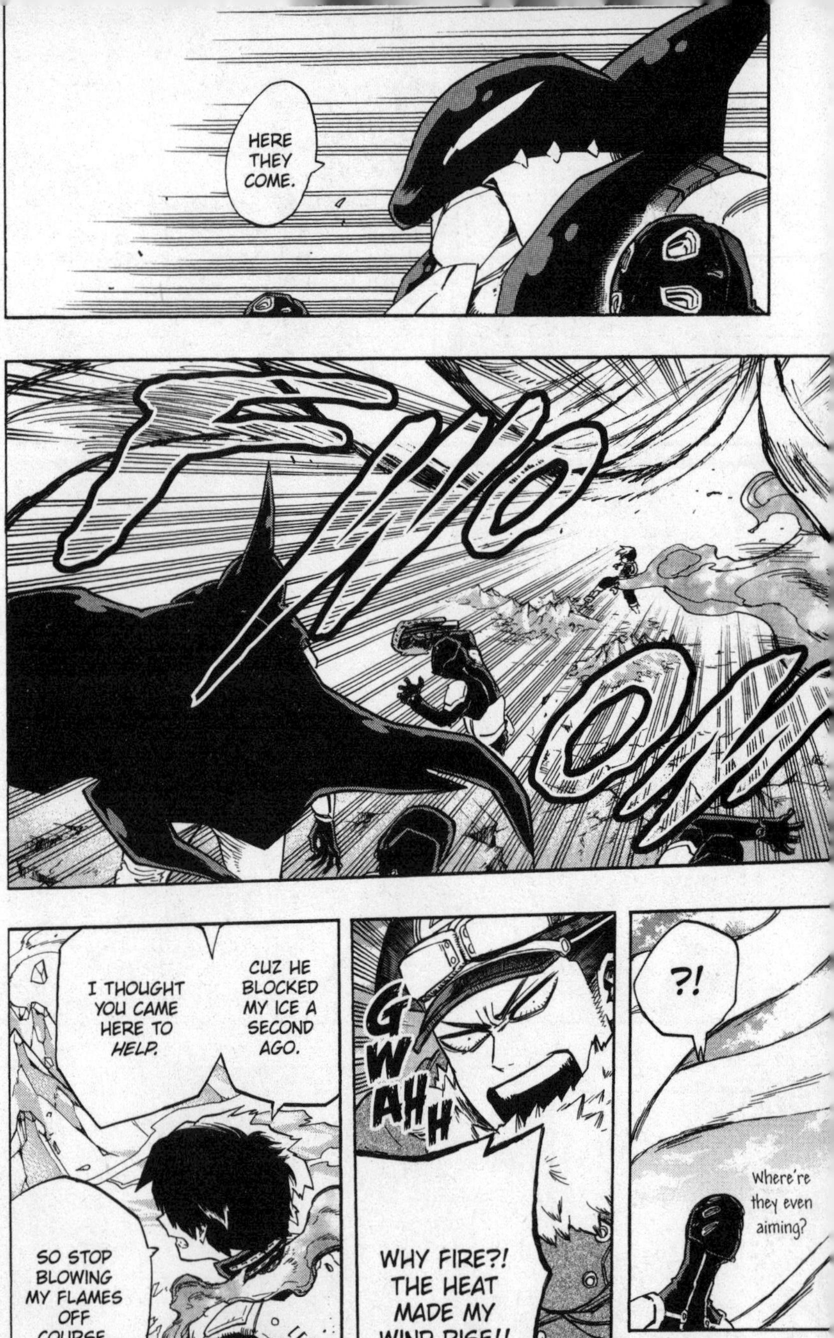
HERE THEY COME.
?!
Where're they even aiming?
GWAHH
WHY FIRE?! THE HEAT MADE MY WIND RISE!!
CUZ HE BLOCKED MY ICE A SECOND AGO.
I THOUGHT YOU CAME HERE TO *HELP.*
SO STOP BLOWING MY FLAMES OFF COURSE.

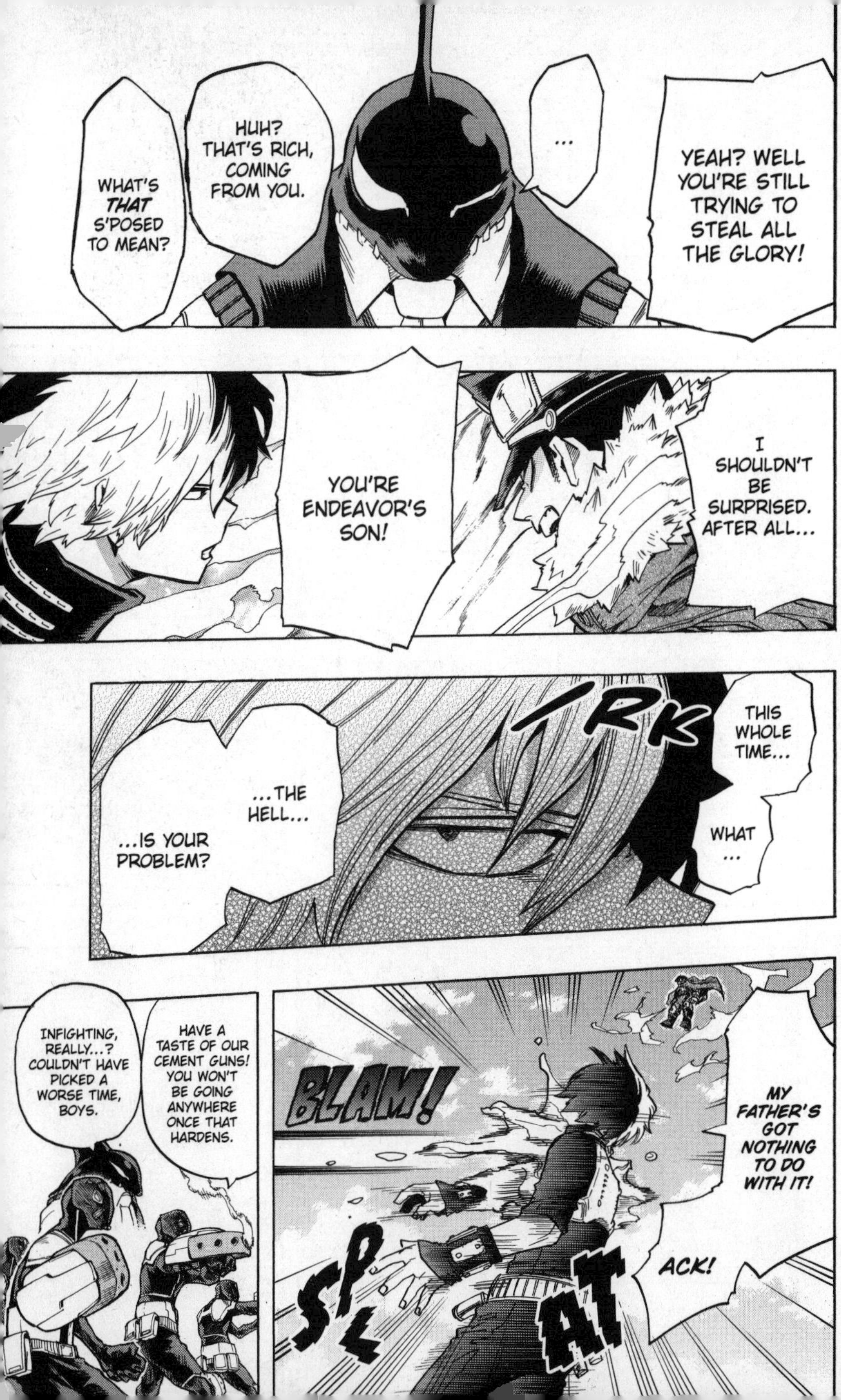
YEAH? WELL YOU'RE STILL TRYING TO STEAL ALL THE GLORY!
...
HUH? THAT'S RICH, COMING FROM YOU.
WHAT'S *THAT* S'POSED TO MEAN?
I SHOULDN'T BE SURPRISED. AFTER ALL...
YOU'RE ENDEAVOR'S SON!
THIS WHOLE TIME...
IRK
WHAT ...
...THE HELL...
...IS YOUR PROBLEM?
MY FATHER'S GOT NOTHING TO DO WITH IT!
BLAM!
ACK!
SPLAT
HAVE A TASTE OF OUR CEMENT GUNS! YOU WON'T BE GOING ANYWHERE ONCE THAT HARDENS.
INFIGHTING, REALLY...? COULDN'T HAVE PICKED A WORSE TIME, BOYS.

FWISH FWISH FW

HE'S GOT EVERYTHING TO DO WITH IT, DARN IT!

YEA HH HH

TO ME, HEROES ARE ALL ABOUT BRINGING THE *HEAT!*

THEIR FIERY SOULS INSPIRE PASSION AND HOPE IN PEOPLE!!

YEA HH HH

MOVE IT.

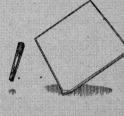

SO IT WAS A REAL LETDOWN WHEN...

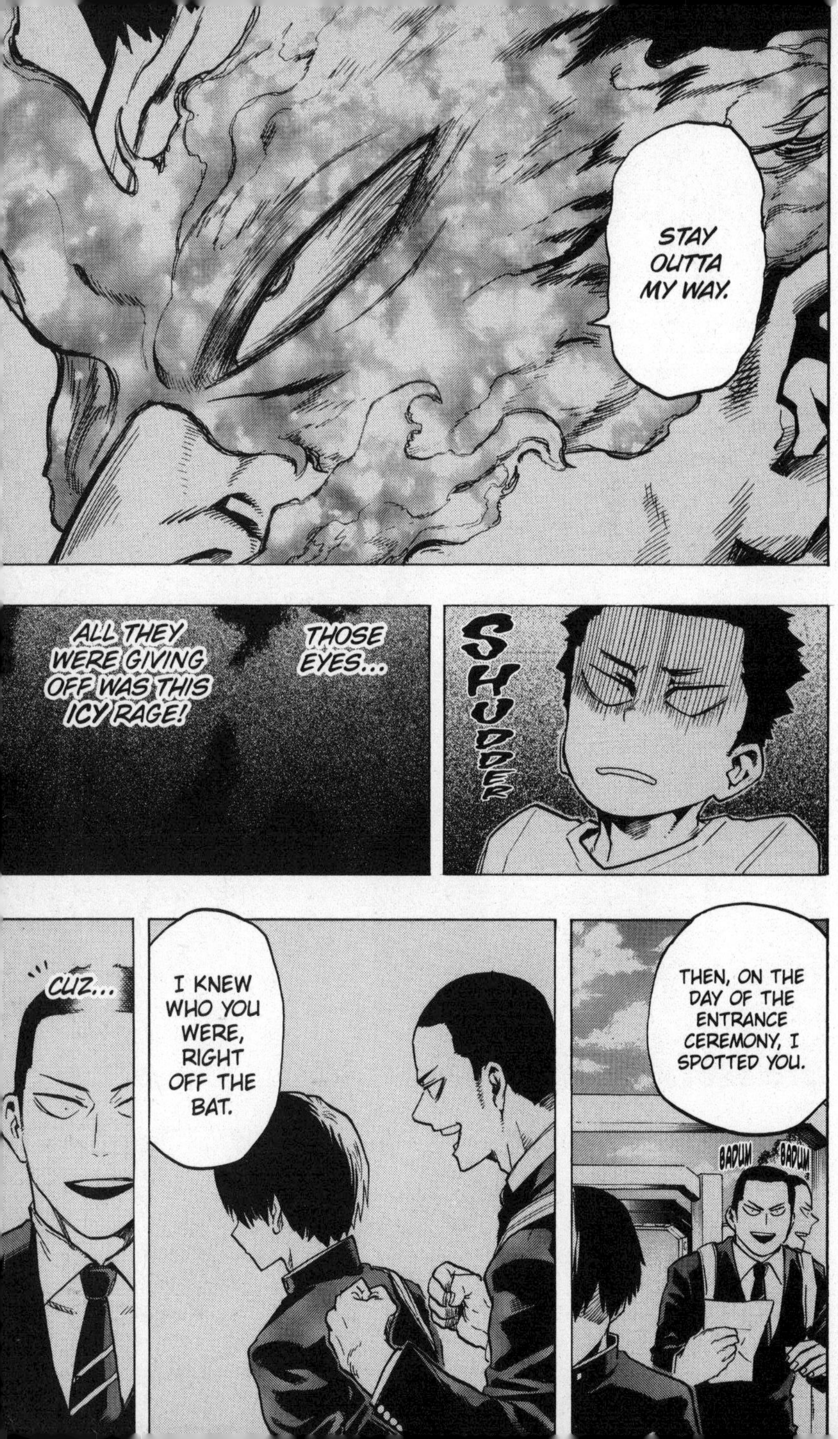
STAY OUTTA MY WAY.
SHUDDER
THOSE EYES...
ALL THEY WERE GIVING OFF WAS THIS ICY RAGE!
THEN, ON THE DAY OF THE ENTRANCE CEREMONY, I SPOTTED YOU.
BADUM
BADUM
I KNEW WHO YOU WERE, RIGHT OFF THE BAT.
CUZ...

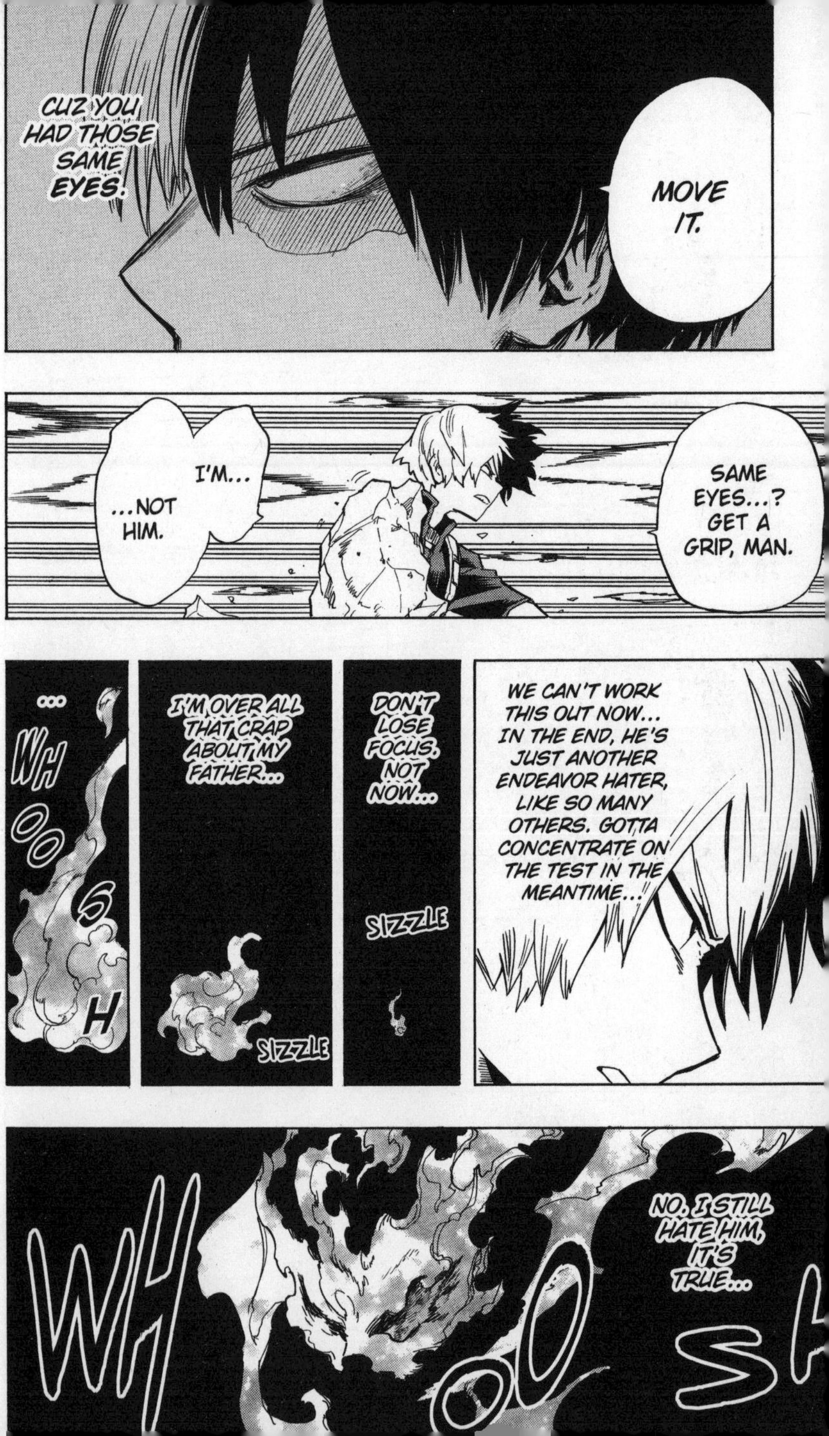
MOVE IT.
CUZ YOU HAD THOSE SAME EYES.
SAME EYES...? GET A GRIP, MAN.
I'M...
...NOT HIM.
WE CAN'T WORK THIS OUT NOW... IN THE END, HE'S JUST ANOTHER ENDEAVOR HATER, LIKE SO MANY OTHERS. GOTTA CONCENTRATE ON THE TEST IN THE MEANTIME...
DON'T LOSE FOCUS. NOT NOW...
SIZZLE
I'M OVER ALL THAT CRAP ABOUT MY FATHER...
SIZZLE
...
WHOOSH
NO. I STILL HATE HIM, IT'S TRUE...
WHOOSH

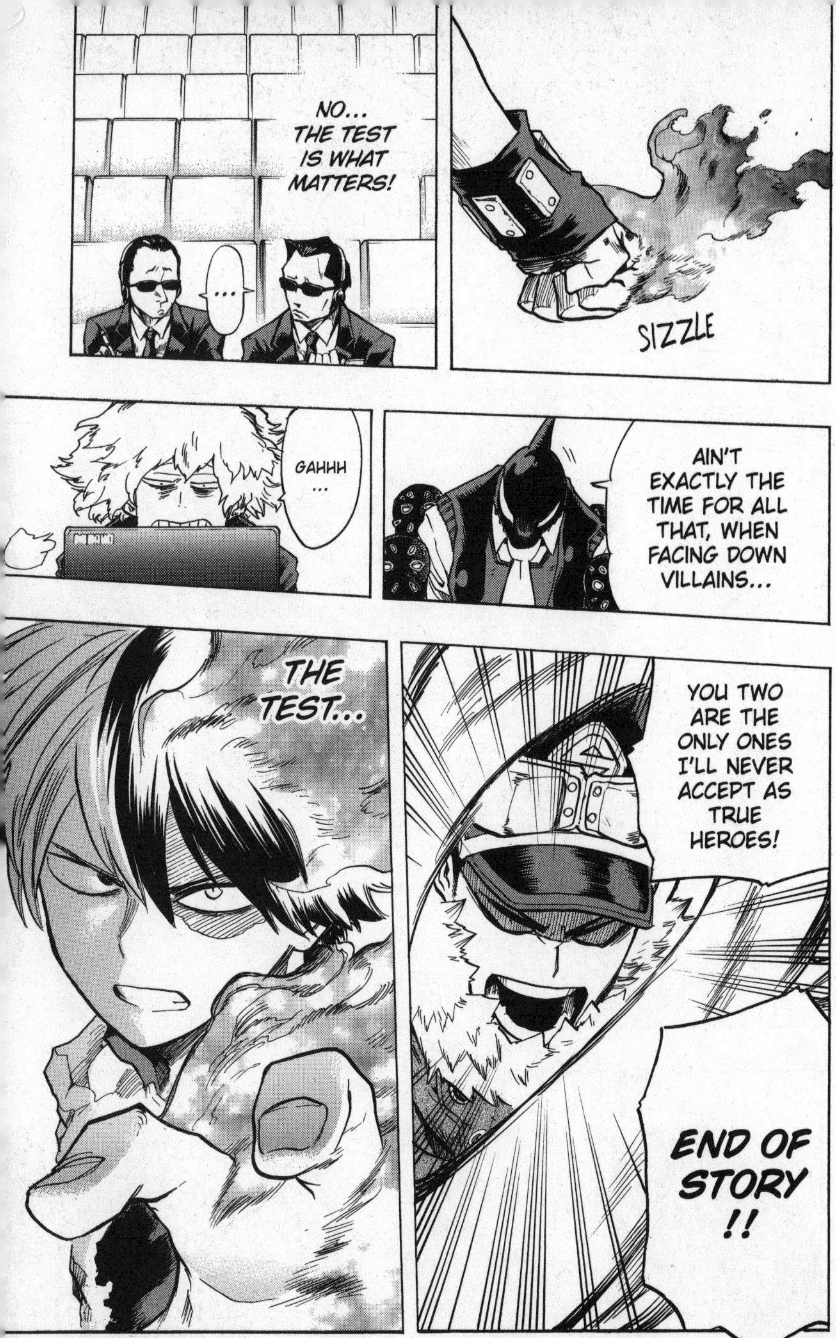
SIZZLE
NO... THE TEST IS WHAT MATTERS!
...
AIN'T EXACTLY THE TIME FOR ALL THAT, WHEN FACING DOWN VILLAINS...
GAHHH ...
YOU TWO ARE THE ONLY ONES I'LL NEVER ACCEPT AS TRUE HEROES!
END OF STORY !!
THE TEST...

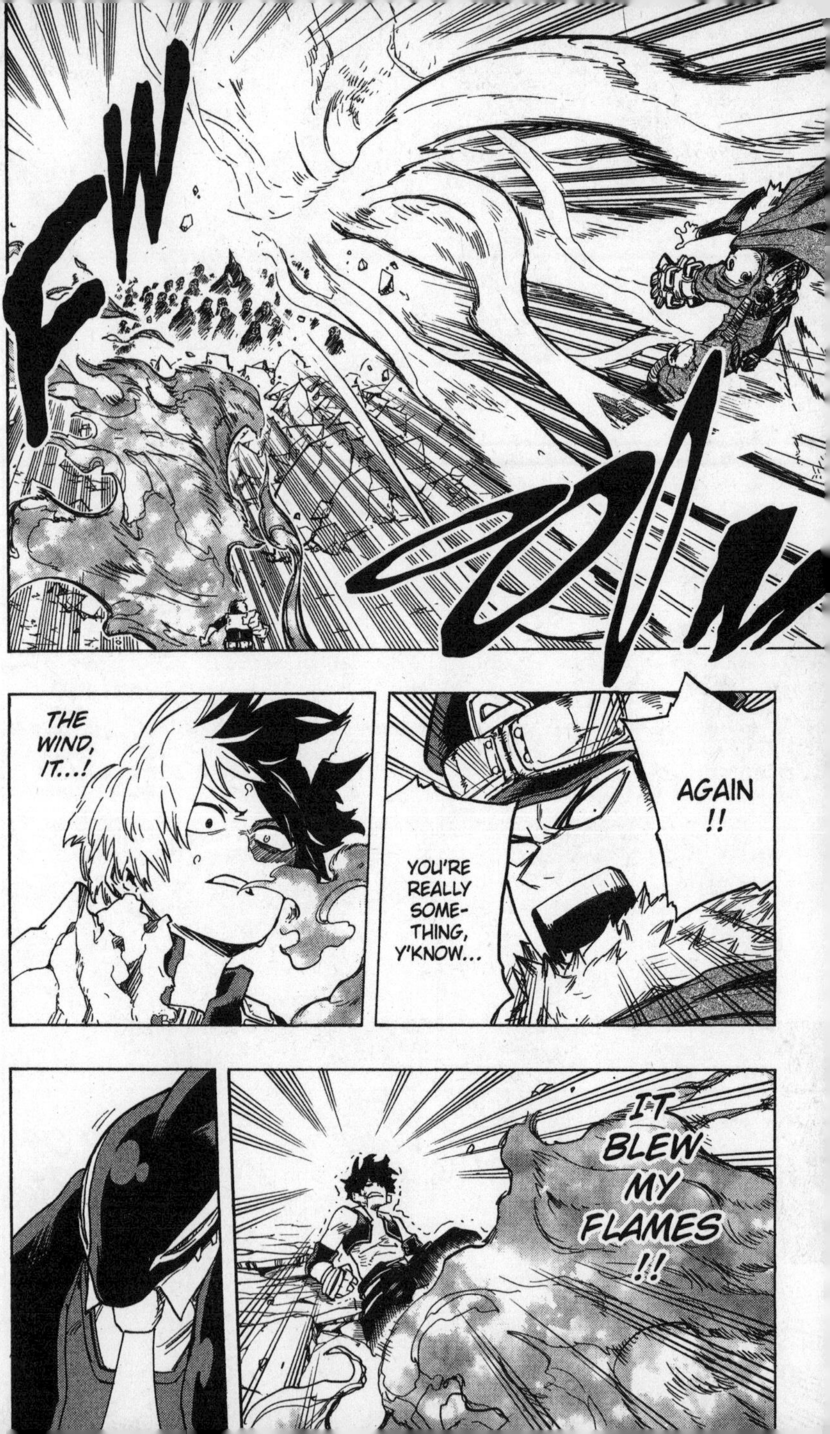
FWOOM
AGAIN!!
YOU'RE REALLY SOMETHING, Y'KNOW...
THE WIND, IT...!
IT BLEW MY FLAMES!!

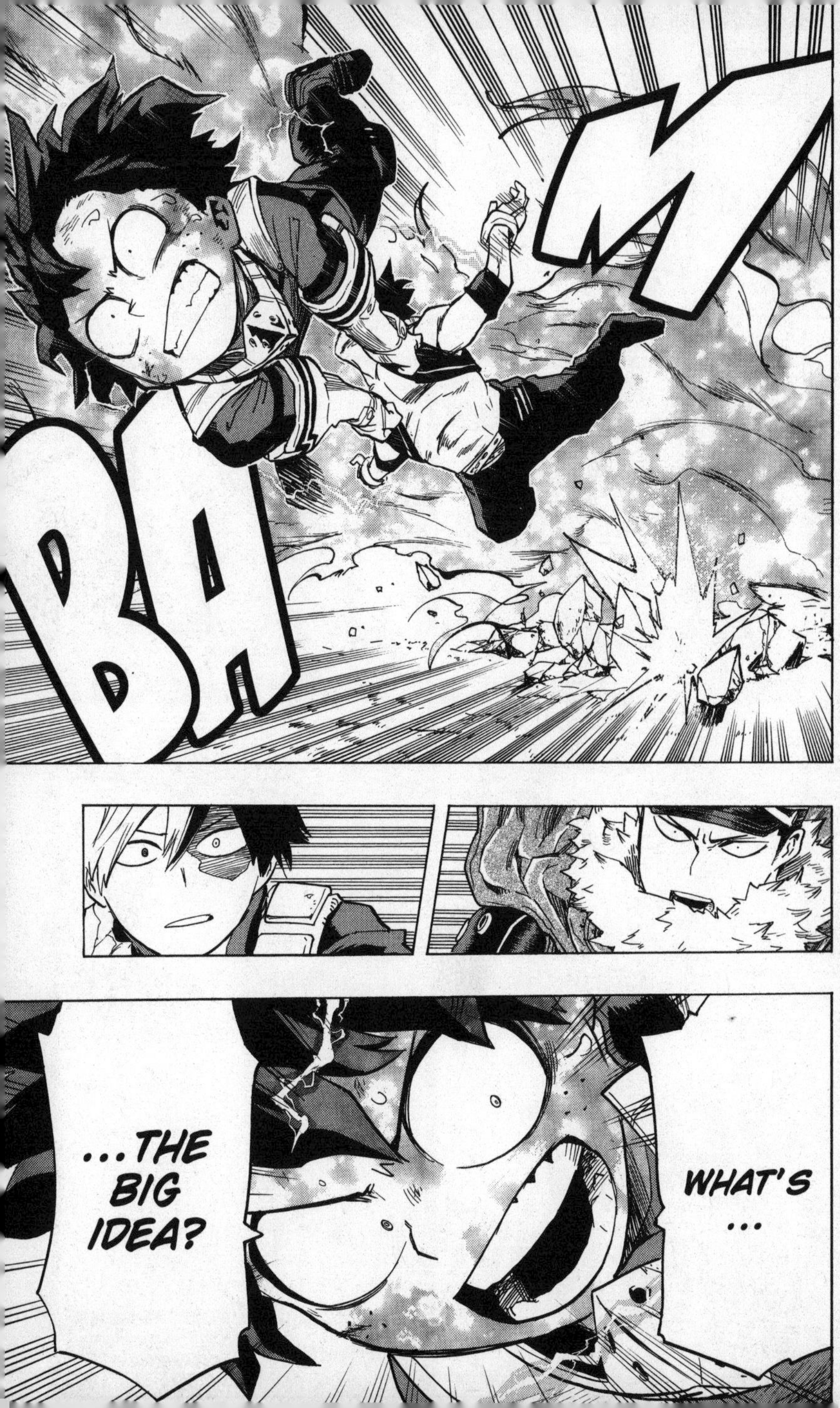
BAM
WHAT'S ...
...THE BIG IDEA?

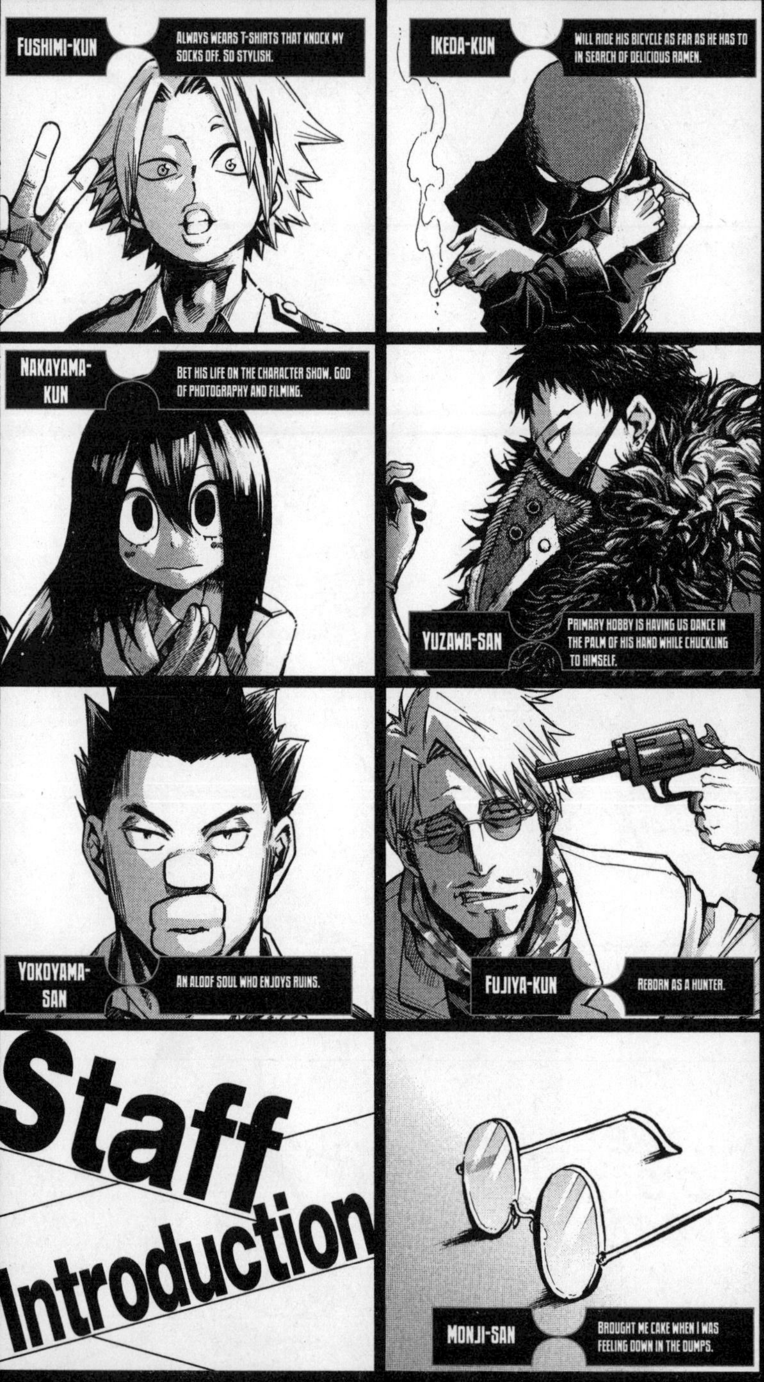
IKEDA-KUN
WILL RIDE HIS BICYCLE AS FAR AS HE HAS TO IN SEARCH OF DELICIOUS RAMEN.
FUSHIMI-KUN
ALWAYS WEARS T-SHIRTS THAT KNOCK MY SOCKS OFF. SO STYLISH.
YUZAWA-SAN
PRIMARY HOBBY IS HAVING US DANCE IN THE PALM OF HIS HAND WHILE CHUCKLING TO HIMSELF.
NAKAYAMA-KUN
BET HIS LIFE ON THE CHARACTER SHOW. GOD OF PHOTOGRAPHY AND FILMING.
FUJIYA-KUN
REBORN AS A HUNTER.
YOKOYAMA-SAN
AN ALOOF SOUL WHO ENJOYS RUINS.
MONJI-SAN
BROUGHT ME CAKE WHEN I WAS FEELING DOWN IN THE DUMPS.
Staff Introduction

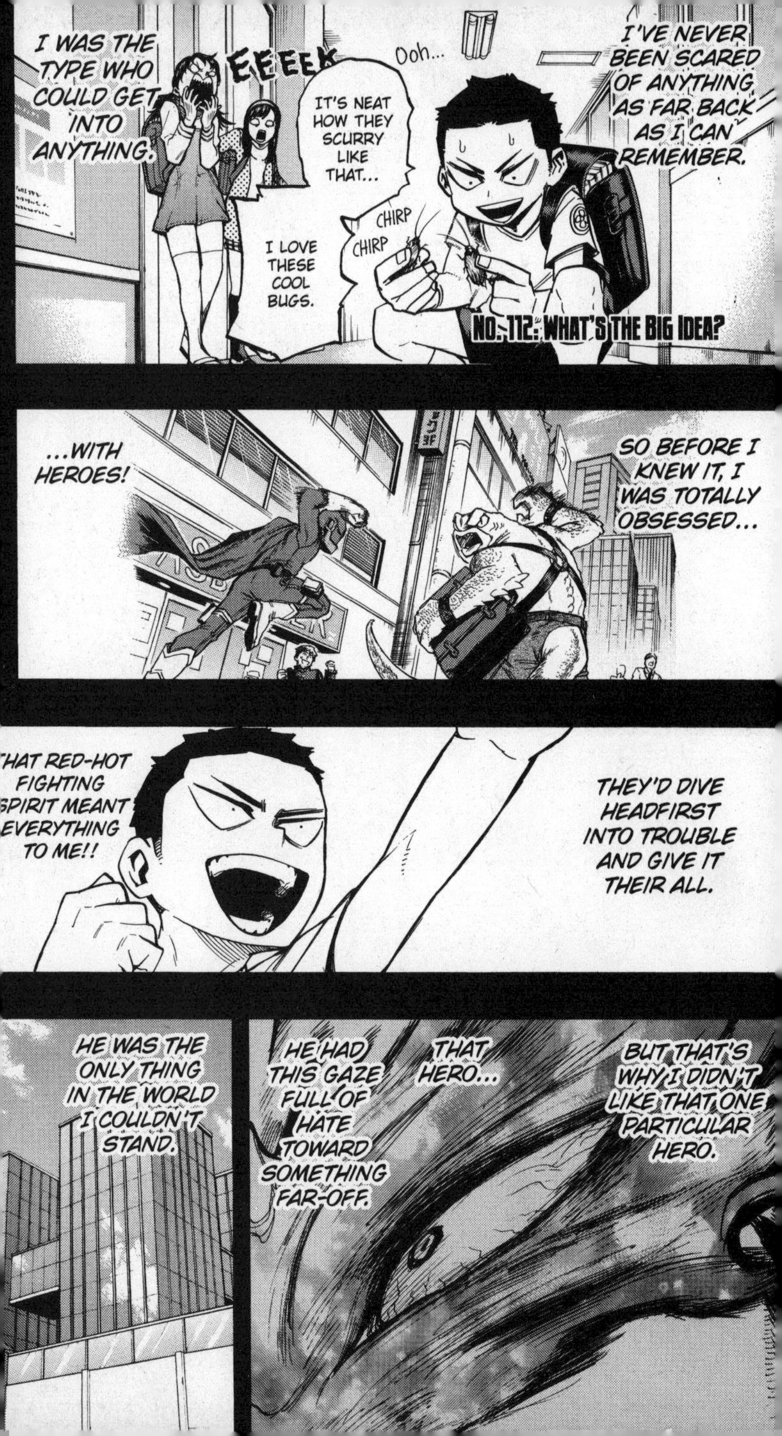
I'VE NEVER BEEN SCARED OF ANYTHING AS FAR BACK AS I CAN REMEMBER.
Ooh...
IT'S NEAT HOW THEY SCURRY LIKE THAT...
CHIRP
CHIRP
I LOVE THESE COOL BUGS.
EEEEK
I WAS THE TYPE WHO COULD GET INTO ANYTHING.
No. 112: What's the Big Idea?
SO BEFORE I KNEW IT, I WAS TOTALLY OBSESSED...
...WITH HEROES!
THEY'D DIVE HEADFIRST INTO TROUBLE AND GIVE IT THEIR ALL.
THAT RED-HOT FIGHTING SPIRIT MEANT EVERYTHING TO ME!!
BUT THAT'S WHY I DIDN'T LIKE THAT ONE PARTICULAR HERO.
THAT HERO...
HE HAD THIS GAZE FULL OF HATE TOWARD SOMETHING FAR-OFF.
HE WAS THE ONLY THING IN THE WORLD I COULDN'T STAND.

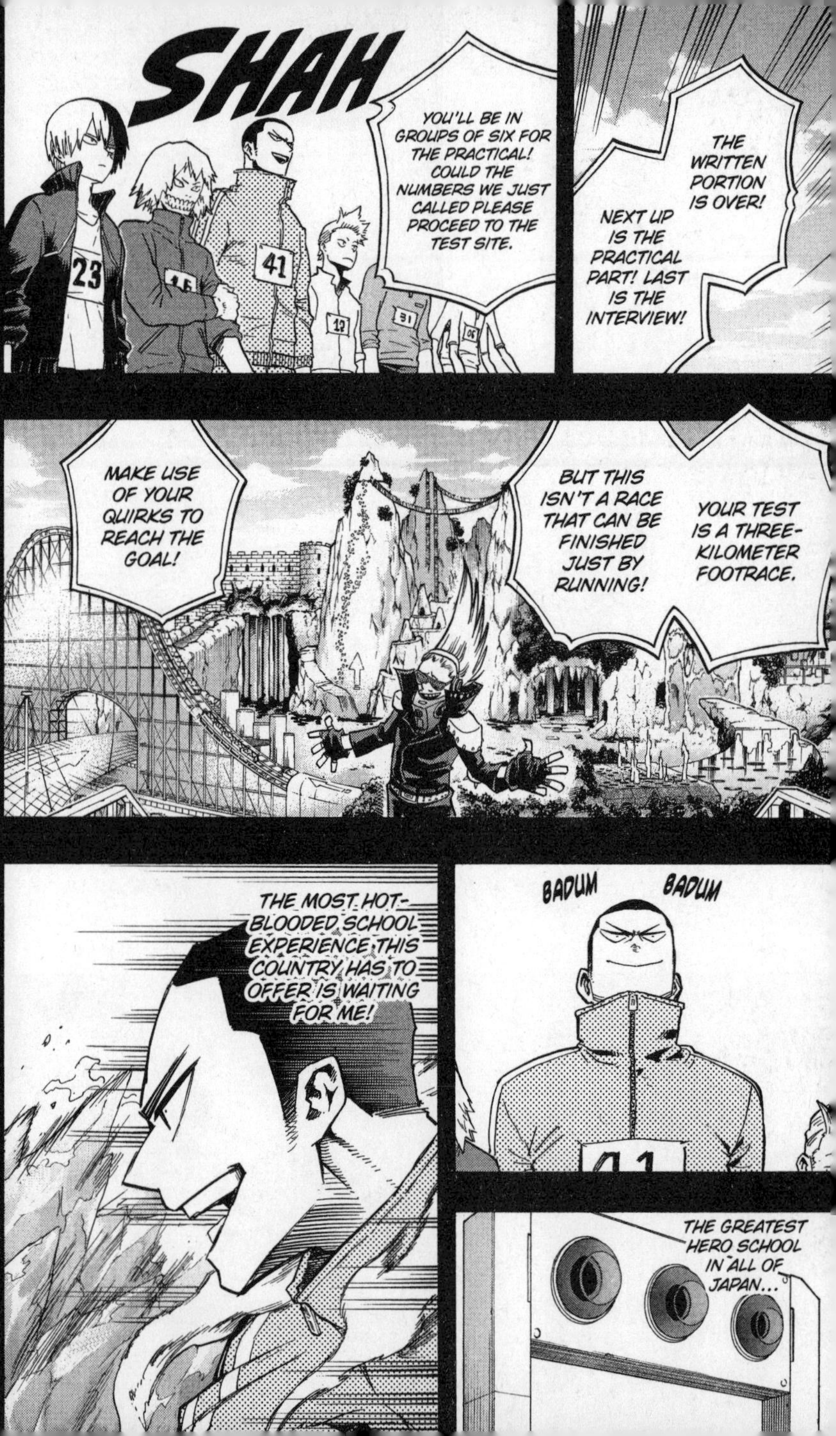
THE WRITTEN PORTION IS OVER!
NEXT UP IS THE PRACTICAL PART! LAST IS THE INTERVIEW!
SHAH
YOU'LL BE IN GROUPS OF SIX FOR THE PRACTICAL! COULD THE NUMBERS WE JUST CALLED PLEASE PROCEED TO THE TEST SITE.
23
41
YOUR TEST IS A THREE-KILOMETER FOOTRACE.
BUT THIS ISN'T A RACE THAT CAN BE FINISHED JUST BY RUNNING!
MAKE USE OF YOUR QUIRKS TO REACH THE GOAL!
BADUM
BADUM
THE GREATEST HERO SCHOOL IN ALL OF JAPAN...
THE MOST HOT-BLOODED SCHOOL EXPERIENCE THIS COUNTRY HAS TO OFFER IS WAITING FOR ME!

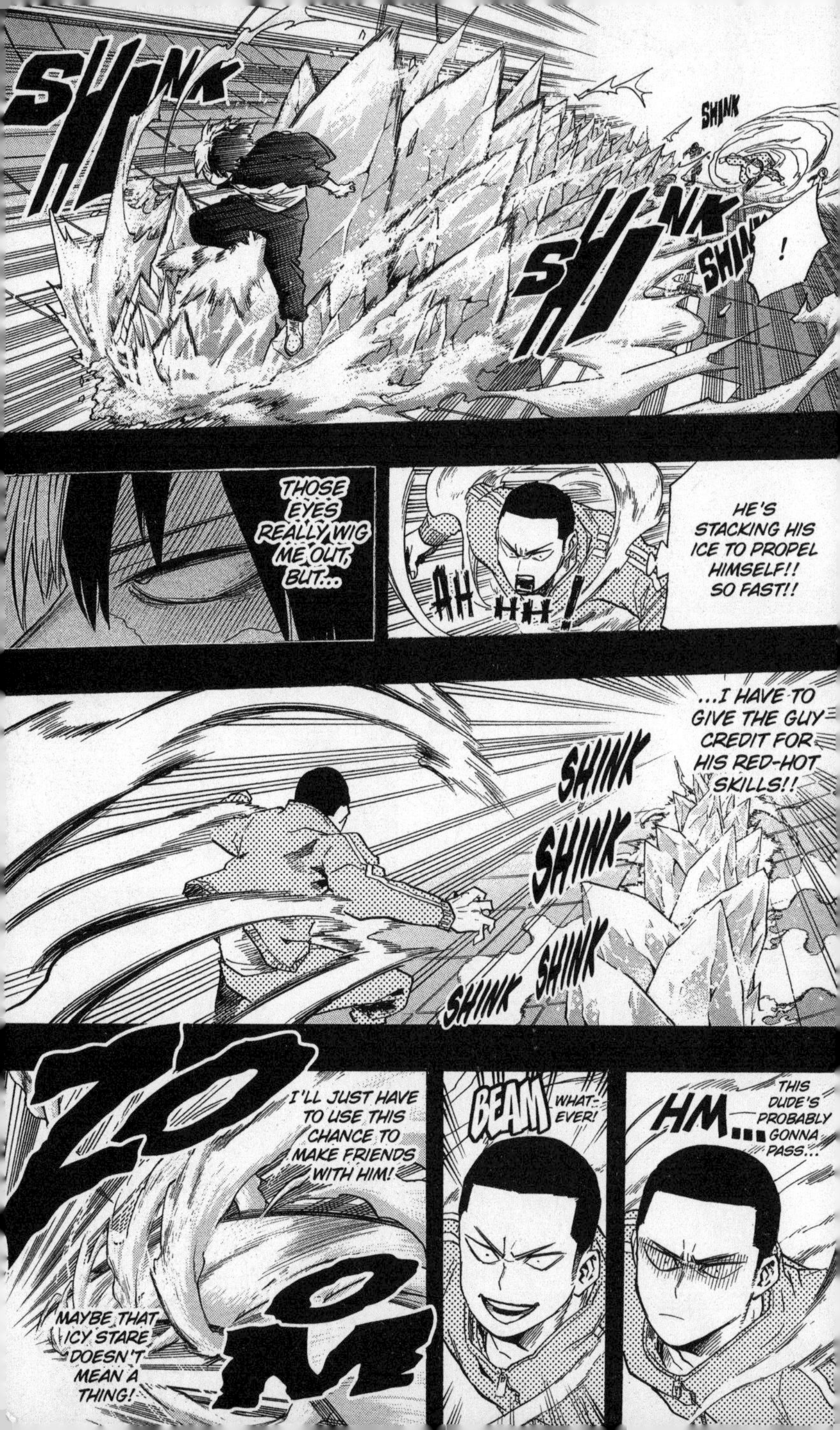
SHINK
!
SHINK
SHINK
SHINK
HE'S STACKING HIS ICE TO PROPEL HIMSELF!! SO FAST!!
AHHH!
THOSE EYES REALLY WIG ME OUT, BUT...
...I HAVE TO GIVE THE GUY CREDIT FOR HIS RED-HOT SKILLS!!
SHINK
SHINK
SHINK
SHINK
THIS DUDE'S PROBABLY GONNA PASS...
HM...
BEAM
WHAT-EVER!
I'LL JUST HAVE TO USE THIS CHANCE TO MAKE FRIENDS WITH HIM!
ZOOM
MAYBE THAT ICY STARE DOESN'T MEAN A THING!

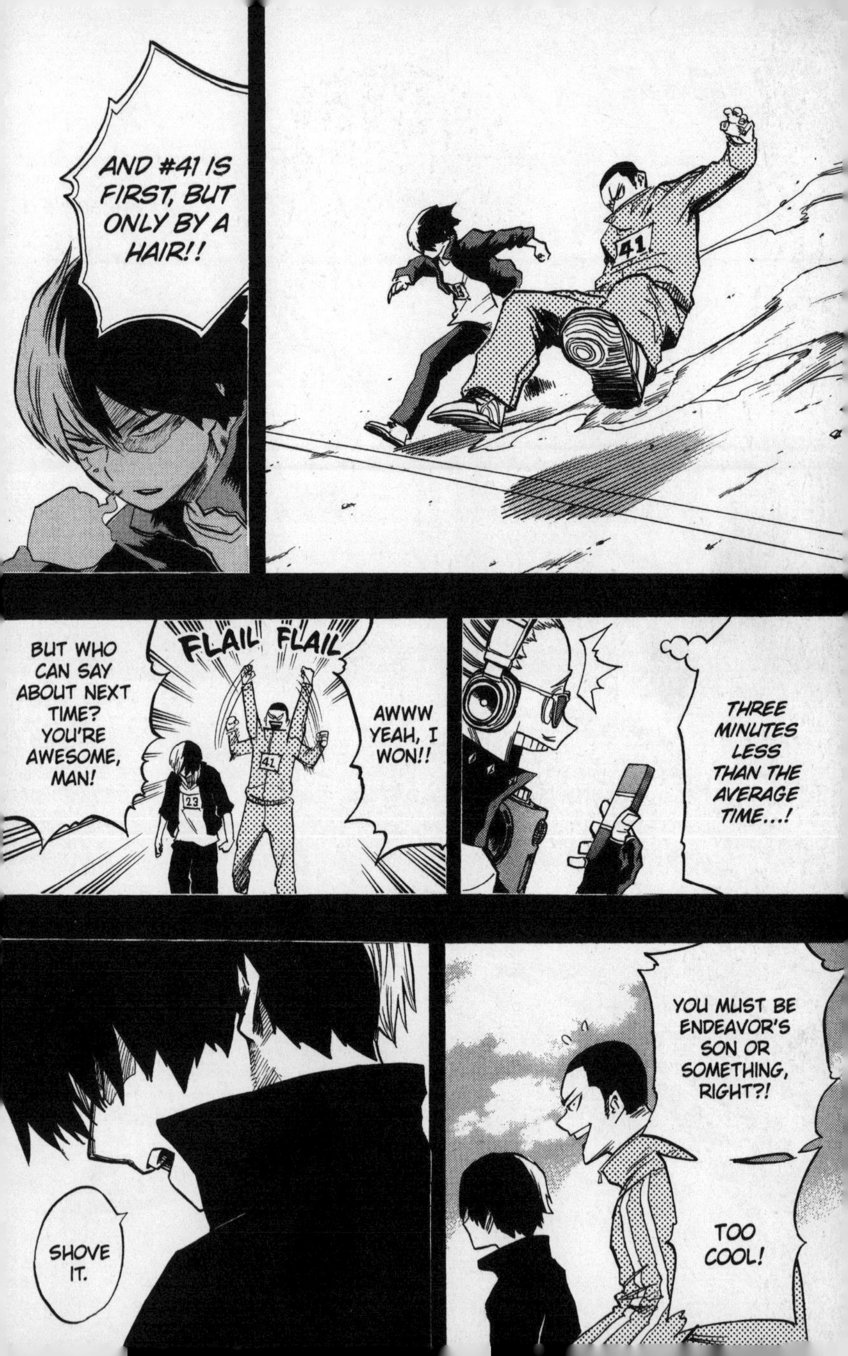
AND #41 IS FIRST, BUT ONLY BY A HAIR!!
THREE MINUTES LESS THAN THE AVERAGE TIME...!
FLAIL FLAIL
AWWW YEAH, I WON!!
BUT WHO CAN SAY ABOUT NEXT TIME? YOU'RE AWESOME, MAN!
YOU MUST BE ENDEAVOR'S SON OR SOMETHING, RIGHT?!
TOO COOL!
SHOVE IT.

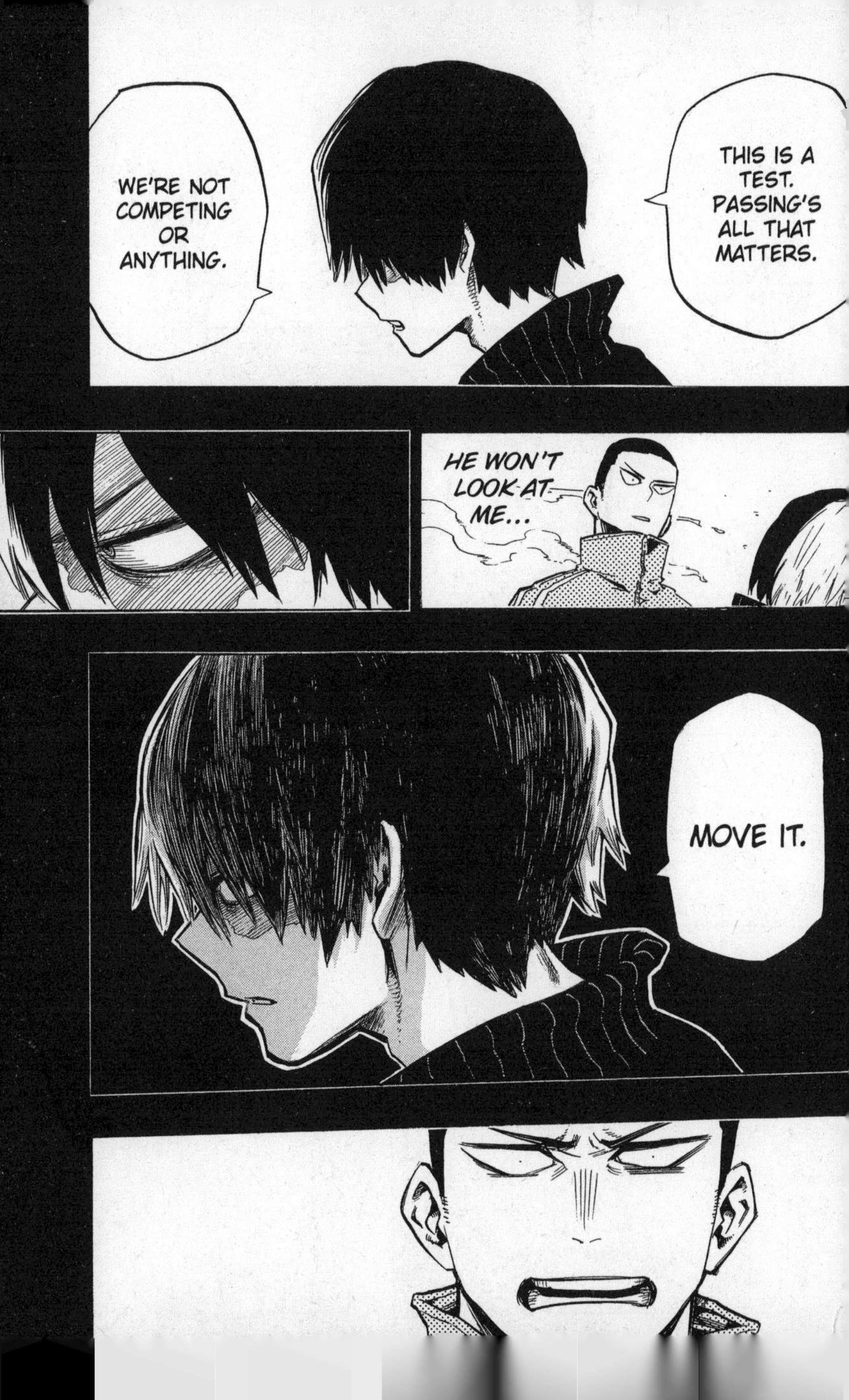
THIS IS A TEST. PASSING'S ALL THAT MATTERS.
WE'RE NOT COMPETING OR ANYTHING.
HE WON'T LOOK AT ME...
MOVE IT.

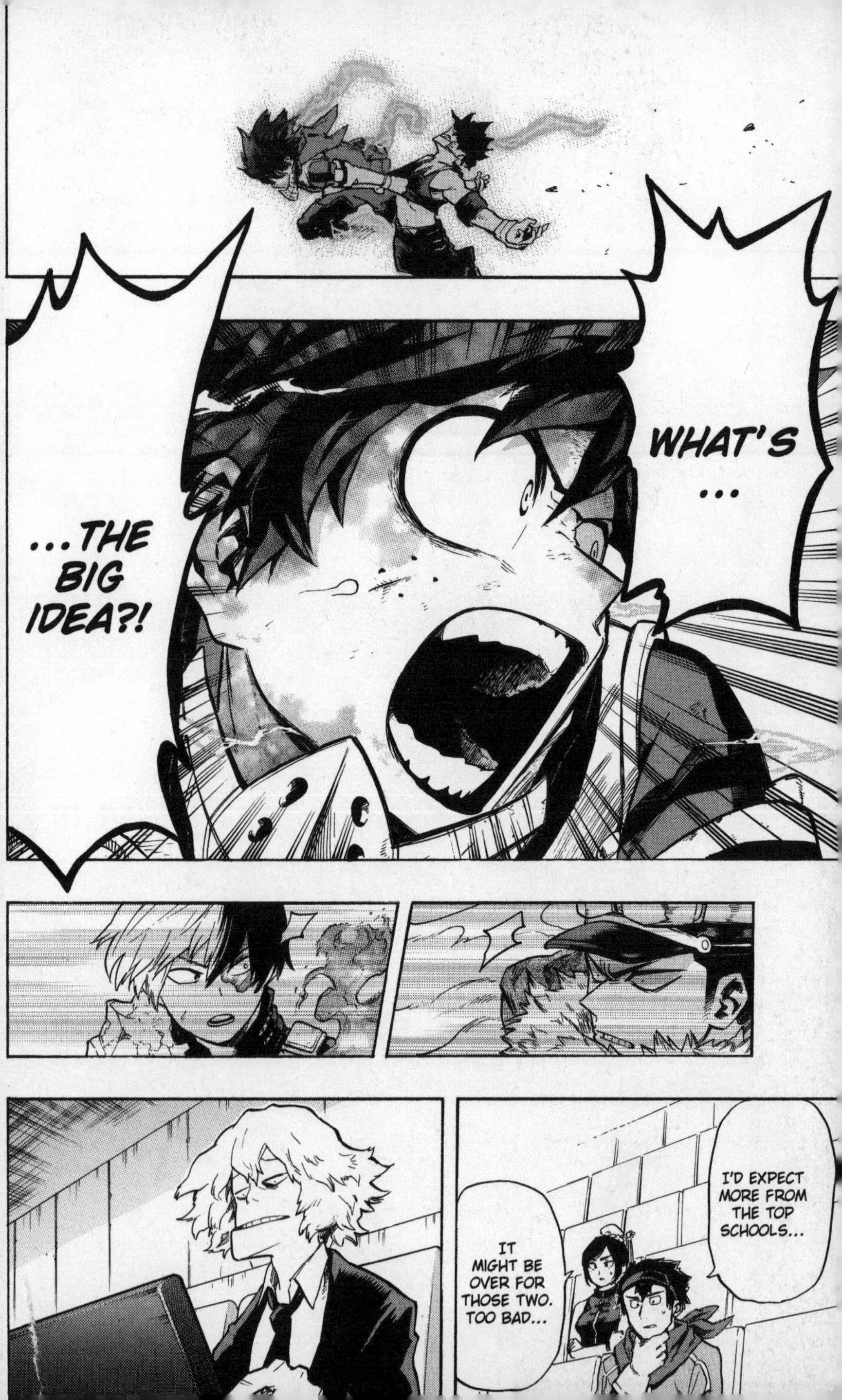
WHAT'S ...
...THE BIG IDEA?!
I'D EXPECT MORE FROM THE TOP SCHOOLS...
IT MIGHT BE OVER FOR THOSE TWO. TOO BAD...

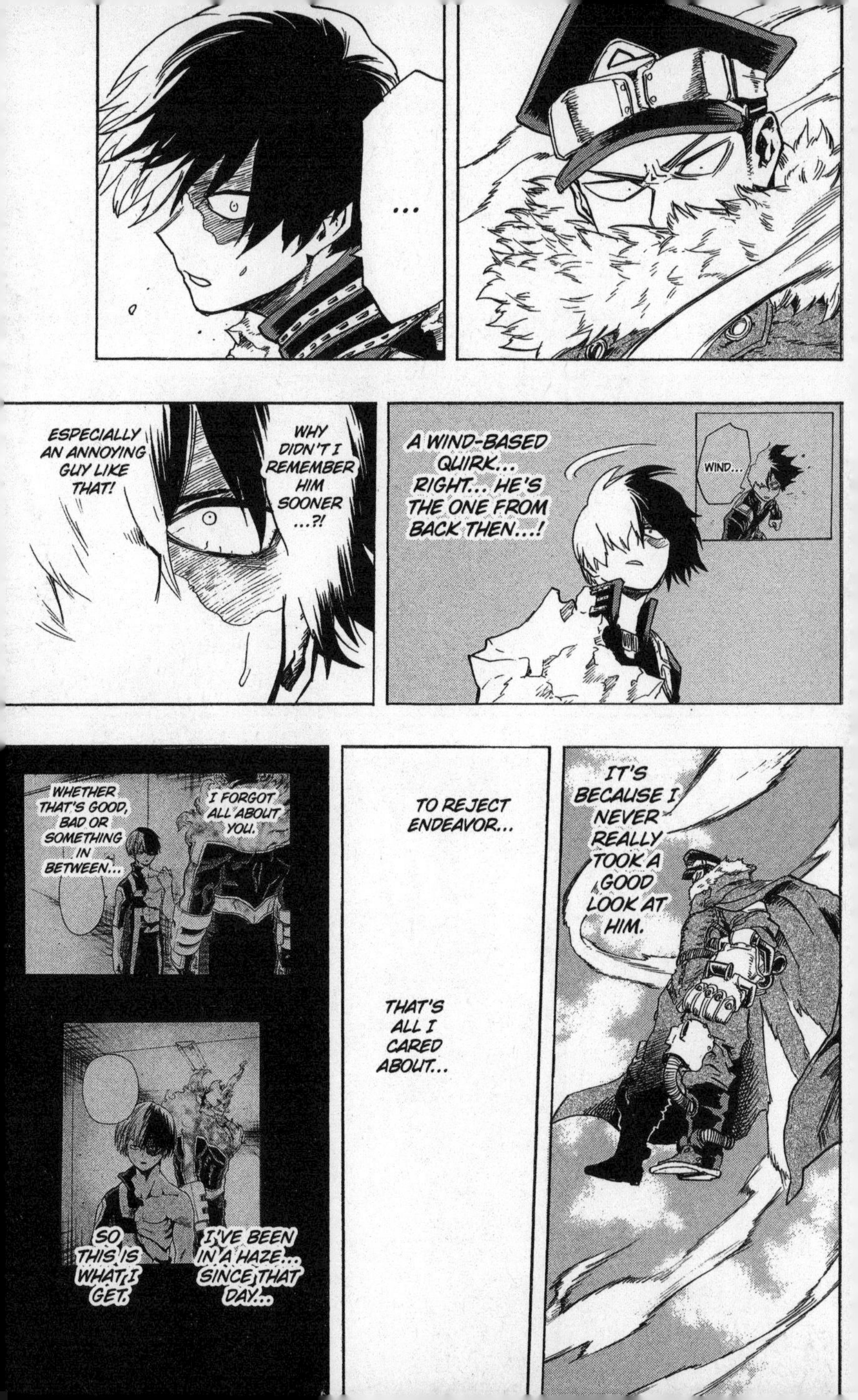
...
WIND...
A WIND-BASED QUIRK... RIGHT... HE'S THE ONE FROM BACK THEN...!
WHY DIDN'T I REMEMBER HIM SOONER ...?!
ESPECIALLY AN ANNOYING GUY LIKE THAT!
IT'S BECAUSE I NEVER REALLY TOOK A GOOD LOOK AT HIM.
TO REJECT ENDEAVOR...
THAT'S ALL I CARED ABOUT...
I FORGOT ALL ABOUT YOU.
WHETHER THAT'S GOOD, BAD OR SOMETHING IN BETWEEN...
I'VE BEEN IN A HAZE... SINCE THAT DAY...
SO THIS IS WHAT I GET.

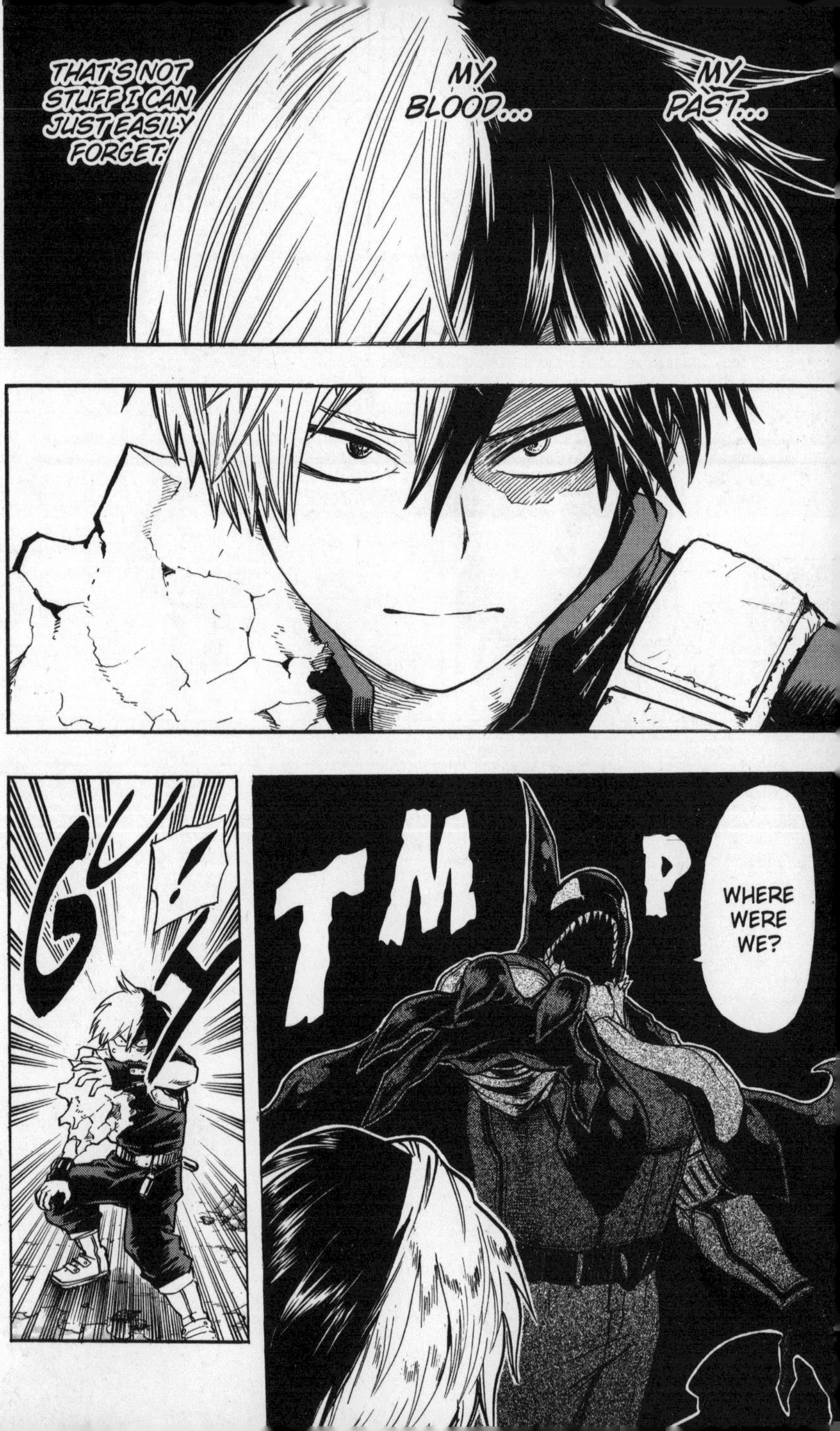
MY PAST...
MY BLOOD...
THAT'S NOT STUFF I CAN JUST EASILY FORGET.
TMP
WHERE WERE WE?

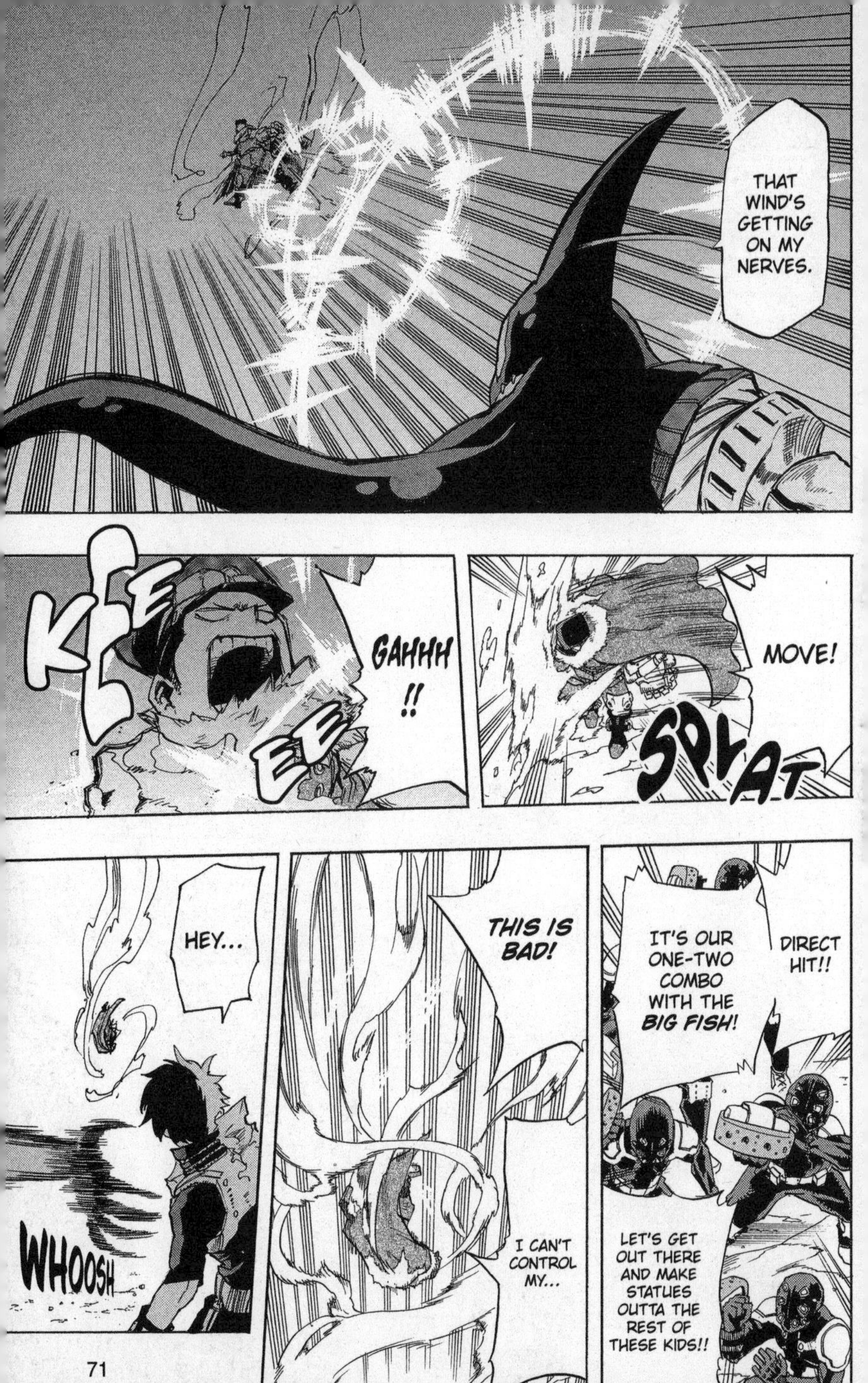
THAT WIND'S GETTING ON MY NERVES.
MOVE!
SPLAT
GAHHH!!
KEEEE
DIRECT HIT!!
IT'S OUR ONE-TWO COMBO WITH THE *BIG FISH*!
LET'S GET OUT THERE AND MAKE STATUES OUTTA THE REST OF THESE KIDS!!
THIS IS BAD!
I CAN'T CONTROL MY...
HEY...
WHOOSH

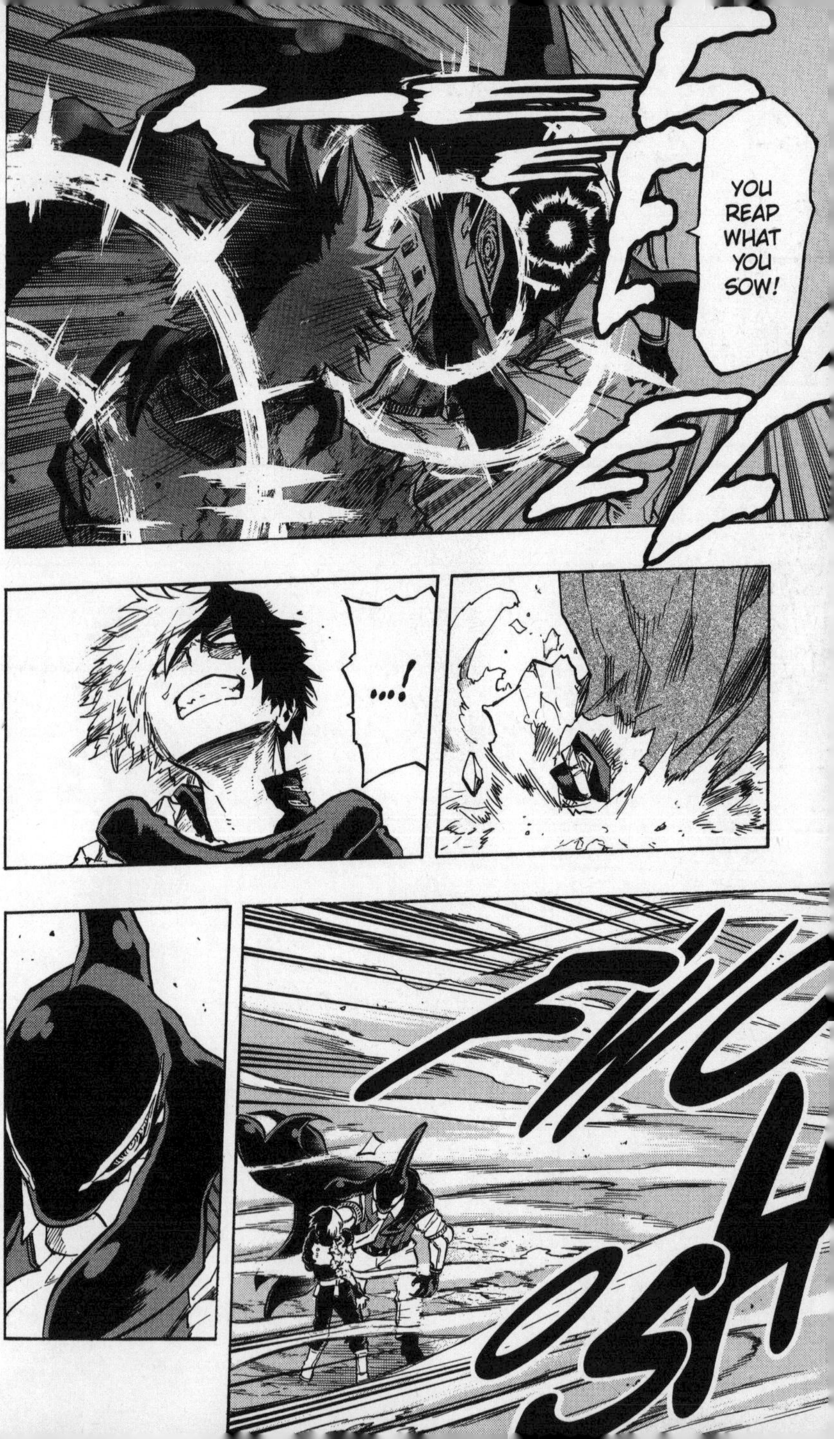
YOU REAP WHAT YOU SOW!
...!

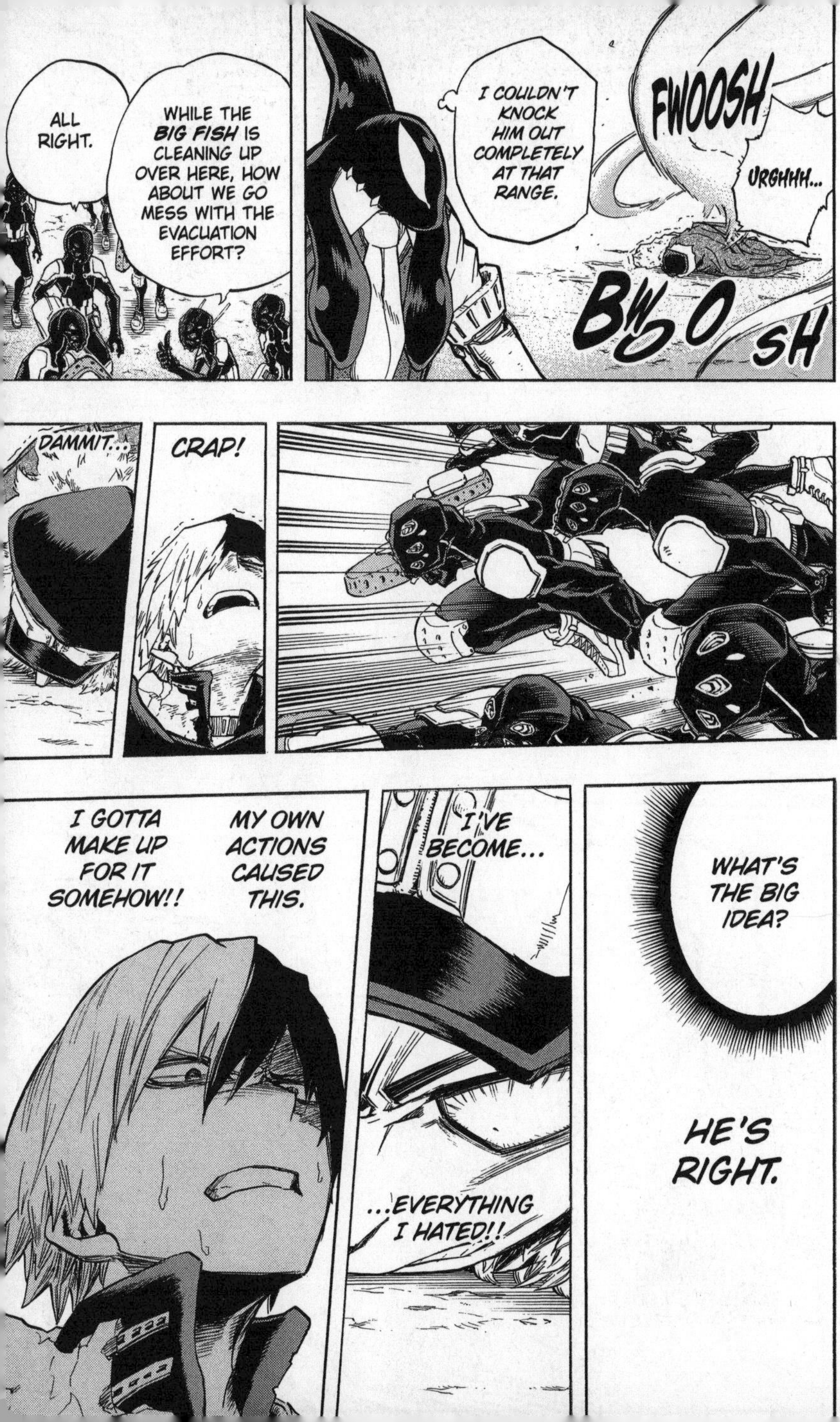
FWOOSH
URGHHH...
I COULDN'T KNOCK HIM OUT COMPLETELY AT THAT RANGE.
BWOOOSH
WHILE THE BIG FISH IS CLEANING UP OVER HERE, HOW ABOUT WE GO MESS WITH THE EVACUATION EFFORT?
ALL RIGHT.
CRAP!
DAMMIT...
WHAT'S THE BIG IDEA?
HE'S RIGHT.
I'VE BECOME...
...EVERYTHING I HATED!!
MY OWN ACTIONS CAUSED THIS.
I GOTTA MAKE UP FOR IT SOMEHOW!!

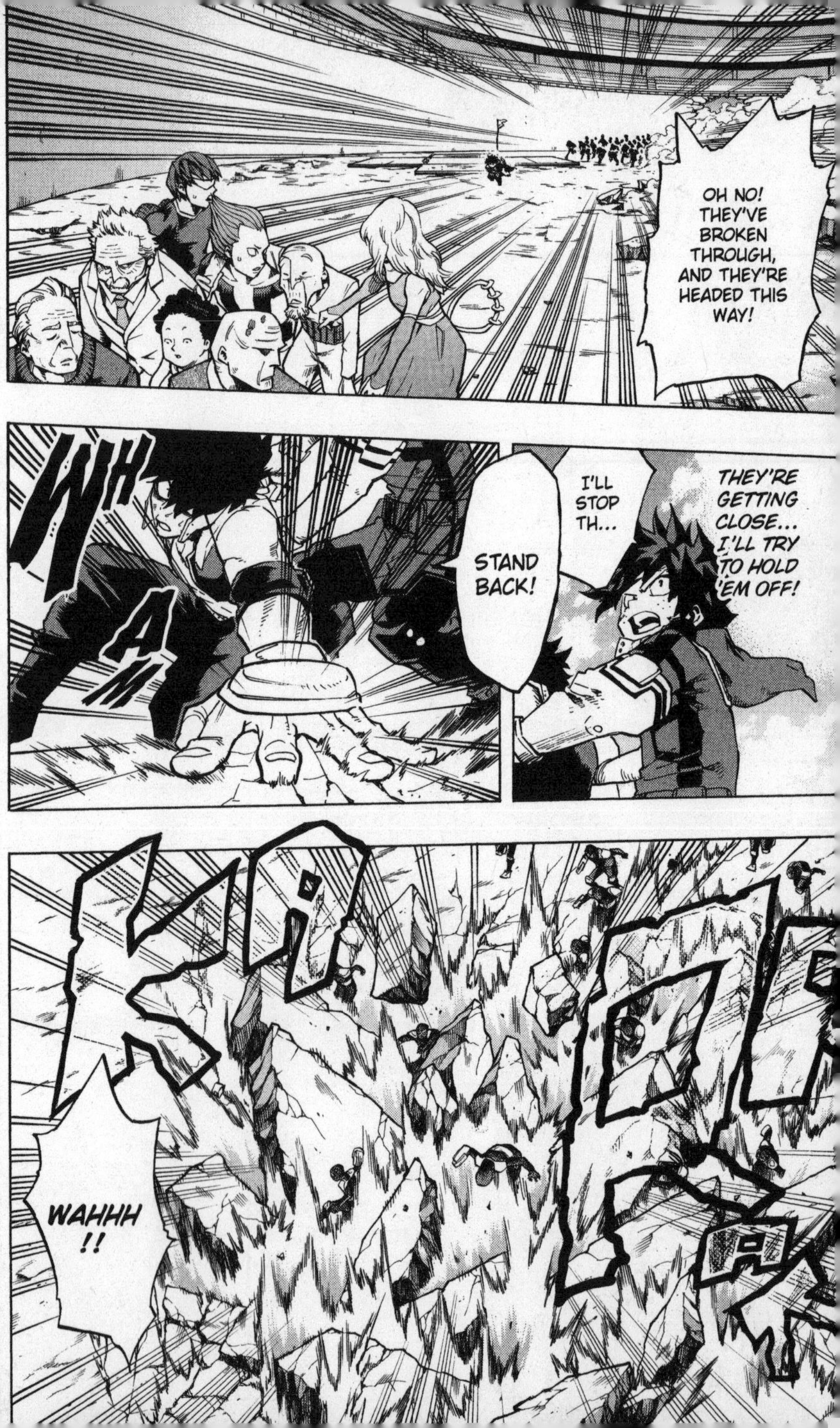
OH NO! THEY'VE BROKEN THROUGH, AND THEY'RE HEADED THIS WAY!
THEY'RE GETTING CLOSE... I'LL TRY TO HOLD 'EM OFF!
I'LL STOP TH...
STAND BACK!
WHAM
WAHHH !!

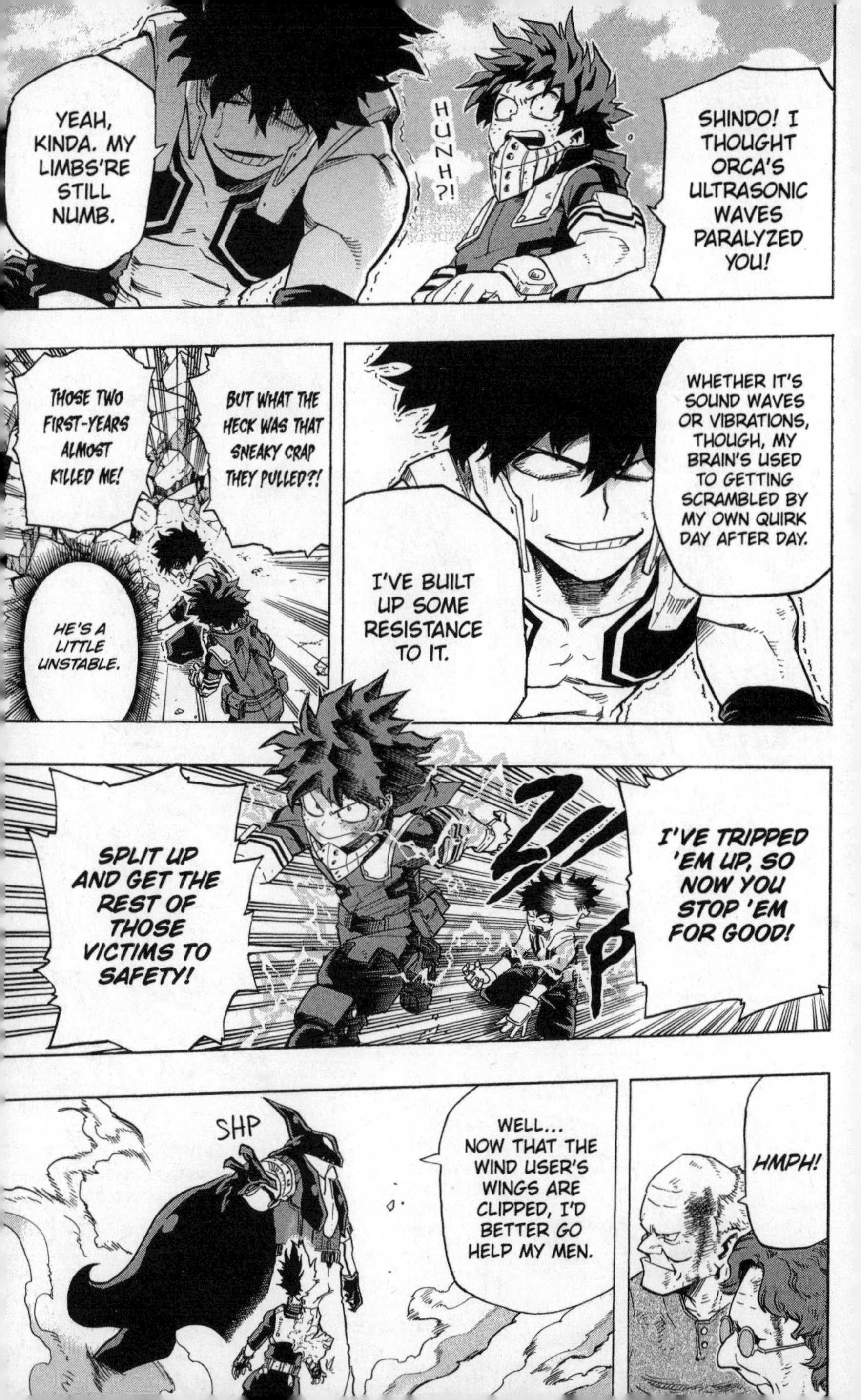
SHINDO! I THOUGHT ORCA'S ULTRASONIC WAVES PARALYZED YOU!
HUNH?!
YEAH, KINDA. MY LIMBS'RE STILL NUMB.
WHETHER IT'S SOUND WAVES OR VIBRATIONS, THOUGH, MY BRAIN'S USED TO GETTING SCRAMBLED BY MY OWN QUIRK DAY AFTER DAY.
I'VE BUILT UP SOME RESISTANCE TO IT.
BUT WHAT THE HECK WAS THAT SNEAKY CRAP THEY PULLED?!
THOSE TWO FIRST-YEARS ALMOST KILLED ME!
HE'S A LITTLE UNSTABLE.
I'VE TRIPPED 'EM UP, SO NOW YOU STOP 'EM FOR GOOD!
ZIP
SPLIT UP AND GET THE REST OF THOSE VICTIMS TO SAFETY!
HMPH!
WELL... NOW THAT THE WIND USER'S WINGS ARE CLIPPED, I'D BETTER GO HELP MY MEN.
SHP

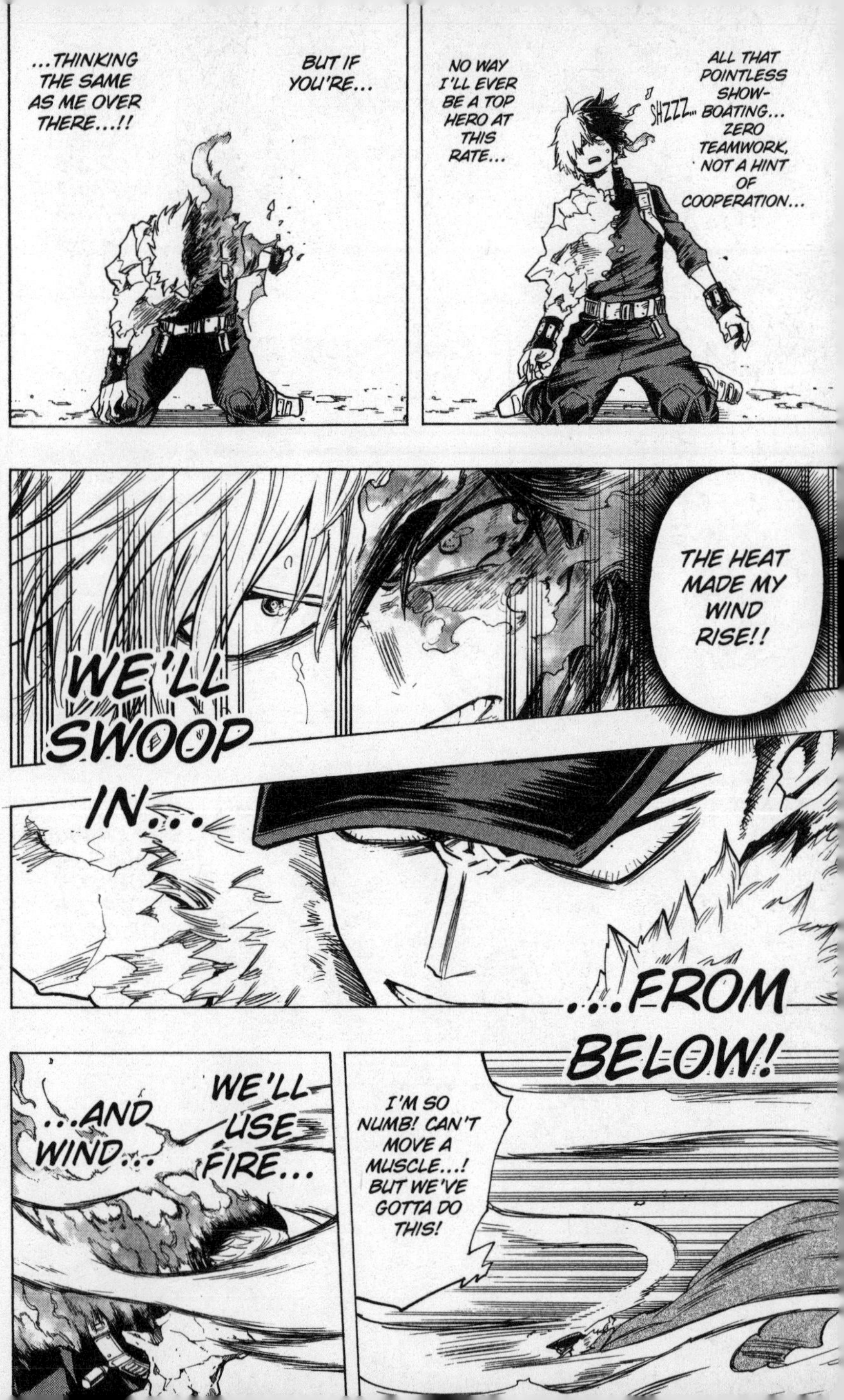
ALL THAT POINTLESS SHOW-BOATING... ZERO TEAMWORK, NOT A HINT OF COOPERATION...
SHZZZ...
NO WAY I'LL EVER BE A TOP HERO AT THIS RATE...
BUT IF YOU'RE...
...THINKING THE SAME AS ME OVER THERE...!!
THE HEAT MADE MY WIND RISE!!
WE'LL SWOOP IN...
...FROM BELOW!
I'M SO NUMB! CAN'T MOVE A MUSCLE...! BUT WE'VE GOTTA DO THIS!
WE'LL USE FIRE...
...AND WIND...

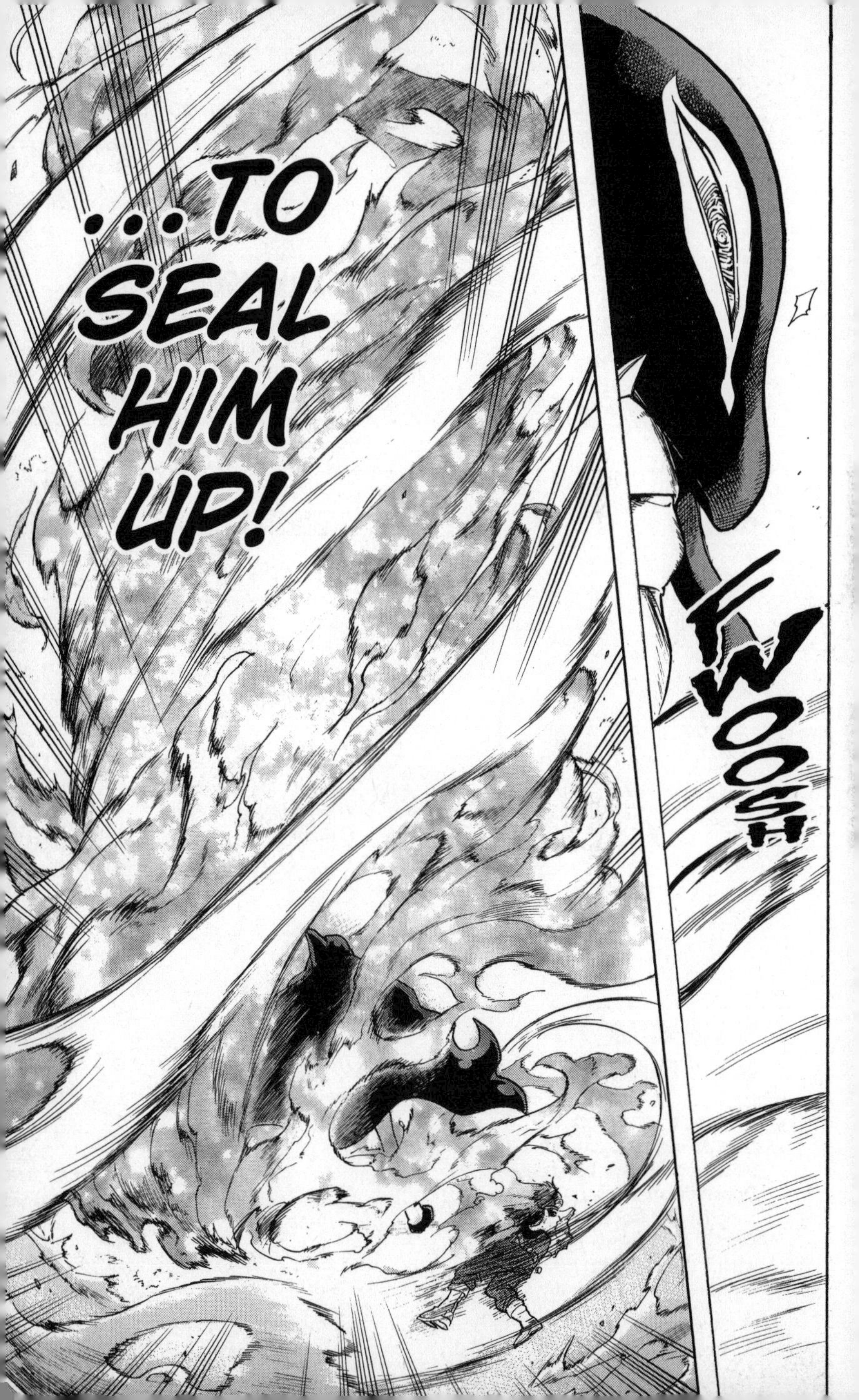
...TO SEAL HIM UP!
FWOOSH

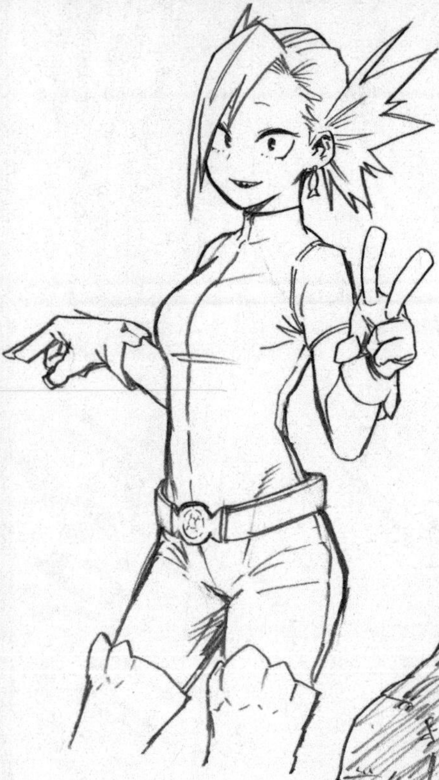

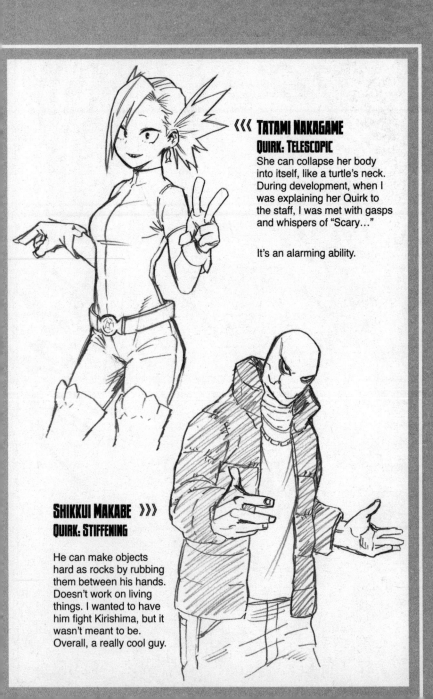

⟪⟪⟪ TATAMI NAKAGAME

QUIRK: TELESCOPIC

She can collapse her body into itself, like a turtle's neck. During development, when I was explaining her Quirk to the staff, I was met with gasps and whispers of "Scary…"

It's an alarming ability.

SHIKKUI MAKABE ⟫⟫⟫

QUIRK: STIFFENING

He can make objects hard as rocks by rubbing them between his hands. Doesn't work on living things. I wanted to have him fight Kirishima, but it wasn't meant to be. Overall, a really cool guy.

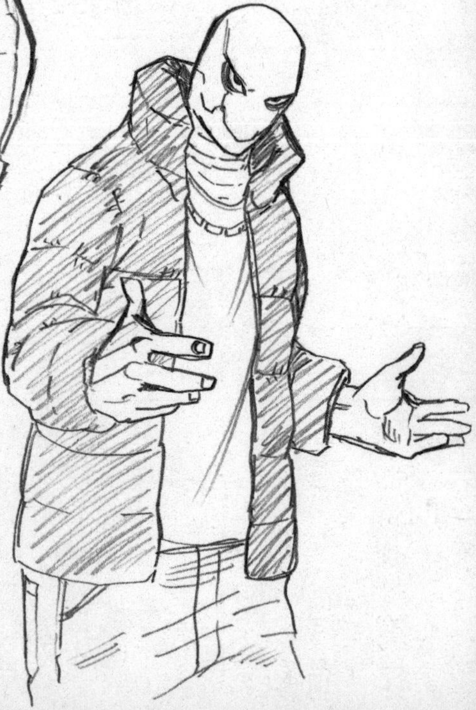

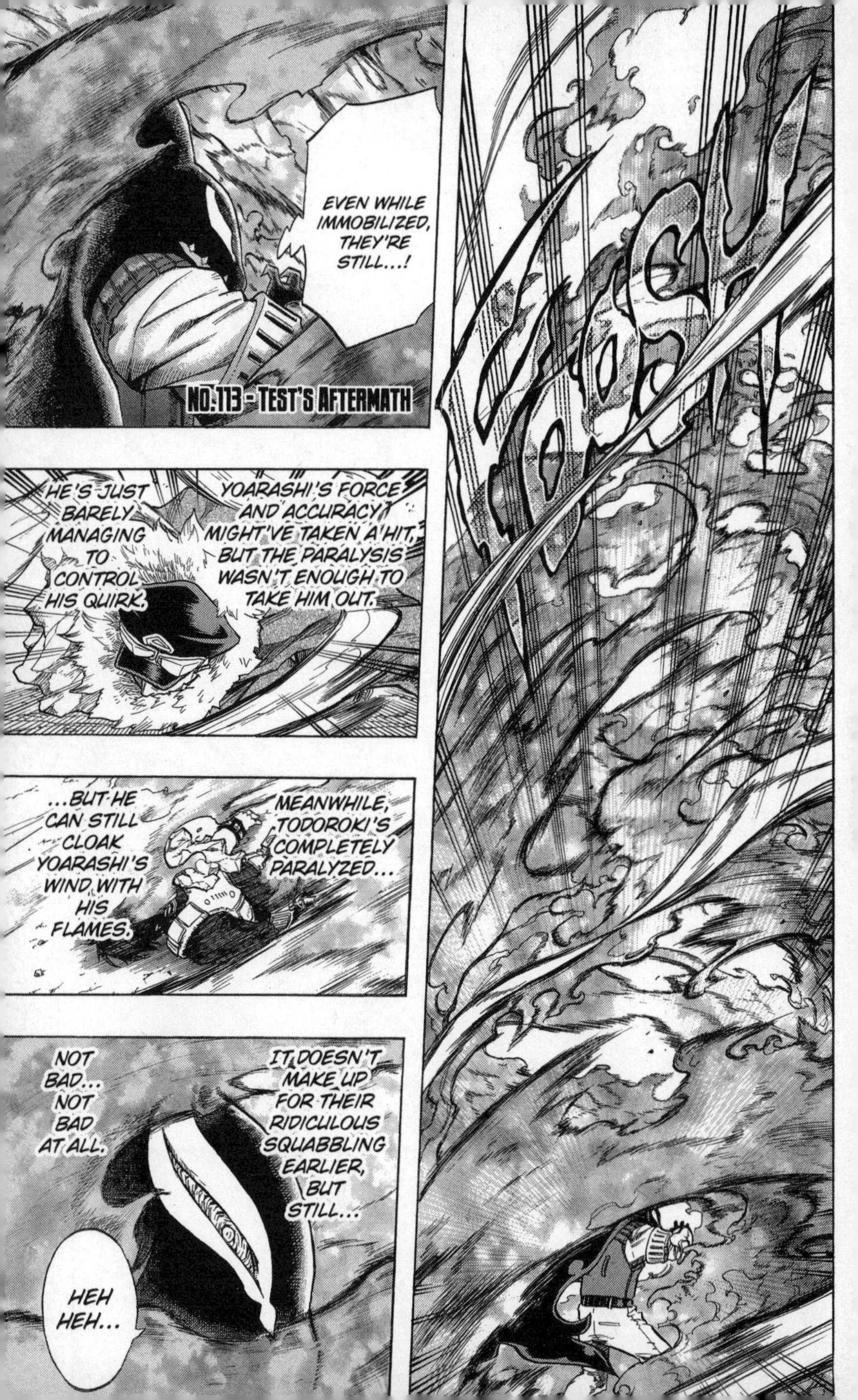
EVEN WHILE IMMOBILIZED, THEY'RE STILL...!
NO. 113 - TEST'S AFTERMATH
YOARASHI'S FORCE AND ACCURACY MIGHT'VE TAKEN A HIT, BUT THE PARALYSIS WASN'T ENOUGH TO TAKE HIM OUT.
HE'S JUST BARELY MANAGING TO CONTROL HIS QUIRK.
MEANWHILE, TODOROKI'S COMPLETELY PARALYZED...
...BUT HE CAN STILL CLOAK YOARASHI'S WIND WITH HIS FLAMES.
IT DOESN'T MAKE UP FOR THEIR RIDICULOUS SQUABBLING EARLIER, BUT STILL...
NOT BAD... NOT BAD AT ALL.
HEH HEH...

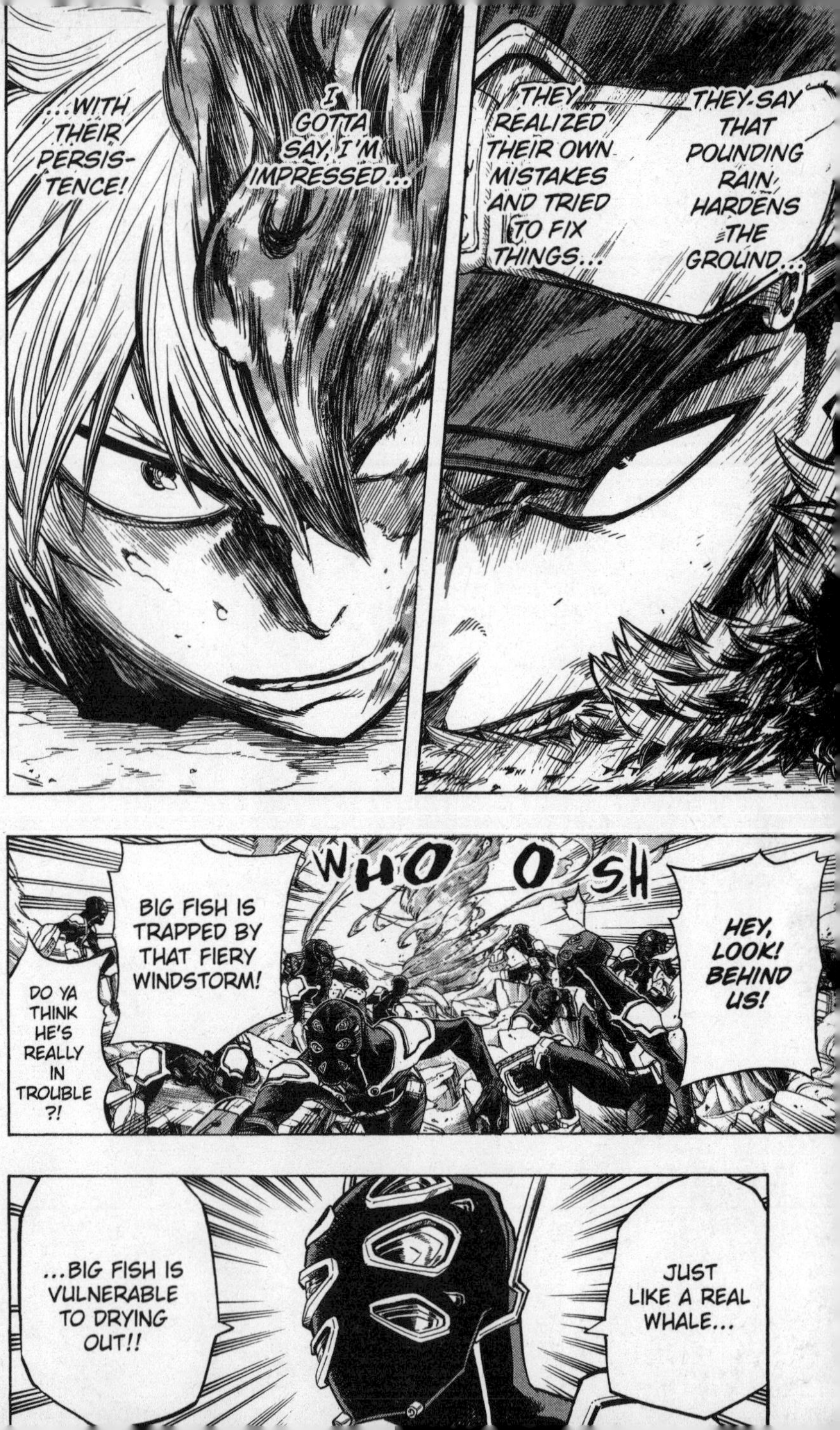
THEY SAY THAT POUNDING RAIN HARDENS THE GROUND...
THEY REALIZED THEIR OWN MISTAKES AND TRIED TO FIX THINGS...
I GOTTA SAY, I'M IMPRESSED...
...WITH THEIR PERSISTENCE!
WHOOSH
HEY, LOOK! BEHIND US!
BIG FISH IS TRAPPED BY THAT FIERY WINDSTORM!
DO YA THINK HE'S REALLY IN TROUBLE?!
JUST LIKE A REAL WHALE...
...BIG FISH IS VULNERABLE TO DRYING OUT!!

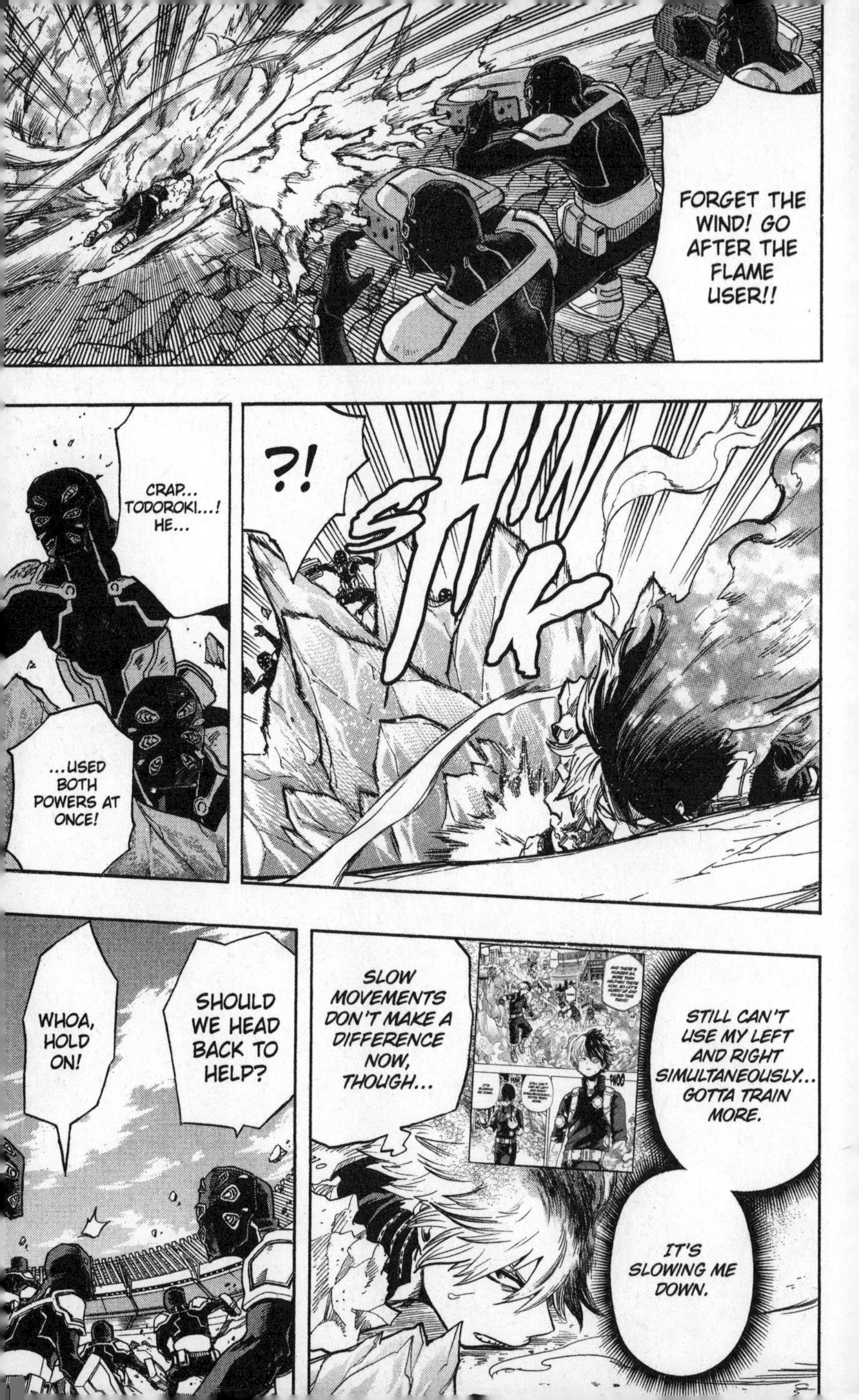
FORGET THE WIND! GO AFTER THE FLAME USER!!
?!
CRAP... TODOROKI...! HE...
...USED BOTH POWERS AT ONCE!
STILL CAN'T USE MY LEFT AND RIGHT SIMULTANEOUSLY... GOTTA TRAIN MORE.
SLOW MOVEMENTS DON'T MAKE A DIFFERENCE NOW, THOUGH...
IT'S SLOWING ME DOWN.
SHOULD WE HEAD BACK TO HELP?
WHOA, HOLD ON!

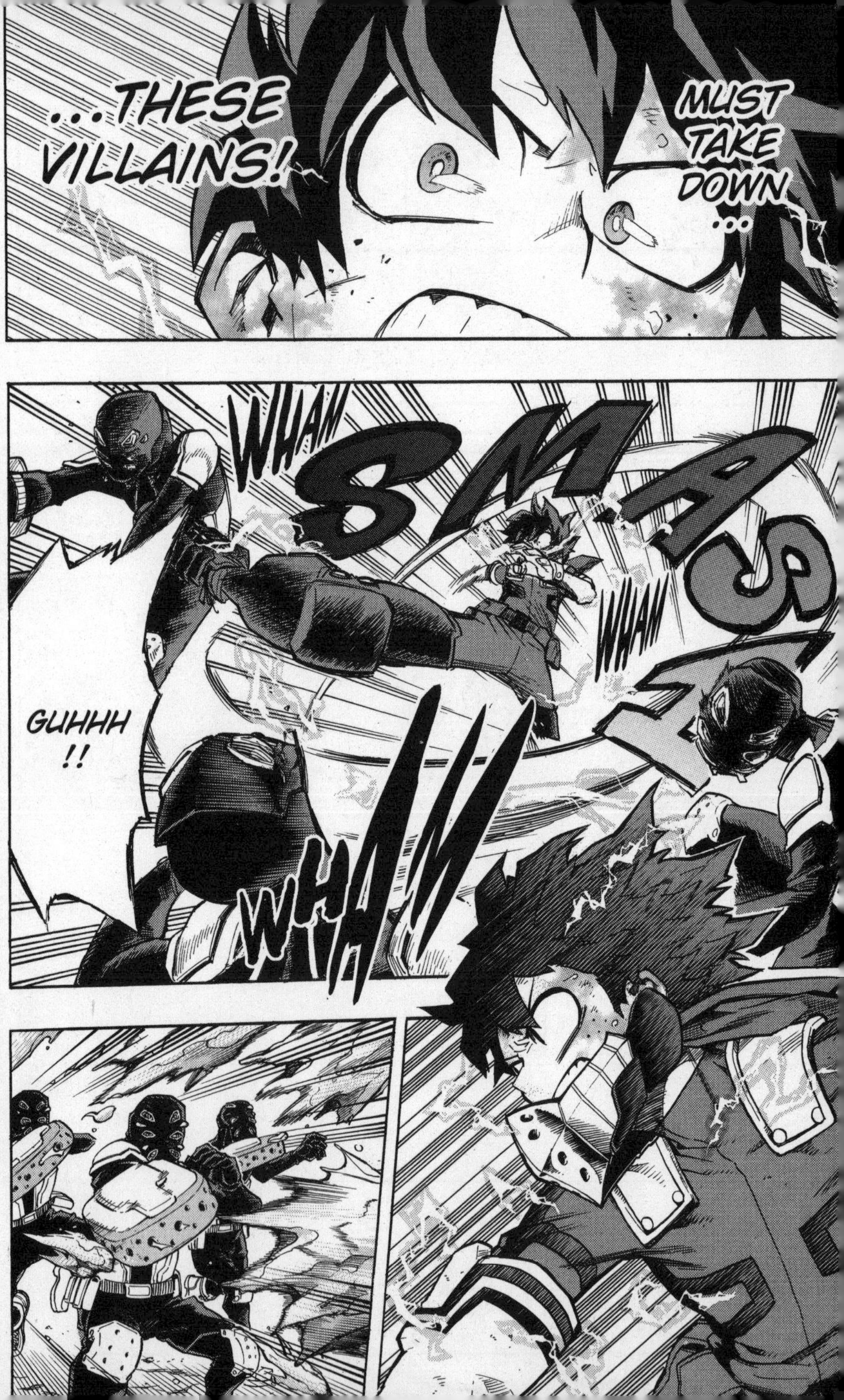
MUST TAKE DOWN...
...THESE VILLAINS!
SMASH
WHAM
WHAM
GUHHH!!
WHAM

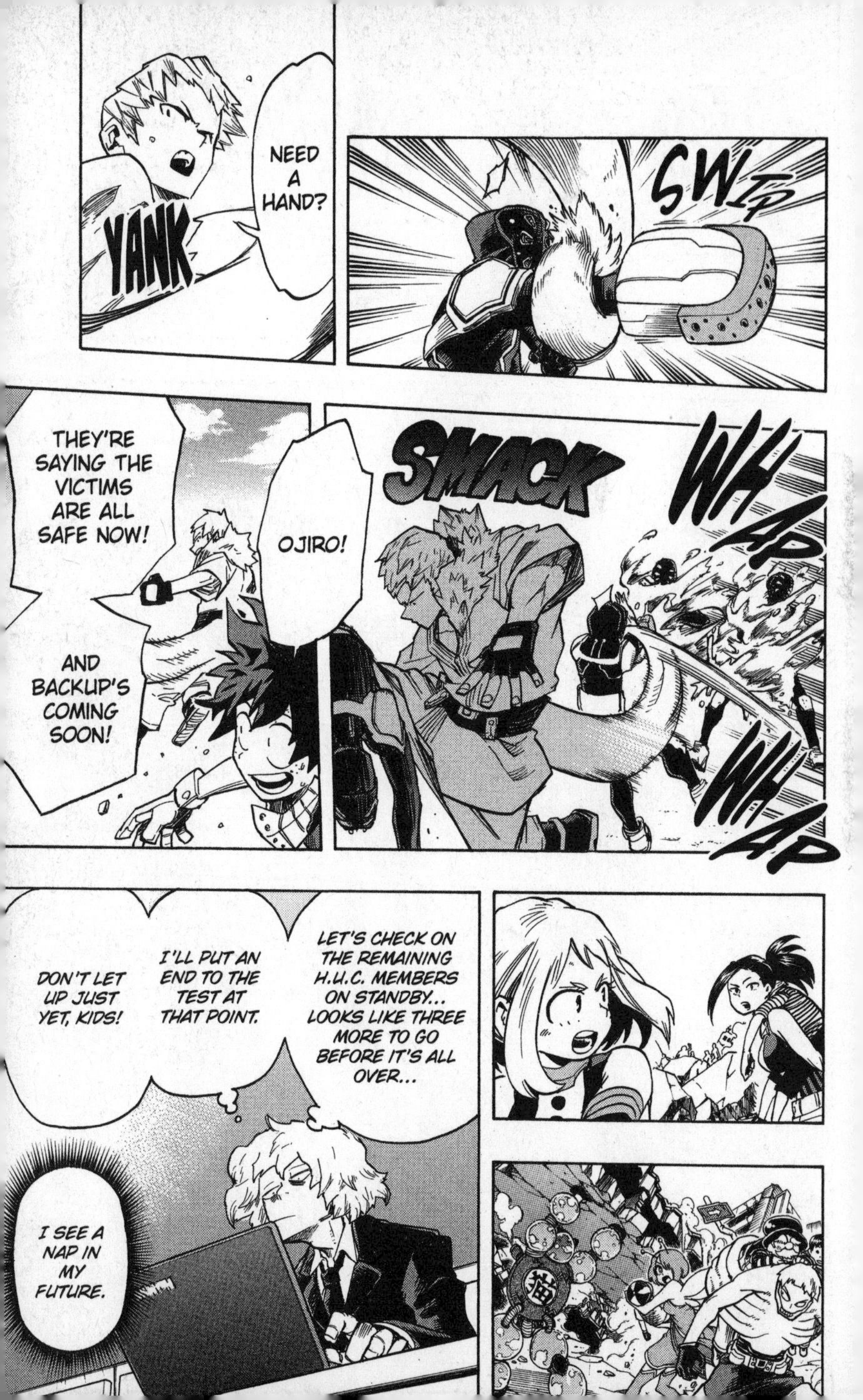
SWIP
NEED A HAND?
YANK
SMACK
WHAP
WHAP
OJIRO!
THEY'RE SAYING THE VICTIMS ARE ALL SAFE NOW!
AND BACKUP'S COMING SOON!
LET'S CHECK ON THE REMAINING H.U.C. MEMBERS ON STANDBY... LOOKS LIKE THREE MORE TO GO BEFORE IT'S ALL OVER...
I'LL PUT AN END TO THE TEST AT THAT POINT.
DON'T LET UP JUST YET, KIDS!
I SEE A NAP IN MY FUTURE.

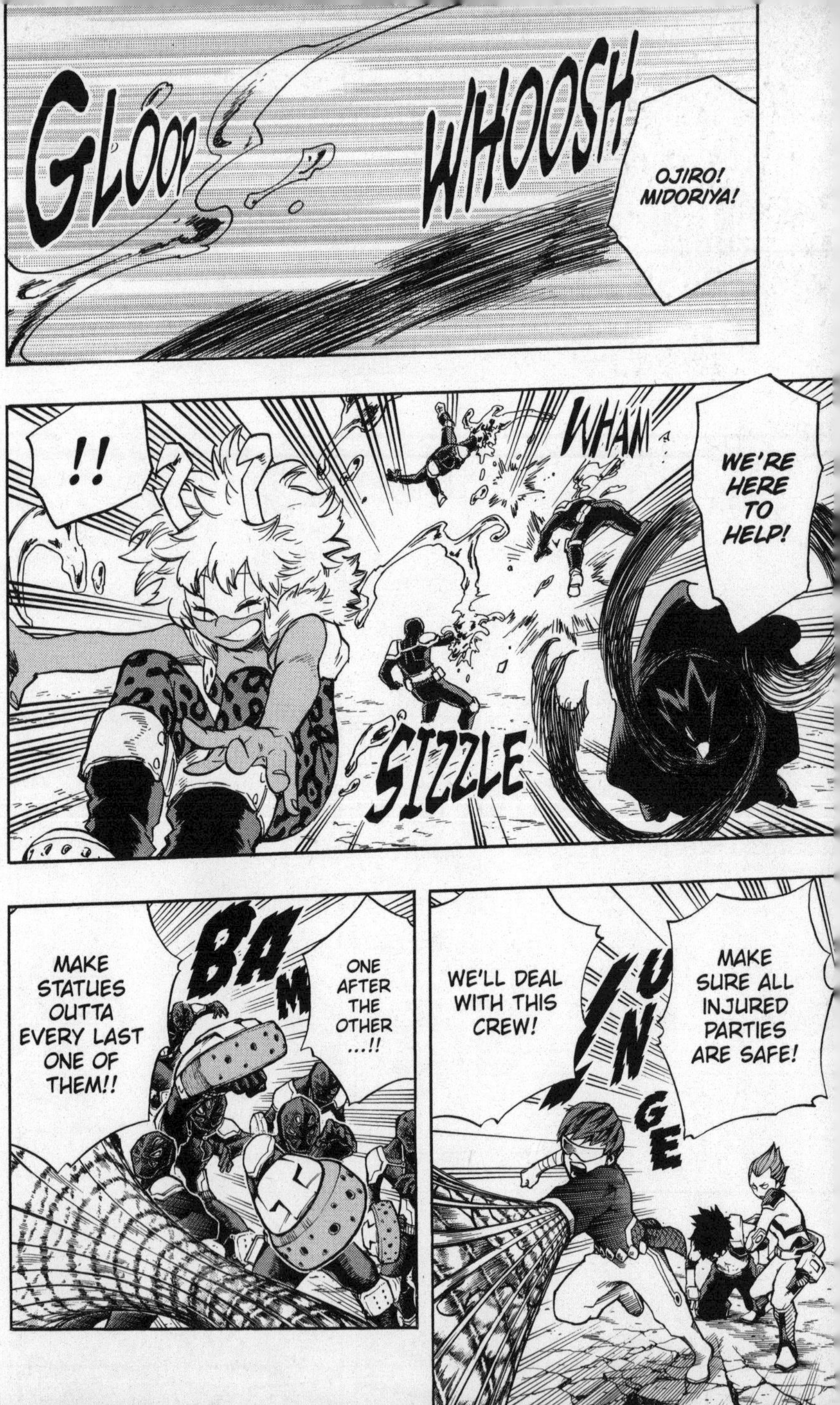
OJIRO! MIDORIYA!
WHOOSH
GLOOP
WE'RE HERE TO HELP!
WHAM
!!
SIZZLE
MAKE SURE ALL INJURED PARTIES ARE SAFE!
LUNGE
WE'LL DEAL WITH THIS CREW!
ONE AFTER THE OTHER ...!!
BAM
MAKE STATUES OUTTA EVERY LAST ONE OF THEM!!

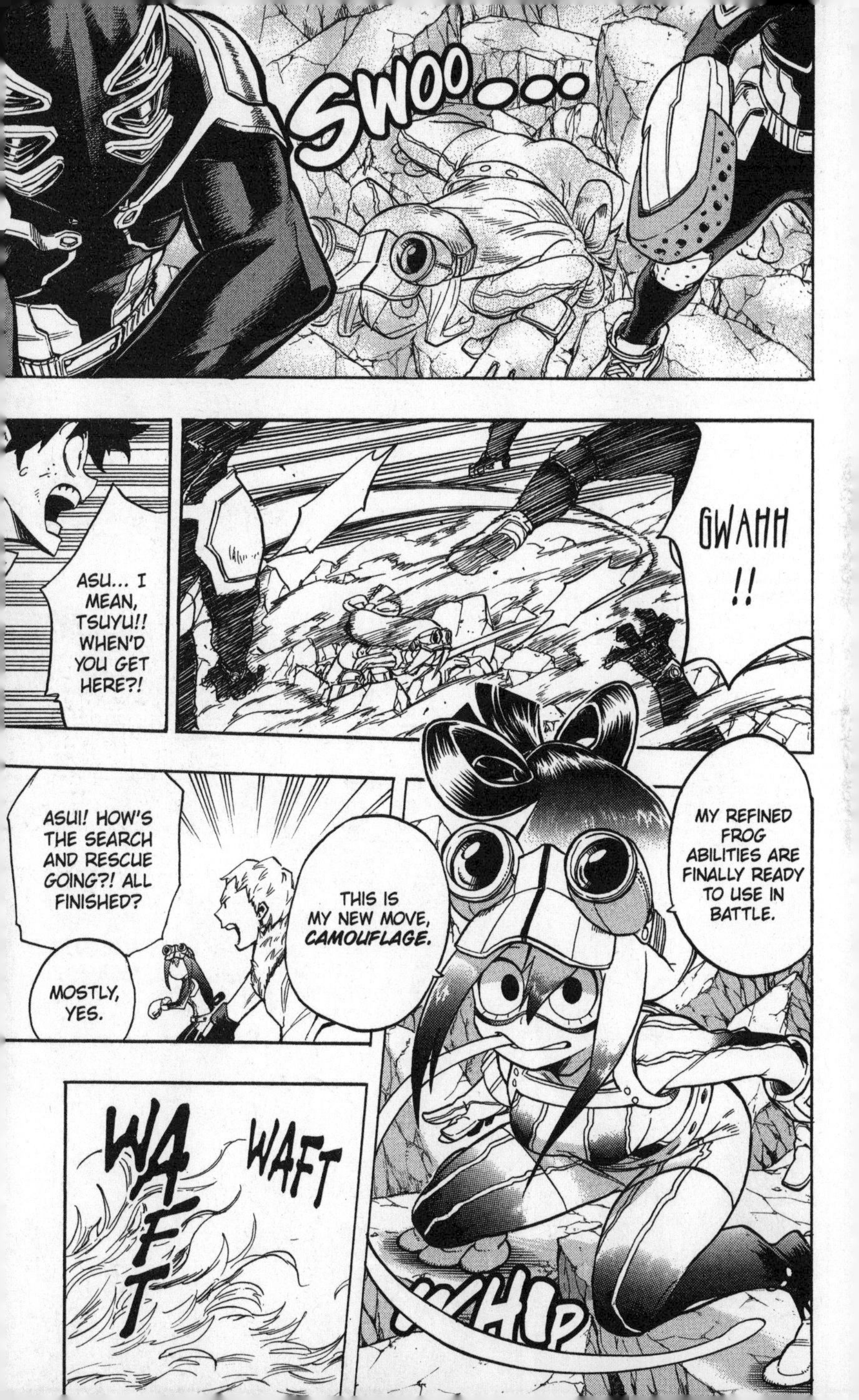
SWOO...
GWAHH!!
ASU... I MEAN, TSUYU!! WHEN'D YOU GET HERE?!
MY REFINED FROG ABILITIES ARE FINALLY READY TO USE IN BATTLE.
THIS IS MY NEW MOVE, **CAMOUFLAGE.**
WHIP
ASUI! HOW'S THE SEARCH AND RESCUE GOING?! ALL FINISHED?
MOSTLY, YES.
WAFT
WAFT

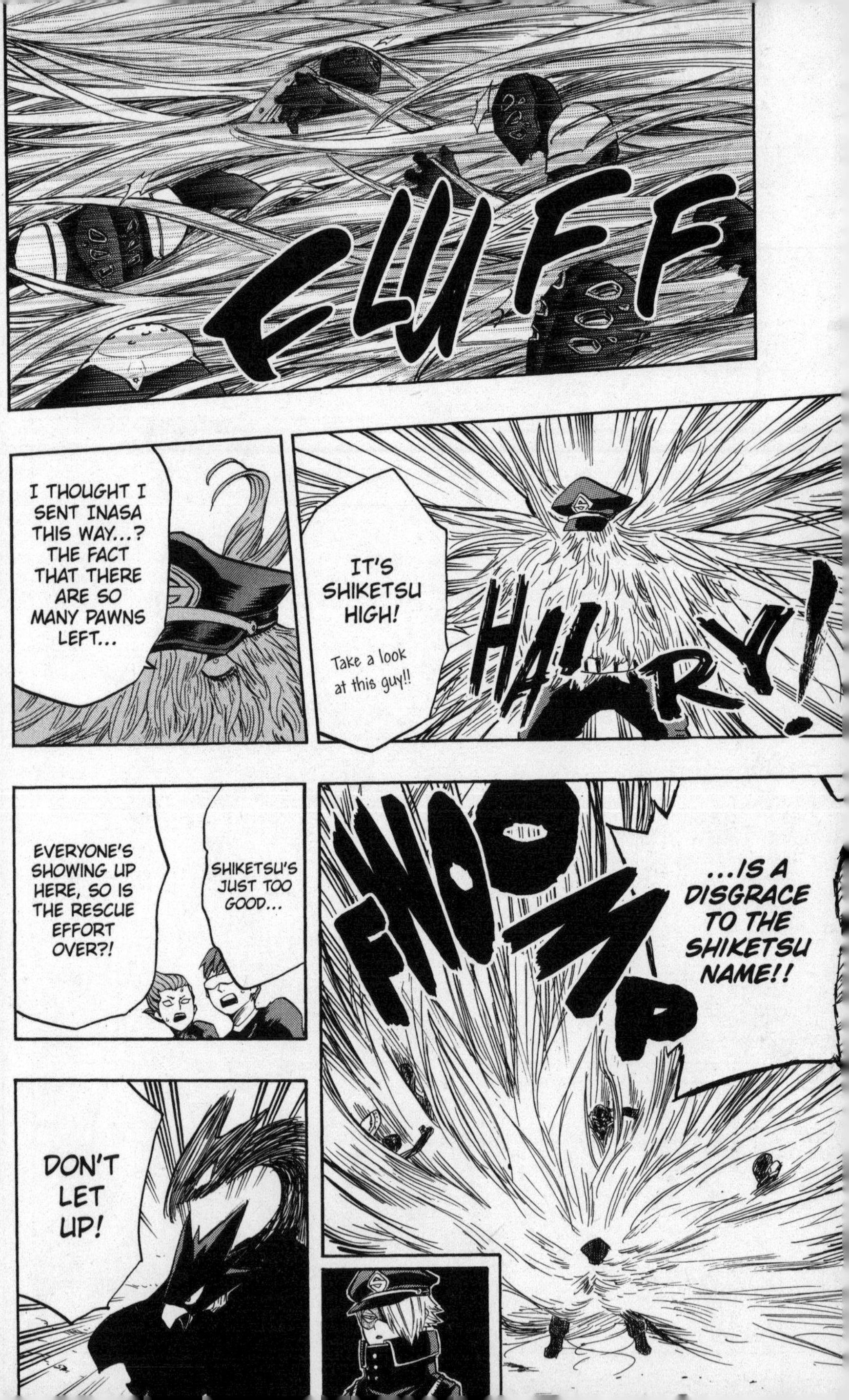

FLUFF
IT'S SHIKETSU HIGH!
Take a look at this guy!!
HAIRY!
I THOUGHT I SENT INASA THIS WAY...? THE FACT THAT THERE ARE SO MANY PAWNS LEFT...
FWOOMP
...IS A DISGRACE TO THE SHIKETSU NAME!!
SHIKETSU'S JUST TOO GOOD...
EVERYONE'S SHOWING UP HERE, SO IS THE RESCUE EFFORT OVER?!
DON'T LET UP!

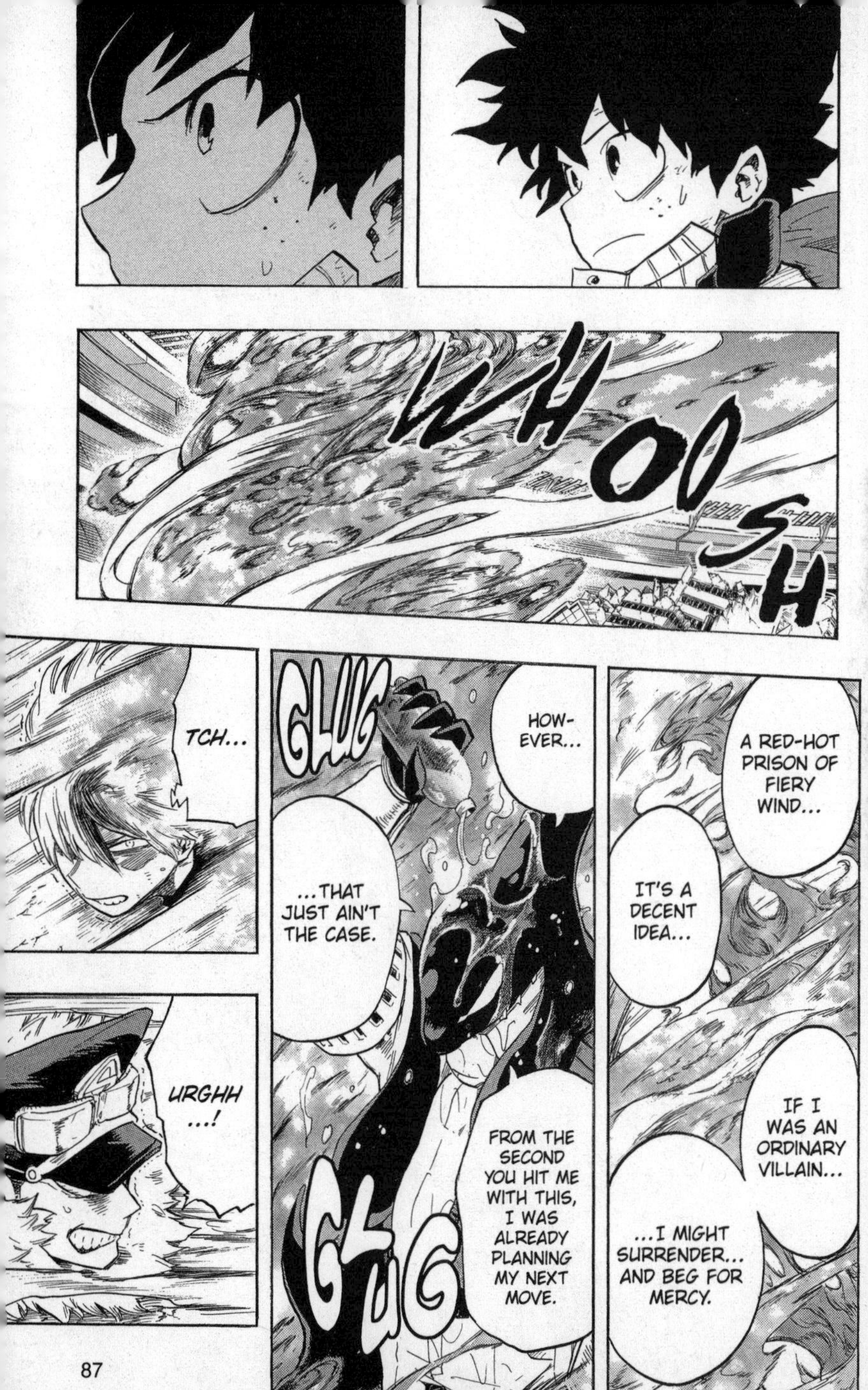
WHOOSH
A RED-HOT PRISON OF FIERY WIND...
IT'S A DECENT IDEA...
IF I WAS AN ORDINARY VILLAIN...
...I MIGHT SURRENDER... AND BEG FOR MERCY.
GLUG
HOW-EVER...
...THAT JUST AIN'T THE CASE.
FROM THE SECOND YOU HIT ME WITH THIS, I WAS ALREADY PLANNING MY NEXT MOVE.
GLUG
TCH...
URGHH ...!

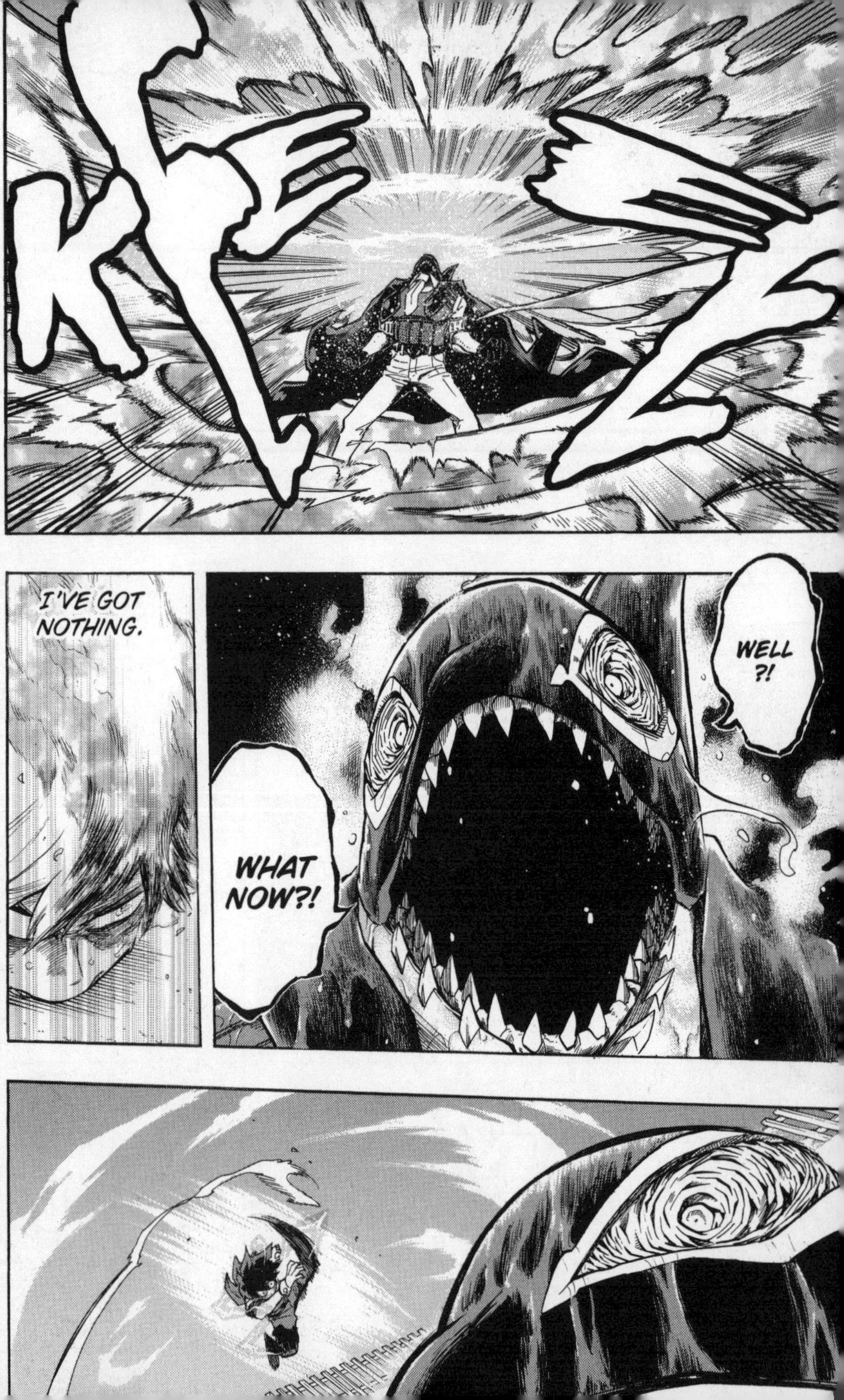
WELL ?!
WHAT NOW?!
I'VE GOT NOTHING.

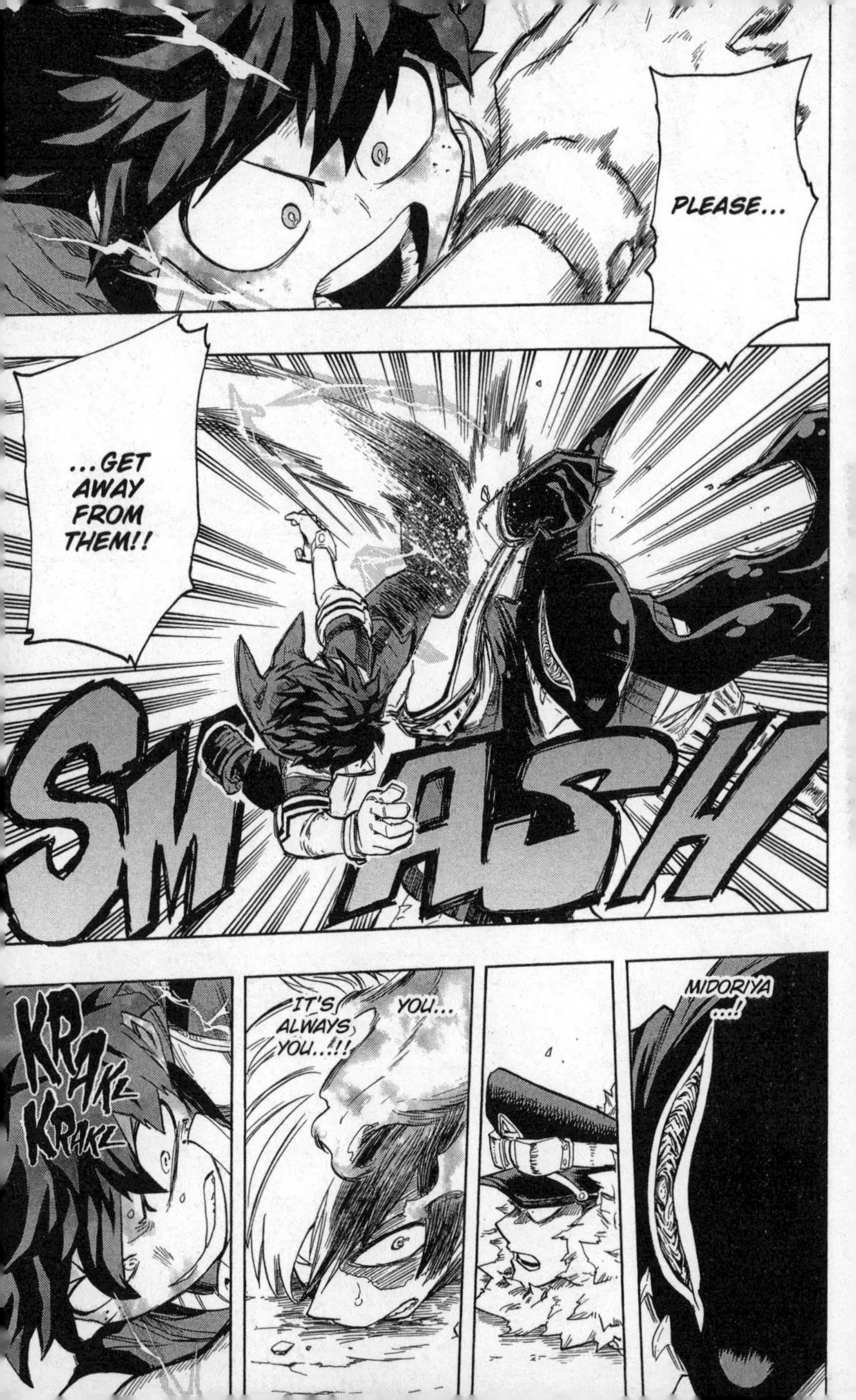
PLEASE...
...GET AWAY FROM THEM!!
SMASH
MIDORIYA ...!
YOU...
IT'S ALWAYS YOU...!!
KRAKL
KRAKL

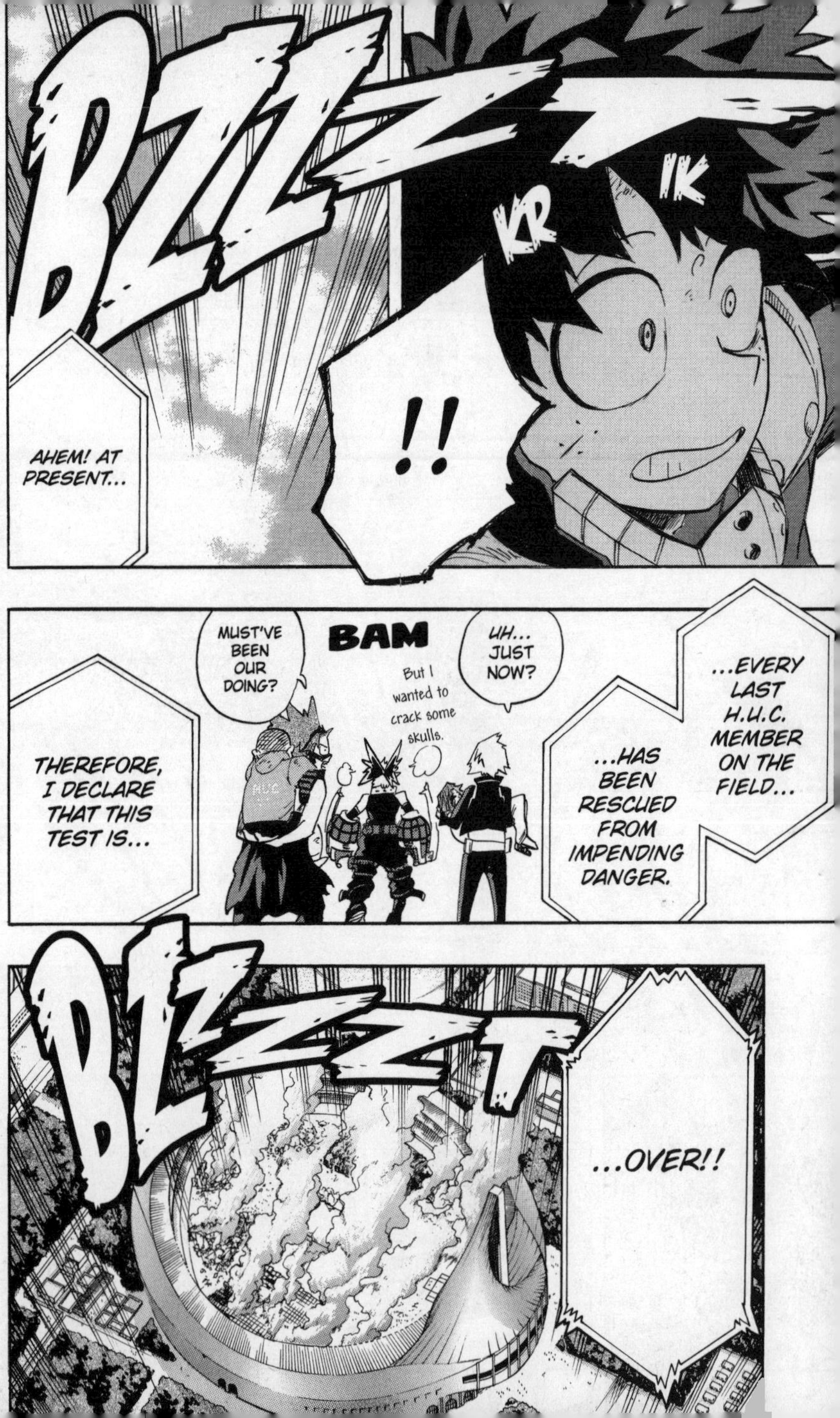
BZZZT
KR IK
!!
AHEM! AT PRESENT...
...EVERY LAST H.U.C. MEMBER ON THE FIELD...
...HAS BEEN RESCUED FROM IMPENDING DANGER.
UH... JUST NOW?
BAM
MUST'VE BEEN OUR DOING?
But I wanted to crack some skulls.
THEREFORE, I DECLARE THAT THIS TEST IS...
...OVER!!
BZZZT

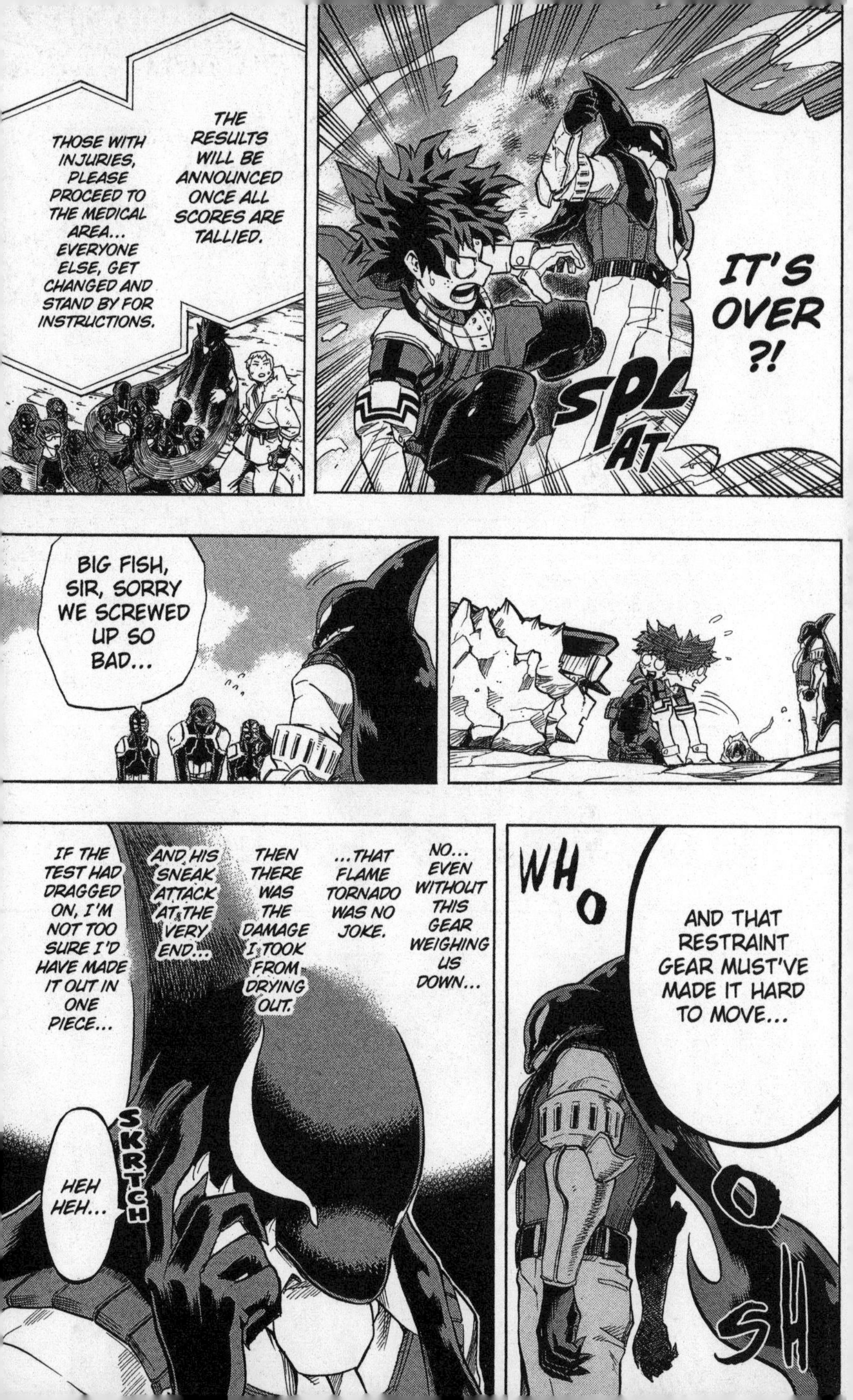
IT'S OVER?!
SPLAT
THE RESULTS WILL BE ANNOUNCED ONCE ALL SCORES ARE TALLIED.
THOSE WITH INJURIES, PLEASE PROCEED TO THE MEDICAL AREA... EVERYONE ELSE, GET CHANGED AND STAND BY FOR INSTRUCTIONS.
BIG FISH, SIR, SORRY WE SCREWED UP SO BAD...
WHOOSH
AND THAT RESTRAINT GEAR MUST'VE MADE IT HARD TO MOVE...
NO... EVEN WITHOUT THIS GEAR WEIGHING US DOWN...
...THAT FLAME TORNADO WAS NO JOKE.
THEN THERE WAS THE DAMAGE I TOOK FROM DRYING OUT.
AND HIS SNEAK ATTACK AT THE VERY END...
IF THE TEST HAD DRAGGED ON, I'M NOT TOO SURE I'D HAVE MADE IT OUT IN ONE PIECE...
SKRTCH
HEH HEH...

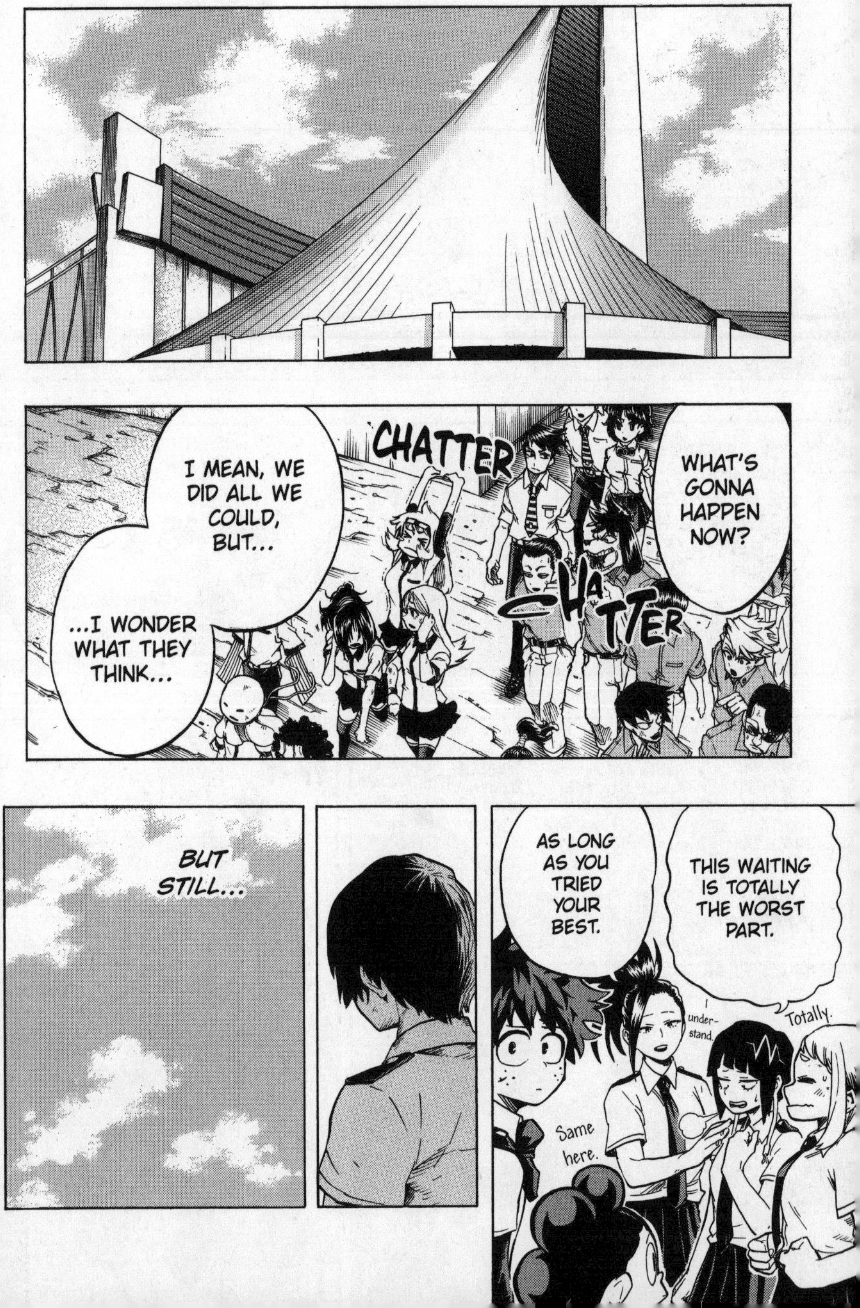
WHAT'S GONNA HAPPEN NOW?
CHATTER
CHATTER
I MEAN, WE DID ALL WE COULD, BUT...
...I WONDER WHAT THEY THINK...
THIS WAITING IS TOTALLY THE WORST PART.
Totally.
AS LONG AS YOU TRIED YOUR BEST.
I understand.
Same here.
BUT STILL...

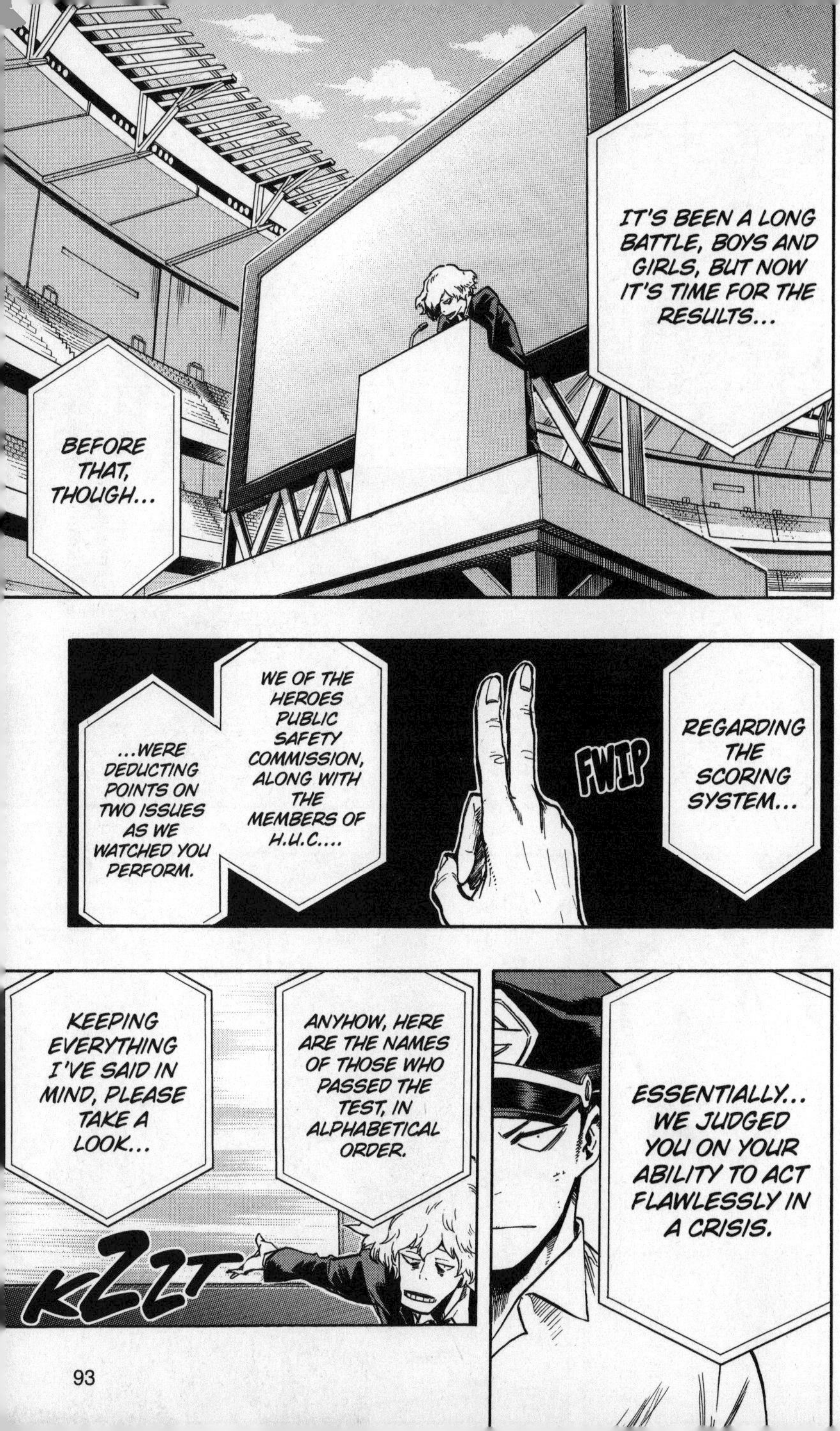
IT'S BEEN A LONG BATTLE, BOYS AND GIRLS, BUT NOW IT'S TIME FOR THE RESULTS...
BEFORE THAT, THOUGH...
REGARDING THE SCORING SYSTEM...
FWIP
WE OF THE HEROES PUBLIC SAFETY COMMISSION, ALONG WITH THE MEMBERS OF H.U.C....
...WERE DEDUCTING POINTS ON TWO ISSUES AS WE WATCHED YOU PERFORM.
ESSENTIALLY... WE JUDGED YOU ON YOUR ABILITY TO ACT FLAWLESSLY IN A CRISIS.
ANYHOW, HERE ARE THE NAMES OF THOSE WHO PASSED THE TEST, IN ALPHABETICAL ORDER.
KEEPING EVERYTHING I'VE SAID IN MIND, PLEASE TAKE A LOOK...
KZZT

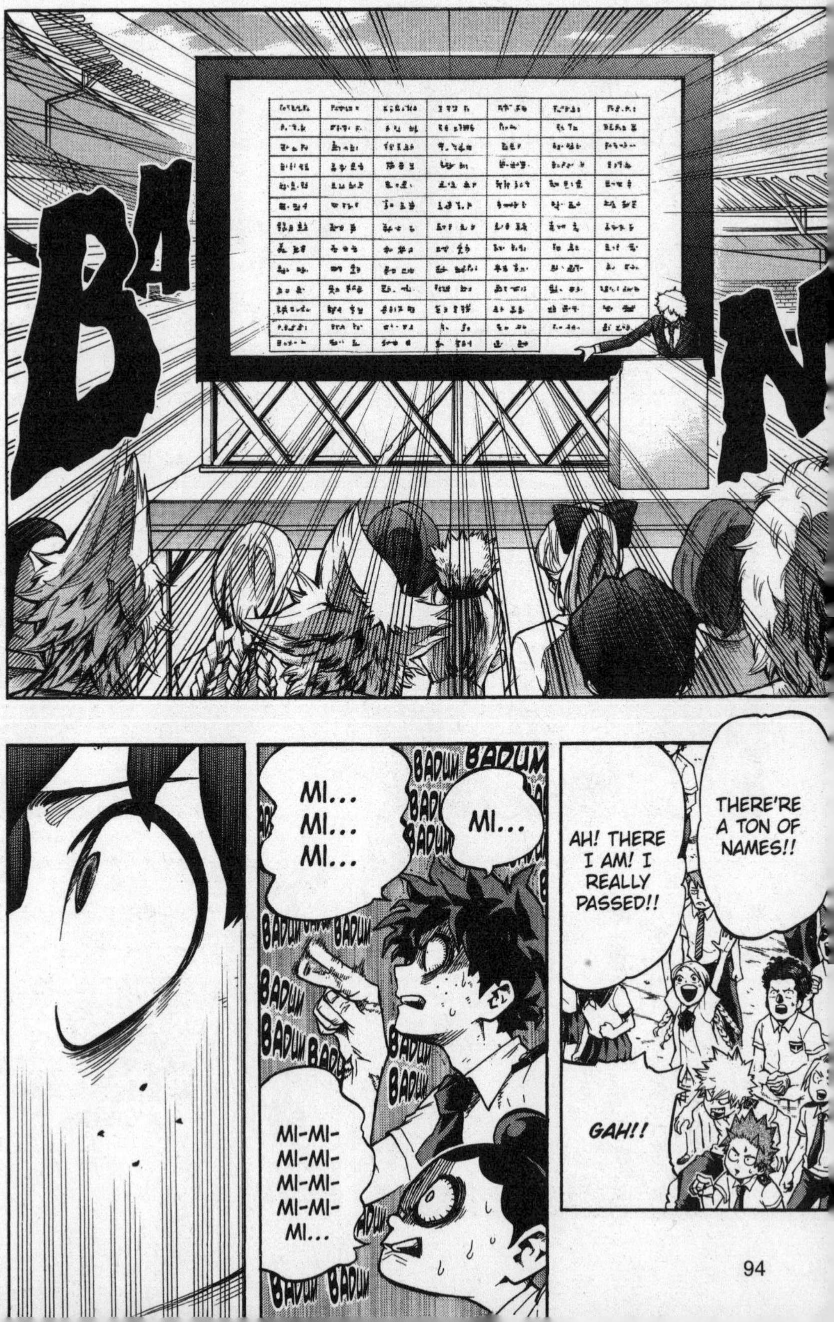
BAN
THERE'RE A TON OF NAMES!!
AH! THERE I AM! I REALLY PASSED!!
GAH!!
MI...
MI... MI... MI...
BADUM BADUM BADUM BADUM
MI-MI-MI-MI-MI-MI-MI-MI-MI...

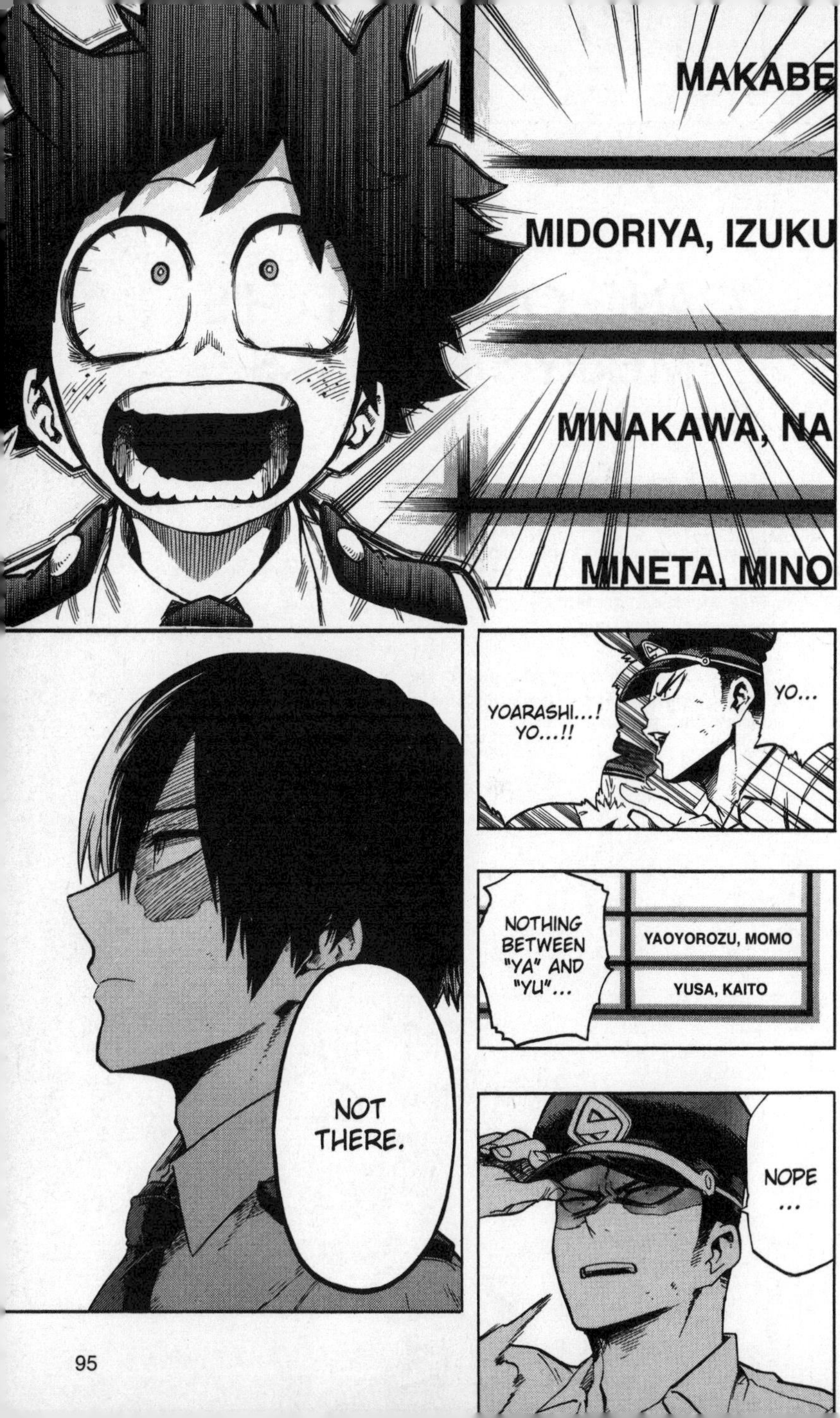
MAKABE
MIDORIYA, IZUKU
MINAKAWA, NA
MINETA, MINO
YO...
YOARASHI...! YO...!!
NOTHING BETWEEN "YA" AND "YU"...
YAOYOROZU, MOMO
YUSA, KAITO
NOPE ...
NOT THERE.

GANG ORCA AND HIS MERRY SIDEKICKS

Most of these fellows are sidekicks who help out Gang Orca with his heroics. That's why they call him "the Big Fish." During the test, they're handicapped in the following three ways: they can't use their Quirks, they can only attack with cement guns and they have to wear restraint gear.

The costumes were prepared just for the testing exercise. These guys have their own lives to live, after all.

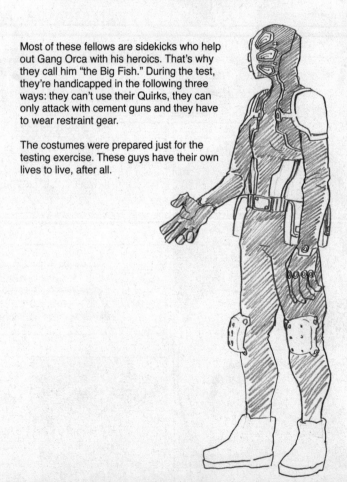

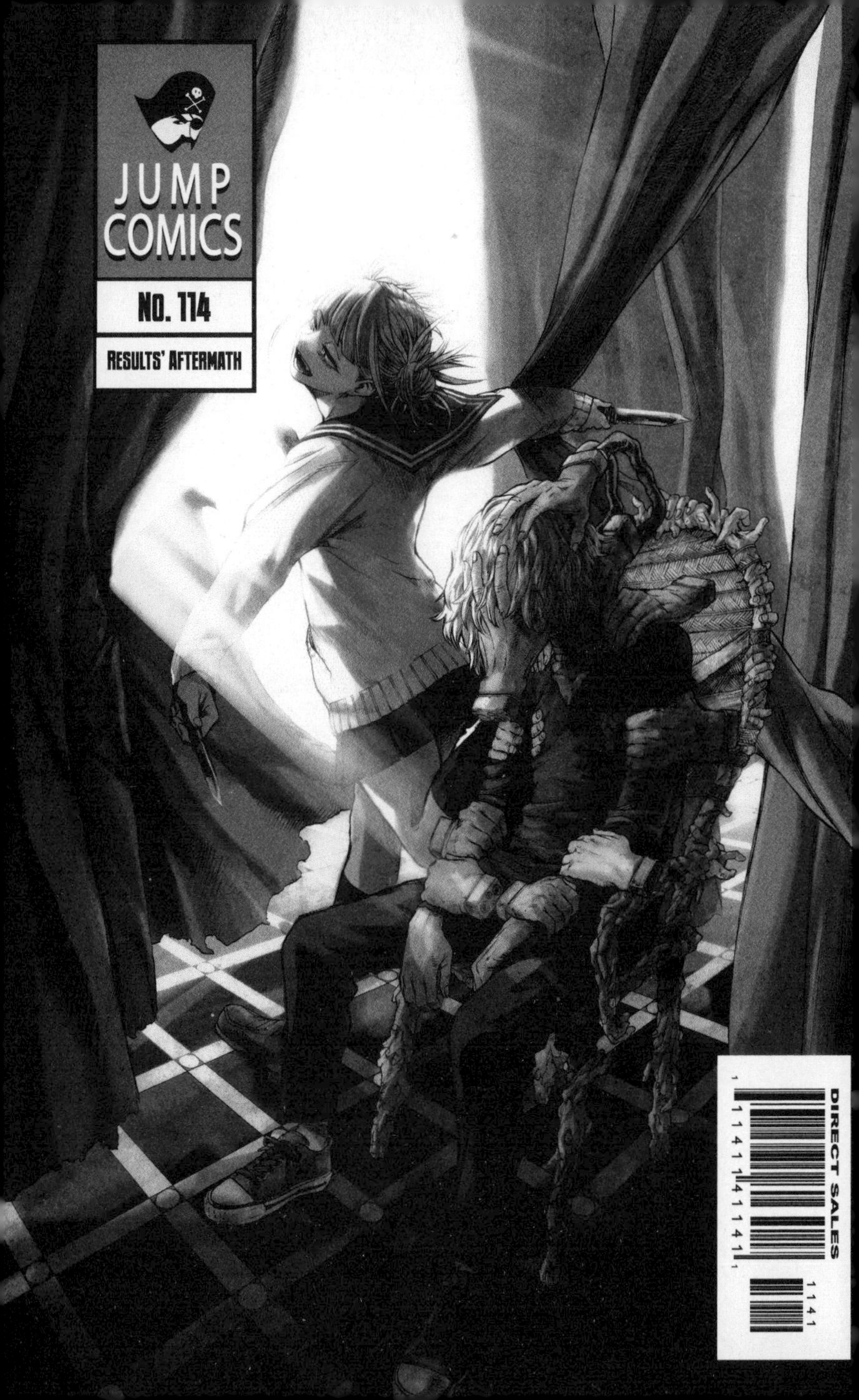
JUMP COMICS
No. 114
RESULTS' AFTERMATH
DIRECT SALES

MY HERO ACADEMIA

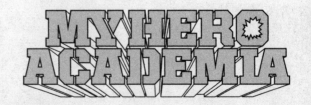

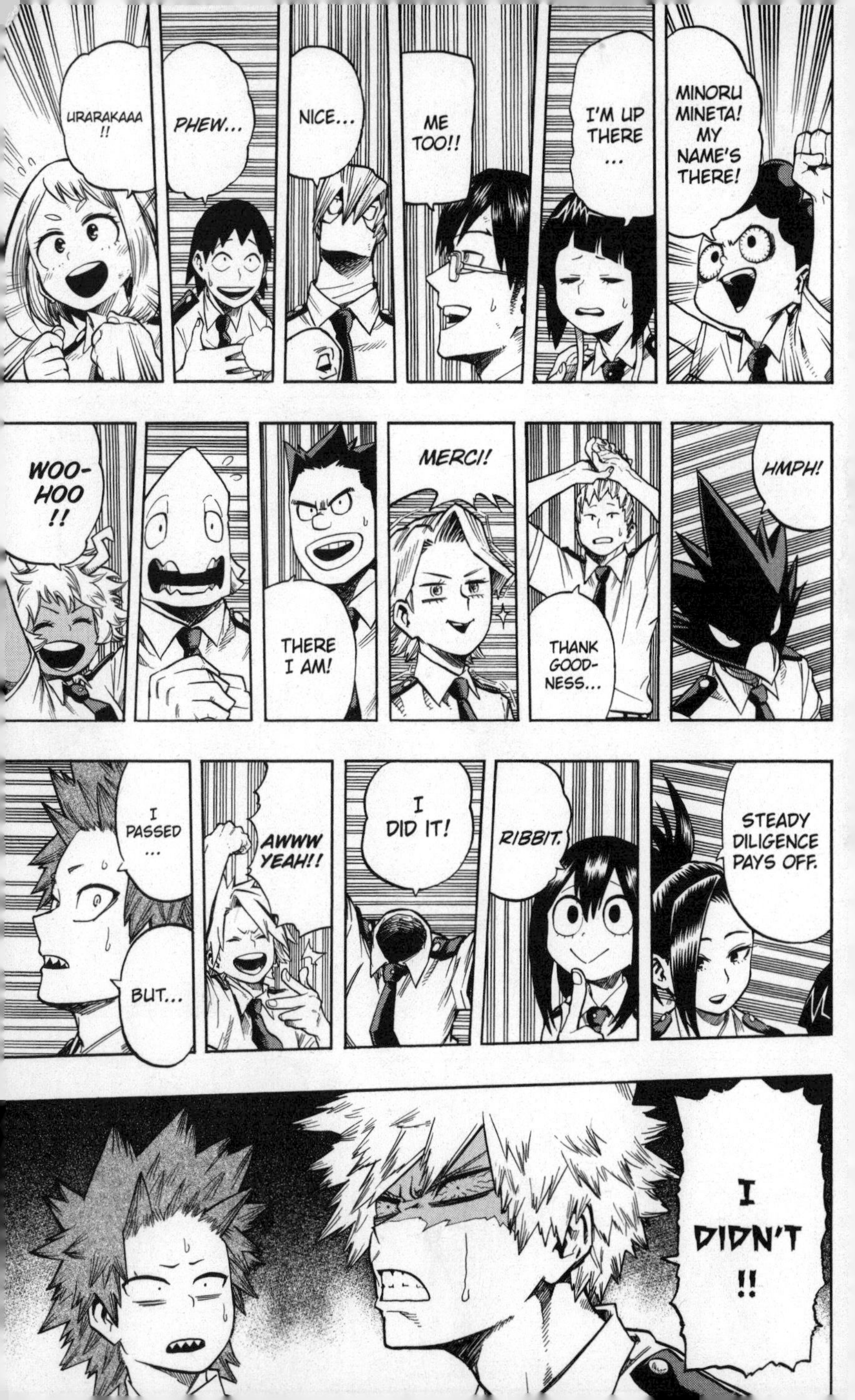
MINORU MINETA! MY NAME'S THERE!
I'M UP THERE ...
ME TOO!!
NICE...
PHEW...
URARAKAAA !!
HMPH!
THANK GOOD-NESS...
MERCI!
THERE I AM!
WOO-HOO !!
STEADY DILIGENCE PAYS OFF.
RIBBIT.
I DID IT!
AWWW YEAH!!
I PASSED ...
BUT...
I DIDN'T !!

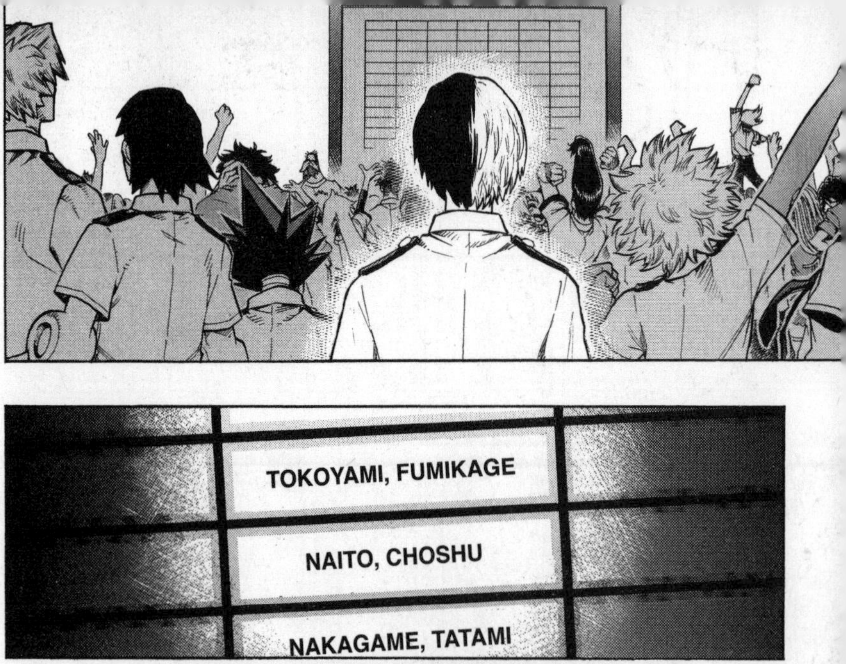
TOKOYAMI, FUMIKAGE
NAITO, CHOSHU
NAKAGAME, TATAMI

*TODOROKI'S NAME WOULD APPEAR BETWEEN TOKOYAMI AND NAITO IN THE JAPANESE ALPHABET.

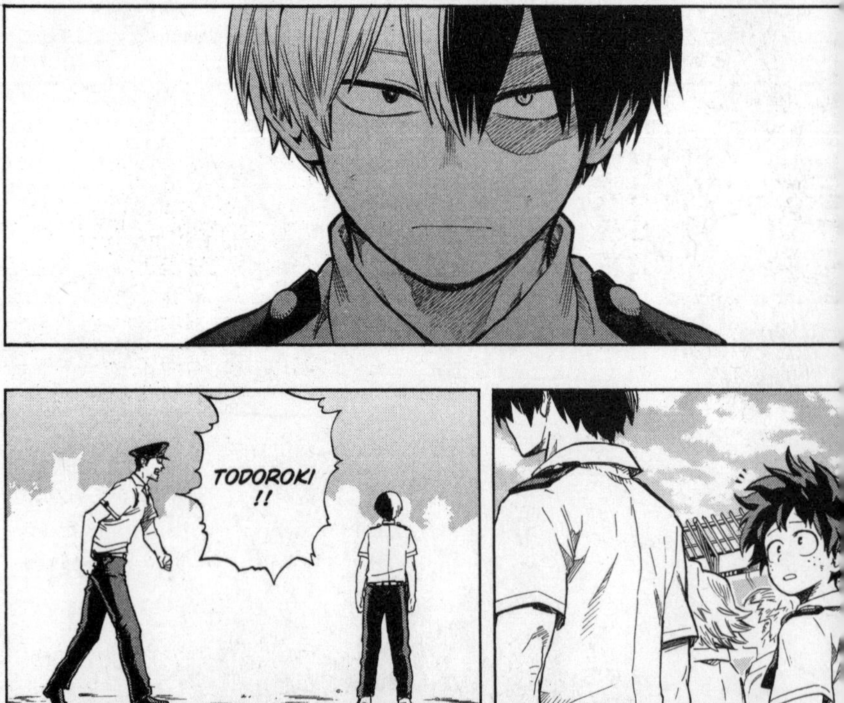
TODOROKI !!

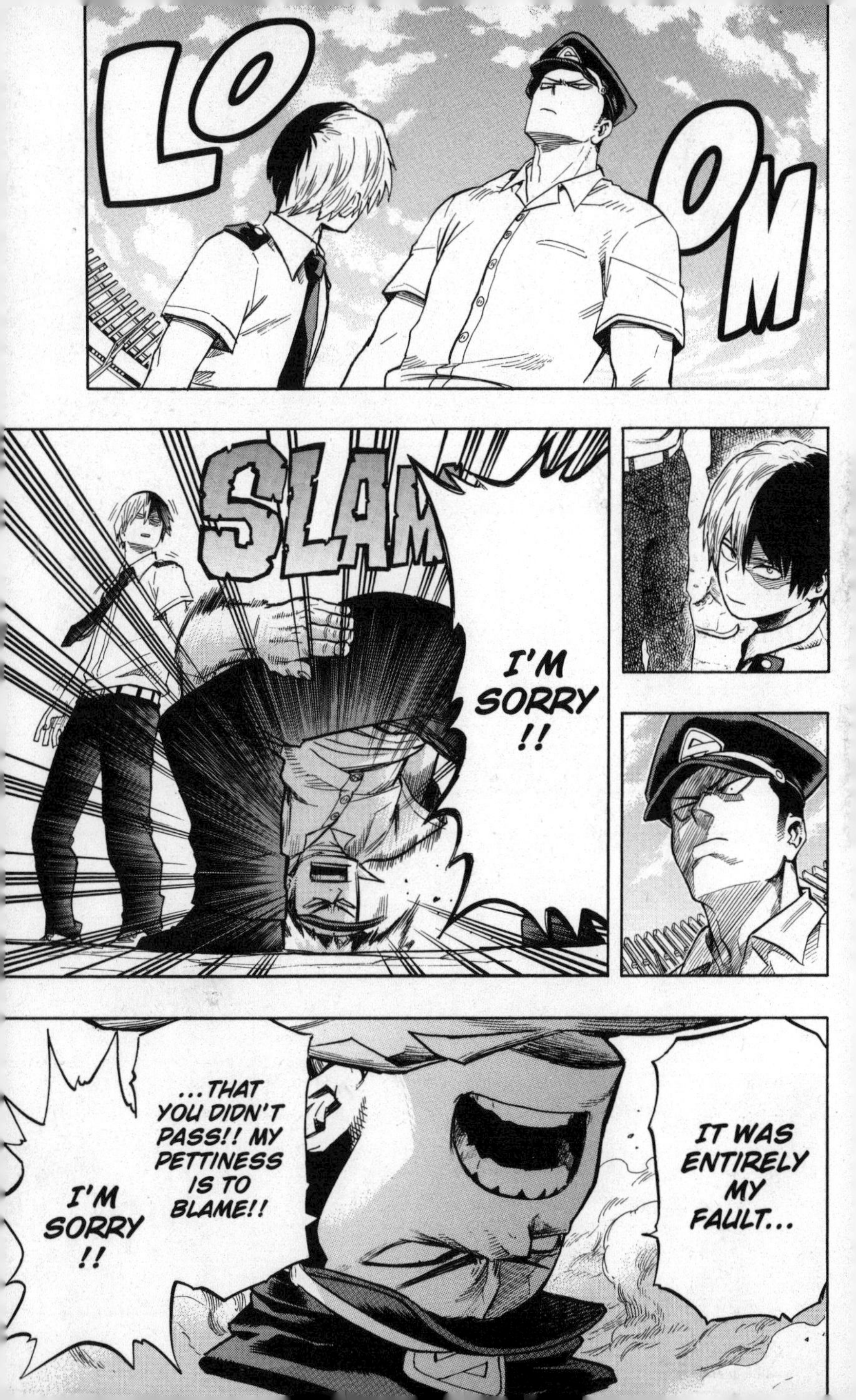
LO OM
SLAM
I'M SORRY!!
IT WAS ENTIRELY MY FAULT...
...THAT YOU DIDN'T PASS!! MY PETTINESS IS TO BLAME!!
I'M SORRY!!

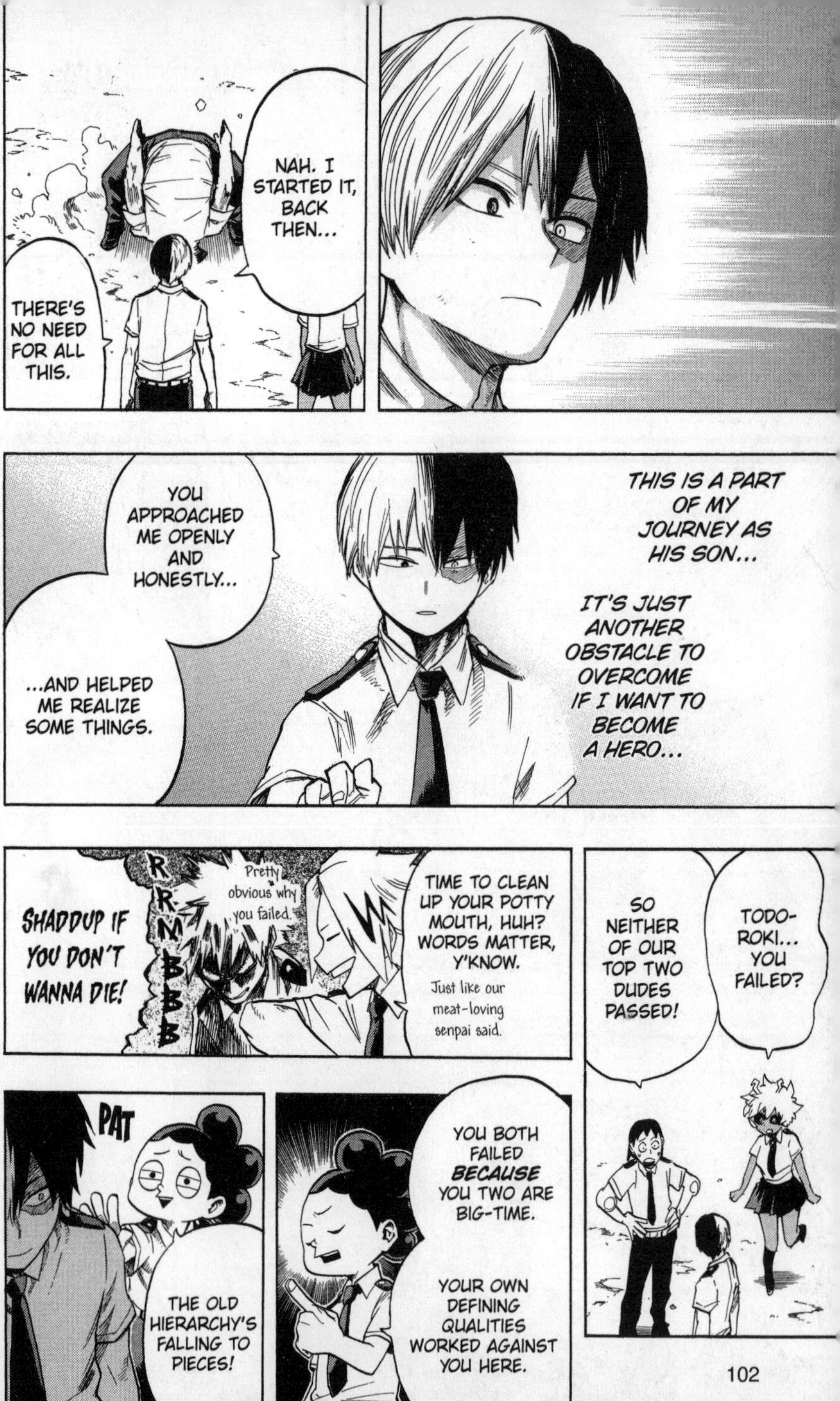
NAH. I STARTED IT, BACK THEN...
THERE'S NO NEED FOR ALL THIS.
THIS IS A PART OF MY JOURNEY AS HIS SON...
IT'S JUST ANOTHER OBSTACLE TO OVERCOME IF I WANT TO BECOME A HERO...
YOU APPROACHED ME OPENLY AND HONESTLY...
...AND HELPED ME REALIZE SOME THINGS.
TODO-ROKI... YOU FAILED?
SO NEITHER OF OUR TOP TWO DUDES PASSED!
TIME TO CLEAN UP YOUR POTTY MOUTH, HUH? WORDS MATTER, Y'KNOW.
Just like our meat-loving senpai said.
Pretty obvious why you failed.
RRMBBB
SHADDUP IF YOU DON'T WANNA DIE!
YOU BOTH FAILED *BECAUSE* YOU TWO ARE BIG-TIME.
YOUR OWN DEFINING QUALITIES WORKED AGAINST YOU HERE.
PAT
THE OLD HIERARCHY'S FALLING TO PIECES!

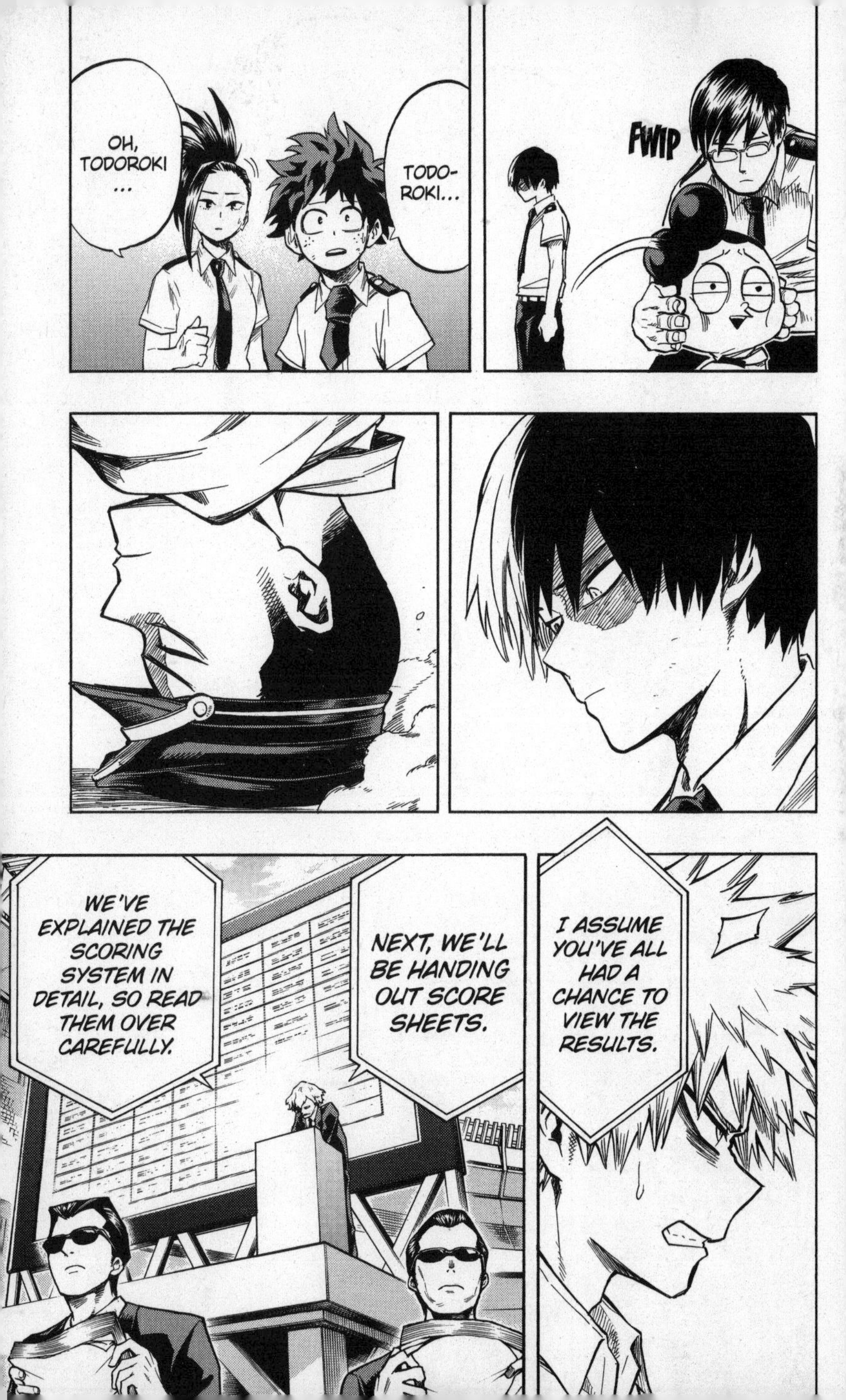
FWIP
TODO-ROKI...
OH, TODOROKI ...
I ASSUME YOU'VE ALL HAD A CHANCE TO VIEW THE RESULTS.
NEXT, WE'LL BE HANDING OUT SCORE SHEETS.
WE'VE EXPLAINED THE SCORING SYSTEM IN DETAIL, SO READ THEM OVER CAREFULLY.

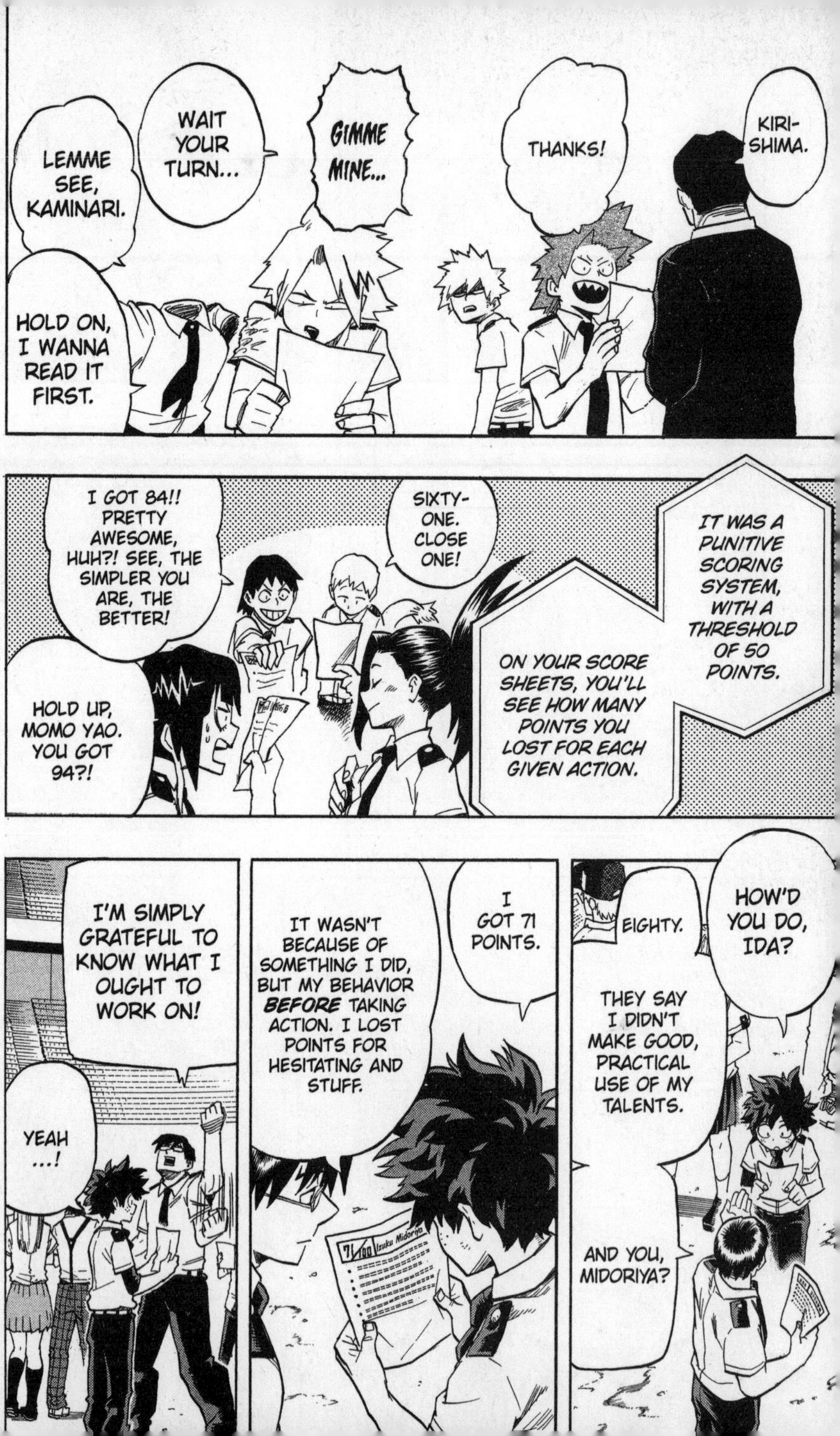
KIRI-SHIMA.
THANKS!
GIMME MINE...
WAIT YOUR TURN...
LEMME SEE, KAMINARI.
HOLD ON, I WANNA READ IT FIRST.
IT WAS A PUNITIVE SCORING SYSTEM, WITH A THRESHOLD OF 50 POINTS.
ON YOUR SCORE SHEETS, YOU'LL SEE HOW MANY POINTS YOU LOST FOR EACH GIVEN ACTION.
SIXTY-ONE. CLOSE ONE!
I GOT 84!! PRETTY AWESOME, HUH?! SEE, THE SIMPLER YOU ARE, THE BETTER!
HOLD UP, MOMO YAO. YOU GOT 94?!
HOW'D YOU DO, IDA?
EIGHTY.
THEY SAY I DIDN'T MAKE GOOD, PRACTICAL USE OF MY TALENTS.
AND YOU, MIDORIYA?
I GOT 71 POINTS.
IT WASN'T BECAUSE OF SOMETHING I DID, BUT MY BEHAVIOR ***BEFORE*** TAKING ACTION. I LOST POINTS FOR HESITATING AND STUFF.
I'M SIMPLY GRATEFUL TO KNOW WHAT I OUGHT TO WORK ON!
YEAH ...!

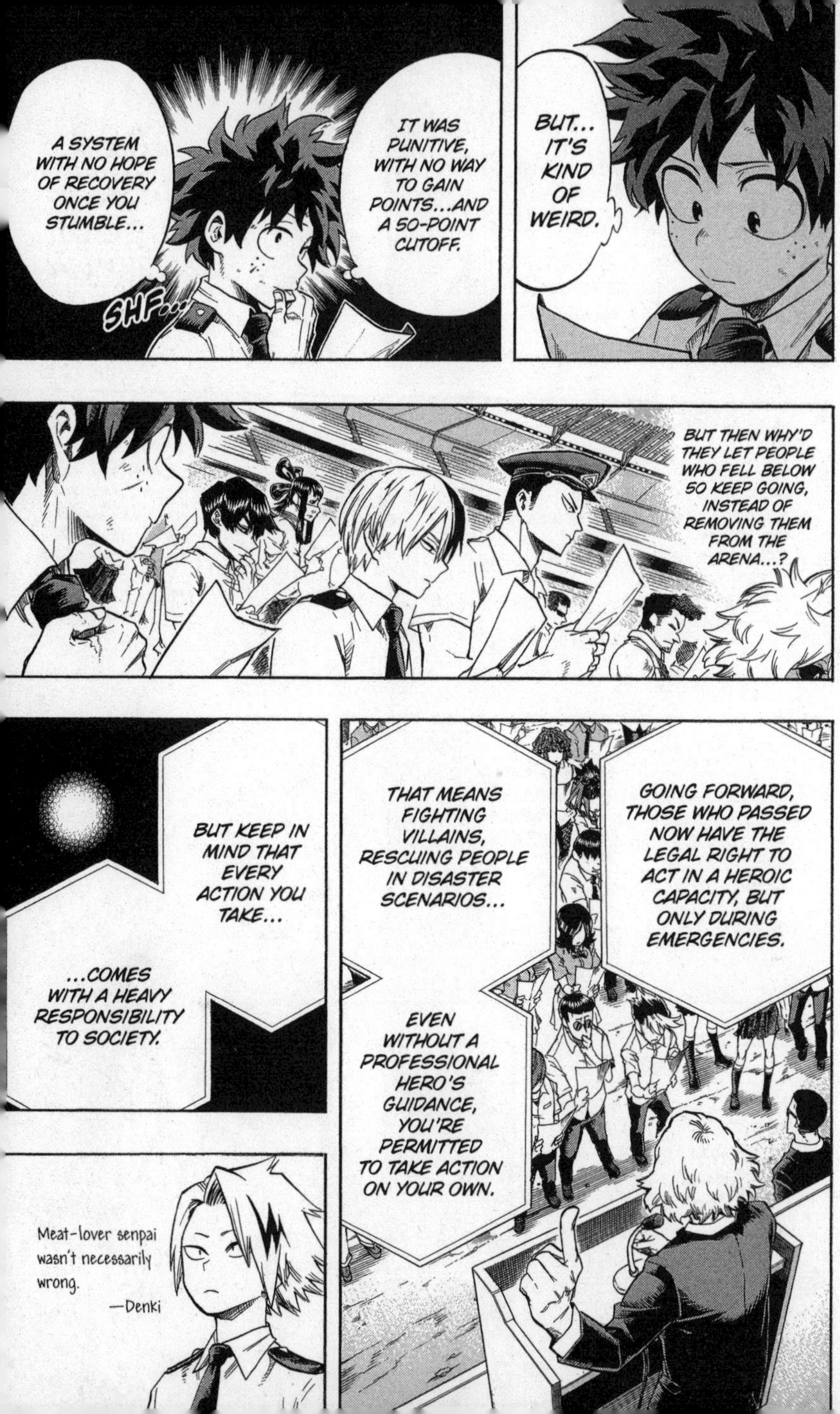
BUT... IT'S KIND OF WEIRD.
IT WAS PUNITIVE, WITH NO WAY TO GAIN POINTS...AND A 50-POINT CUTOFF.
A SYSTEM WITH NO HOPE OF RECOVERY ONCE YOU STUMBLE...
SHF...
BUT THEN WHY'D THEY LET PEOPLE WHO FELL BELOW 50 KEEP GOING, INSTEAD OF REMOVING THEM FROM THE ARENA...?
GOING FORWARD, THOSE WHO PASSED NOW HAVE THE LEGAL RIGHT TO ACT IN A HEROIC CAPACITY, BUT ONLY DURING EMERGENCIES.
THAT MEANS FIGHTING VILLAINS, RESCUING PEOPLE IN DISASTER SCENARIOS...
EVEN WITHOUT A PROFESSIONAL HERO'S GUIDANCE, YOU'RE PERMITTED TO TAKE ACTION ON YOUR OWN.
BUT KEEP IN MIND THAT EVERY ACTION YOU TAKE...
...COMES WITH A HEAVY RESPONSIBILITY TO SOCIETY.
Meat-lover senpai wasn't necessarily wrong.
—Denki

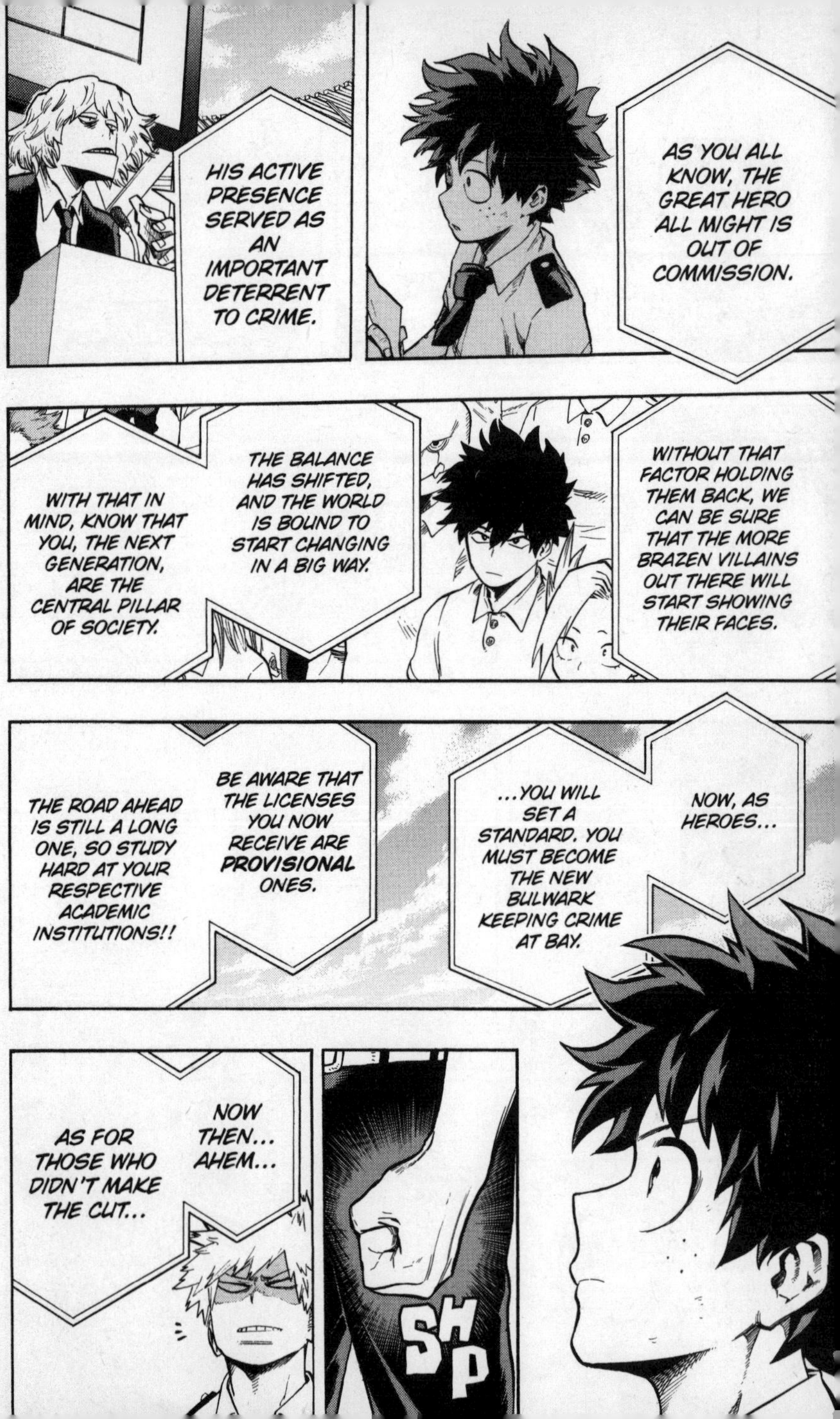
AS YOU ALL KNOW, THE GREAT HERO ALL MIGHT IS OUT OF COMMISSION.
HIS ACTIVE PRESENCE SERVED AS AN IMPORTANT DETERRENT TO CRIME.
WITHOUT THAT FACTOR HOLDING THEM BACK, WE CAN BE SURE THAT THE MORE BRAZEN VILLAINS OUT THERE WILL START SHOWING THEIR FACES.
THE BALANCE HAS SHIFTED, AND THE WORLD IS BOUND TO START CHANGING IN A BIG WAY.
WITH THAT IN MIND, KNOW THAT YOU, THE NEXT GENERATION, ARE THE CENTRAL PILLAR OF SOCIETY.
NOW, AS HEROES...
...YOU WILL SET A STANDARD. YOU MUST BECOME THE NEW BULWARK KEEPING CRIME AT BAY.
BE AWARE THAT THE LICENSES YOU NOW RECEIVE ARE **PROVISIONAL** ONES.
THE ROAD AHEAD IS STILL A LONG ONE, SO STUDY HARD AT YOUR RESPECTIVE ACADEMIC INSTITUTIONS!!
SHP
NOW THEN... AHEM...
AS FOR THOSE WHO DIDN'T MAKE THE CUT...

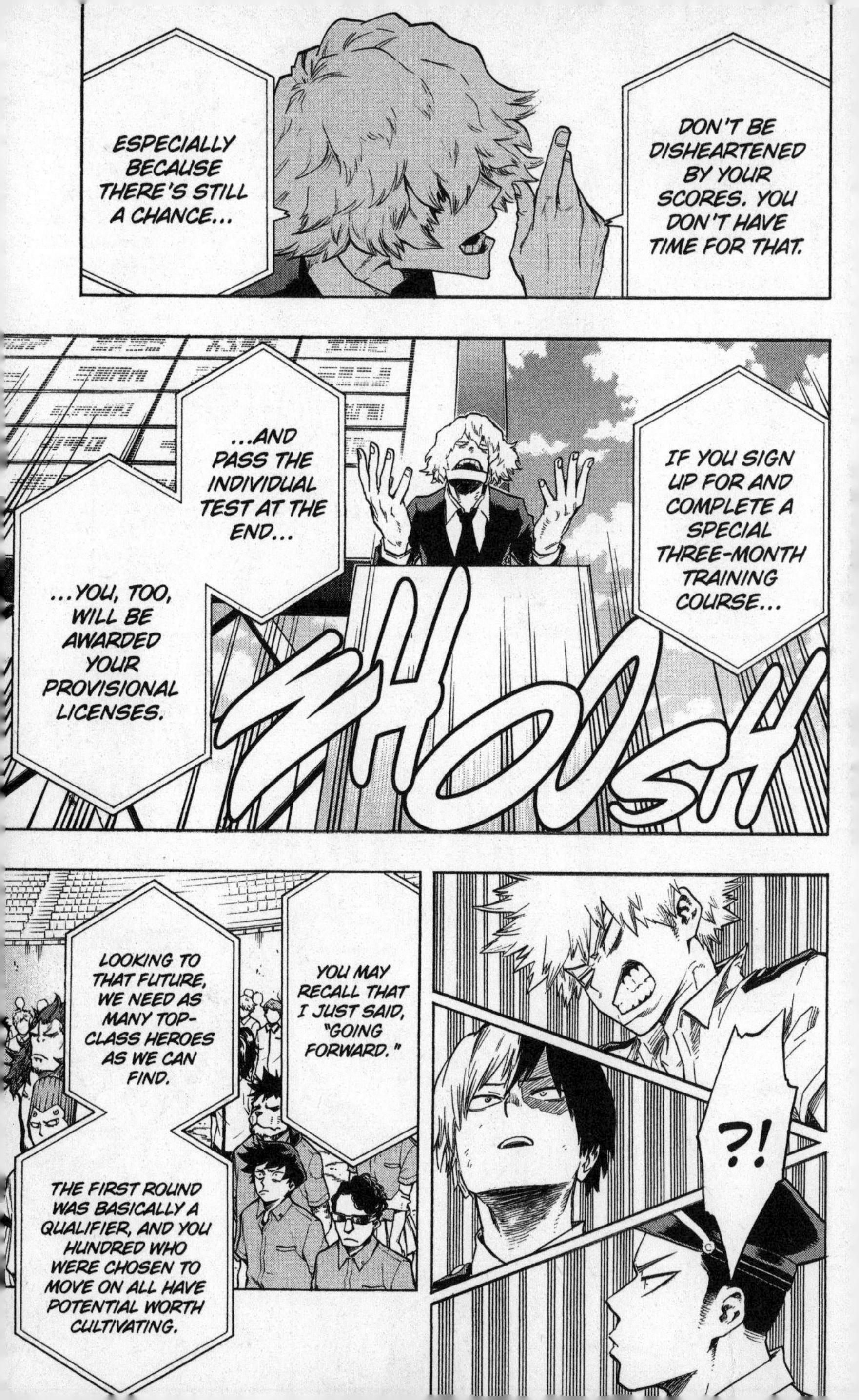
DON'T BE DISHEARTENED BY YOUR SCORES. YOU DON'T HAVE TIME FOR THAT.
ESPECIALLY BECAUSE THERE'S STILL A CHANCE...
IF YOU SIGN UP FOR AND COMPLETE A SPECIAL THREE-MONTH TRAINING COURSE...
...AND PASS THE INDIVIDUAL TEST AT THE END...
...YOU, TOO, WILL BE AWARDED YOUR PROVISIONAL LICENSES.
WHOOSH
?!
YOU MAY RECALL THAT I JUST SAID, "GOING FORWARD."
LOOKING TO THAT FUTURE, WE NEED AS MANY TOP-CLASS HEROES AS WE CAN FIND.
THE FIRST ROUND WAS BASICALLY A QUALIFIER, AND YOU HUNDRED WHO WERE CHOSEN TO MOVE ON ALL HAVE POTENTIAL WORTH CULTIVATING.

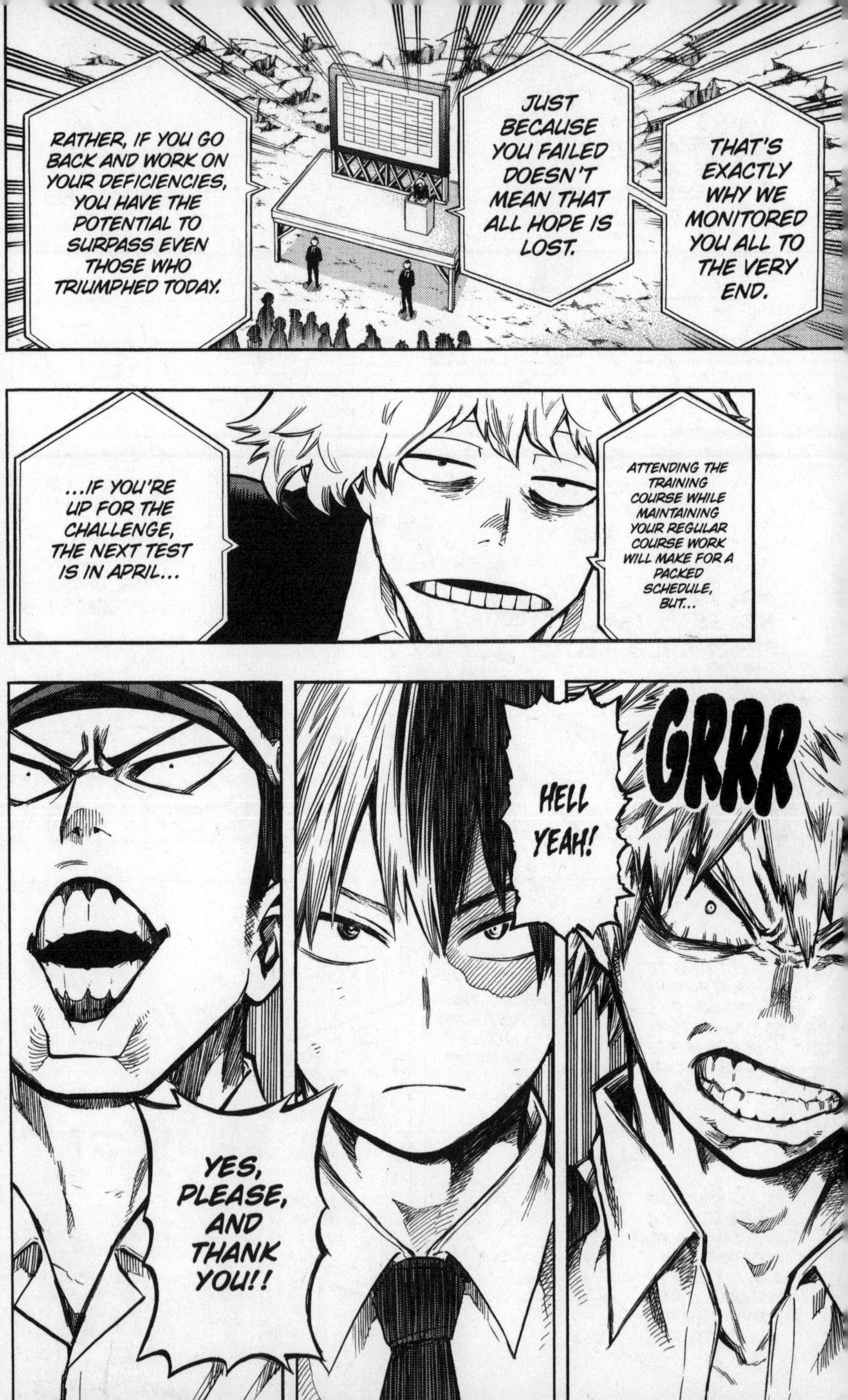
THAT'S EXACTLY WHY WE MONITORED YOU ALL TO THE VERY END.
JUST BECAUSE YOU FAILED DOESN'T MEAN THAT ALL HOPE IS LOST.
RATHER, IF YOU GO BACK AND WORK ON YOUR DEFICIENCIES, YOU HAVE THE POTENTIAL TO SURPASS EVEN THOSE WHO TRIUMPHED TODAY.
ATTENDING THE TRAINING COURSE WHILE MAINTAINING YOUR REGULAR COURSE WORK WILL MAKE FOR A PACKED SCHEDULE, BUT...
...IF YOU'RE UP FOR THE CHALLENGE, THE NEXT TEST IS IN APRIL...
GRRR
HELL YEAH!
YES, PLEASE, AND THANK YOU!!

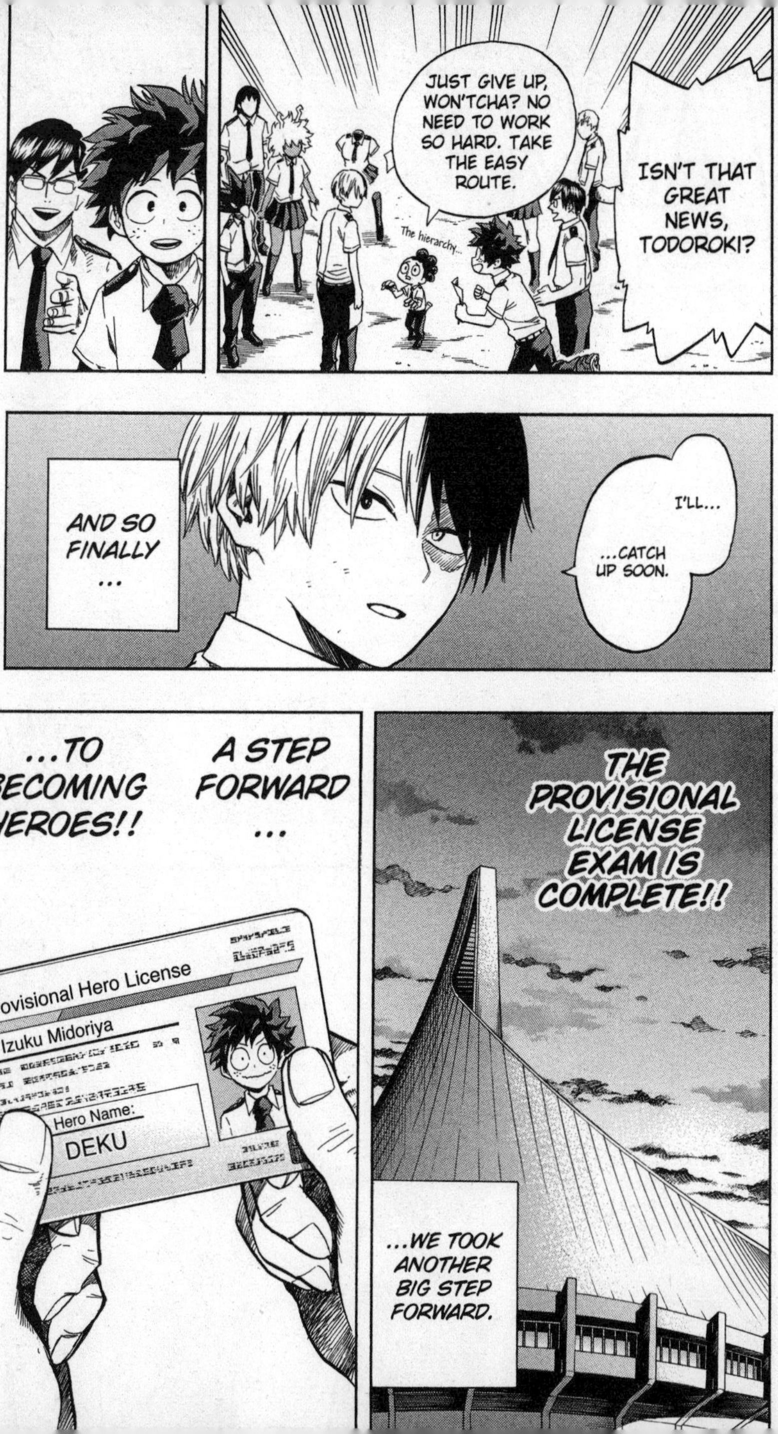
ISN'T THAT GREAT NEWS, TODOROKI?
JUST GIVE UP, WON'TCHA? NO NEED TO WORK SO HARD. TAKE THE EASY ROUTE.
The hierarchy...
I'LL...
...CATCH UP SOON.
AND SO FINALLY ...
THE PROVISIONAL LICENSE EXAM IS COMPLETE!!
...WE TOOK ANOTHER BIG STEP FORWARD.
A STEP FORWARD ...
...TO BECOMING HEROES!!
Provisional Hero License
Izuku Midoriya
Hero Name:
DEKU

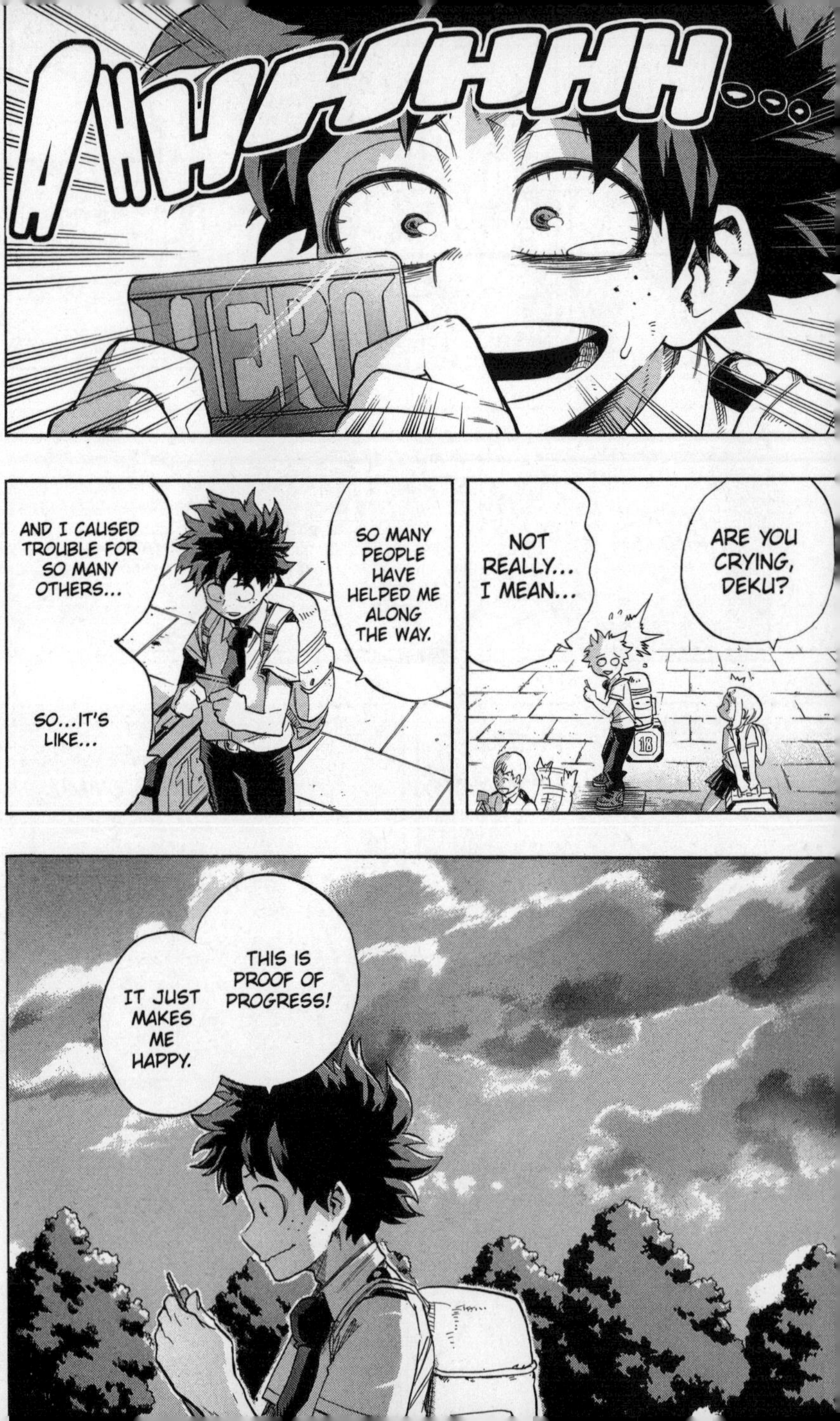
AHHHHHHH...
ARE YOU CRYING, DEKU?
NOT REALLY... I MEAN...
SO MANY PEOPLE HAVE HELPED ME ALONG THE WAY.
AND I CAUSED TROUBLE FOR SO MANY OTHERS...
SO...IT'S LIKE...
THIS IS PROOF OF PROGRESS!
IT JUST MAKES ME HAPPY.

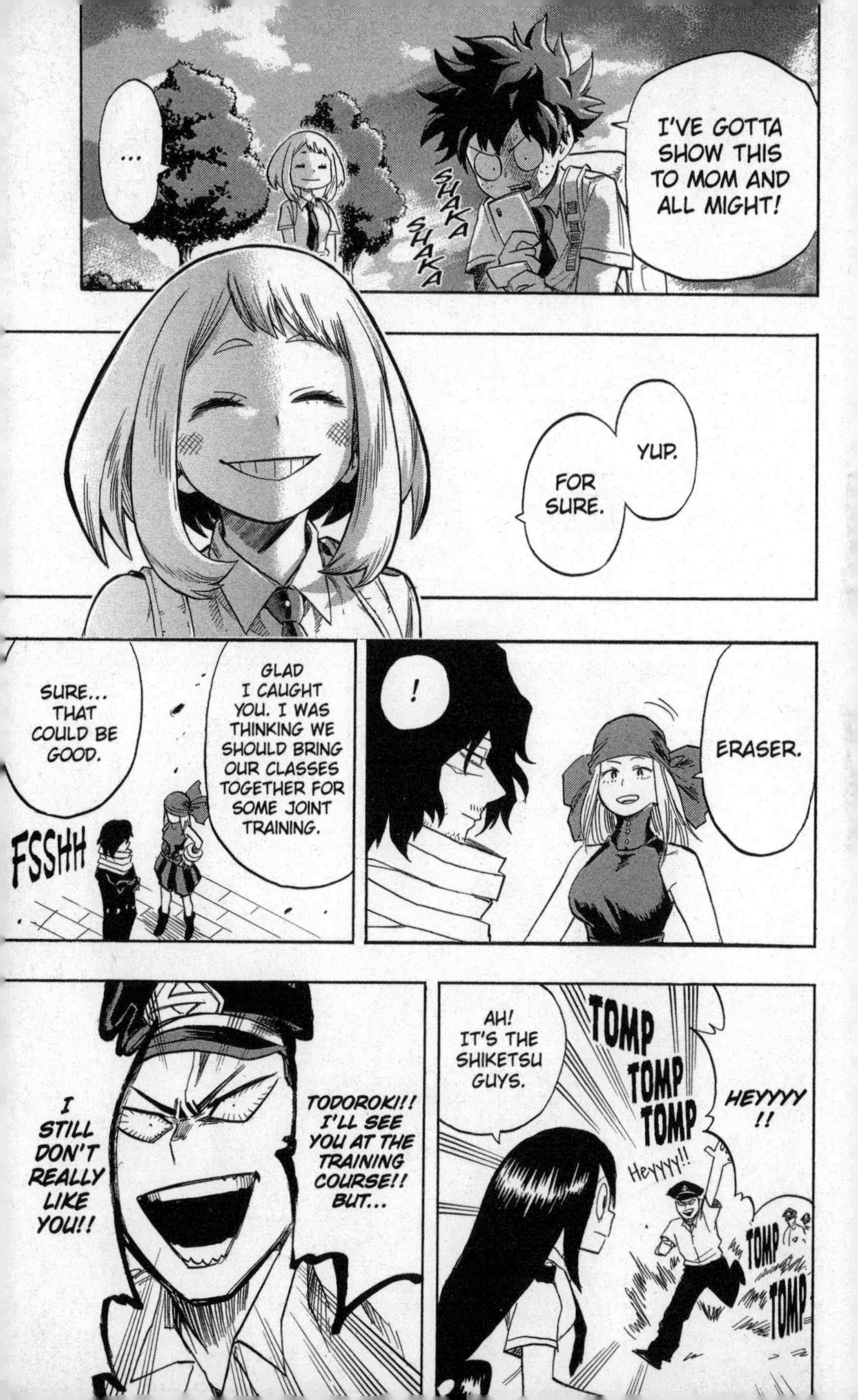
I'VE GOTTA SHOW THIS TO MOM AND ALL MIGHT!
SHAKA SHAKA
...
YUP.
FOR SURE.
ERASER.
!
GLAD I CAUGHT YOU. I WAS THINKING WE SHOULD BRING OUR CLASSES TOGETHER FOR SOME JOINT TRAINING.
SURE... THAT COULD BE GOOD.
FSSHH
HEYYYY !!
TOMP TOMP TOMP
AH! IT'S THE SHIKETSU GUYS.
Heyyyy!!
TOMP TOMP
TODOROKI!! I'LL SEE YOU AT THE TRAINING COURSE!! BUT...
I STILL DON'T REALLY LIKE YOU!!

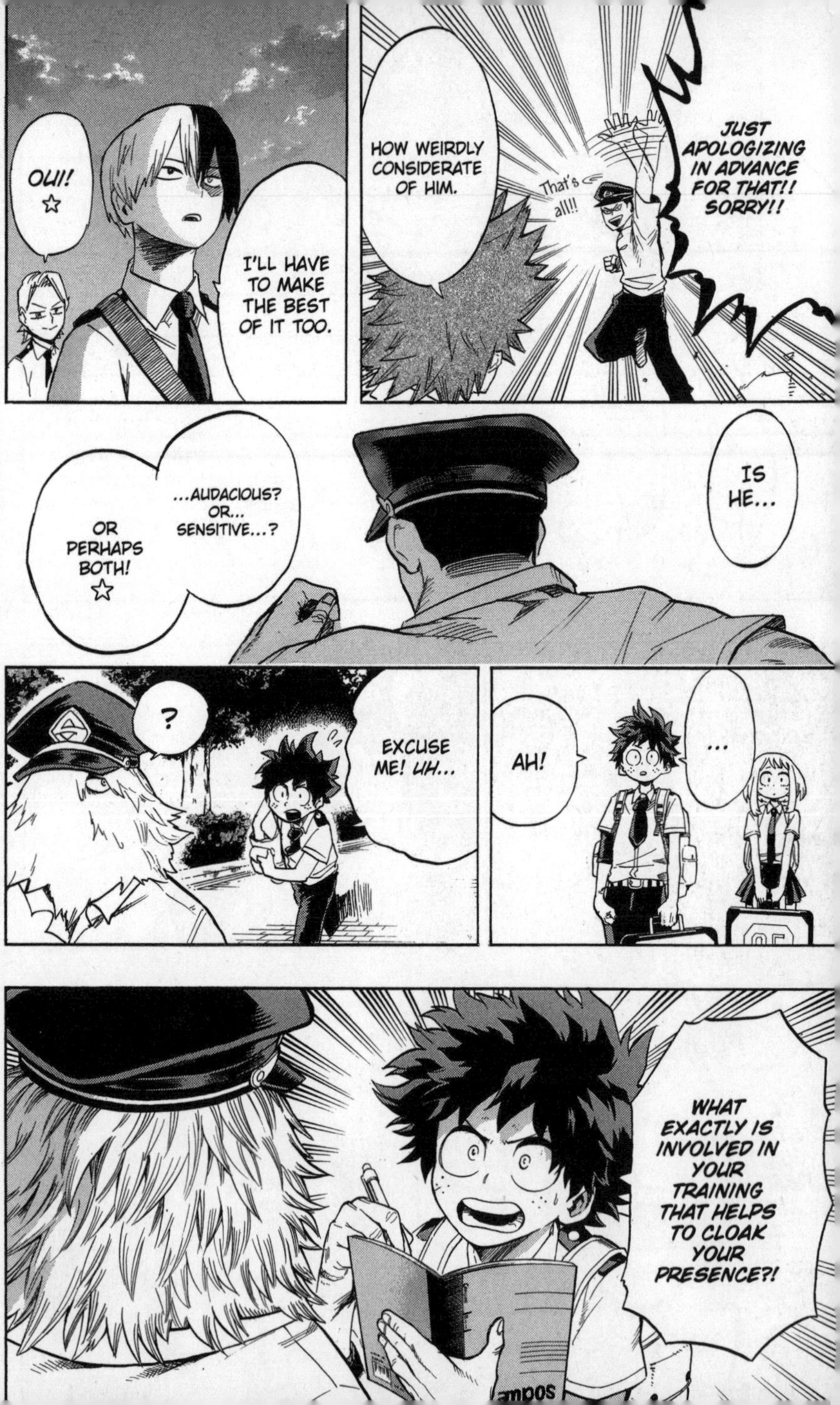
JUST APOLOGIZING IN ADVANCE FOR THAT!! SORRY!!
That's all!!!
HOW WEIRDLY CONSIDERATE OF HIM.
I'LL HAVE TO MAKE THE BEST OF IT TOO.
OUI! ☆
IS HE...
...AUDACIOUS? OR... SENSITIVE...?
OR PERHAPS BOTH! ☆
...
AH!
EXCUSE ME! UH...
?
WHAT EXACTLY IS INVOLVED IN YOUR TRAINING THAT HELPS TO CLOAK YOUR PRESENCE?!

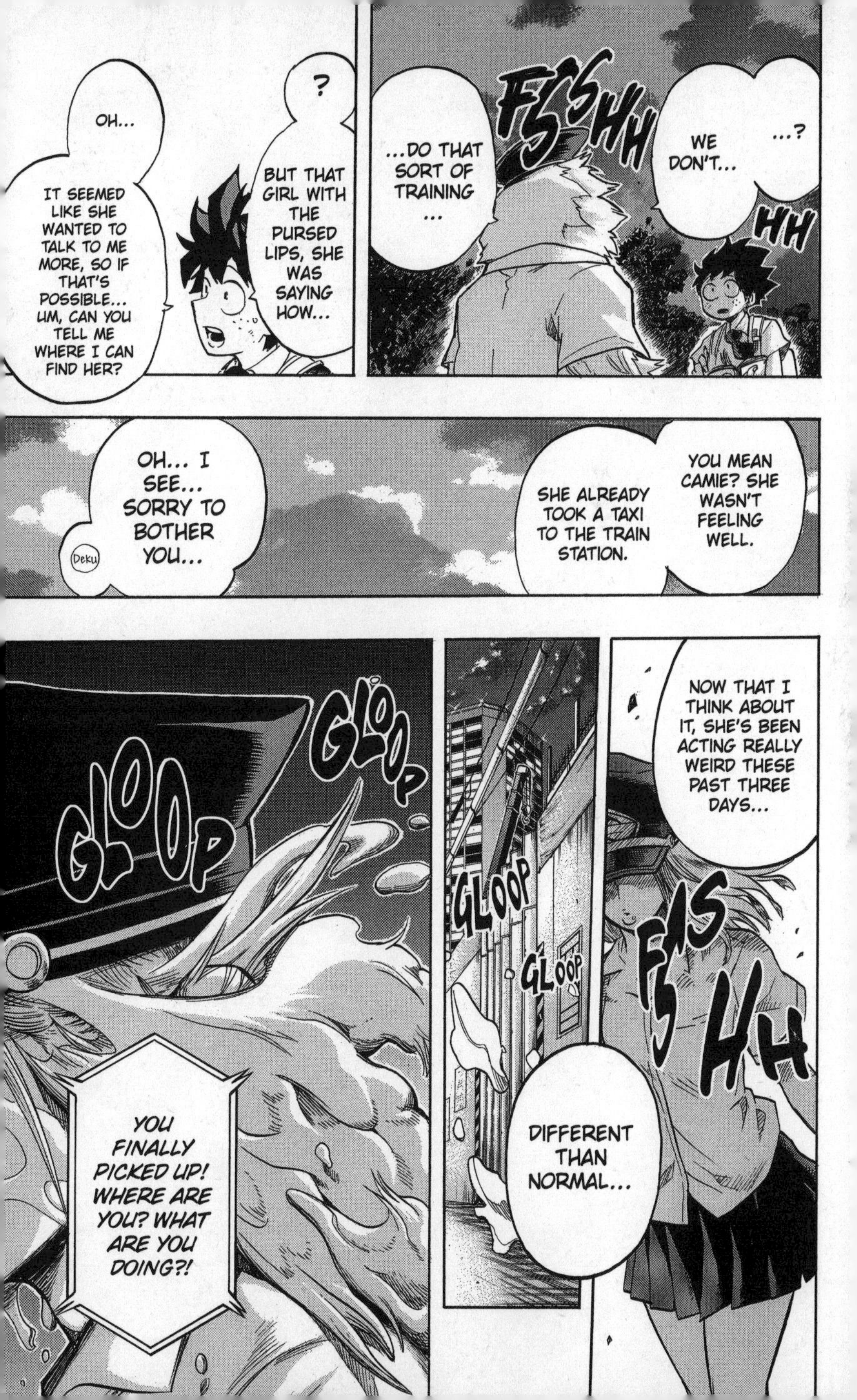
...?
WE DON'T...
FSSHH
...DO THAT SORT OF TRAINING...
HH
?
BUT THAT GIRL WITH THE PURSED LIPS, SHE WAS SAYING HOW...
OH...
IT SEEMED LIKE SHE WANTED TO TALK TO ME MORE, SO IF THAT'S POSSIBLE... UM, CAN YOU TELL ME WHERE I CAN FIND HER?
YOU MEAN CAMIE? SHE WASN'T FEELING WELL.
SHE ALREADY TOOK A TAXI TO THE TRAIN STATION.
OH... I SEE... SORRY TO BOTHER YOU...
Deku
NOW THAT I THINK ABOUT IT, SHE'S BEEN ACTING REALLY WEIRD THESE PAST THREE DAYS...
FSSHH
DIFFERENT THAN NORMAL...
GLOOP
GLOOP
GLOOP
GLOOP
YOU FINALLY PICKED UP! WHERE ARE YOU? WHAT ARE YOU DOING?!

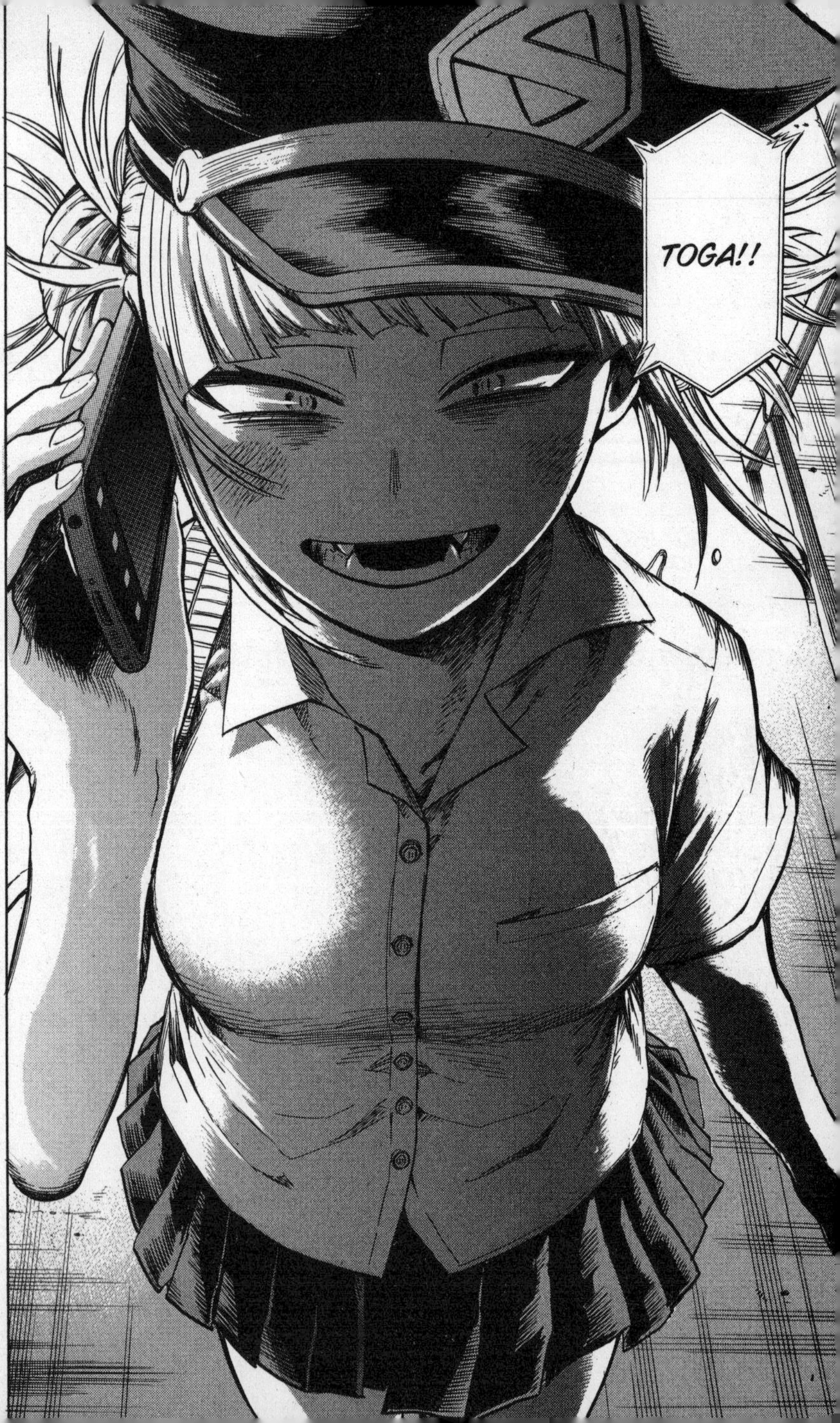
TOGA!!

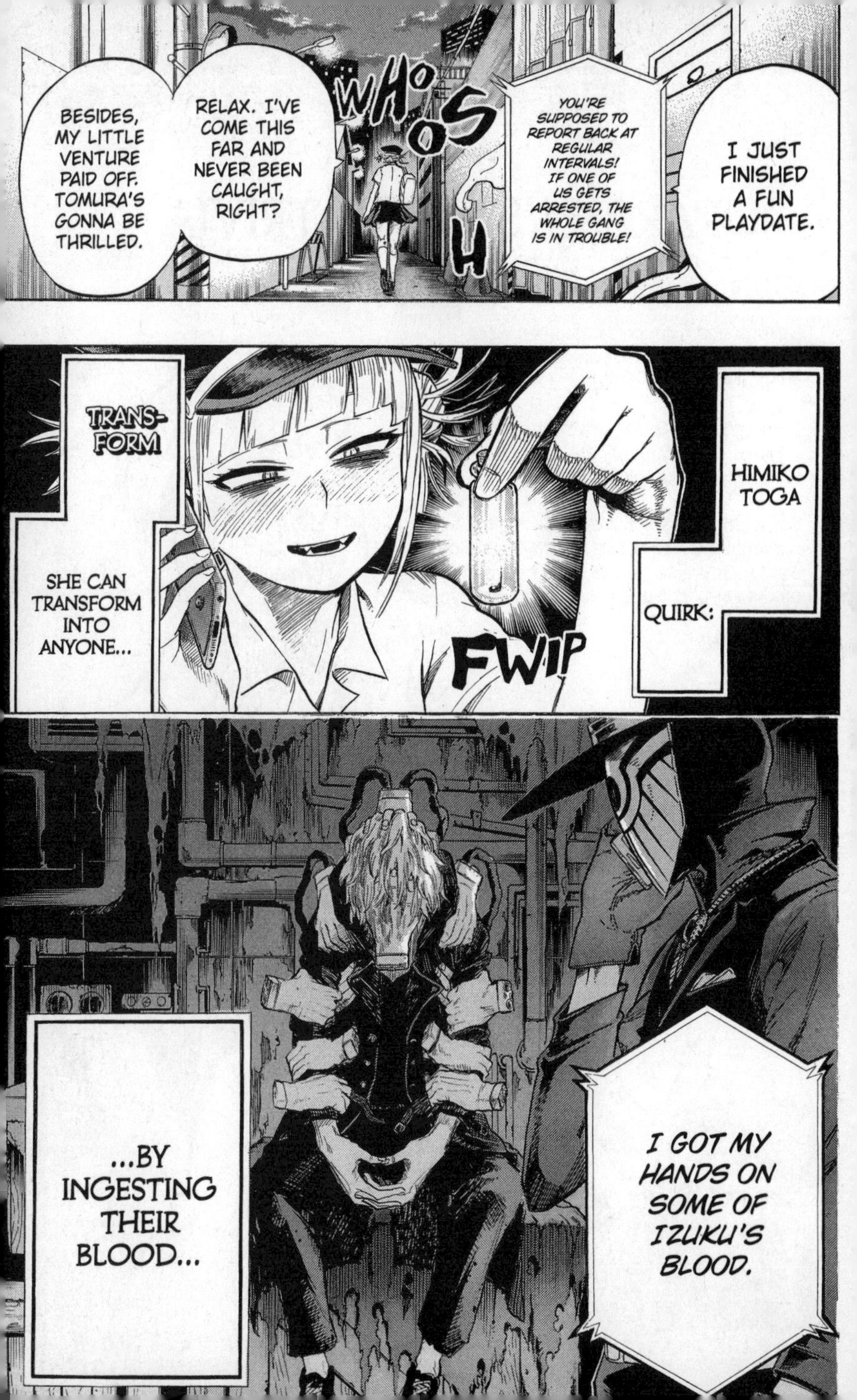
I JUST FINISHED A FUN PLAYDATE.
YOU'RE SUPPOSED TO REPORT BACK AT REGULAR INTERVALS! IF ONE OF US GETS ARRESTED, THE WHOLE GANG IS IN TROUBLE!
WHOOSH
RELAX. I'VE COME THIS FAR AND NEVER BEEN CAUGHT, RIGHT?
BESIDES, MY LITTLE VENTURE PAID OFF. TOMURA'S GONNA BE THRILLED.
HIMIKO TOGA
QUIRK:
TRANSFORM
SHE CAN TRANSFORM INTO ANYONE...
FWIP
I GOT MY HANDS ON SOME OF IZUKU'S BLOOD.
...BY INGESTING THEIR BLOOD...

URARAKA'S DOTS TRIVIA

Bakugo and Ochaco's costumes were produced by the same designer at the same support company.

Same goes for Sero + Kirishima, Yaoyorozu + Tsuyu + Ashido + Mineta, Kaminari + Jiro, and Izuku + Todoroki.

Some designers insist on inserting their own personal touches, while others don't. Some want their artistic voices to be heard, but others keep it all business. It takes all types.

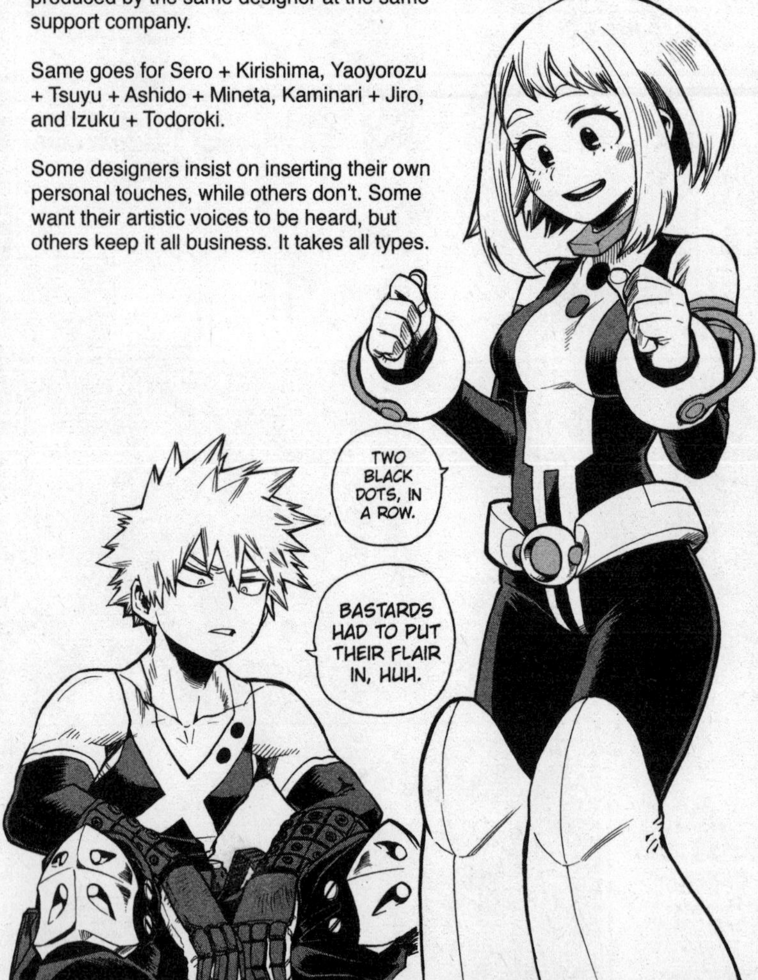
TWO BLACK DOTS, IN A ROW.
BASTARDS HAD TO PUT THEIR FLAIR IN, HUH.

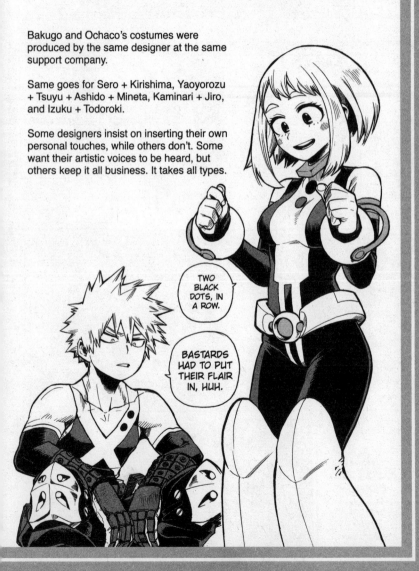

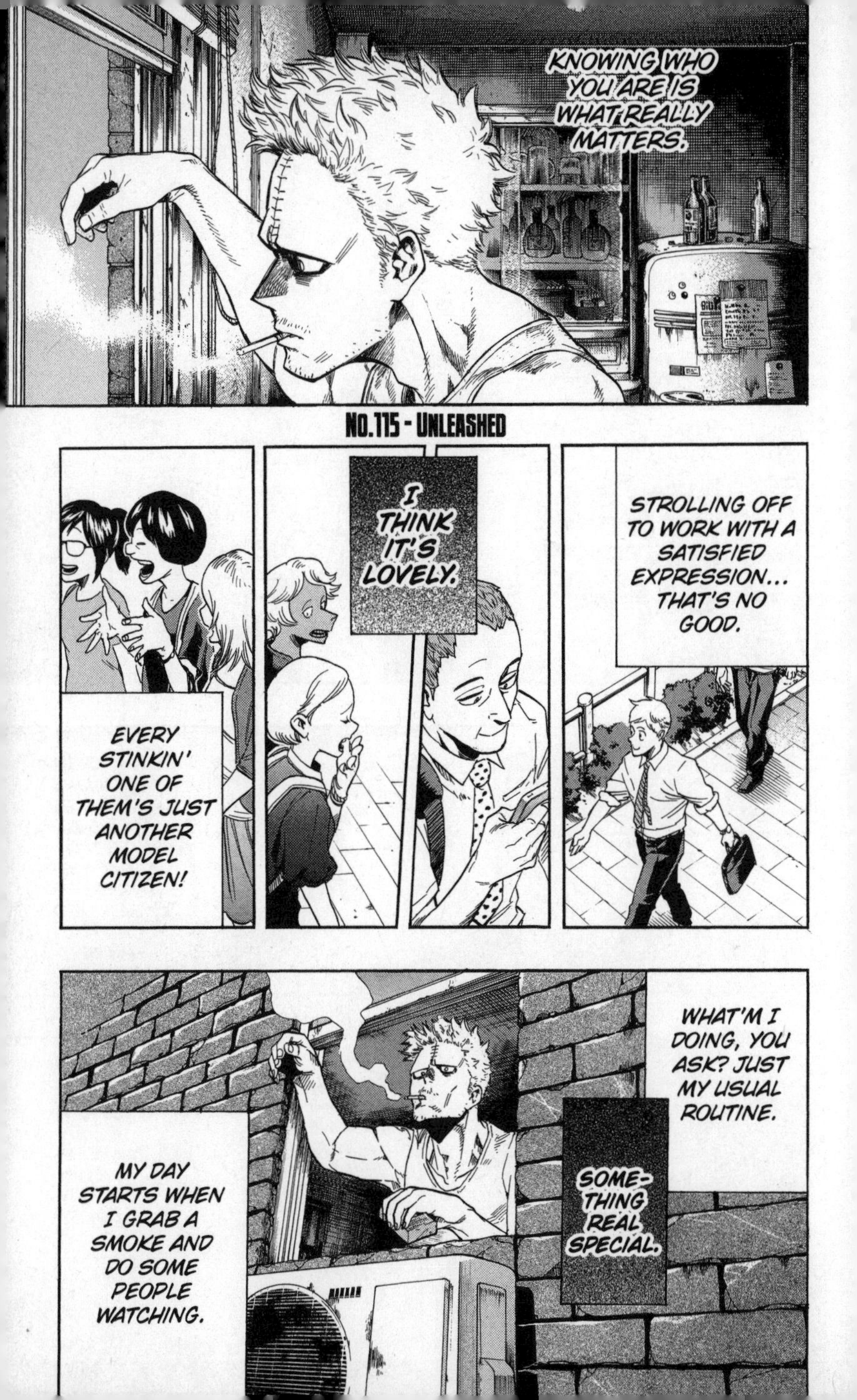
KNOWING WHO YOU ARE IS WHAT REALLY MATTERS.
NO.115 - UNLEASHED
STROLLING OFF TO WORK WITH A SATISFIED EXPRESSION... THAT'S NO GOOD.
I THINK IT'S LOVELY.
EVERY STINKIN' ONE OF THEM'S JUST ANOTHER MODEL CITIZEN!
WHAT'M I DOING, YOU ASK? JUST MY USUAL ROUTINE.
SOME-THING REAL SPECIAL.
MY DAY STARTS WHEN I GRAB A SMOKE AND DO SOME PEOPLE WATCHING.

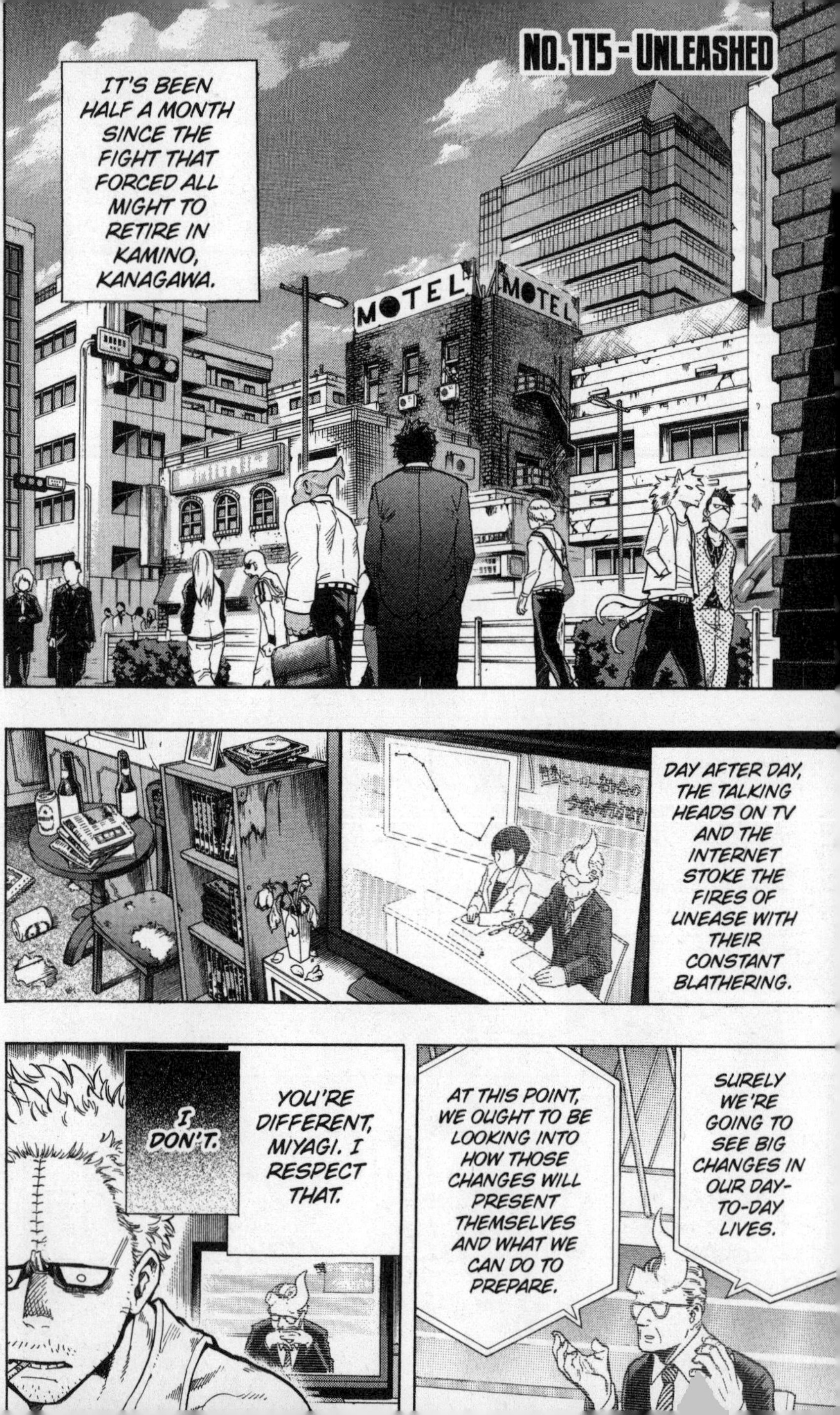
NO. 115 - UNLEASHED
IT'S BEEN HALF A MONTH SINCE THE FIGHT THAT FORCED ALL MIGHT TO RETIRE IN KAMINO, KANAGAWA.
MOTEL
MOTEL
DAY AFTER DAY, THE TALKING HEADS ON TV AND THE INTERNET STOKE THE FIRES OF UNEASE WITH THEIR CONSTANT BLATHERING.
SURELY WE'RE GOING TO SEE BIG CHANGES IN OUR DAY-TO-DAY LIVES.
AT THIS POINT, WE OUGHT TO BE LOOKING INTO HOW THOSE CHANGES WILL PRESENT THEMSELVES AND WHAT WE CAN DO TO PREPARE.
YOU'RE DIFFERENT, MIYAGI. I RESPECT THAT.
I DON'T.

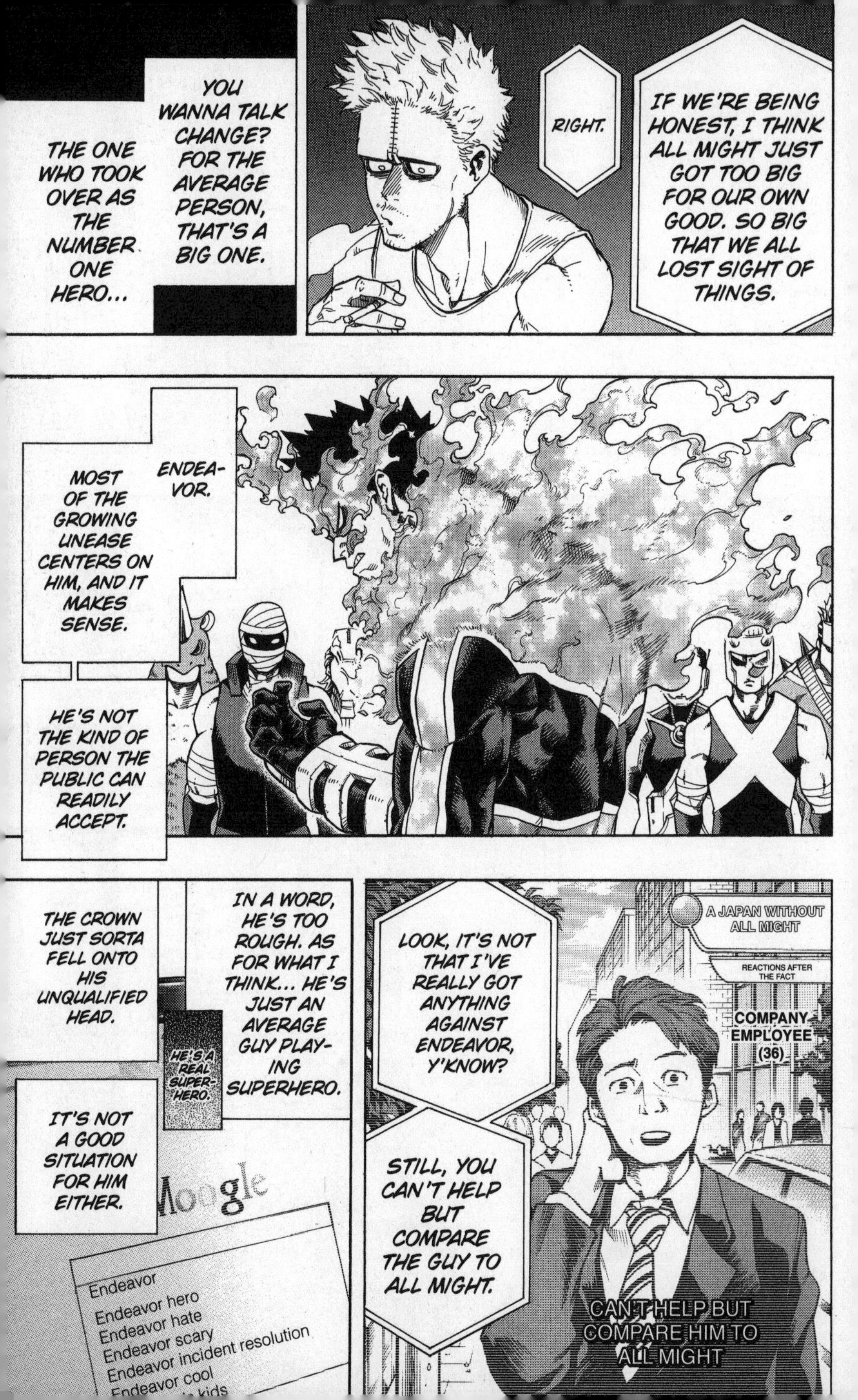
IF WE'RE BEING HONEST, I THINK ALL MIGHT JUST GOT TOO BIG FOR OUR OWN GOOD. SO BIG THAT WE ALL LOST SIGHT OF THINGS.
RIGHT.
YOU WANNA TALK CHANGE? FOR THE AVERAGE PERSON, THAT'S A BIG ONE.
THE ONE WHO TOOK OVER AS THE NUMBER ONE HERO...
ENDEAVOR.
MOST OF THE GROWING UNEASE CENTERS ON HIM, AND IT MAKES SENSE.
HE'S NOT THE KIND OF PERSON THE PUBLIC CAN READILY ACCEPT.
A JAPAN WITHOUT ALL MIGHT
REACTIONS AFTER THE FACT
COMPANY EMPLOYEE (36)
LOOK, IT'S NOT THAT I'VE REALLY GOT ANYTHING AGAINST ENDEAVOR, Y'KNOW?
STILL, YOU CAN'T HELP BUT COMPARE THE GUY TO ALL MIGHT.
CAN'T HELP BUT COMPARE HIM TO ALL MIGHT
IN A WORD, HE'S TOO ROUGH. AS FOR WHAT I THINK... HE'S JUST AN AVERAGE GUY PLAYING SUPERHERO.
THE CROWN JUST SORTA FELL ONTO HIS UNQUALIFIED HEAD.
HE'S A REAL SUPER-HERO.
IT'S NOT A GOOD SITUATION FOR HIM EITHER.
Moogle
Endeavor
Endeavor hero
Endeavor hate
Endeavor scary
Endeavor incident resolution
Endeavor cool

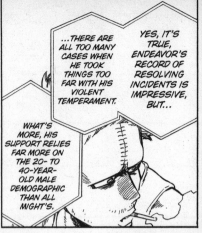

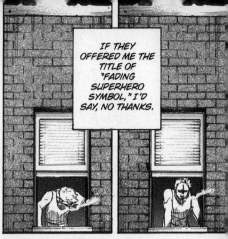

IF THEY OFFERED ME THE TITLE OF "FADING SUPERHERO SYMBOL," I'D SAY, NO THANKS.
YES, IT'S TRUE, ENDEAVOR'S RECORD OF RESOLVING INCIDENTS IS IMPRESSIVE, BUT...
...THERE ARE ALL TOO MANY CASES WHEN HE TOOK THINGS TOO FAR WITH HIS VIOLENT TEMPERAMENT.
WHAT'S MORE, HIS SUPPORT RELIES FAR MORE ON THE 20- TO 40-YEAR-OLD MALE DEMOGRAPHIC THAN ALL MIGHT'S.
AS FOR US, WE SHOULDN'T JUST PASSIVELY PROTECT THE STATUS QUO.
ISN'T IT OUR DUTY TO BRING BACK A CULTURE OF EXCITEMENT AROUND HEROES?
?!
RATHER THAN HARPING ON THE NEGATIVES, LET'S THINK ABOUT THE POSITIVES THAT-
KZZT
TIME TO GO...
THE FADING SYMBOL THING ISN'T ABOUT POWER, THOUGH. IT'S ABOUT PEOPLE'S HEARTS AND MINDS. MIYAGI KNOWS THAT.
IT'S ABOUT POWER.
SHUT UP...! JUST SHUT UP ALREADY...!
"I AM HERE."
INSPIRATIONAL WORDS FOR THOSE ON THE RIGHT SIDE OF THE LAW. FOR OTHERS, THOUGH, THAT PHRASE WAS LIKE A CURSE.

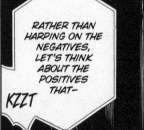

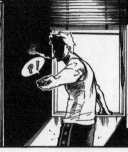

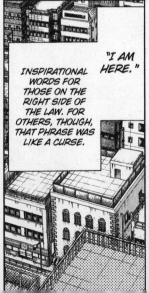

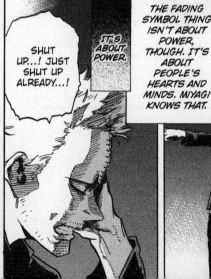

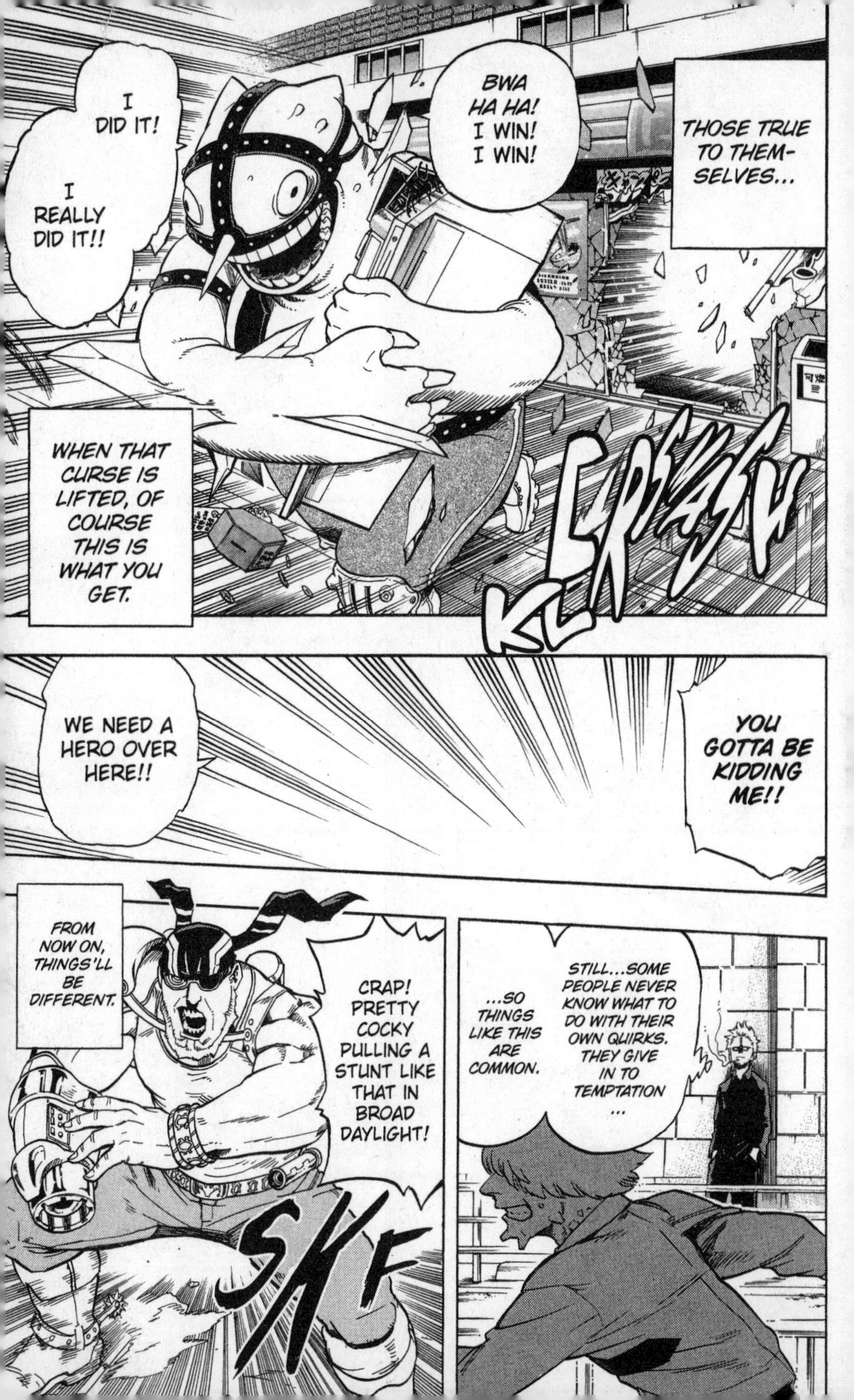
THOSE TRUE TO THEMSELVES...
BWA HA HA! I WIN! I WIN!
I DID IT!
I REALLY DID IT!!
WHEN THAT CURSE IS LIFTED, OF COURSE THIS IS WHAT YOU GET.
YOU GOTTA BE KIDDING ME!!
WE NEED A HERO OVER HERE!!
STILL...SOME PEOPLE NEVER KNOW WHAT TO DO WITH THEIR OWN QUIRKS. THEY GIVE IN TO TEMPTATION ...
...SO THINGS LIKE THIS ARE COMMON.
FROM NOW ON, THINGS'LL BE DIFFERENT.
CRAP! PRETTY COCKY PULLING A STUNT LIKE THAT IN BROAD DAYLIGHT!

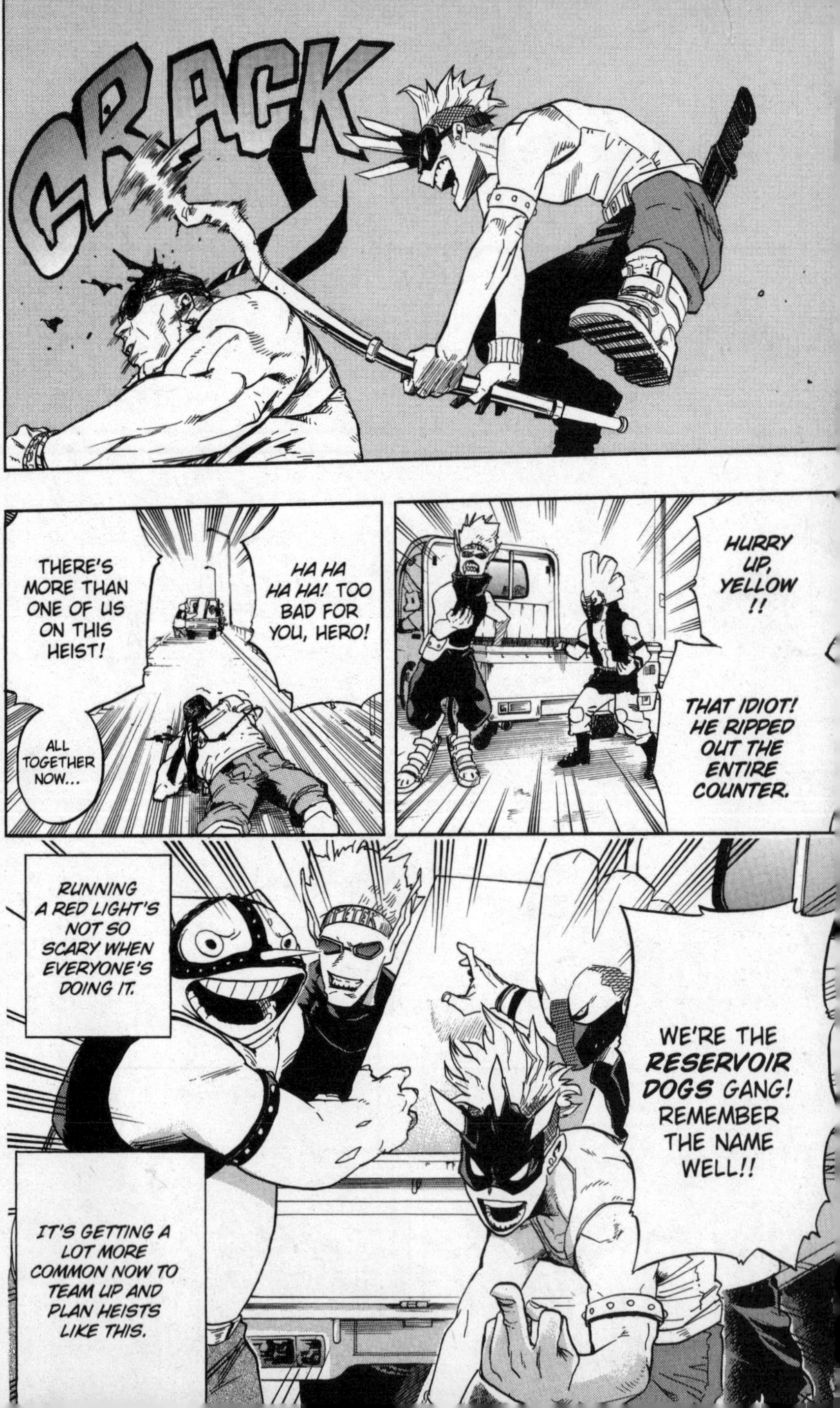
CRACK
HURRY UP, YELLOW!!
THAT IDIOT! HE RIPPED OUT THE ENTIRE COUNTER.
HA HA HA HA! TOO BAD FOR YOU, HERO!
THERE'S MORE THAN ONE OF US ON THIS HEIST!
ALL TOGETHER NOW...
WE'RE THE RESERVOIR DOGS GANG! REMEMBER THE NAME WELL!!
RUNNING A RED LIGHT'S NOT SO SCARY WHEN EVERYONE'S DOING IT.
IT'S GETTING A LOT MORE COMMON NOW TO TEAM UP AND PLAN HEISTS LIKE THIS.

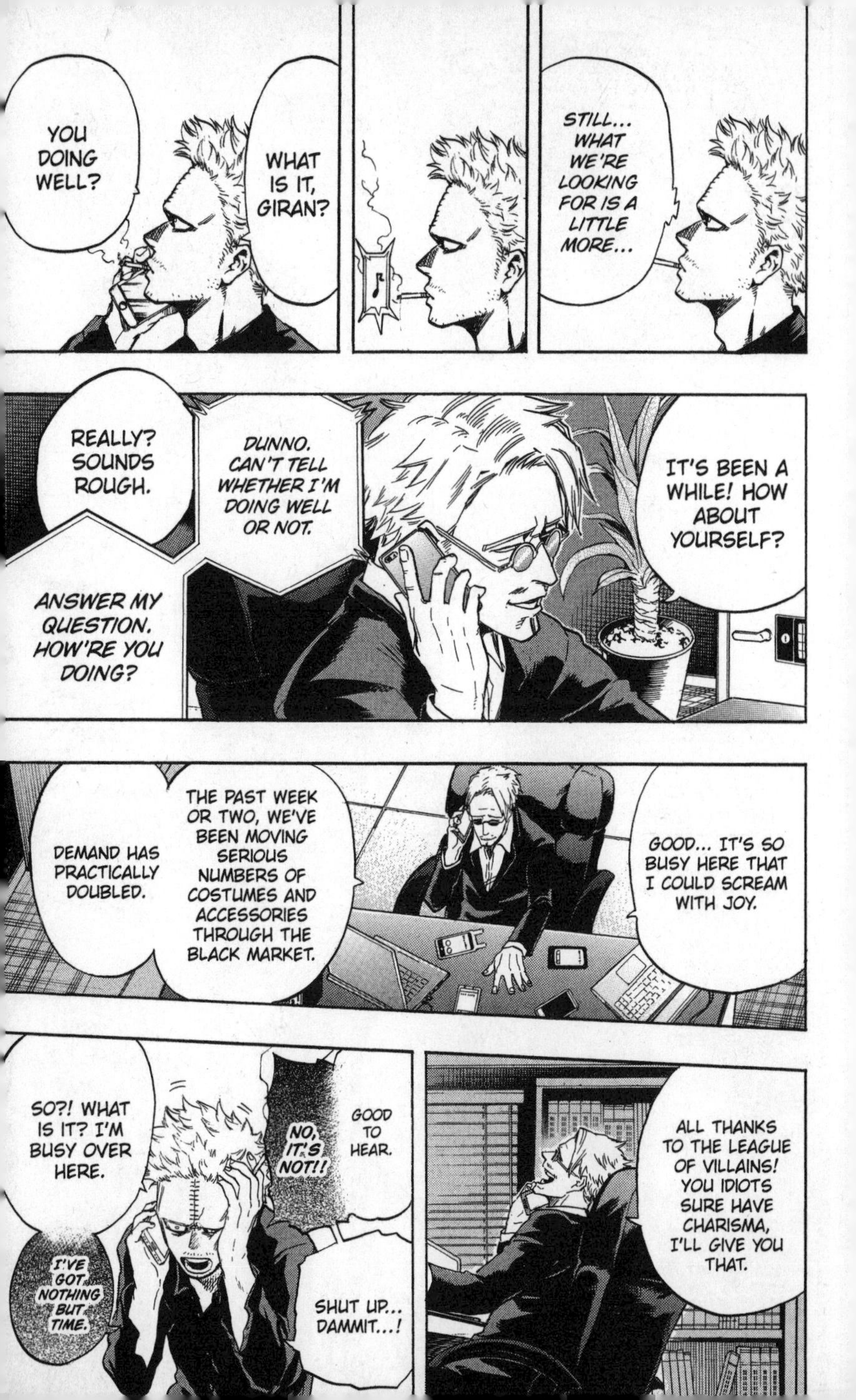
STILL... WHAT WE'RE LOOKING FOR IS A LITTLE MORE...
WHAT IS IT, GIRAN?
YOU DOING WELL?
IT'S BEEN A WHILE! HOW ABOUT YOURSELF?
DUNNO. CAN'T TELL WHETHER I'M DOING WELL OR NOT.
REALLY? SOUNDS ROUGH.
ANSWER MY QUESTION. HOW'RE YOU DOING?
GOOD... IT'S SO BUSY HERE THAT I COULD SCREAM WITH JOY.
THE PAST WEEK OR TWO, WE'VE BEEN MOVING SERIOUS NUMBERS OF COSTUMES AND ACCESSORIES THROUGH THE BLACK MARKET.
DEMAND HAS PRACTICALLY DOUBLED.
ALL THANKS TO THE LEAGUE OF VILLAINS! YOU IDIOTS SURE HAVE CHARISMA, I'LL GIVE YOU THAT.
GOOD TO HEAR.
NO, IT'S NOT!!
SO?! WHAT IS IT? I'M BUSY OVER HERE.
I'VE GOT NOTHING BUT TIME.
SHUT UP... DAMMIT...!

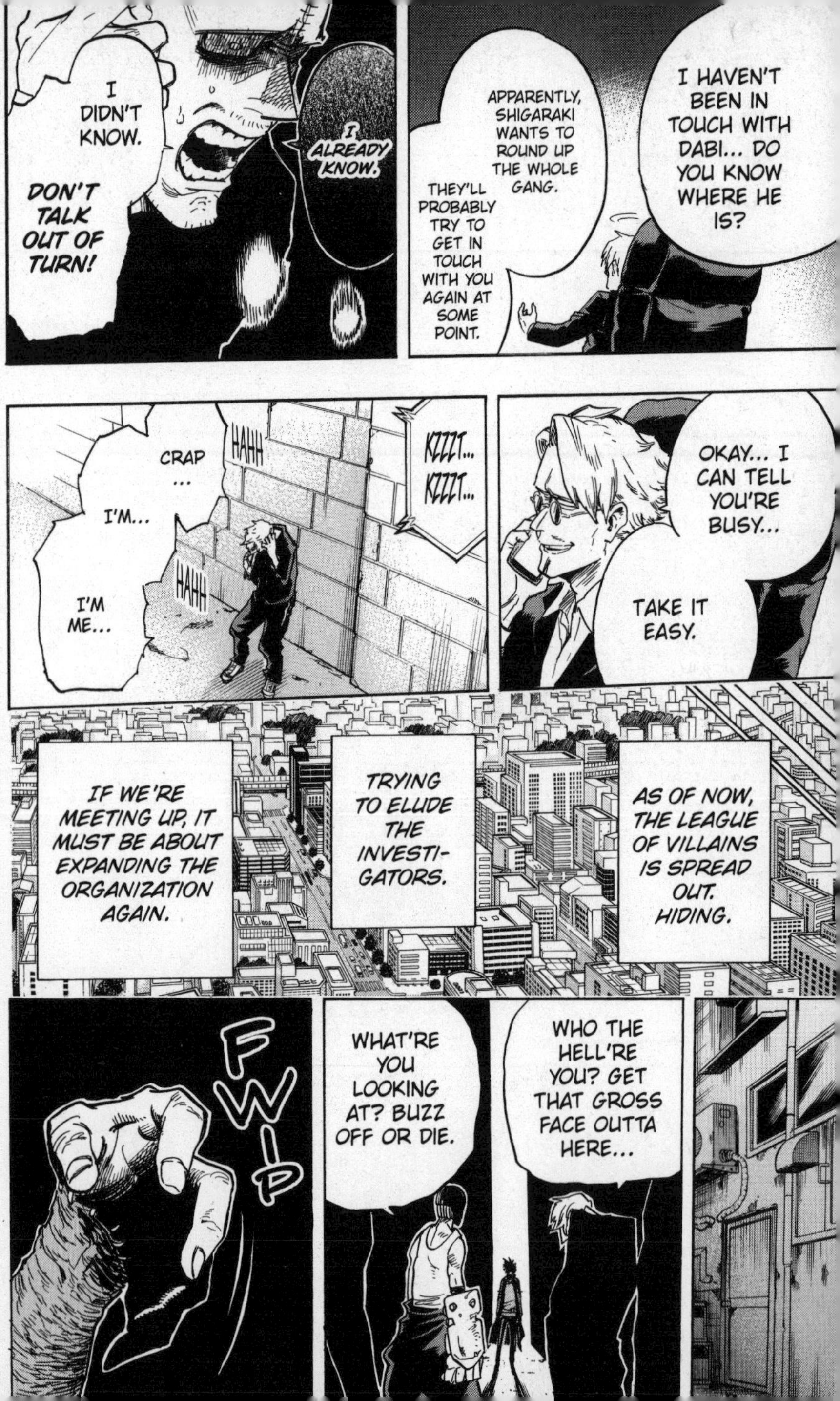
I HAVEN'T BEEN IN TOUCH WITH DABI... DO YOU KNOW WHERE HE IS?
APPARENTLY, SHIGARAKI WANTS TO ROUND UP THE WHOLE GANG.
THEY'LL PROBABLY TRY TO GET IN TOUCH WITH YOU AGAIN AT SOME POINT.
I ALREADY KNOW.
I DIDN'T KNOW.
DON'T TALK OUT OF TURN!
OKAY... I CAN TELL YOU'RE BUSY...
TAKE IT EASY.
KZZZT... KZZZT...
HAHH
CRAP...
I'M...
HAHH
I'M ME...
AS OF NOW, THE LEAGUE OF VILLAINS IS SPREAD OUT. HIDING.
TRYING TO ELUDE THE INVESTIGATORS.
IF WE'RE MEETING UP, IT MUST BE ABOUT EXPANDING THE ORGANIZATION AGAIN.
WHO THE HELL'RE YOU? GET THAT GROSS FACE OUTTA HERE...
WHAT'RE YOU LOOKING AT? BUZZ OFF OR DIE.
FWIP

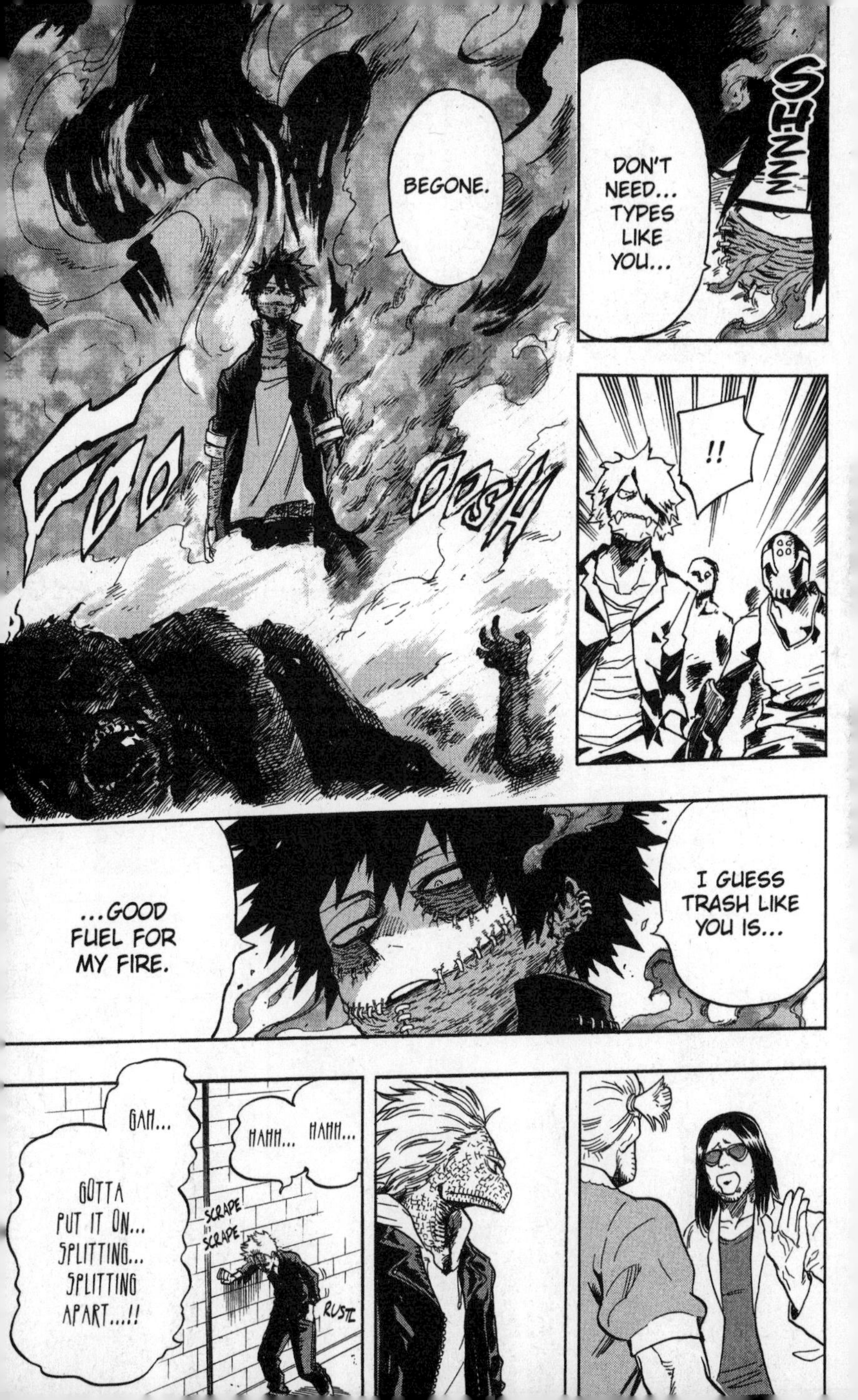
SHUNNN
DON'T NEED... TYPES LIKE YOU...
!!
BEGONE.
FOOO
OOSH
I GUESS TRASH LIKE YOU IS...
...GOOD FUEL FOR MY FIRE.
HAHH... HAHH...
GAH...
GOTTA PUT IT ON... SPLITTING... SPLITTING APART...!!
SCRAPE SCRAPE
RUSTLE

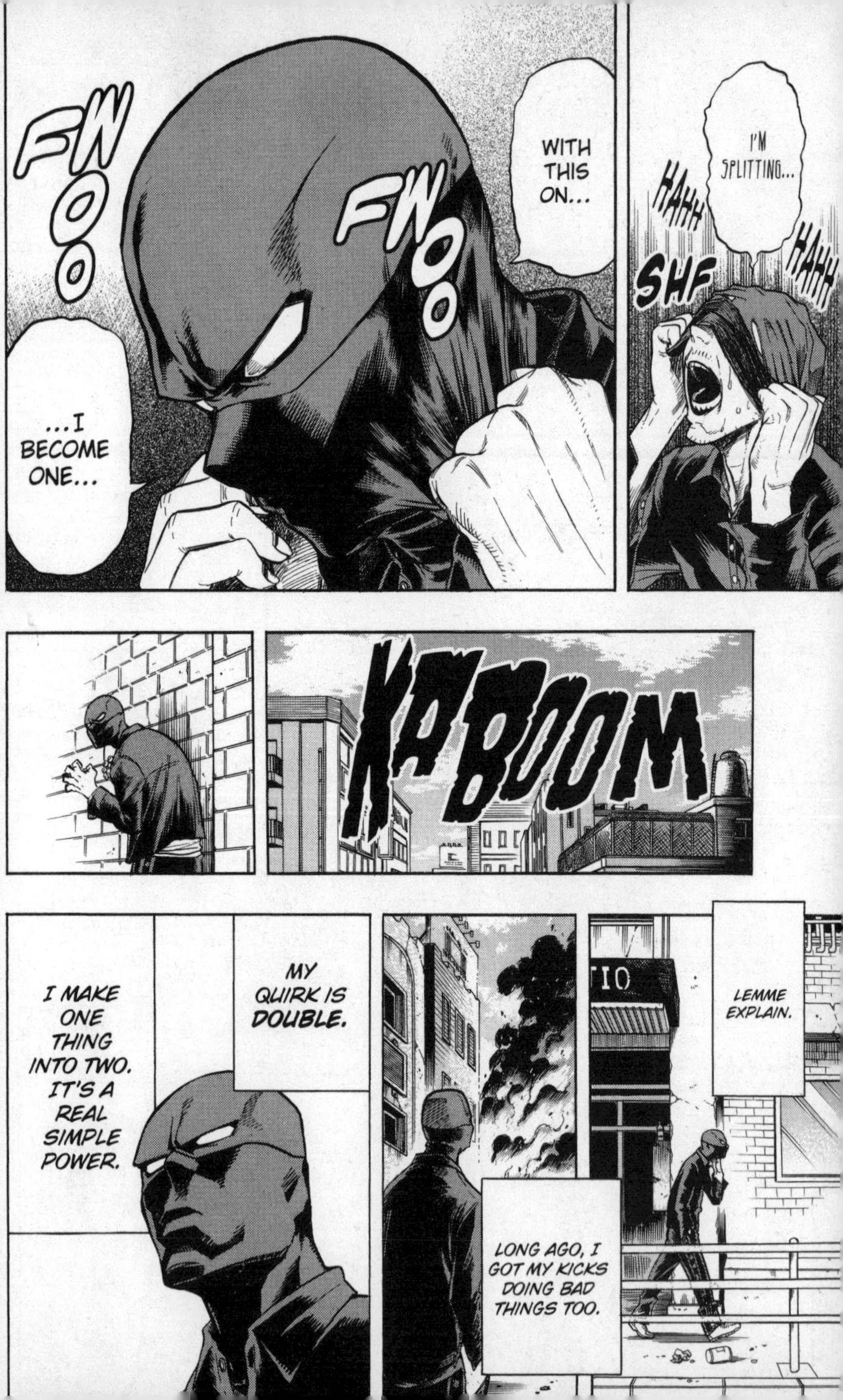
I'M SPLITTING...
HAHH
SHF
HAHH
WITH THIS ON...
FWOOO
...I BECOME ONE...
FWOOO
KABOOM
LEMME EXPLAIN.
LONG AGO, I GOT MY KICKS DOING BAD THINGS TOO.
MY QUIRK IS DOUBLE.
I MAKE ONE THING INTO TWO. IT'S A REAL SIMPLE POWER.

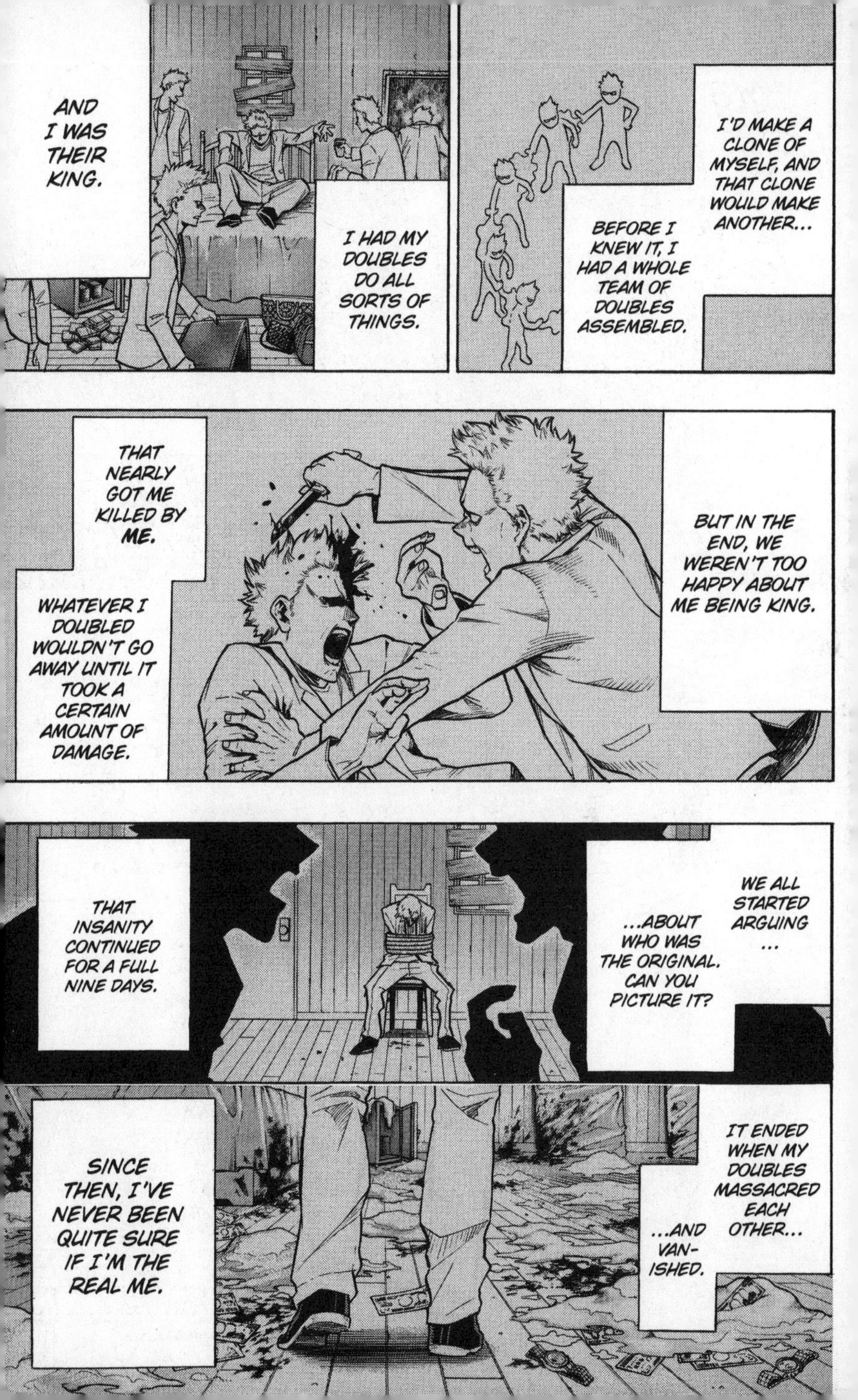
I'D MAKE A CLONE OF MYSELF, AND THAT CLONE WOULD MAKE ANOTHER...
BEFORE I KNEW IT, I HAD A WHOLE TEAM OF DOUBLES ASSEMBLED.
AND I WAS THEIR KING.
I HAD MY DOUBLES DO ALL SORTS OF THINGS.
BUT IN THE END, WE WEREN'T TOO HAPPY ABOUT ME BEING KING.
THAT NEARLY GOT ME KILLED BY ME.
WHATEVER I DOUBLED WOULDN'T GO AWAY UNTIL IT TOOK A CERTAIN AMOUNT OF DAMAGE.
WE ALL STARTED ARGUING...
...ABOUT WHO WAS THE ORIGINAL. CAN YOU PICTURE IT?
THAT INSANITY CONTINUED FOR A FULL NINE DAYS.
IT ENDED WHEN MY DOUBLES MASSACRED EACH OTHER...
...AND VAN-ISHED.
SINCE THEN, I'VE NEVER BEEN QUITE SURE IF I'M THE REAL ME.

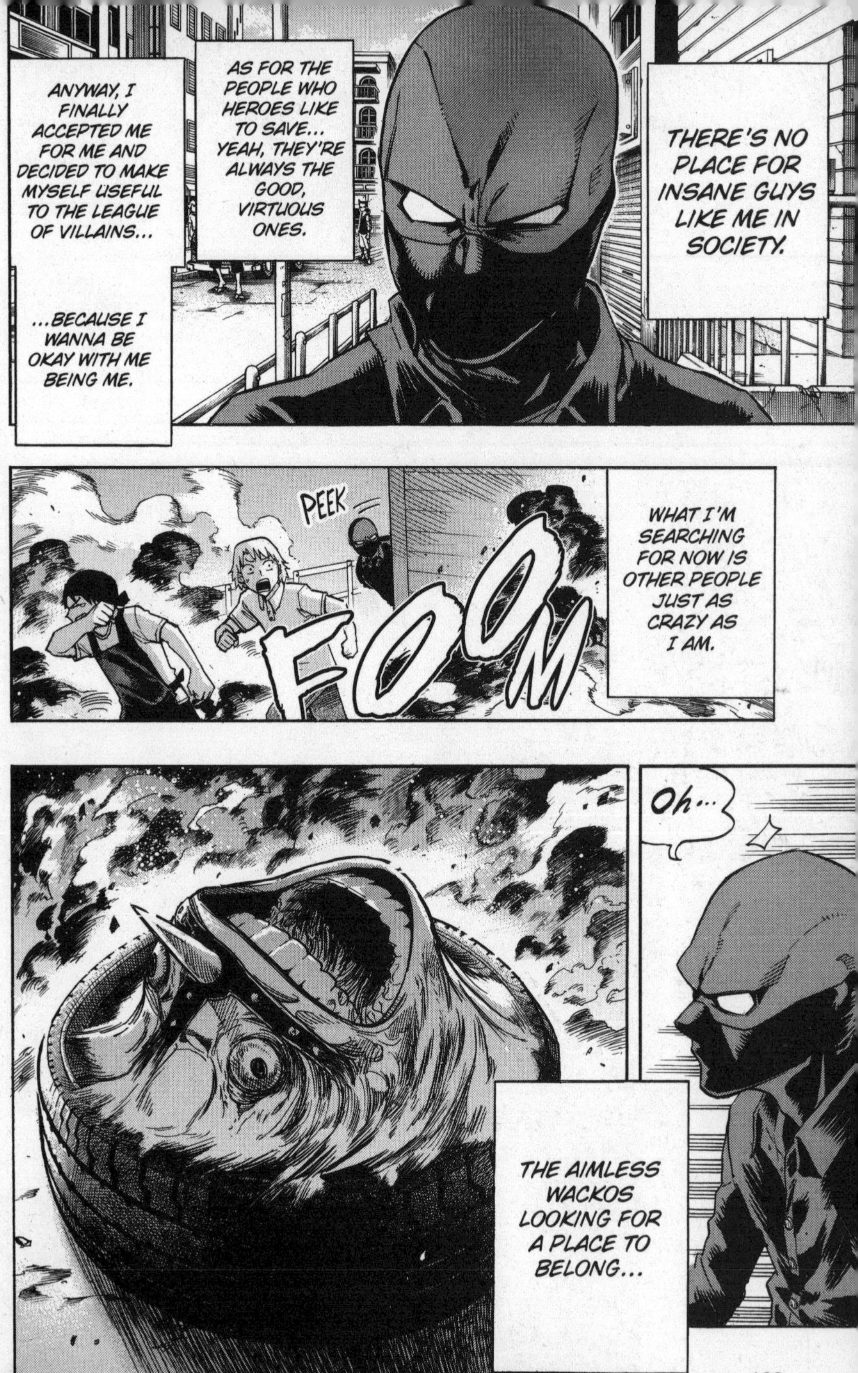
THERE'S NO PLACE FOR INSANE GUYS LIKE ME IN SOCIETY.
AS FOR THE PEOPLE WHO HEROES LIKE TO SAVE... YEAH, THEY'RE ALWAYS THE GOOD, VIRTUOUS ONES.
ANYWAY, I FINALLY ACCEPTED ME FOR ME AND DECIDED TO MAKE MYSELF USEFUL TO THE LEAGUE OF VILLAINS...
...BECAUSE I WANNA BE OKAY WITH ME BEING ME.
WHAT I'M SEARCHING FOR NOW IS OTHER PEOPLE JUST AS CRAZY AS I AM.
PEEK
FOOM
Oh...
THE AIMLESS WACKOS LOOKING FOR A PLACE TO BELONG...

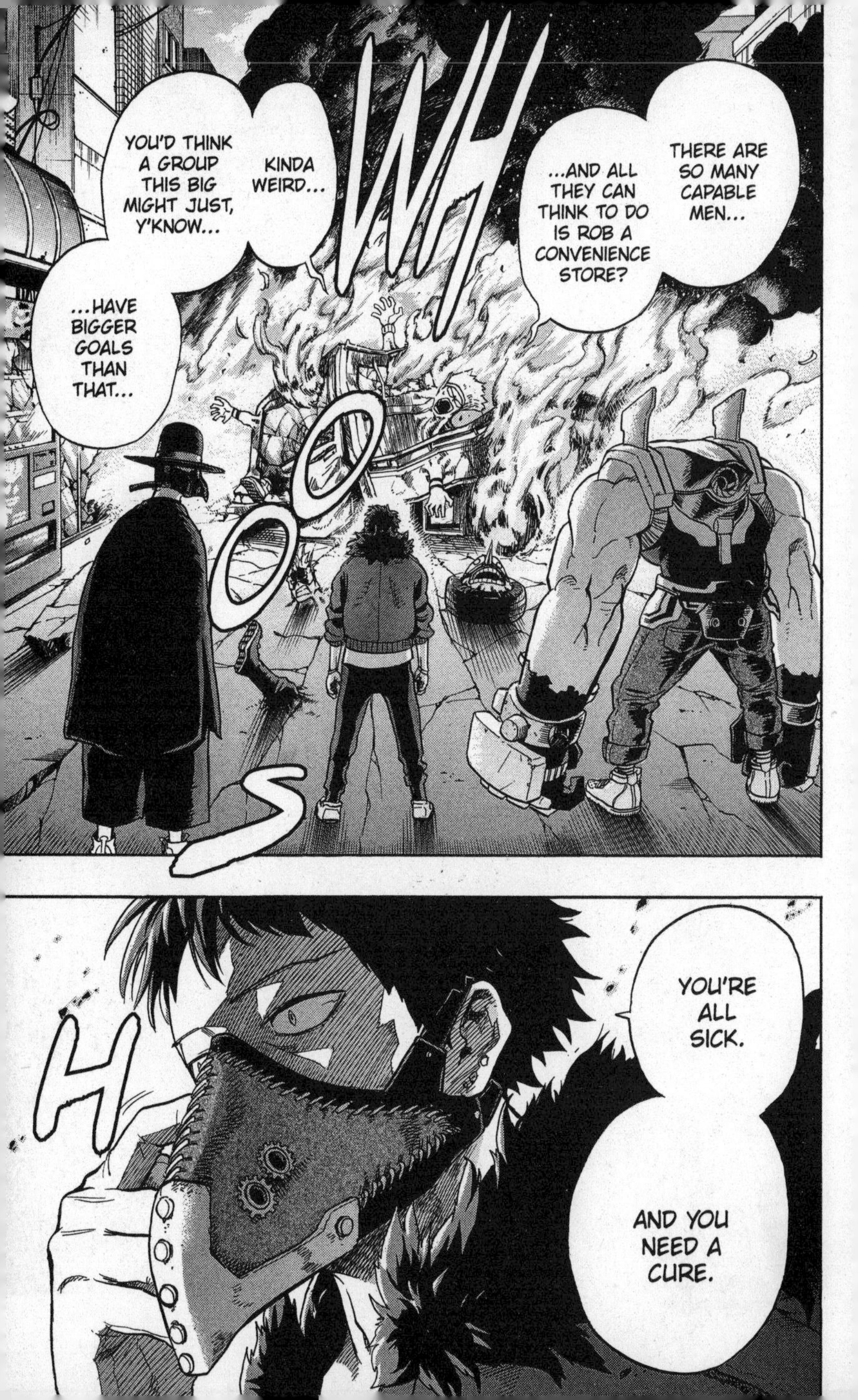

THERE ARE SO MANY CAPABLE MEN...
...AND ALL THEY CAN THINK TO DO IS ROB A CONVENIENCE STORE?
KINDA WEIRD...
YOU'D THINK A GROUP THIS BIG MIGHT JUST, Y'KNOW...
...HAVE BIGGER GOALS THAN THAT...
WHOOSH
YOU'RE ALL SICK.
AND YOU NEED A CURE.

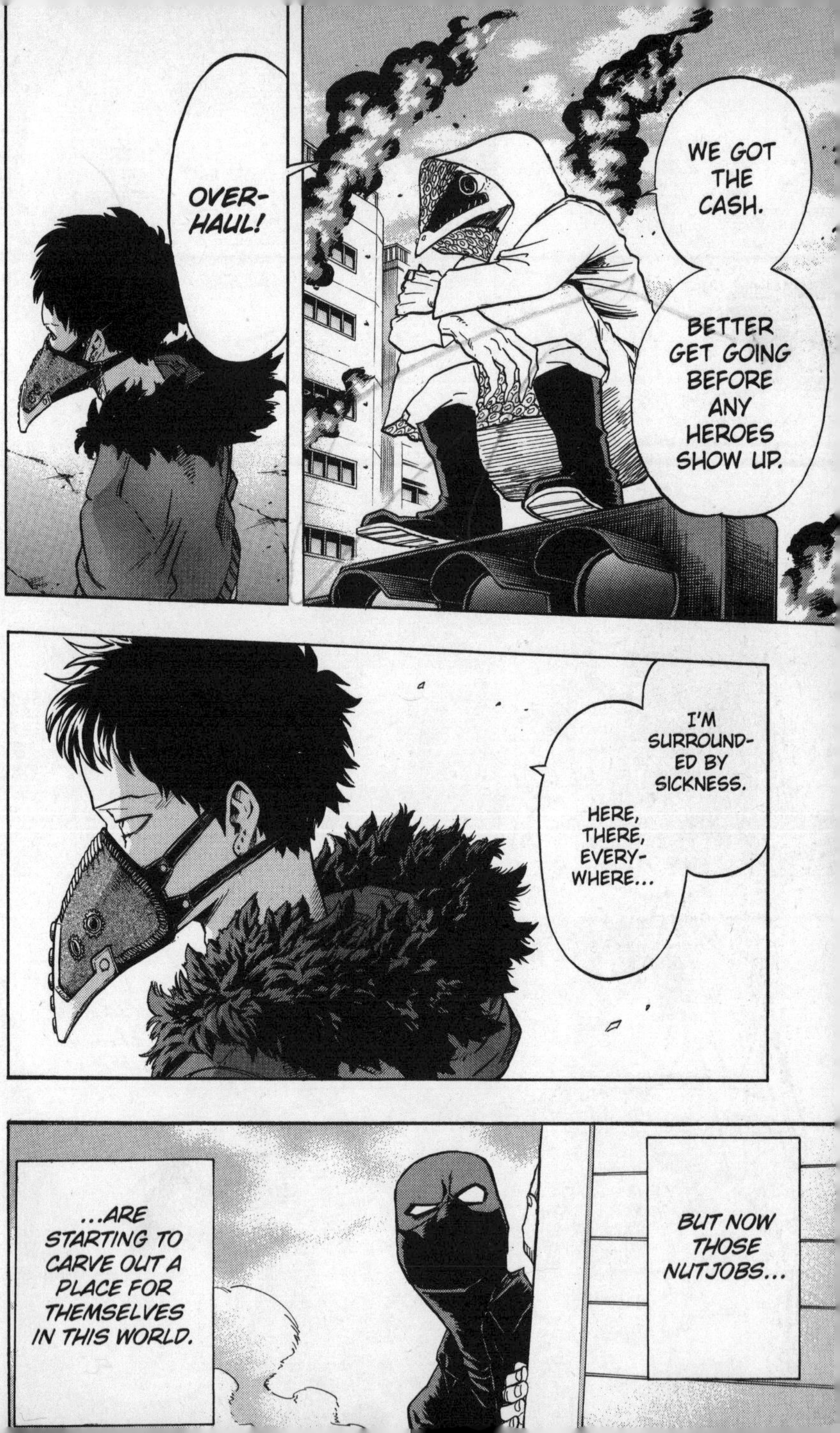
WE GOT THE CASH.
BETTER GET GOING BEFORE ANY HEROES SHOW UP.
OVER-HAUL!
I'M SURROUND-ED BY SICKNESS.
HERE, THERE, EVERY-WHERE...
BUT NOW THOSE NUTJOBS...
...ARE STARTING TO CARVE OUT A PLACE FOR THEMSELVES IN THIS WORLD.

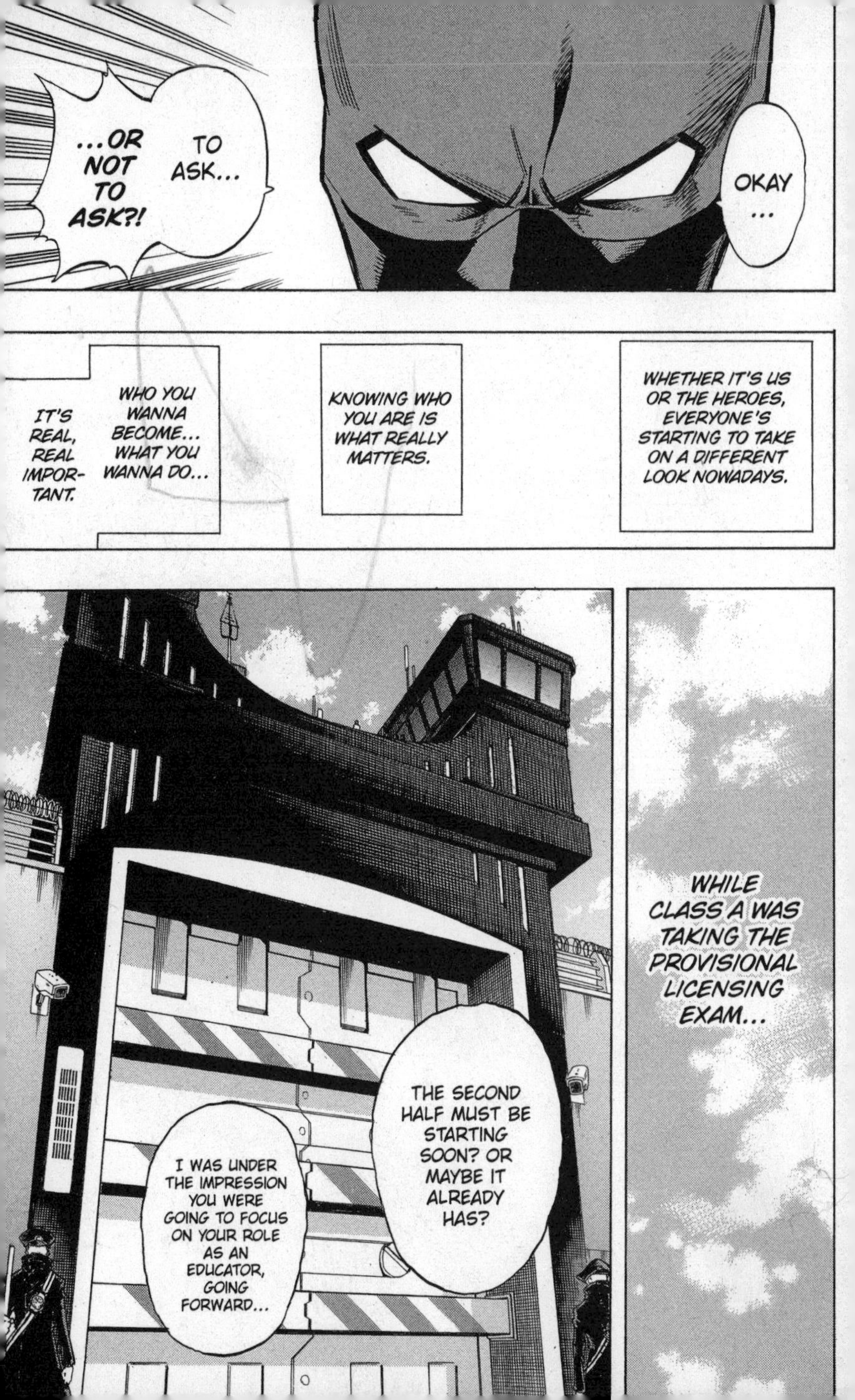
OKAY...
TO ASK... ...OR NOT TO ASK?!
WHETHER IT'S US OR THE HEROES, EVERYONE'S STARTING TO TAKE ON A DIFFERENT LOOK NOWADAYS.
KNOWING WHO YOU ARE IS WHAT REALLY MATTERS.
WHO YOU WANNA BECOME... WHAT YOU WANNA DO...
IT'S REAL, REAL IMPOR-TANT.
WHILE CLASS A WAS TAKING THE PROVISIONAL LICENSING EXAM...
THE SECOND HALF MUST BE STARTING SOON? OR MAYBE IT ALREADY HAS?
I WAS UNDER THE IMPRESSION YOU WERE GOING TO FOCUS ON YOUR ROLE AS AN EDUCATOR, GOING FORWARD...

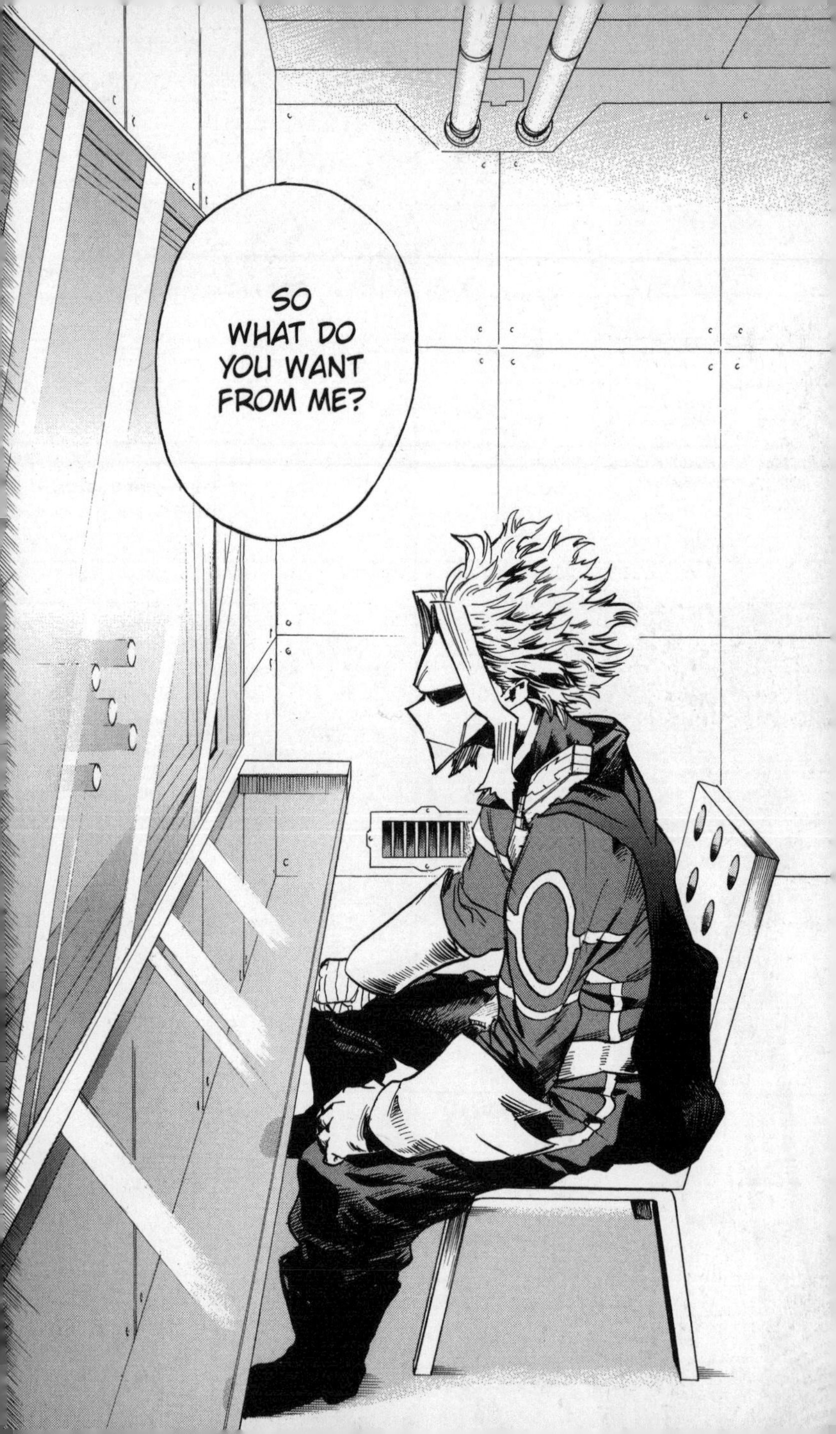
SO WHAT DO YOU WANT FROM ME?

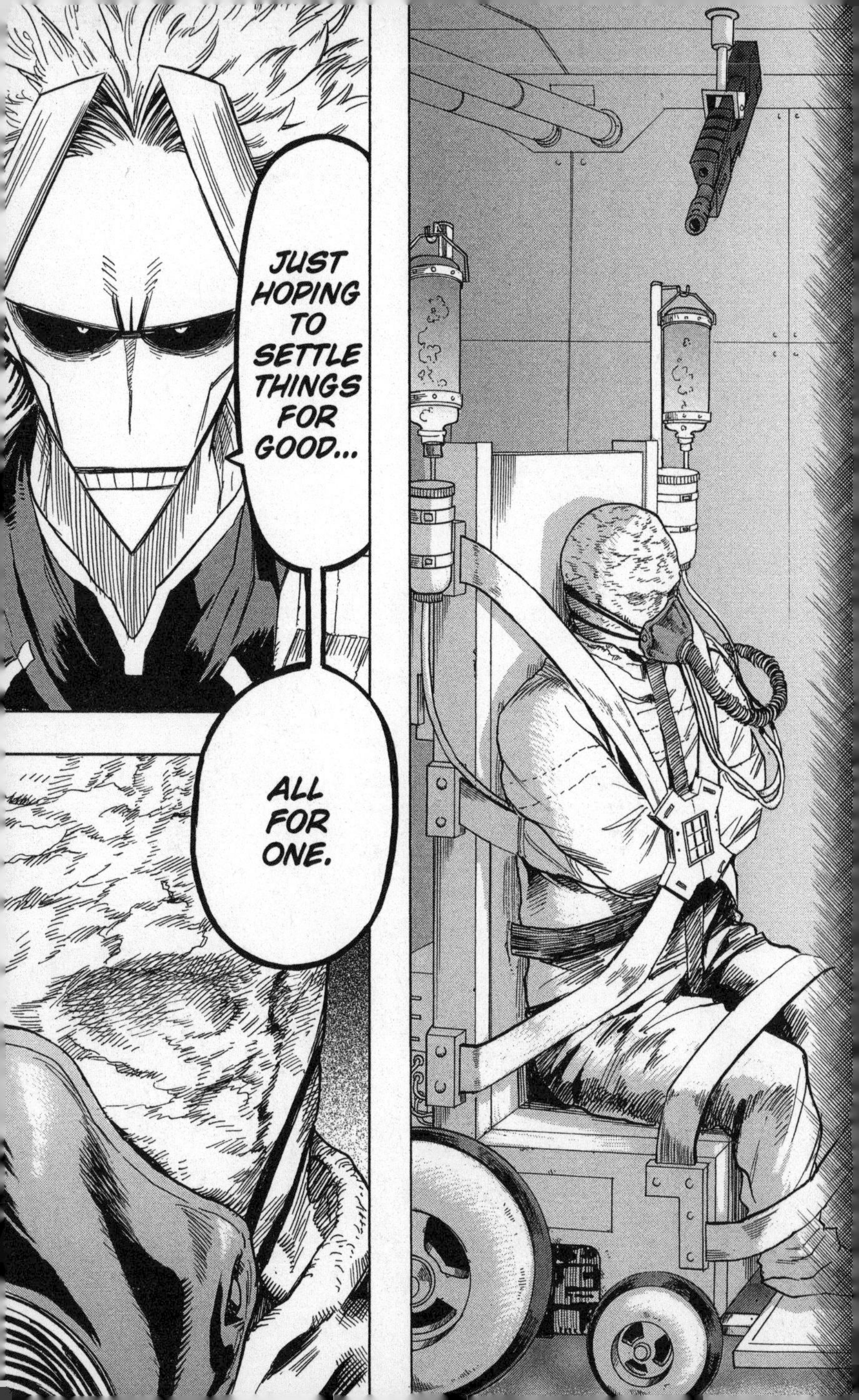
JUST HOPING TO SETTLE THINGS FOR GOOD...
ALL FOR ONE.

THE SPIN-OFFS

Amazingly enough, *My Hero Academia* now has two separate spin-off manga series. The first is a four-panel gag-based comedy called *My Hero Academia Smash!!* It's a lighthearted, occasionally serious take on the main story, retooled in a hilarious way! The series also features a surreal look at aspects of everyday life that we don't get a glimpse at otherwise!

The other is *My Hero Academia: Vigilantes*. That one is a spin-off that takes a look at Deku's society from another angle altogether. It takes place in the same *My Hero* universe and sometimes features pro heroes from the core story, starting with Eraser Head! *Vigilantes* provides an even closer close-up of the *My Hero* world! It's incredible!

Along with this page—which seems to have turned into an advertisement—I also managed to get the authors of these spin-offs to contribute some content for this volume! On page 152, you'll find an awesome illustration from the *Vigilantes* artist, Betten Court Sensei, along with some groovy comments from the writer, Hideyuki Furuhashi Sensei.

Then, on page 168, we have a pair of hilarious four-panel strips from *Smash!!* author Hirofumi Neda Sensei.

I'm so grateful! Not to mention excited. All my thanks to these fabulous authors!

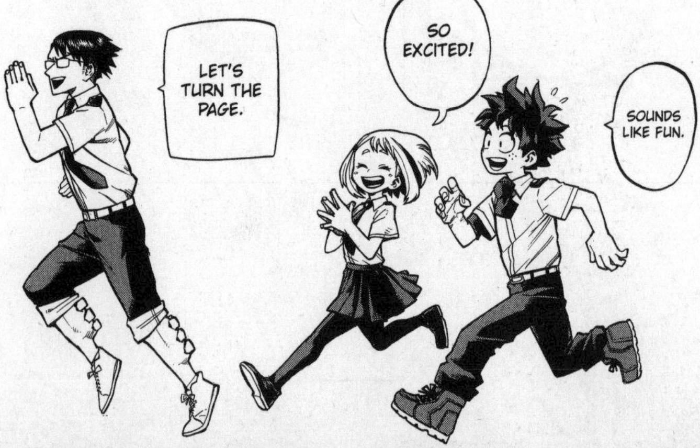
SOUNDS LIKE FUN.
SO EXCITED!
LET'S TURN THE PAGE.

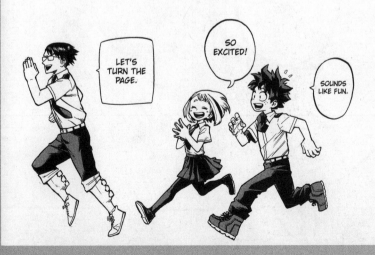

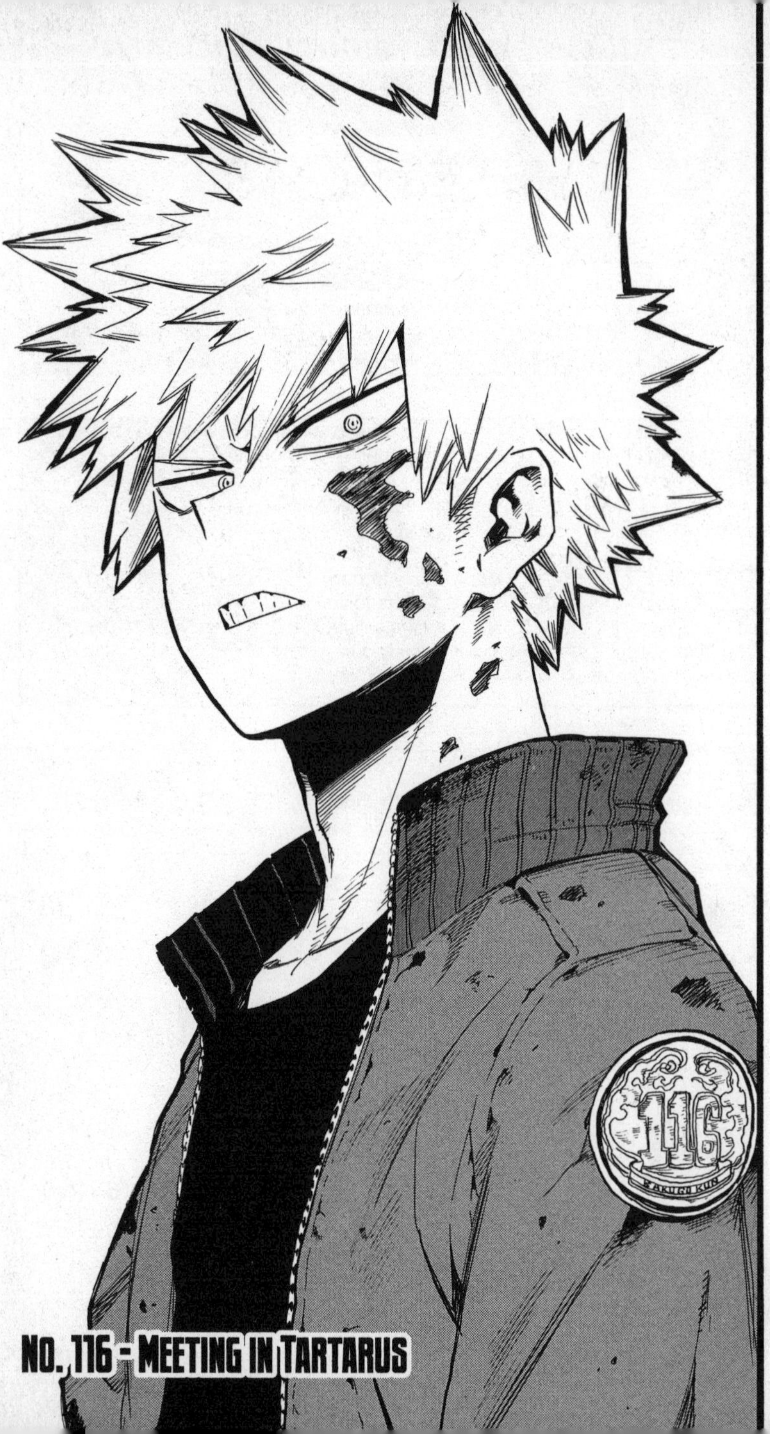
116

No. 116 - Meeting in Tartarus

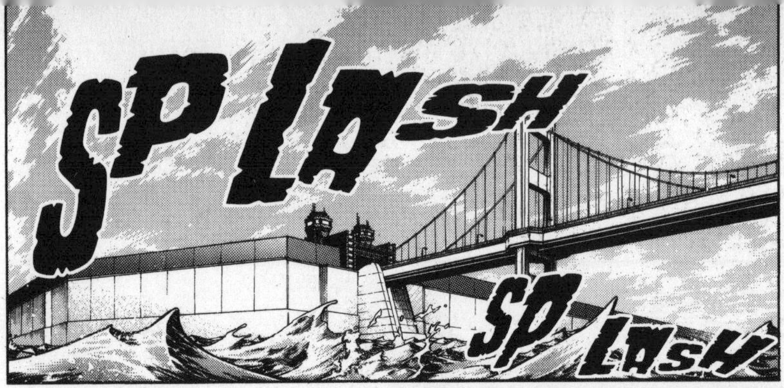
SPLASH
SPLASH
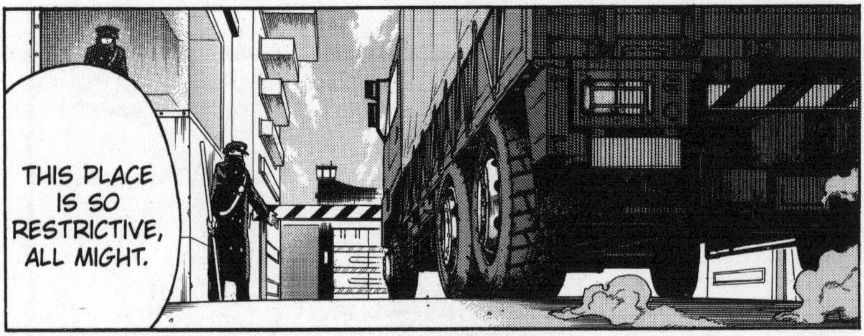
THIS PLACE IS SO RESTRICTIVE, ALL MIGHT.
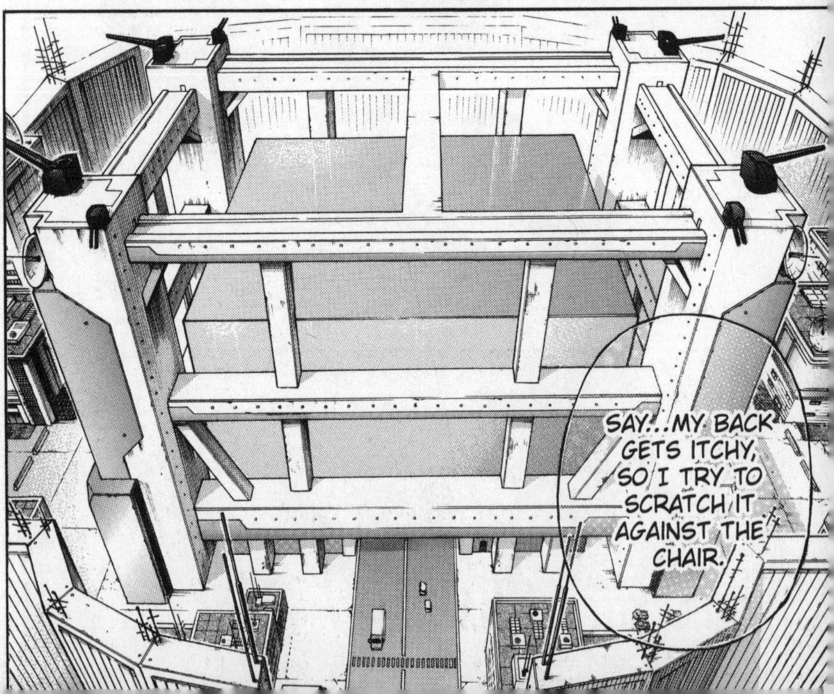
SAY... MY BACK GETS ITCHY, SO I TRY TO SCRATCH IT AGAINST THE CHAIR.

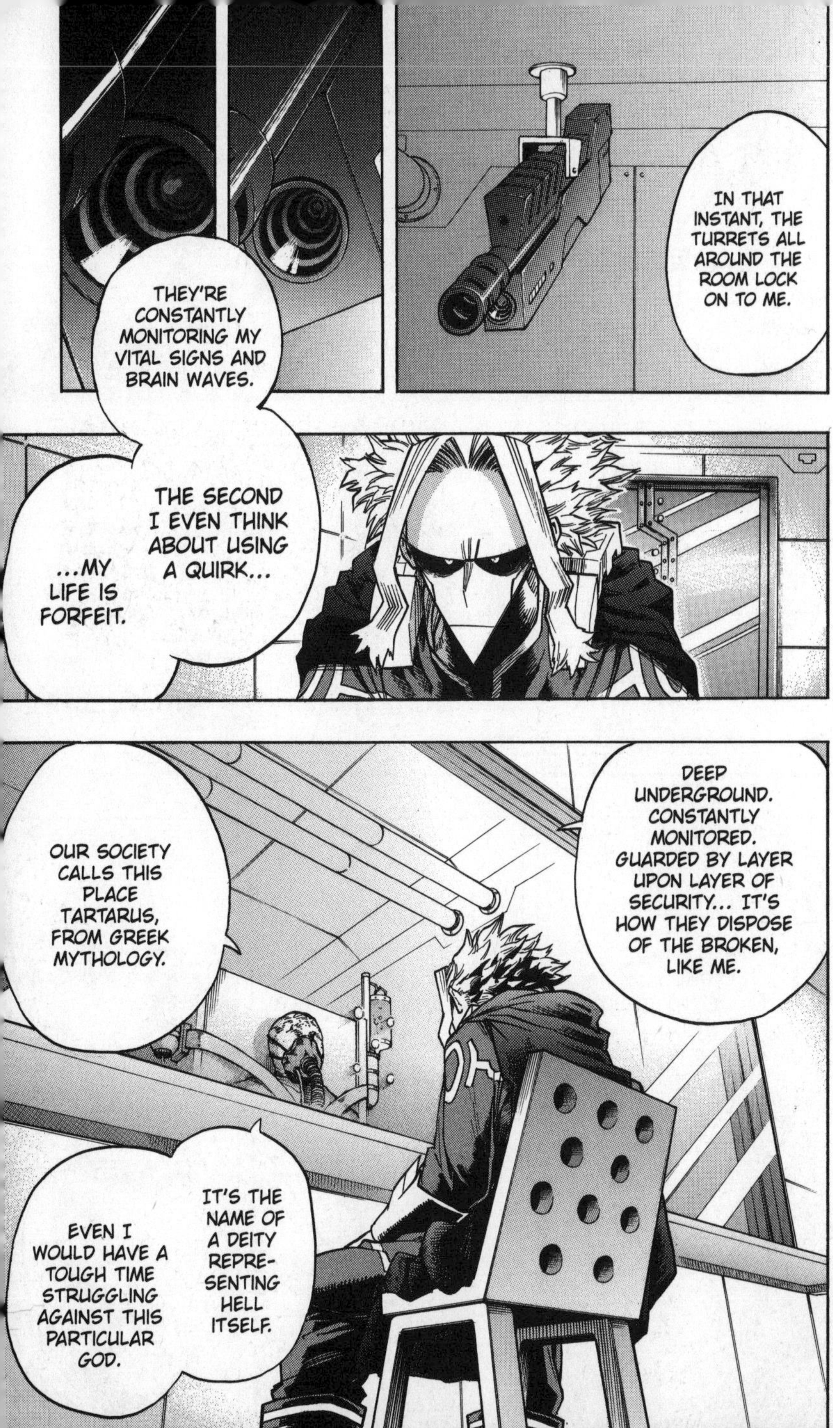
IN THAT INSTANT, THE TURRETS ALL AROUND THE ROOM LOCK ON TO ME.
THEY'RE CONSTANTLY MONITORING MY VITAL SIGNS AND BRAIN WAVES.
THE SECOND I EVEN THINK ABOUT USING A QUIRK...
...MY LIFE IS FORFEIT.
DEEP UNDERGROUND. CONSTANTLY MONITORED. GUARDED BY LAYER UPON LAYER OF SECURITY... IT'S HOW THEY DISPOSE OF THE BROKEN, LIKE ME.
OUR SOCIETY CALLS THIS PLACE TARTARUS, FROM GREEK MYTHOLOGY.
IT'S THE NAME OF A DEITY REPRE-SENTING HELL ITSELF.
EVEN I WOULD HAVE A TOUGH TIME STRUGGLING AGAINST THIS PARTICULAR GOD.

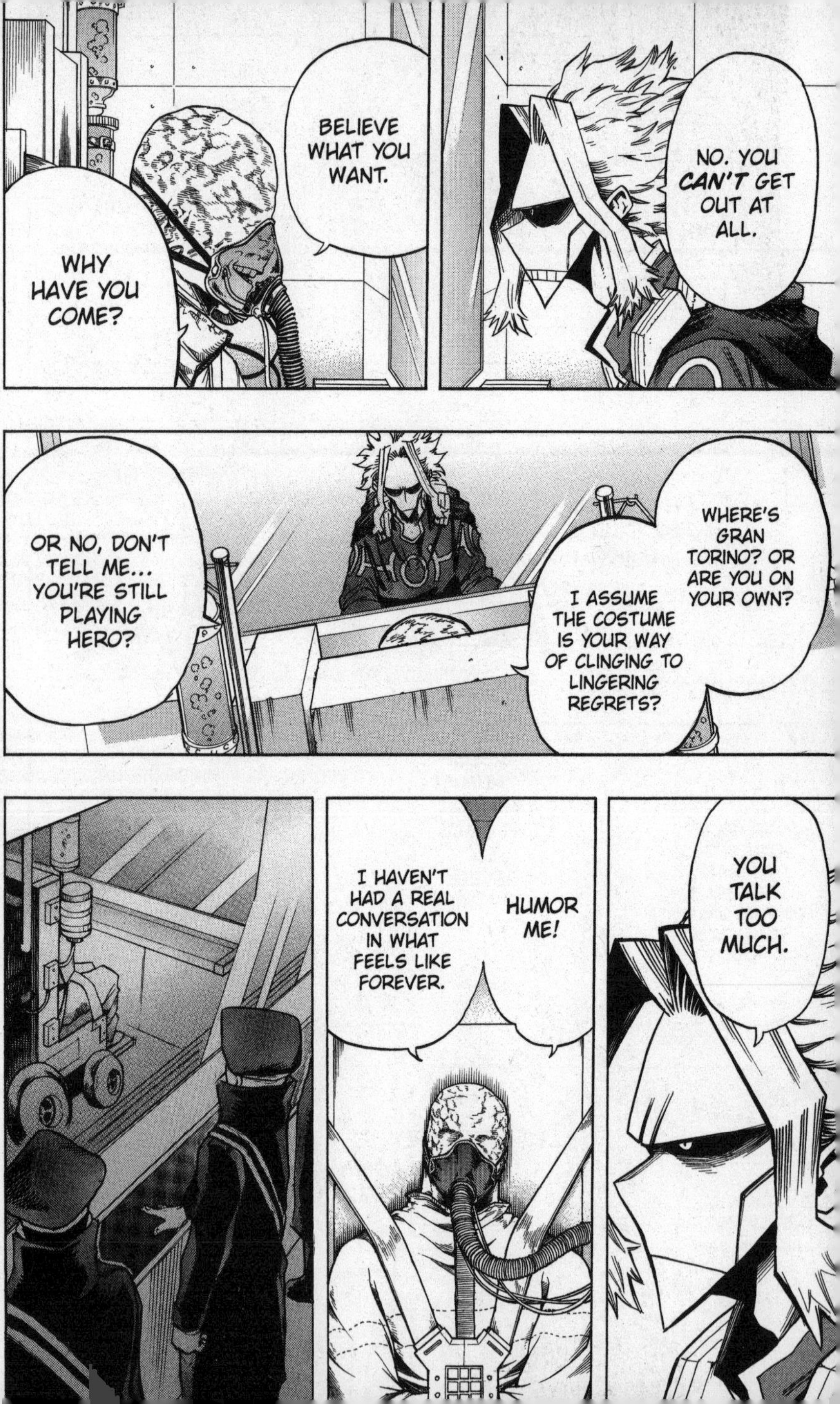
NO. YOU *CAN'T* GET OUT AT ALL.
BELIEVE WHAT YOU WANT.
WHY HAVE YOU COME?
WHERE'S GRAN TORINO? OR ARE YOU ON YOUR OWN?
I ASSUME THE COSTUME IS YOUR WAY OF CLINGING TO LINGERING REGRETS?
OR NO, DON'T TELL ME... YOU'RE STILL PLAYING HERO?
YOU TALK TOO MUCH.
HUMOR ME!
I HAVEN'T HAD A REAL CONVERSATION IN WHAT FEELS LIKE FOREVER.

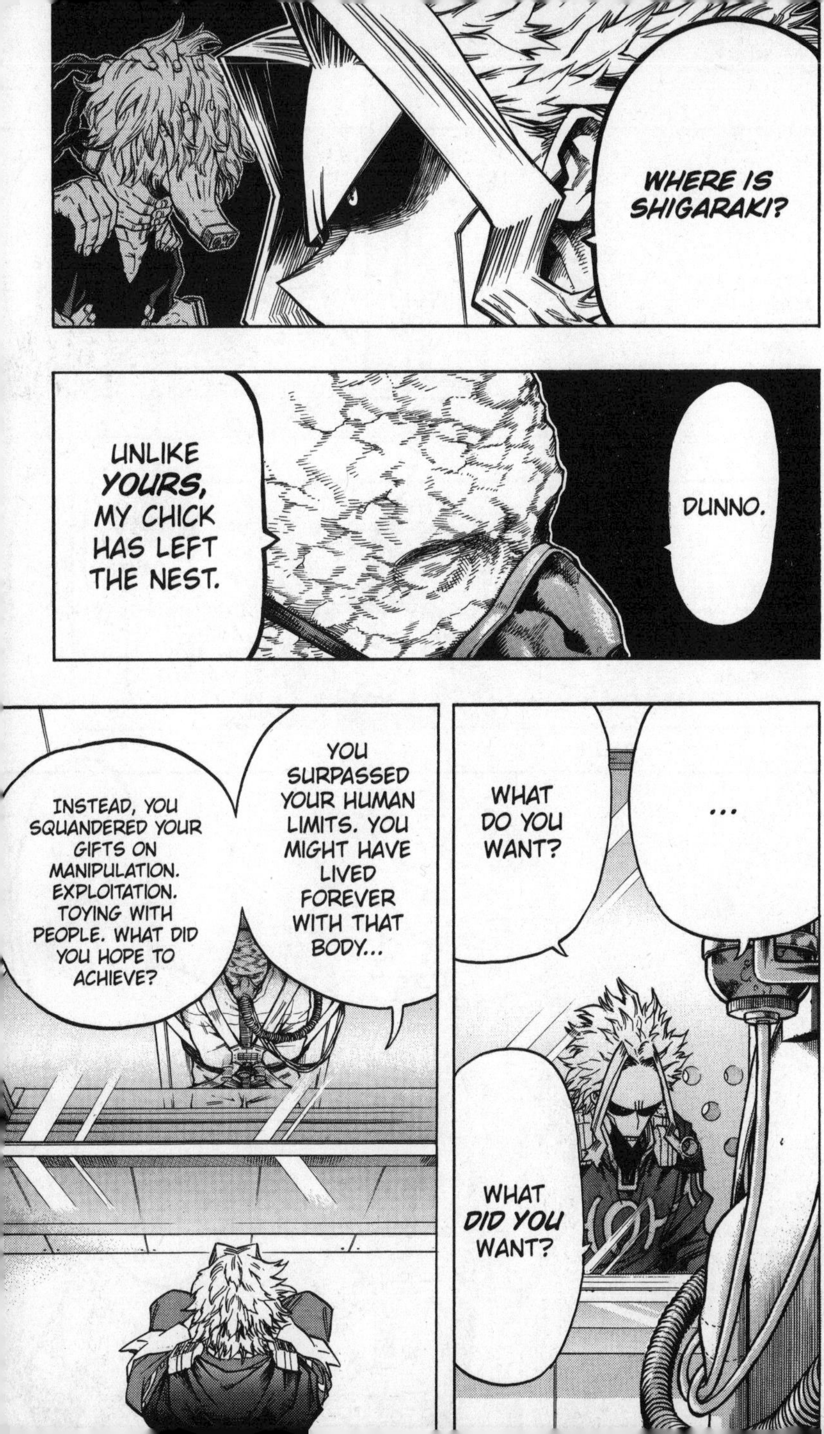
WHERE IS SHIGARAKI?
DUNNO.
UNLIKE *YOURS,* MY CHICK HAS LEFT THE NEST.
...
WHAT DO YOU WANT?
WHAT *DID YOU* WANT?
YOU SURPASSED YOUR HUMAN LIMITS. YOU MIGHT HAVE LIVED FOREVER WITH THAT BODY...
INSTEAD, YOU SQUANDERED YOUR GIFTS ON MANIPULATION. EXPLOITATION. TOYING WITH PEOPLE. WHAT DID YOU HOPE TO ACHIEVE?

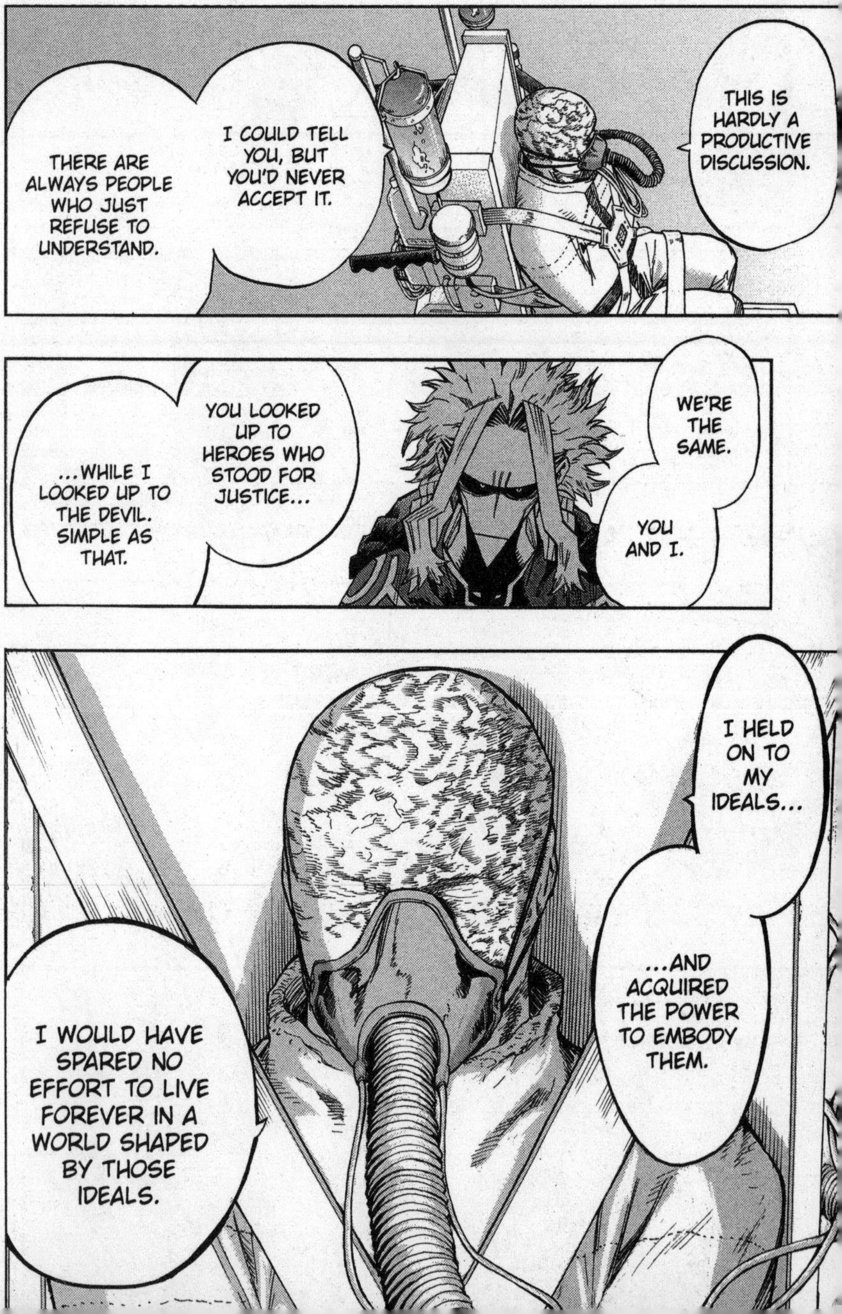
THIS IS HARDLY A PRODUCTIVE DISCUSSION.
I COULD TELL YOU, BUT YOU'D NEVER ACCEPT IT.
THERE ARE ALWAYS PEOPLE WHO JUST REFUSE TO UNDERSTAND.
WE'RE THE SAME.
YOU AND I.
YOU LOOKED UP TO HEROES WHO STOOD FOR JUSTICE...
...WHILE I LOOKED UP TO THE DEVIL. SIMPLE AS THAT.
I HELD ON TO MY IDEALS...
...AND ACQUIRED THE POWER TO EMBODY THEM.
I WOULD HAVE SPARED NO EFFORT TO LIVE FOREVER IN A WORLD SHAPED BY THOSE IDEALS.

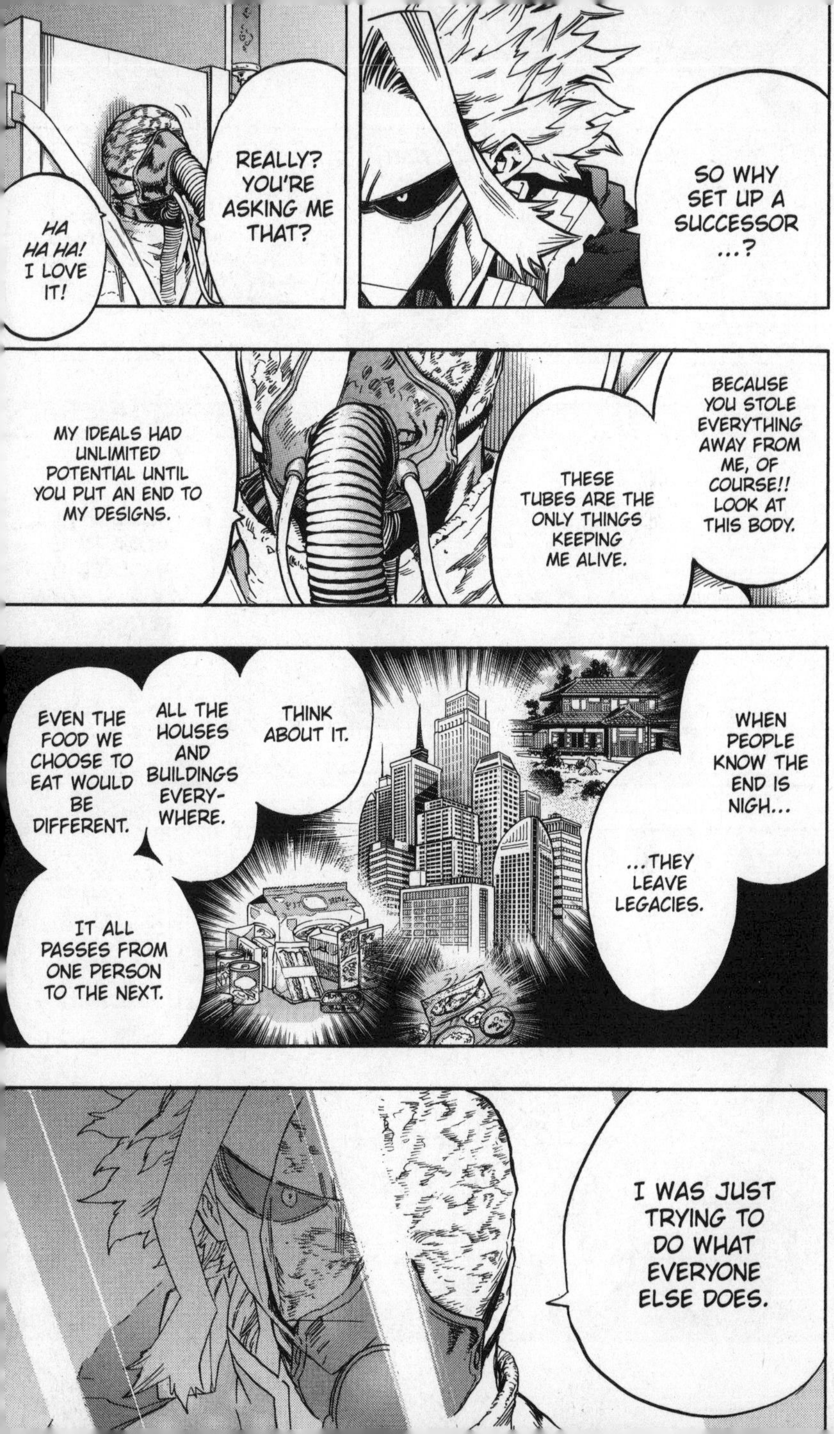
SO WHY SET UP A SUCCESSOR ...?
REALLY? YOU'RE ASKING ME THAT?
HA HA HA! I LOVE IT!
BECAUSE YOU STOLE EVERYTHING AWAY FROM ME, OF COURSE!! LOOK AT THIS BODY.
THESE TUBES ARE THE ONLY THINGS KEEPING ME ALIVE.
MY IDEALS HAD UNLIMITED POTENTIAL UNTIL YOU PUT AN END TO MY DESIGNS.
WHEN PEOPLE KNOW THE END IS NIGH...
...THEY LEAVE LEGACIES.
THINK ABOUT IT.
ALL THE HOUSES AND BUILDINGS EVERY-WHERE.
EVEN THE FOOD WE CHOOSE TO EAT WOULD BE DIFFERENT.
IT ALL PASSES FROM ONE PERSON TO THE NEXT.
I WAS JUST TRYING TO DO WHAT EVERYONE ELSE DOES.

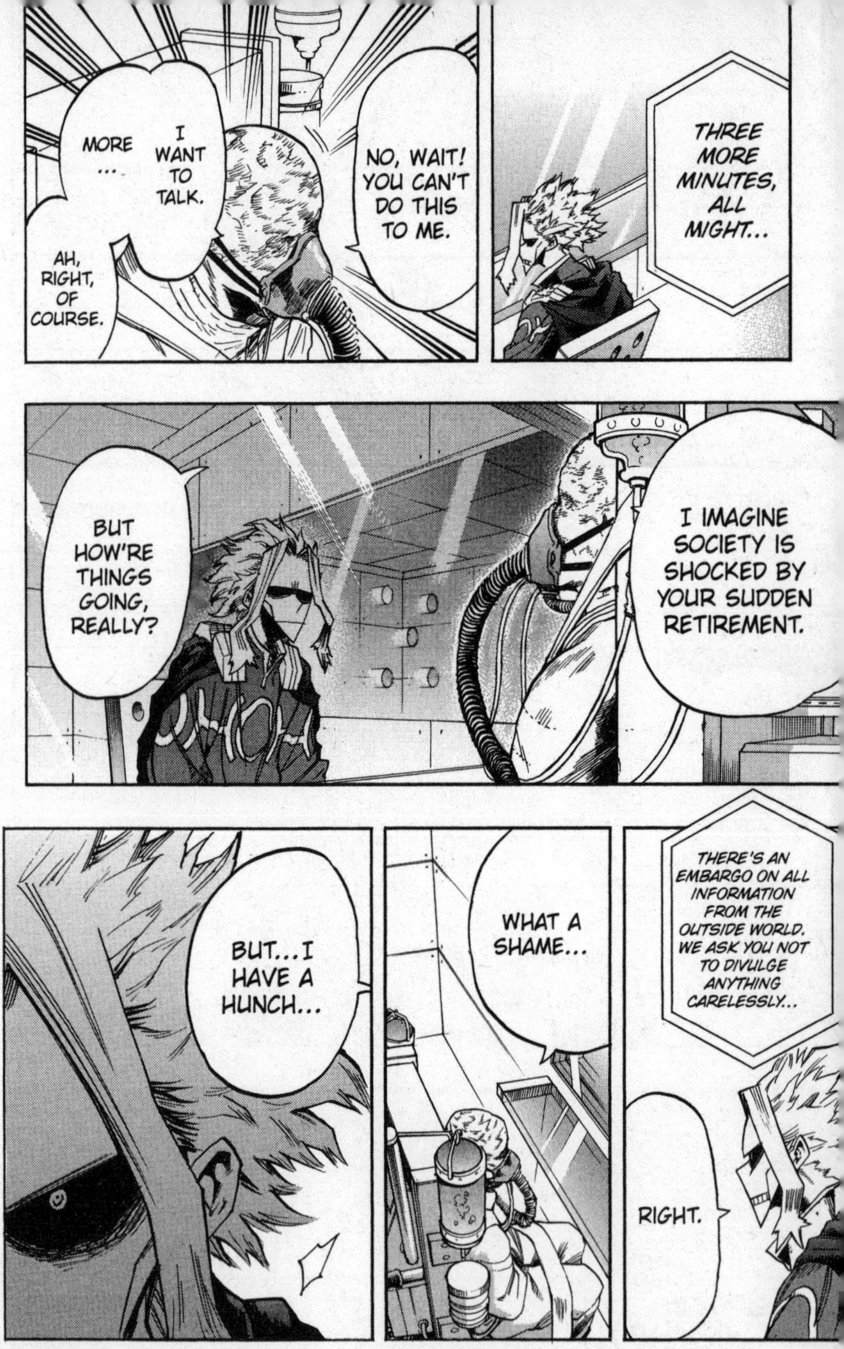
THREE MORE MINUTES, ALL MIGHT...
NO, WAIT! YOU CAN'T DO THIS TO ME.
I WANT TO TALK.
MORE ...
AH, RIGHT, OF COURSE.
I IMAGINE SOCIETY IS SHOCKED BY YOUR SUDDEN RETIREMENT.
BUT HOW'RE THINGS GOING, REALLY?
THERE'S AN EMBARGO ON ALL INFORMATION FROM THE OUTSIDE WORLD. WE ASK YOU NOT TO DIVULGE ANYTHING CARELESSLY...
RIGHT.
WHAT A SHAME...
BUT...I HAVE A HUNCH...

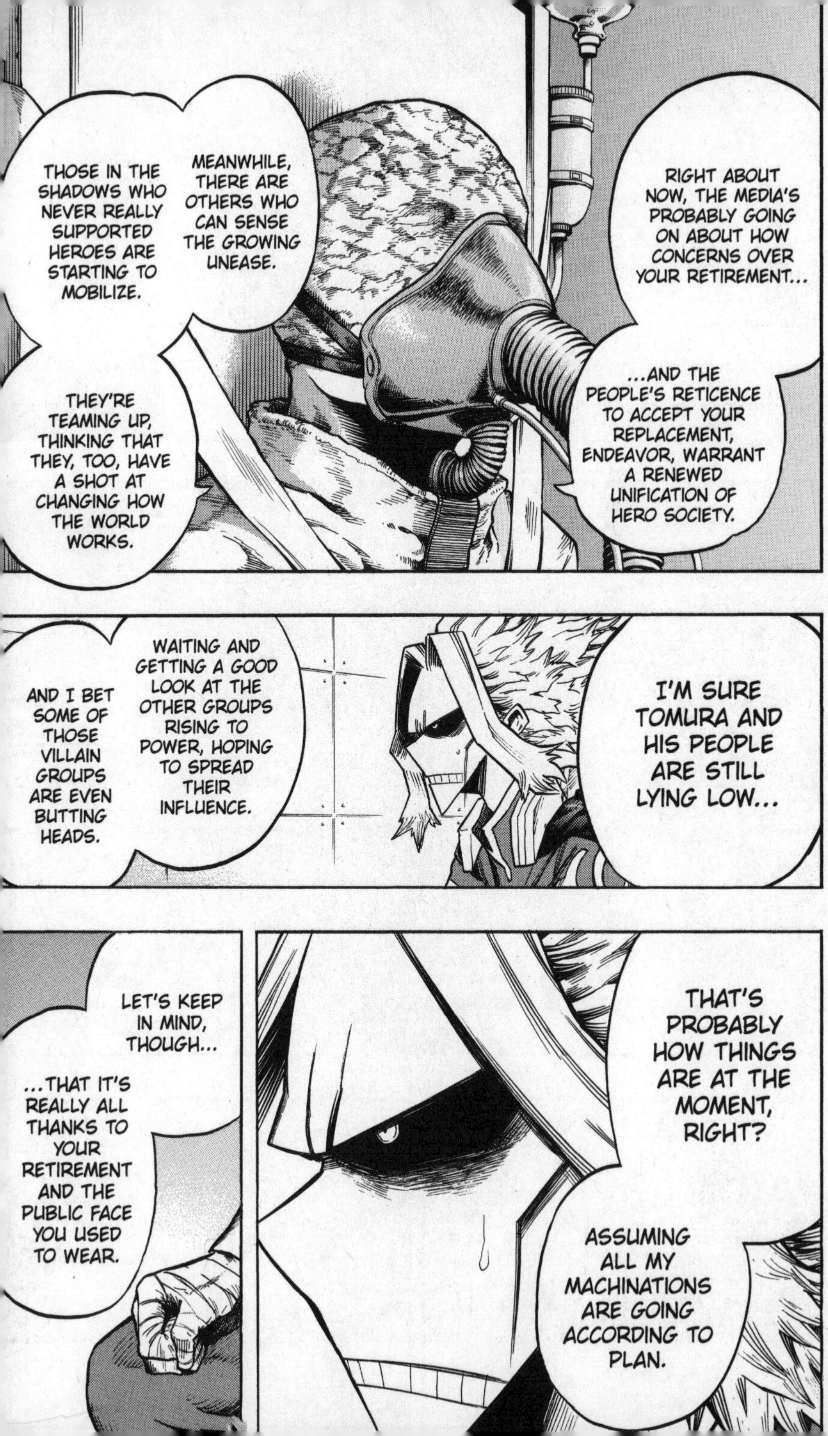
RIGHT ABOUT NOW, THE MEDIA'S PROBABLY GOING ON ABOUT HOW CONCERNS OVER YOUR RETIREMENT...
...AND THE PEOPLE'S RETICENCE TO ACCEPT YOUR REPLACEMENT, ENDEAVOR, WARRANT A RENEWED UNIFICATION OF HERO SOCIETY.
MEANWHILE, THERE ARE OTHERS WHO CAN SENSE THE GROWING UNEASE.
THOSE IN THE SHADOWS WHO NEVER REALLY SUPPORTED HEROES ARE STARTING TO MOBILIZE.
THEY'RE TEAMING UP, THINKING THAT THEY, TOO, HAVE A SHOT AT CHANGING HOW THE WORLD WORKS.
I'M SURE TOMURA AND HIS PEOPLE ARE STILL LYING LOW...
WAITING AND GETTING A GOOD LOOK AT THE OTHER GROUPS RISING TO POWER, HOPING TO SPREAD THEIR INFLUENCE.
AND I BET SOME OF THOSE VILLAIN GROUPS ARE EVEN BUTTING HEADS.
THAT'S PROBABLY HOW THINGS ARE AT THE MOMENT, RIGHT?
ASSUMING ALL MY MACHINATIONS ARE GOING ACCORDING TO PLAN.
LET'S KEEP IN MIND, THOUGH...
...THAT IT'S REALLY ALL THANKS TO YOUR RETIREMENT AND THE PUBLIC FACE YOU USED TO WEAR.

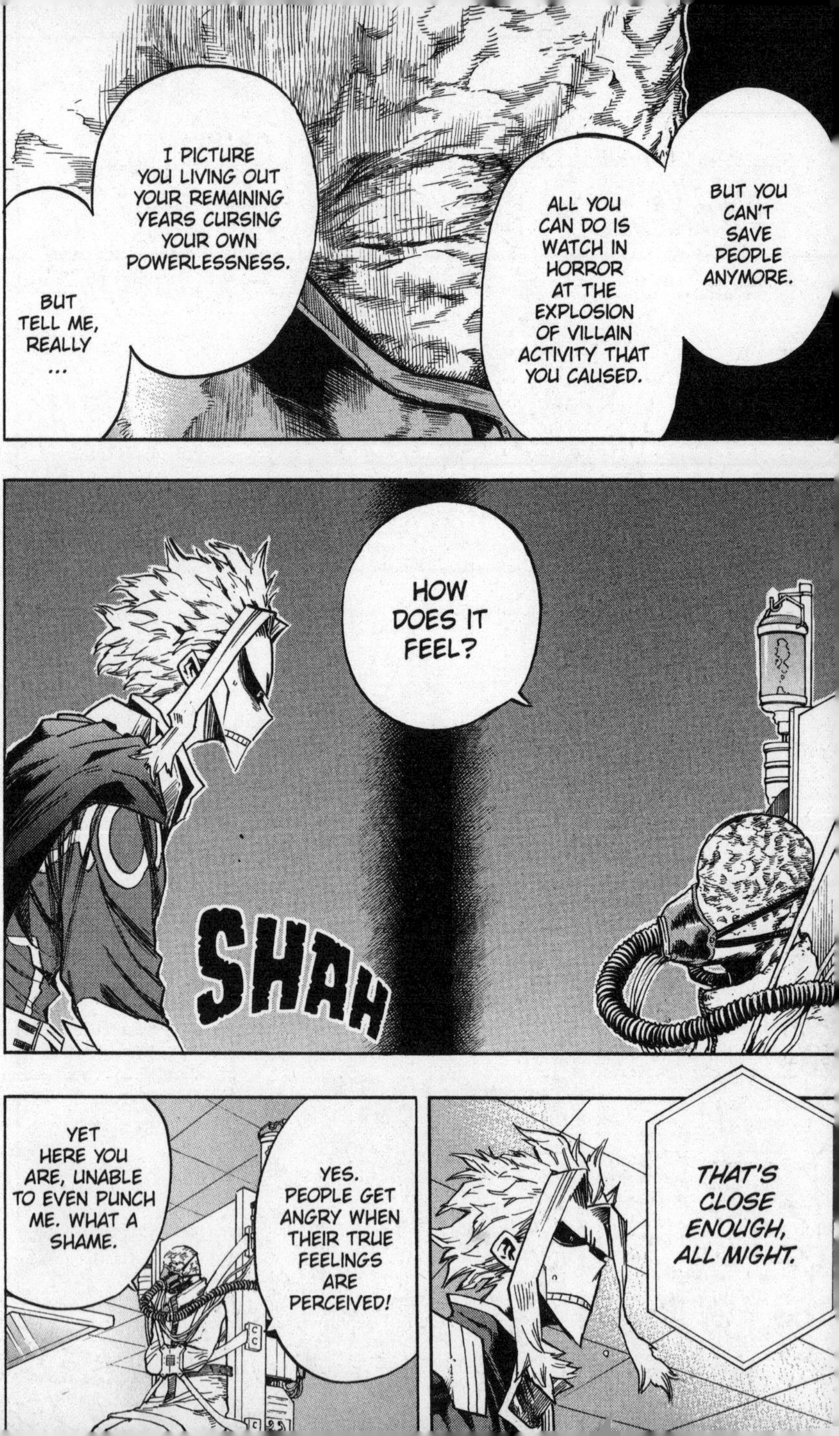
BUT YOU CAN'T SAVE PEOPLE ANYMORE.
ALL YOU CAN DO IS WATCH IN HORROR AT THE EXPLOSION OF VILLAIN ACTIVITY THAT YOU CAUSED.
I PICTURE YOU LIVING OUT YOUR REMAINING YEARS CURSING YOUR OWN POWERLESSNESS.
BUT TELL ME, REALLY ...
HOW DOES IT FEEL?
SHAH
THAT'S CLOSE ENOUGH, ALL MIGHT.
YES. PEOPLE GET ANGRY WHEN THEIR TRUE FEELINGS ARE PERCEIVED!
YET HERE YOU ARE, UNABLE TO EVEN PUNCH ME. WHAT A SHAME.

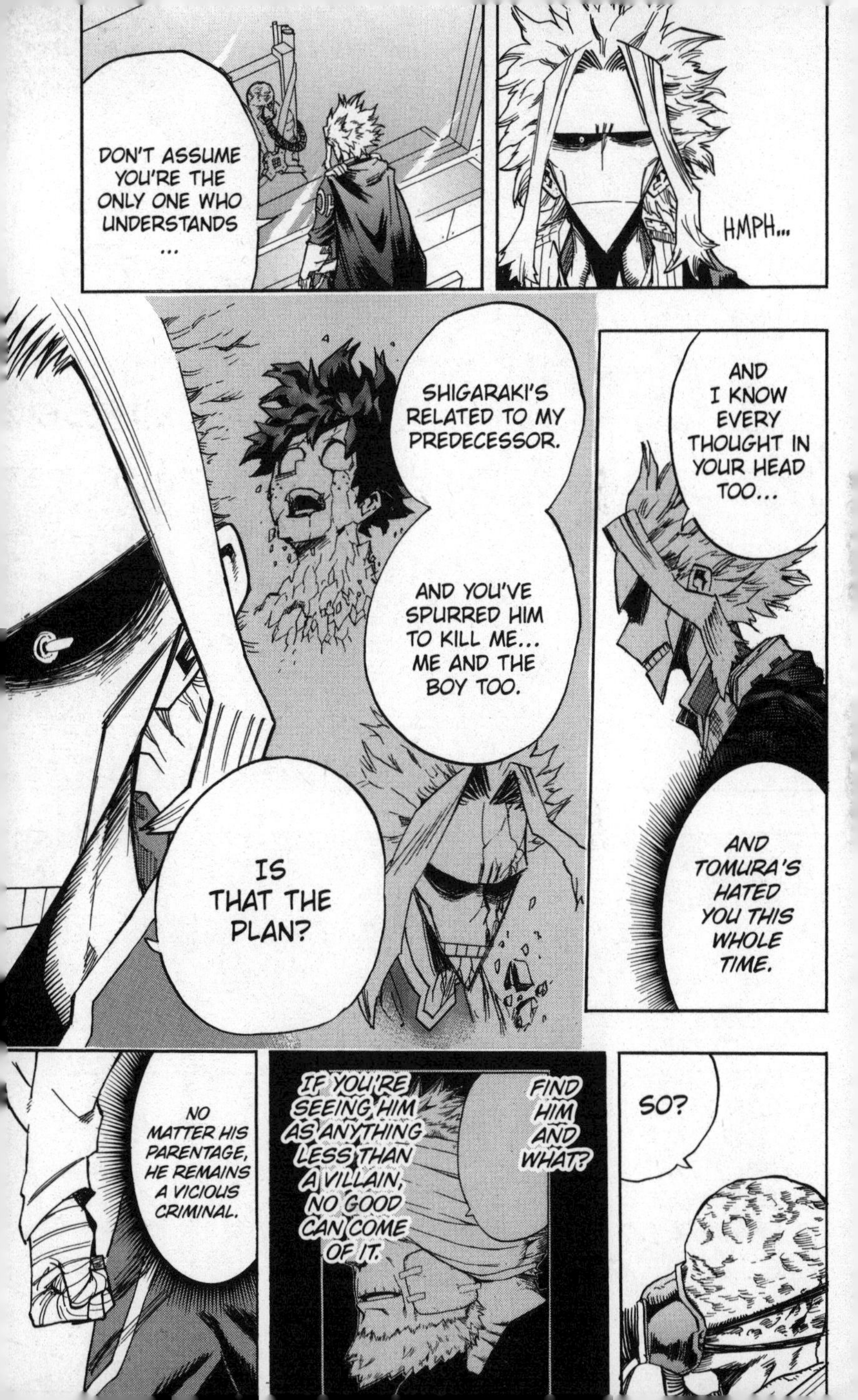
HMPH...
DON'T ASSUME YOU'RE THE ONLY ONE WHO UNDERSTANDS...
AND I KNOW EVERY THOUGHT IN YOUR HEAD TOO...
AND TOMURA'S HATED YOU THIS WHOLE TIME.
SHIGARAKI'S RELATED TO MY PREDECESSOR.
AND YOU'VE SPURRED HIM TO KILL ME... ME AND THE BOY TOO.
IS THAT THE PLAN?
SO?
FIND HIM AND WHAT?
IF YOU'RE SEEING HIM AS ANYTHING LESS THAN A VILLAIN, NO GOOD CAN COME OF IT.
NO MATTER HIS PARENTAGE, HE REMAINS A VICIOUS CRIMINAL.

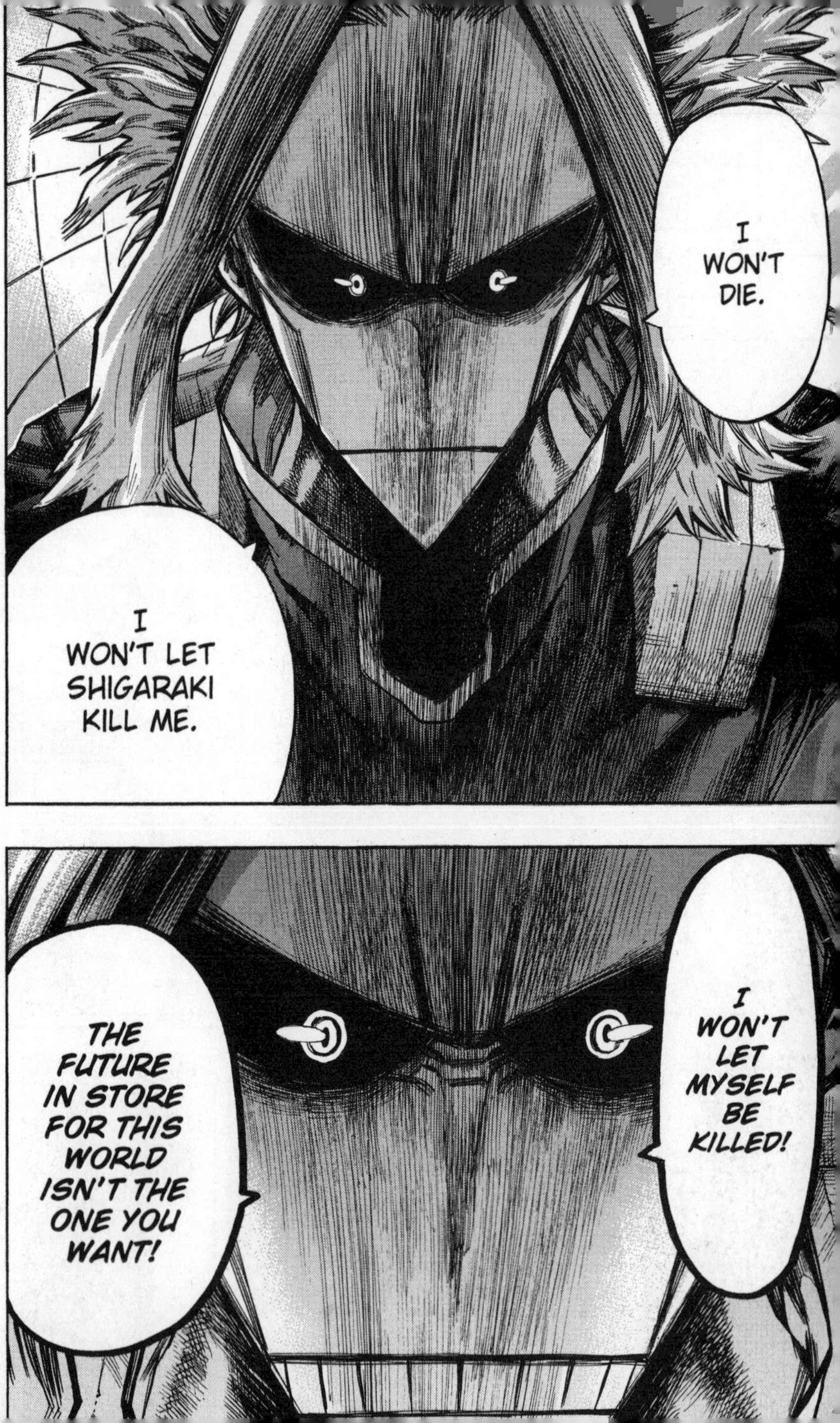
I WON'T DIE.
I WON'T LET SHIGARAKI KILL ME.
I WON'T LET MYSELF BE KILLED!
THE FUTURE IN STORE FOR THIS WORLD ISN'T THE ONE YOU WANT!

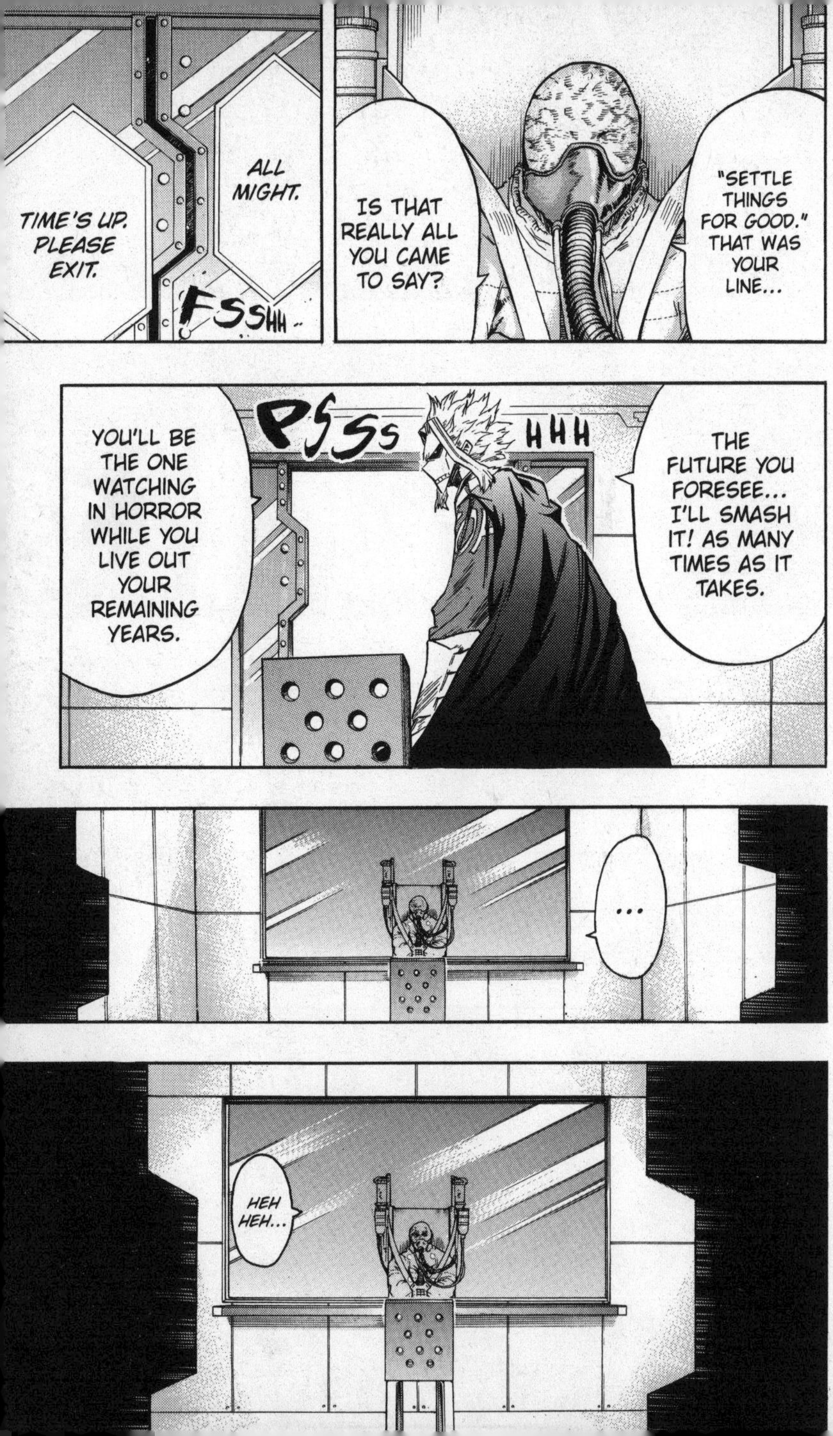
"SETTLE THINGS FOR GOOD." THAT WAS YOUR LINE...
IS THAT REALLY ALL YOU CAME TO SAY?
ALL MIGHT.
TIME'S UP. PLEASE EXIT.
FSSHH...
PSSSHHH
THE FUTURE YOU FORESEE... I'LL SMASH IT! AS MANY TIMES AS IT TAKES.
YOU'LL BE THE ONE WATCHING IN HORROR WHILE YOU LIVE OUT YOUR REMAINING YEARS.
...
HEH HEH...

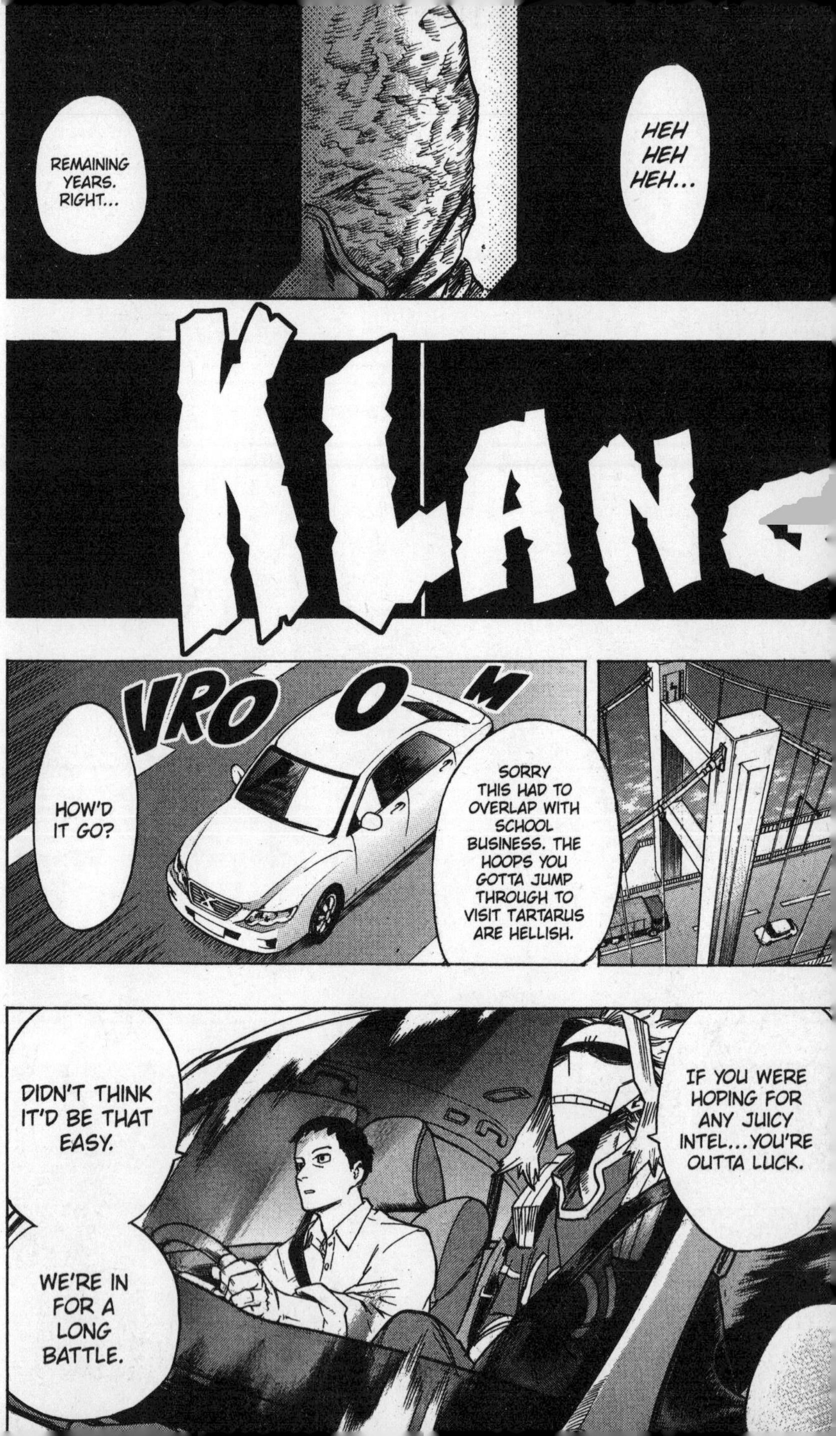
HEH HEH HEH...
REMAINING YEARS. RIGHT...
KLANG
VROOOM
SORRY THIS HAD TO OVERLAP WITH SCHOOL BUSINESS. THE HOOPS YOU GOTTA JUMP THROUGH TO VISIT TARTARUS ARE HELLISH.
HOW'D IT GO?
IF YOU WERE HOPING FOR ANY JUICY INTEL...YOU'RE OUTTA LUCK.
DIDN'T THINK IT'D BE THAT EASY.
WE'RE IN FOR A LONG BATTLE.

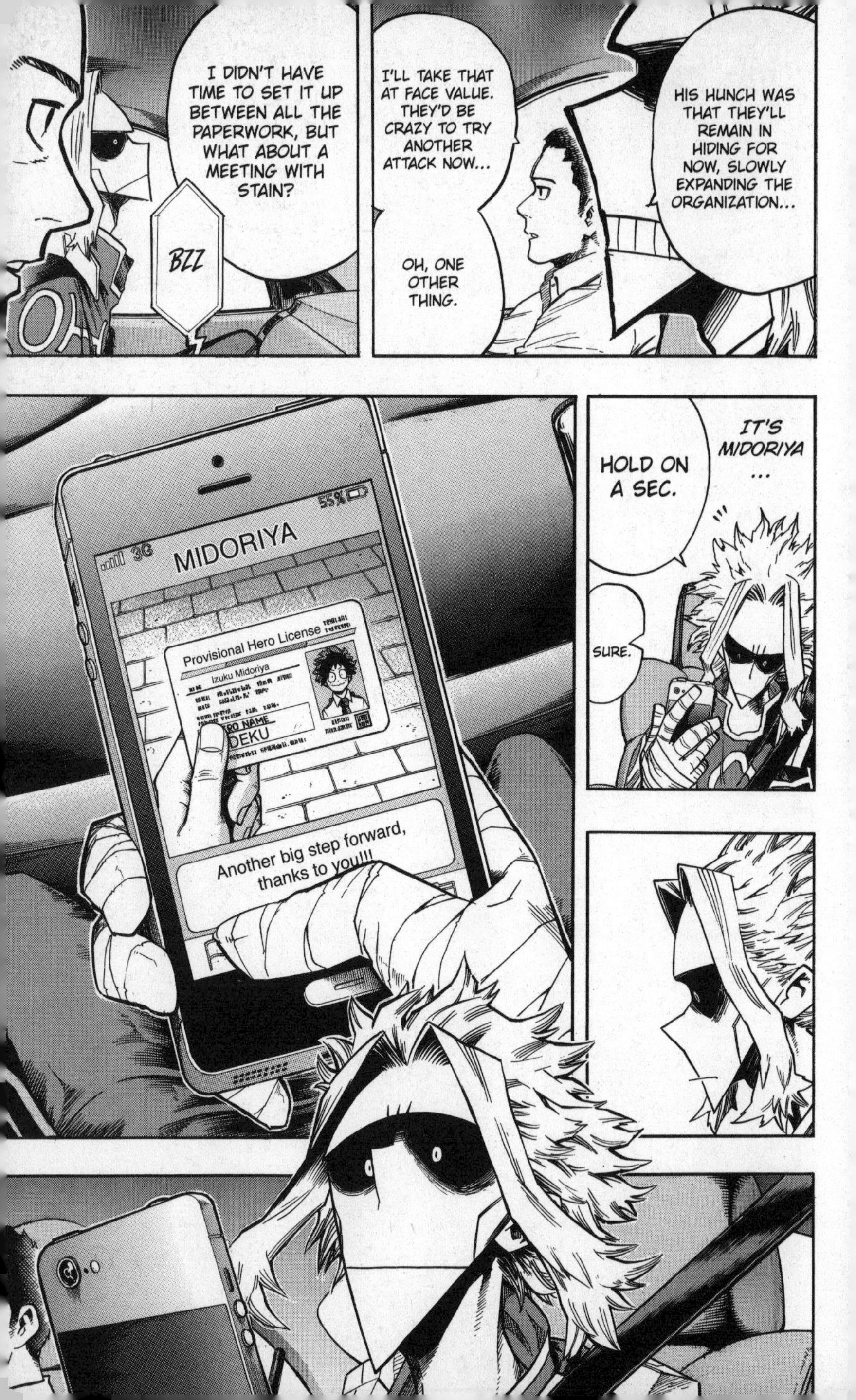
HIS HUNCH WAS THAT THEY'LL REMAIN IN HIDING FOR NOW, SLOWLY EXPANDING THE ORGANIZATION...
I'LL TAKE THAT AT FACE VALUE. THEY'D BE CRAZY TO TRY ANOTHER ATTACK NOW...
OH, ONE OTHER THING.
I DIDN'T HAVE TIME TO SET IT UP BETWEEN ALL THE PAPERWORK, BUT WHAT ABOUT A MEETING WITH STAIN?
BZZ
IT'S MIDORIYA...
HOLD ON A SEC.
SURE.
55%
3G
MIDORIYA
Provisional Hero License
Izuku Midoriya
HERO NAME
DEKU
Another big step forward, thanks to you!!!

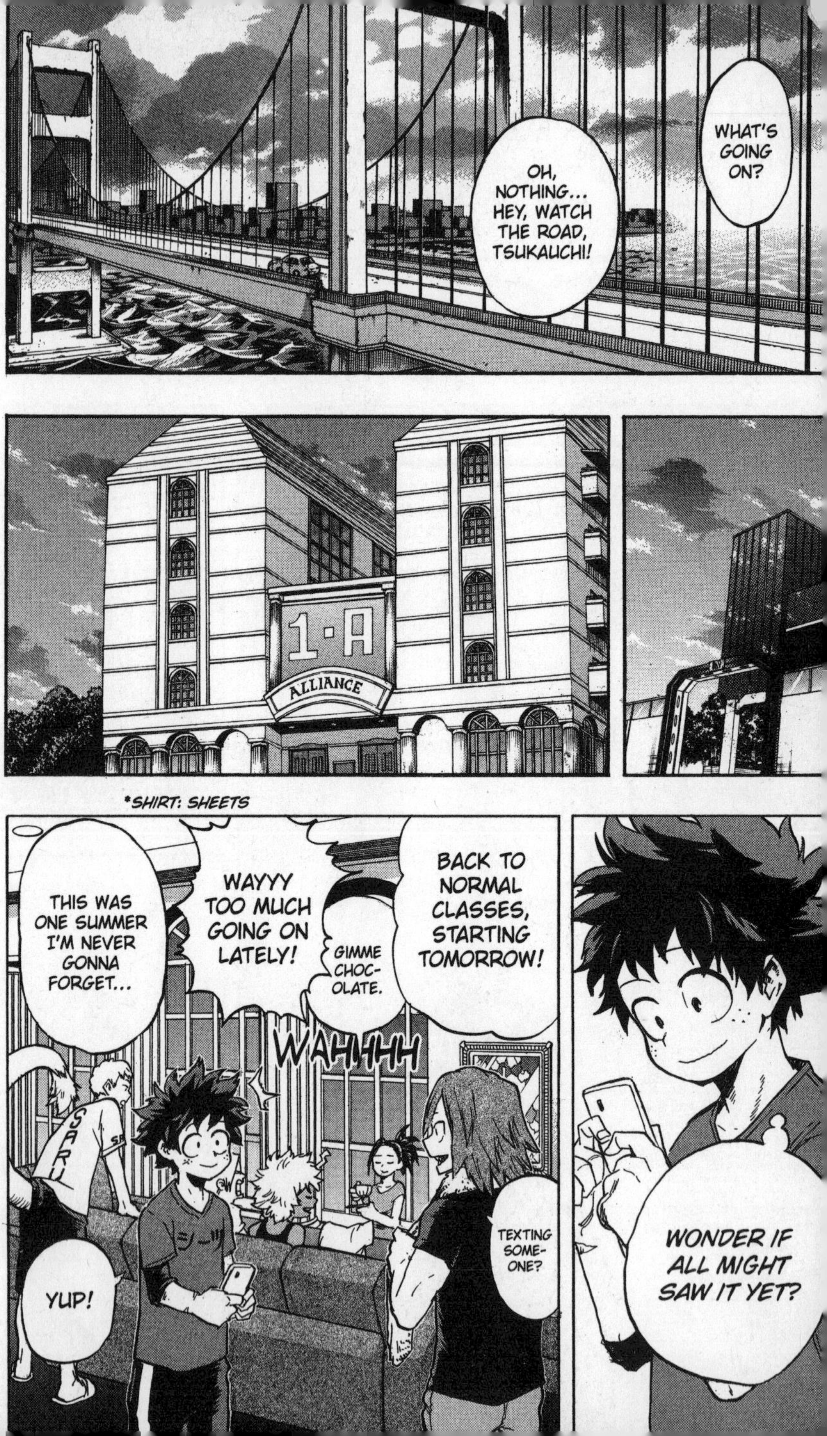
WHAT'S GOING ON?
OH, NOTHING… HEY, WATCH THE ROAD, TSUKAUCHI!
1-A
ALLIANCE
WONDER IF ALL MIGHT SAW IT YET?
BACK TO NORMAL CLASSES, STARTING TOMORROW!
GIMME CHOCOLATE.
WAYYY TOO MUCH GOING ON LATELY!
THIS WAS ONE SUMMER I'M NEVER GONNA FORGET…
WAHHHH
TEXTING SOMEONE?
YUP!

*SHIRT: SHEETS

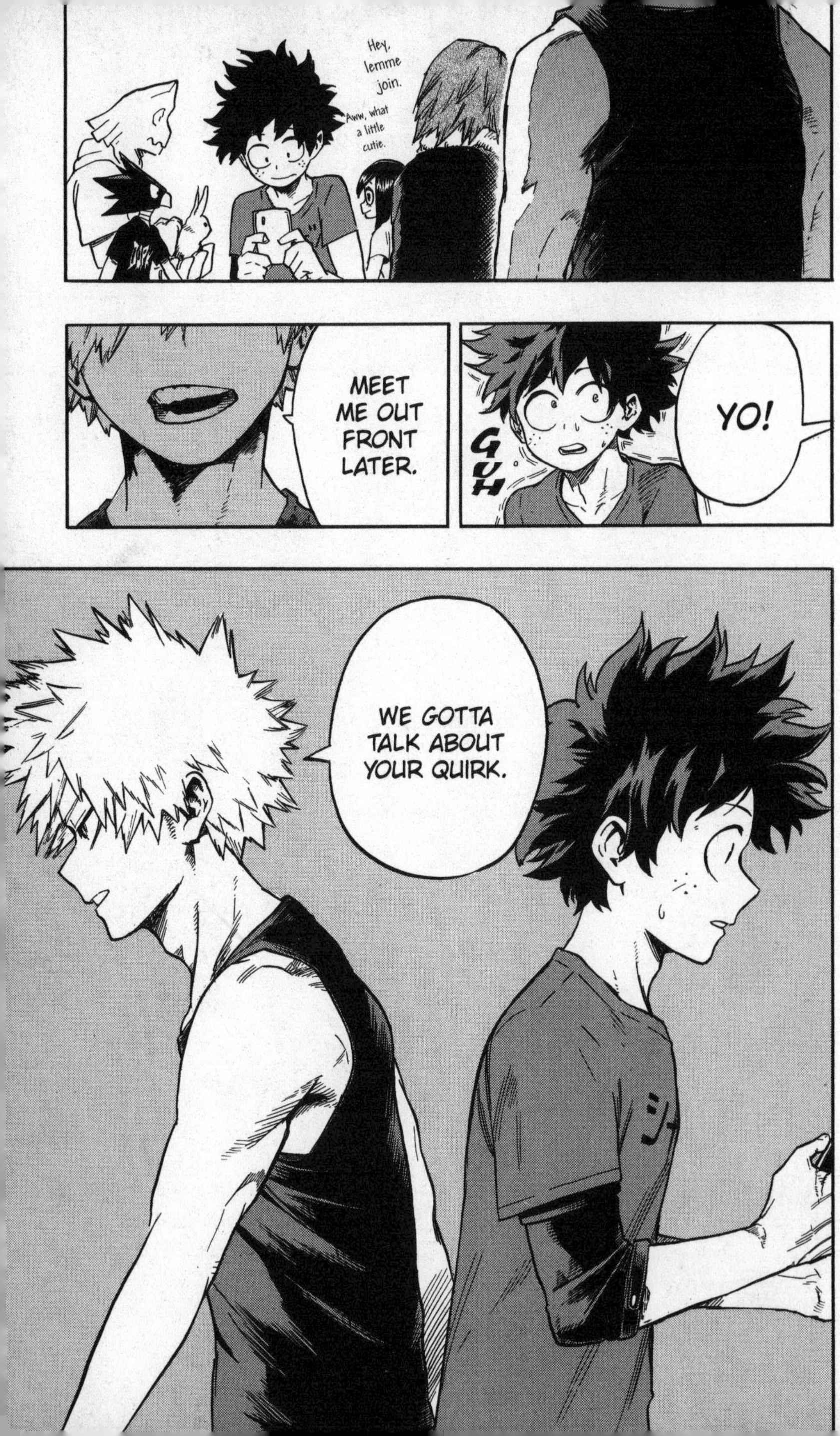
Hey, lemme join.
Aww, what a little cutie.
YO!
GUH
MEET ME OUT FRONT LATER.
WE GOTTA TALK ABOUT YOUR QUIRK.

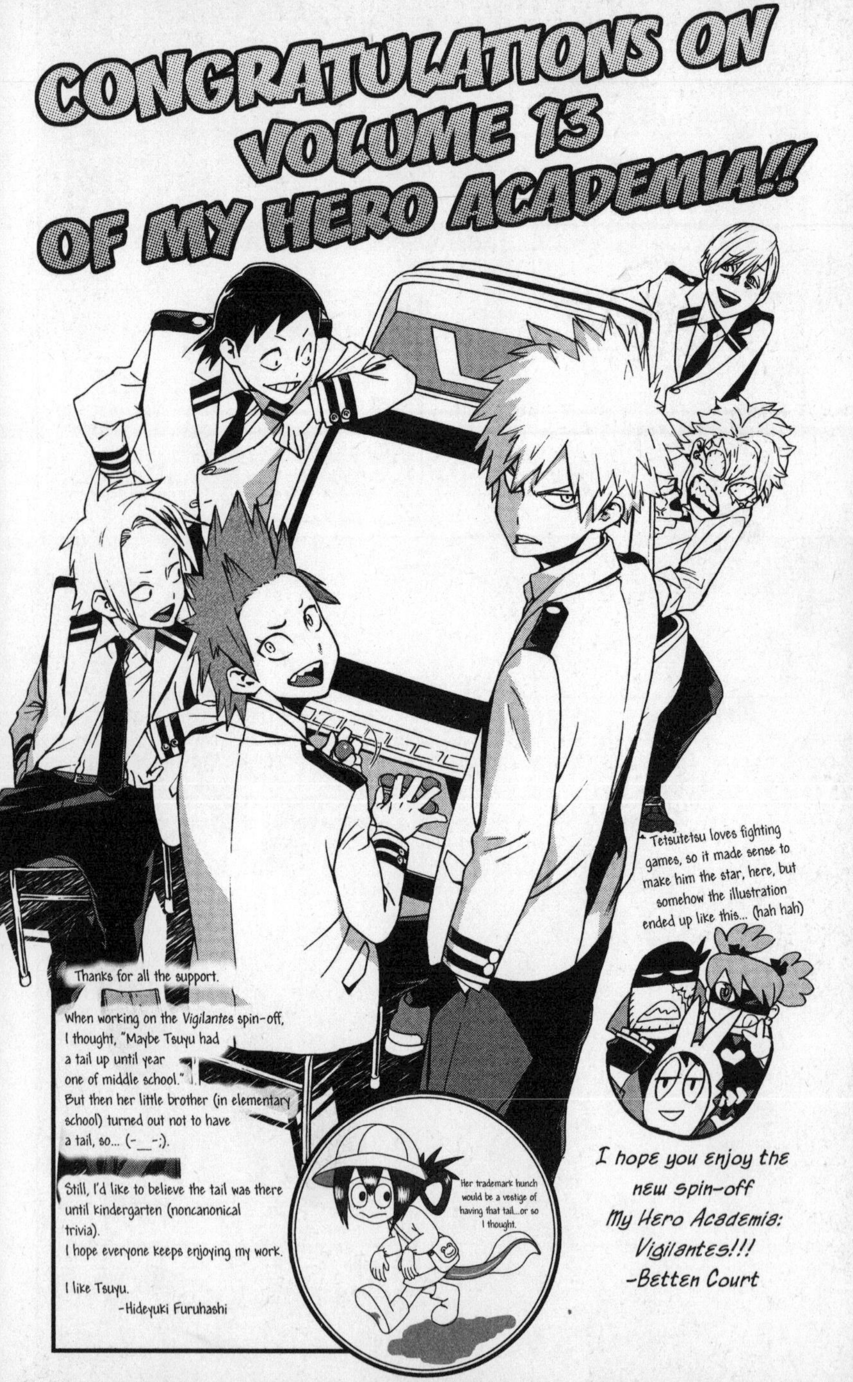
CONGRATULATIONS ON VOLUME 13 OF MY HERO ACADEMIA!!
Tetsutetsu loves fighting games, so it made sense to make him the star, here, but somehow the illustration ended up like this... (hah hah)
Thanks for all the support.
When working on the *Vigilantes* spin-off, I thought, "Maybe Tsuyu had a tail up until year one of middle school."
But then her little brother (in elementary school) turned out not to have a tail, so... (-_-;).
Still, I'd like to believe the tail was there until kindergarten (noncanonical trivia).
I hope everyone keeps enjoying my work.
I like Tsuyu.
-Hideyuki Furuhashi
Her trademark hunch would be a vestige of having that tail...or so I thought.
I hope you enjoy the new spin-off My Hero Academia: Vigilantes!!!
-Betten Court

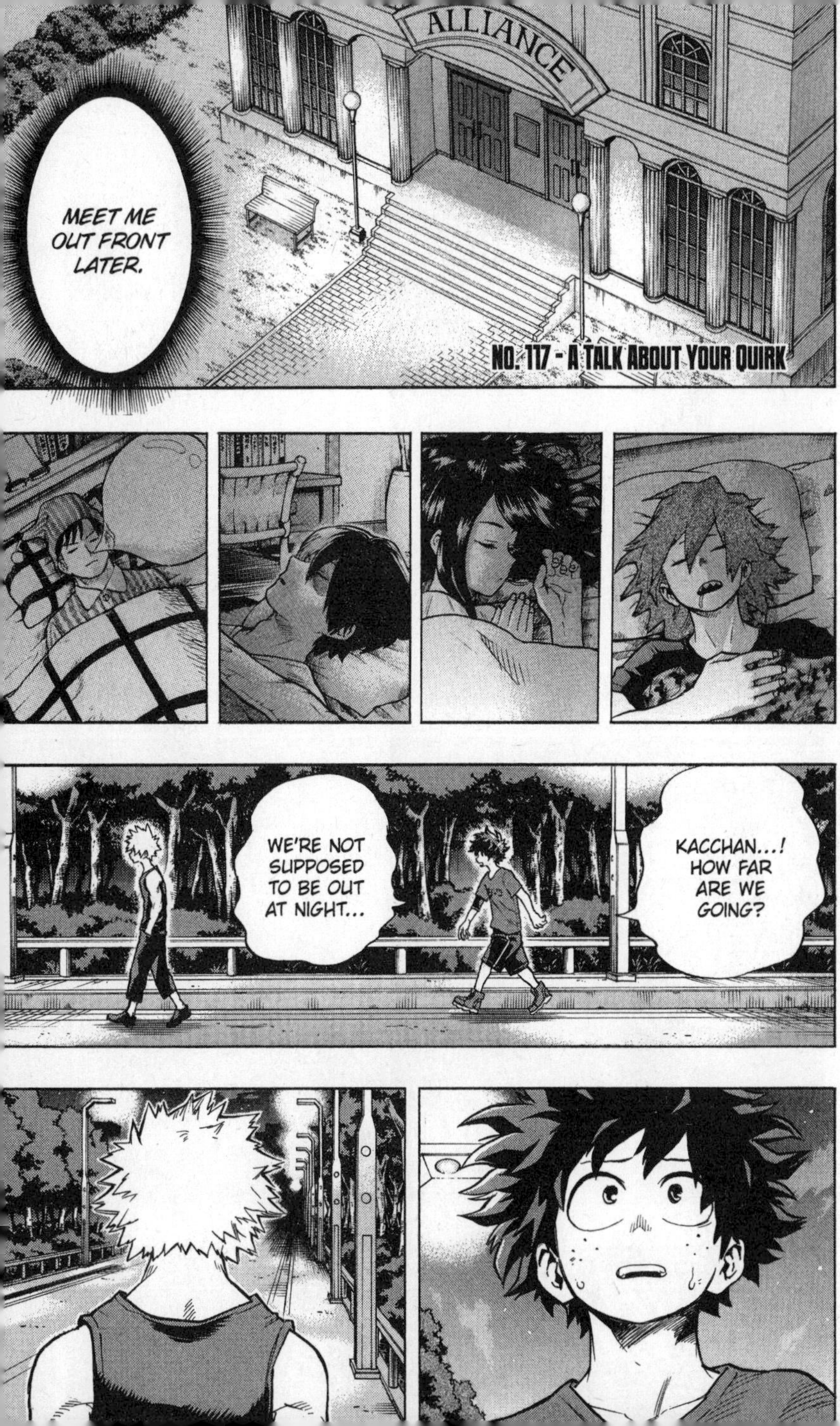
ALLIANCE
MEET ME OUT FRONT LATER.
No. 117 - A Talk About Your Quirk
KACCHAN...! HOW FAR ARE WE GOING?
WE'RE NOT SUPPOSED TO BE OUT AT NIGHT...

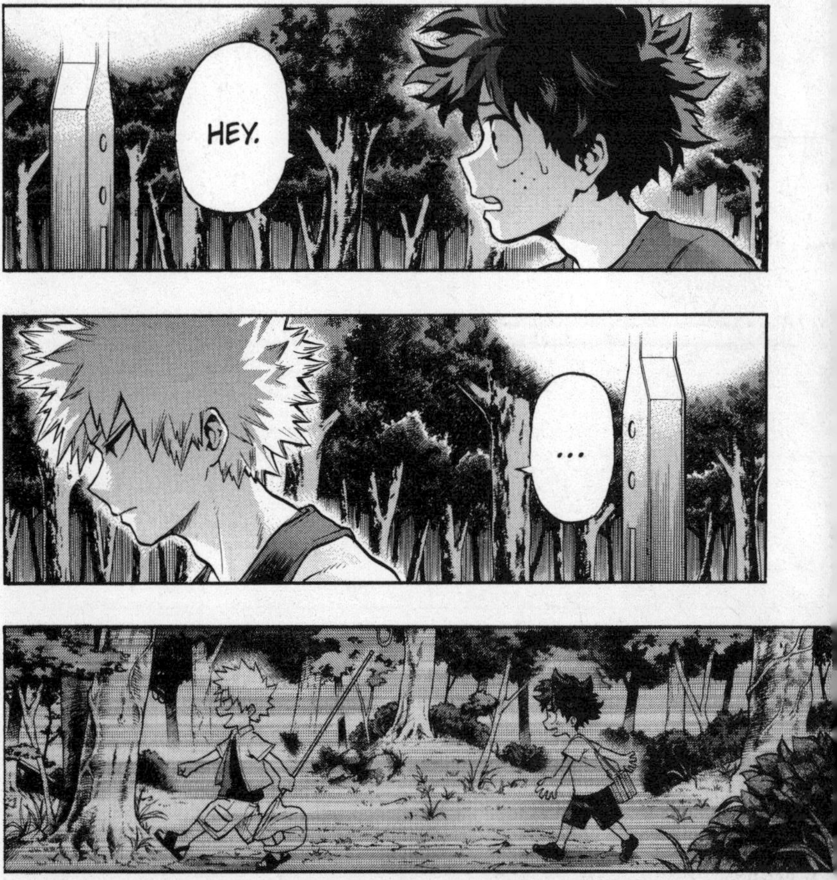
HEY.
...

No. 117 - A Talk About Your Quirk

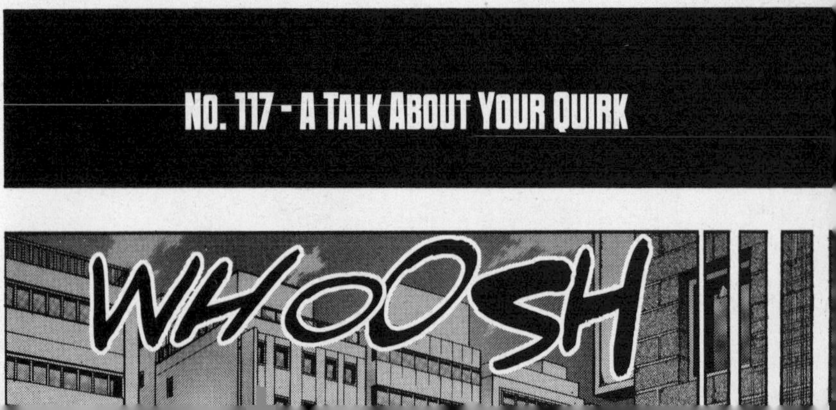
WHOOSH

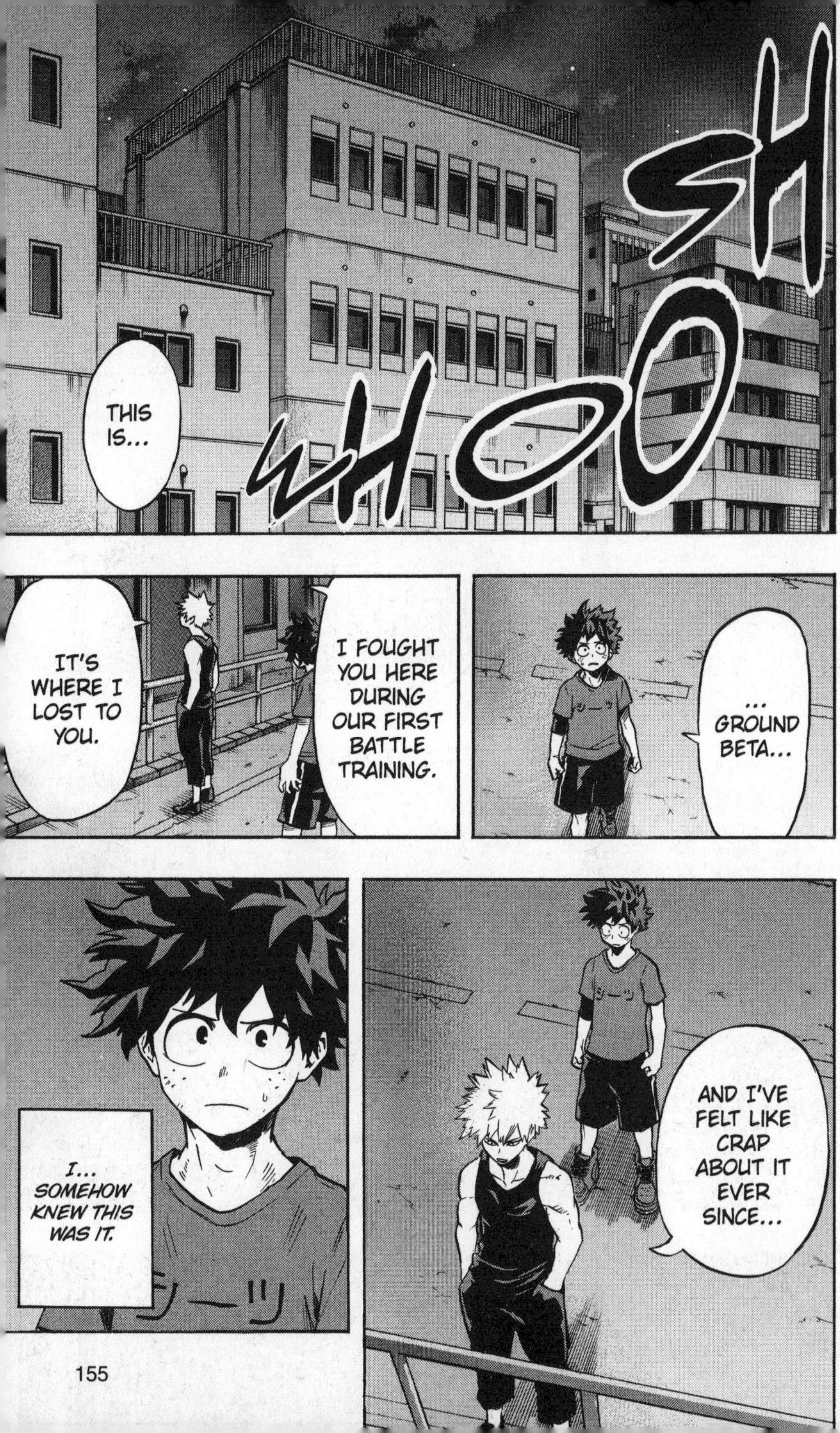
WHOOSH
THIS IS...
... GROUND BETA...
I FOUGHT YOU HERE DURING OUR FIRST BATTLE TRAINING.
IT'S WHERE I LOST TO YOU.
AND I'VE FELT LIKE CRAP ABOUT IT EVER SINCE...
I... SOMEHOW KNEW THIS WAS IT.

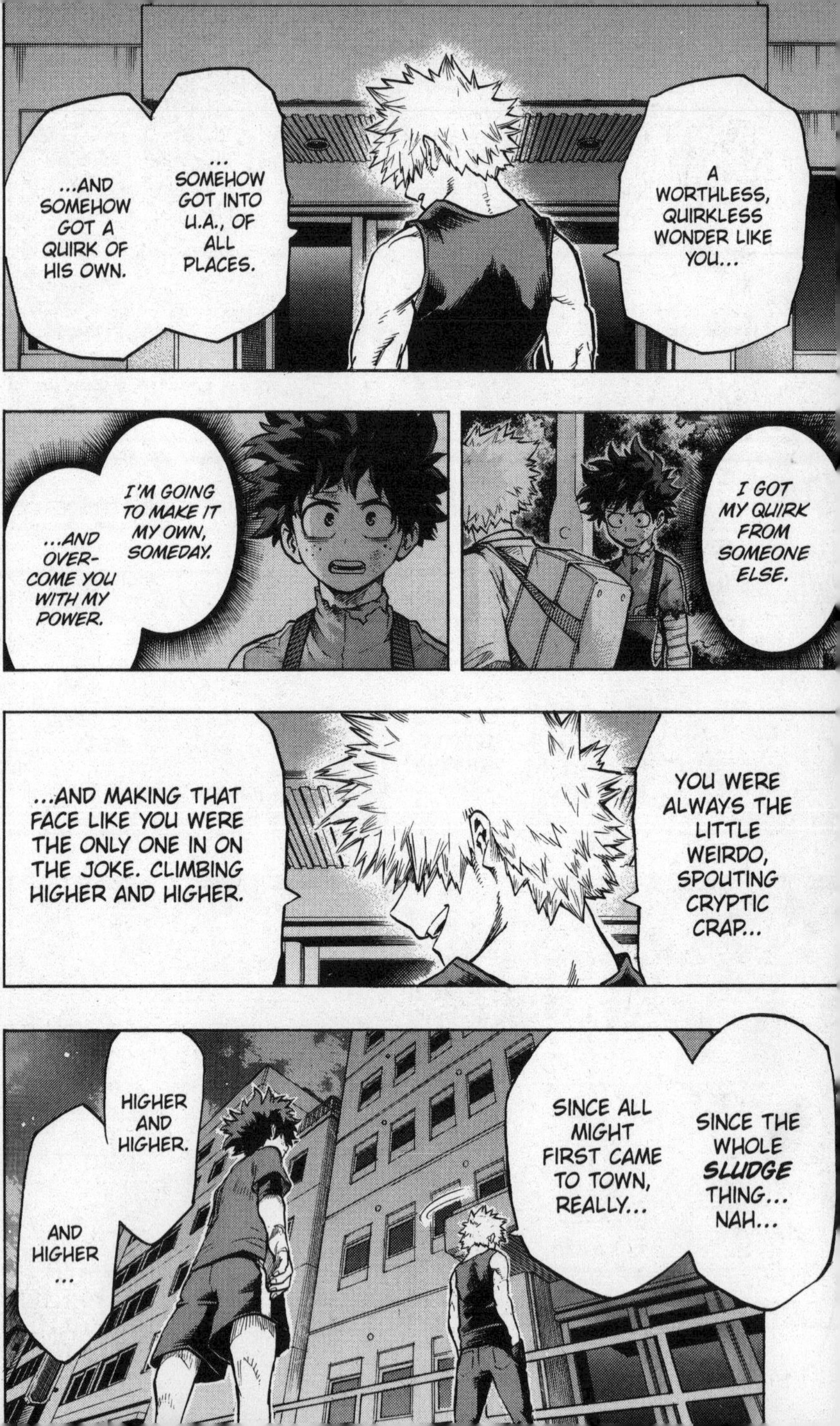
A WORTHLESS, QUIRKLESS WONDER LIKE YOU...
... SOMEHOW GOT INTO U.A., OF ALL PLACES.
...AND SOMEHOW GOT A QUIRK OF HIS OWN.
I GOT MY QUIRK FROM SOMEONE ELSE.
I'M GOING TO MAKE IT MY OWN, SOMEDAY.
...AND OVER-COME YOU WITH MY POWER.
YOU WERE ALWAYS THE LITTLE WEIRDO, SPOUTING CRYPTIC CRAP...
...AND MAKING THAT FACE LIKE YOU WERE THE ONLY ONE IN ON THE JOKE. CLIMBING HIGHER AND HIGHER.
SINCE THE WHOLE SLUDGE THING... NAH...
SINCE ALL MIGHT FIRST CAME TO TOWN, REALLY...
HIGHER AND HIGHER.
AND HIGHER ...

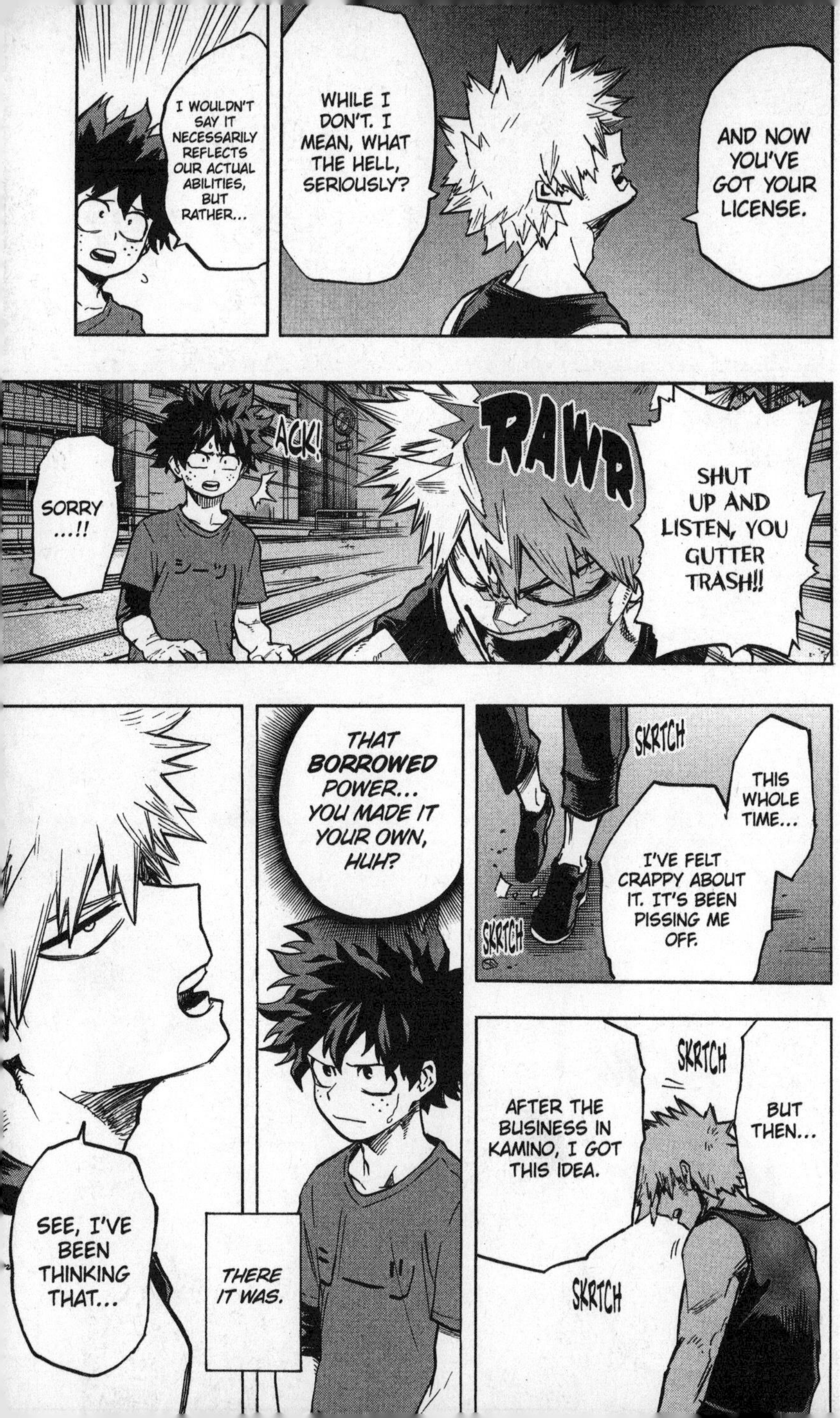
AND NOW YOU'VE GOT YOUR LICENSE.
WHILE I DON'T. I MEAN, WHAT THE HELL, SERIOUSLY?
I WOULDN'T SAY IT NECESSARILY REFLECTS OUR ACTUAL ABILITIES, BUT RATHER...
SHUT UP AND LISTEN, YOU GUTTER TRASH!!
RAWR
ACK!
SORRY ...!!
SKRTCH
THIS WHOLE TIME...
I'VE FELT CRAPPY ABOUT IT. IT'S BEEN PISSING ME OFF.
SKRTCH
SKRTCH
BUT THEN...
AFTER THE BUSINESS IN KAMINO, I GOT THIS IDEA.
SKRTCH
THAT **BORROWED** POWER... YOU MADE IT YOUR OWN, HUH?
THERE IT WAS.
SEE, I'VE BEEN THINKING THAT...

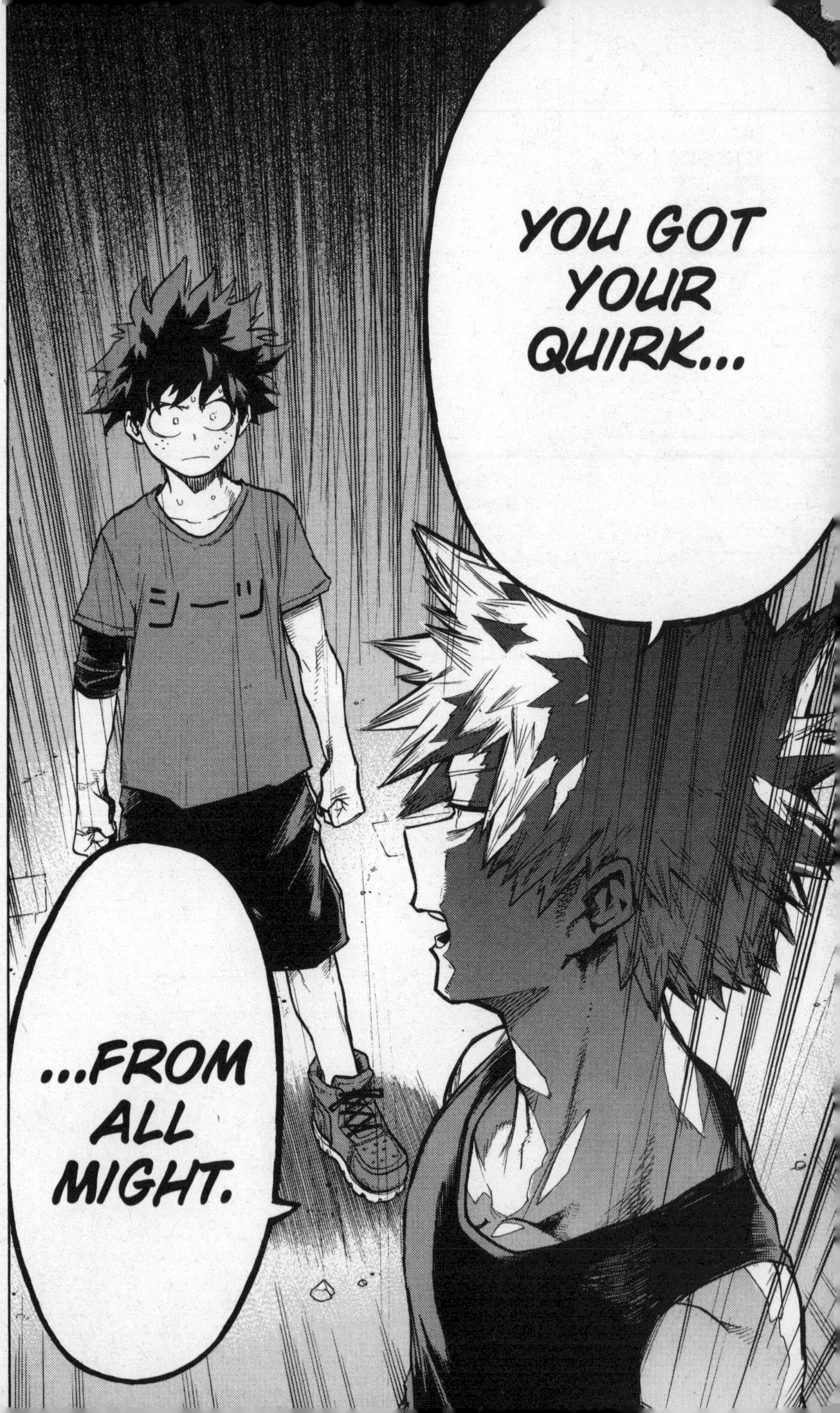
YOU GOT YOUR QUIRK...
...FROM ALL MIGHT.

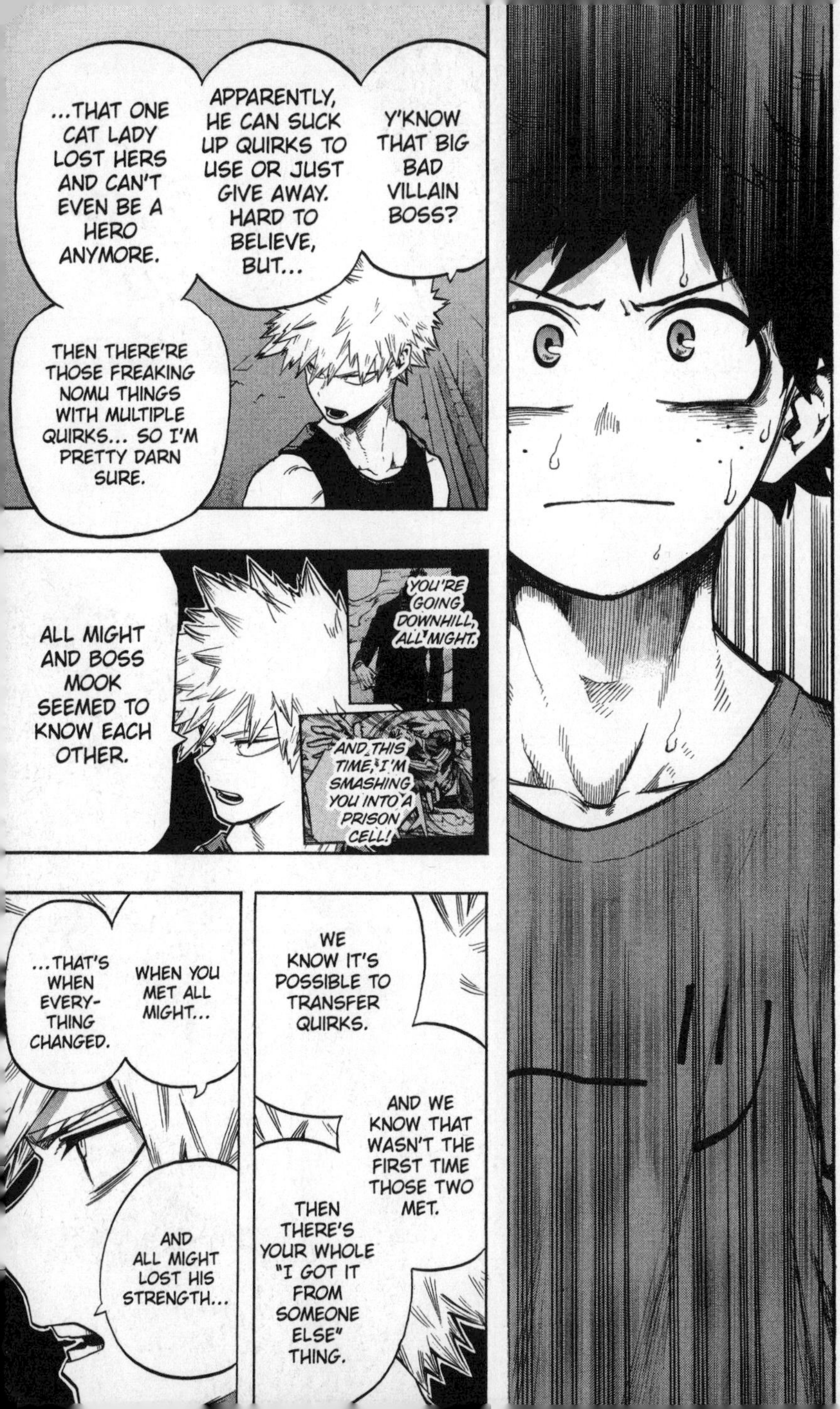
Y'KNOW THAT BIG BAD VILLAIN BOSS?
APPARENTLY, HE CAN SUCK UP QUIRKS TO USE OR JUST GIVE AWAY. HARD TO BELIEVE, BUT...
...THAT ONE CAT LADY LOST HERS AND CAN'T EVEN BE A HERO ANYMORE.
THEN THERE'RE THOSE FREAKING NOMU THINGS WITH MULTIPLE QUIRKS... SO I'M PRETTY DARN SURE.
YOU'RE GOING DOWNHILL, ALL MIGHT.
AND THIS TIME, I'M SMASHING YOU INTO A PRISON CELL!
ALL MIGHT AND BOSS MOOK SEEMED TO KNOW EACH OTHER.
WE KNOW IT'S POSSIBLE TO TRANSFER QUIRKS.
AND WE KNOW THAT WASN'T THE FIRST TIME THOSE TWO MET.
THEN THERE'S YOUR WHOLE "I GOT IT FROM SOMEONE ELSE" THING.
WHEN YOU MET ALL MIGHT...
...THAT'S WHEN EVERY-THING CHANGED.
AND ALL MIGHT LOST HIS STRENGTH...

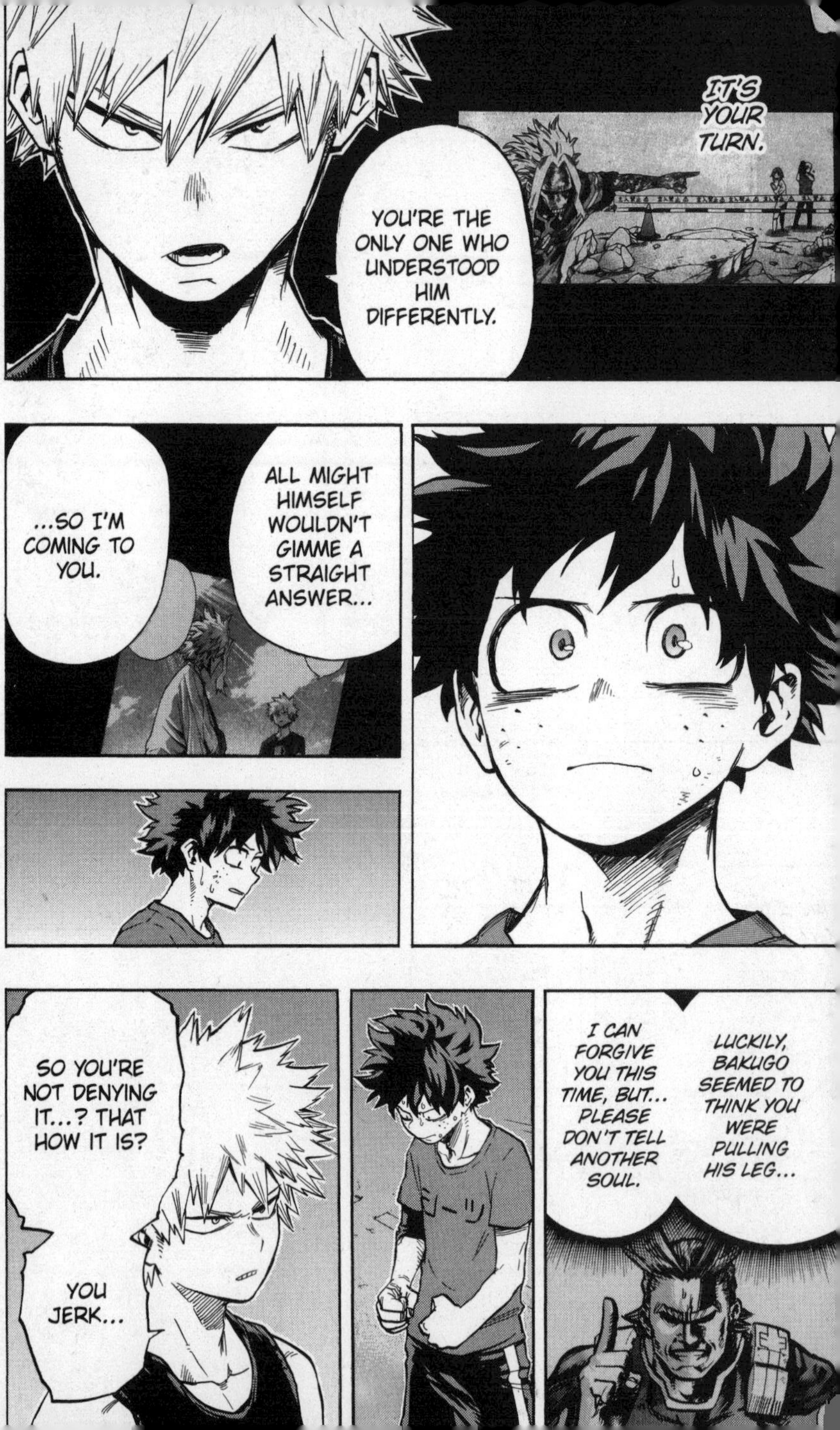
IT'S YOUR TURN.
YOU'RE THE ONLY ONE WHO UNDERSTOOD HIM DIFFERENTLY.
ALL MIGHT HIMSELF WOULDN'T GIMME A STRAIGHT ANSWER...
...SO I'M COMING TO YOU.
LUCKILY, BAKUGO SEEMED TO THINK YOU WERE PULLING HIS LEG...
I CAN FORGIVE YOU THIS TIME, BUT... PLEASE DON'T TELL ANOTHER SOUL.
SO YOU'RE NOT DENYING IT...? THAT HOW IT IS?
YOU JERK...

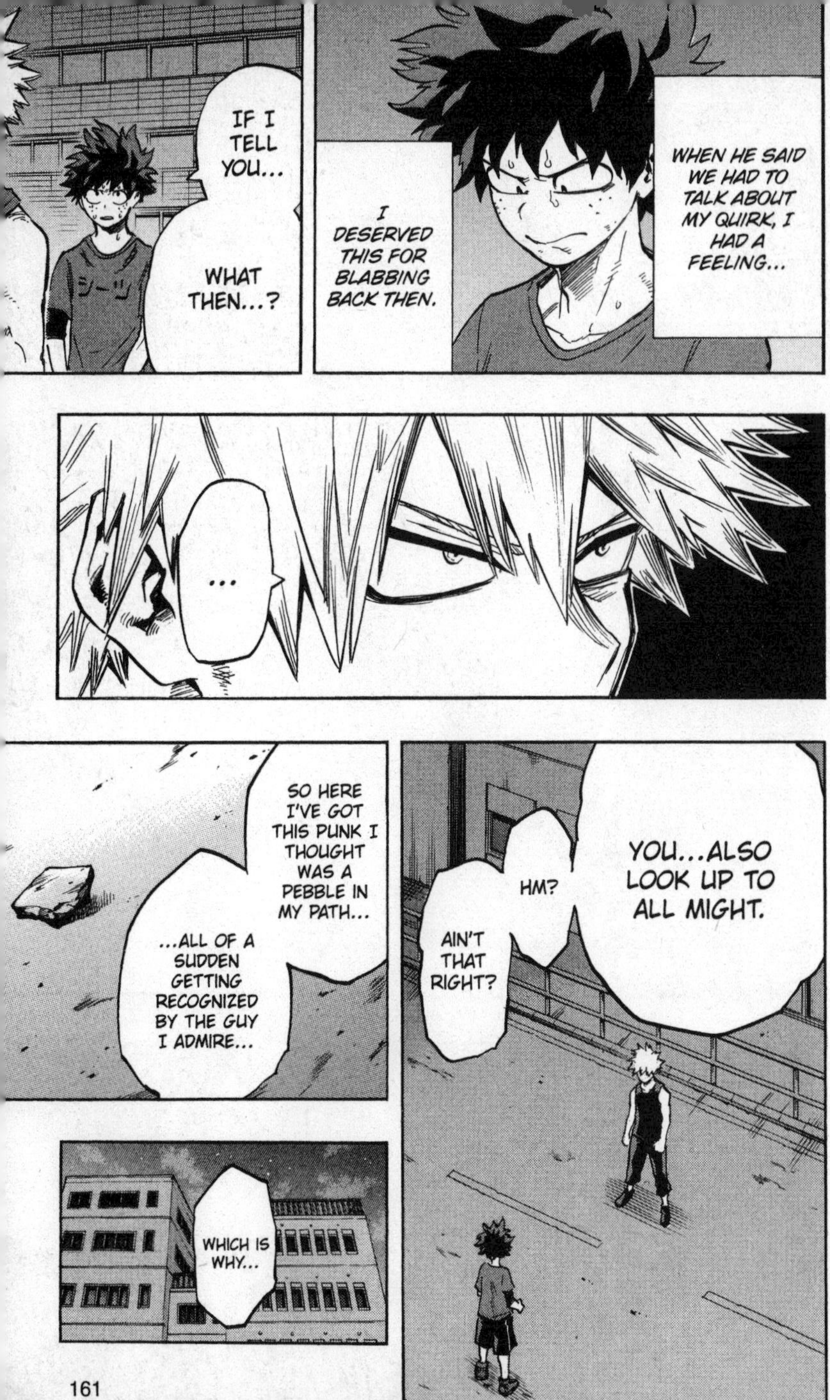
WHEN HE SAID WE HAD TO TALK ABOUT MY QUIRK, I HAD A FEELING...
I DESERVED THIS FOR BLABBING BACK THEN.
IF I TELL YOU...
WHAT THEN...?
...
YOU...ALSO LOOK UP TO ALL MIGHT.
HM?
AIN'T THAT RIGHT?
SO HERE I'VE GOT THIS PUNK I THOUGHT WAS A PEBBLE IN MY PATH...
...ALL OF A SUDDEN GETTING RECOGNIZED BY THE GUY I ADMIRE...
WHICH IS WHY...

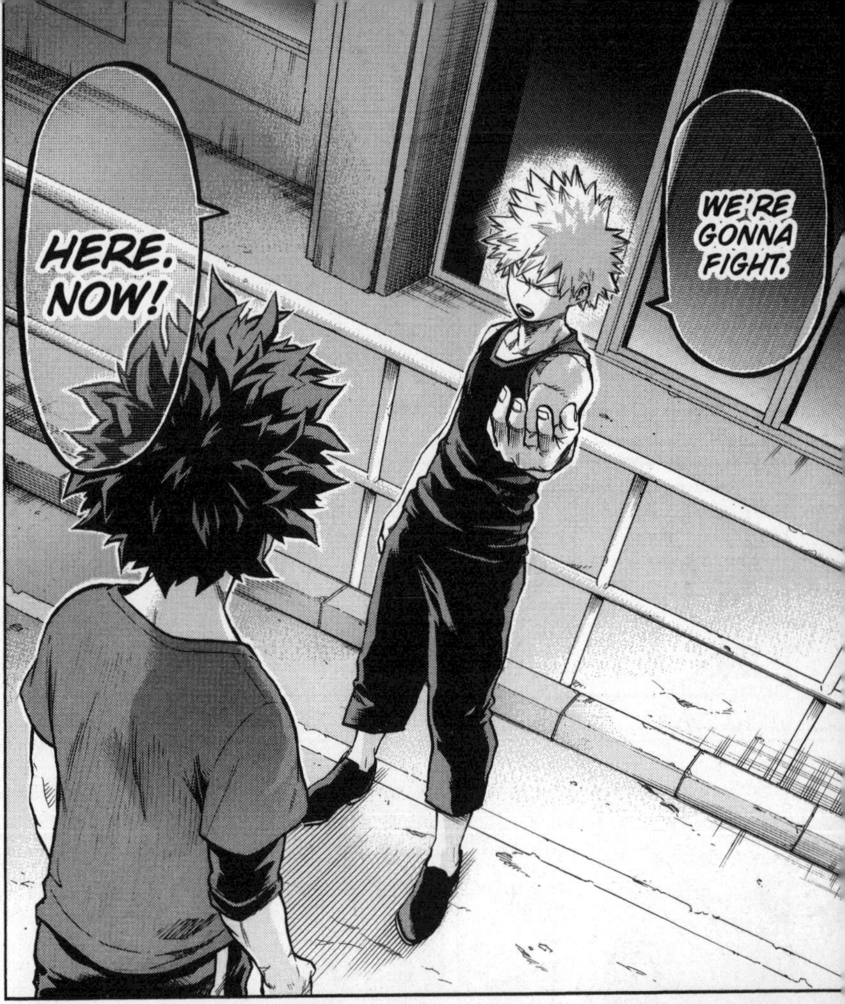
WE'RE GONNA FIGHT.
HERE. NOW!
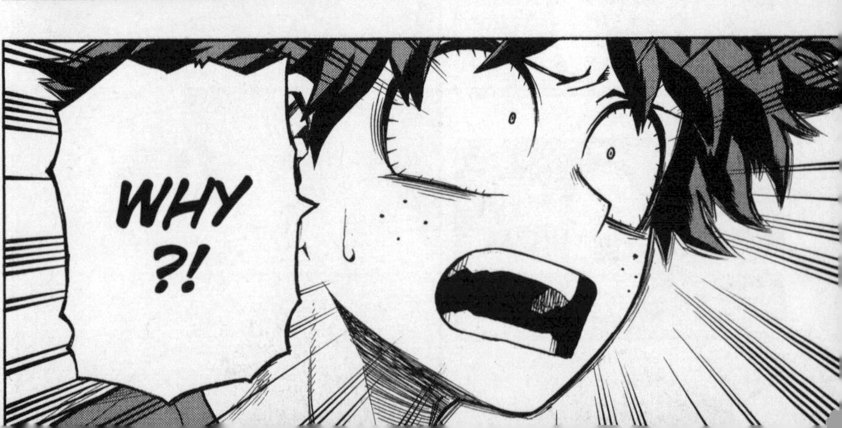
WHY ?!

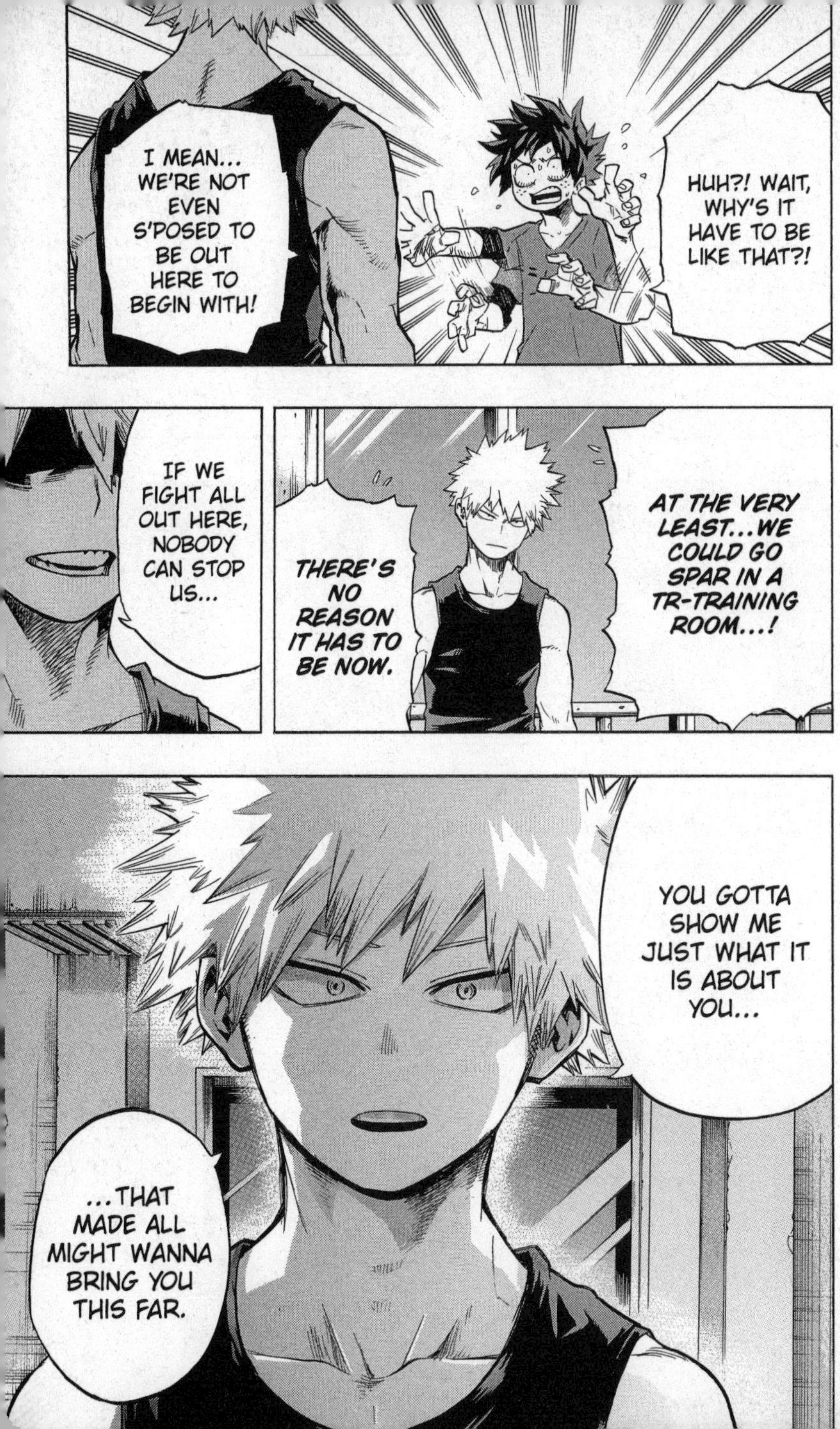
HUH?! WAIT, WHY'S IT HAVE TO BE LIKE THAT?!
I MEAN... WE'RE NOT EVEN S'POSED TO BE OUT HERE TO BEGIN WITH!
AT THE VERY LEAST...WE COULD GO SPAR IN A TR-TRAINING ROOM...!
THERE'S NO REASON IT HAS TO BE NOW.
IF WE FIGHT ALL OUT HERE, NOBODY CAN STOP US...
YOU GOTTA SHOW ME JUST WHAT IT IS ABOUT YOU...
...THAT MADE ALL MIGHT WANNA BRING YOU THIS FAR.

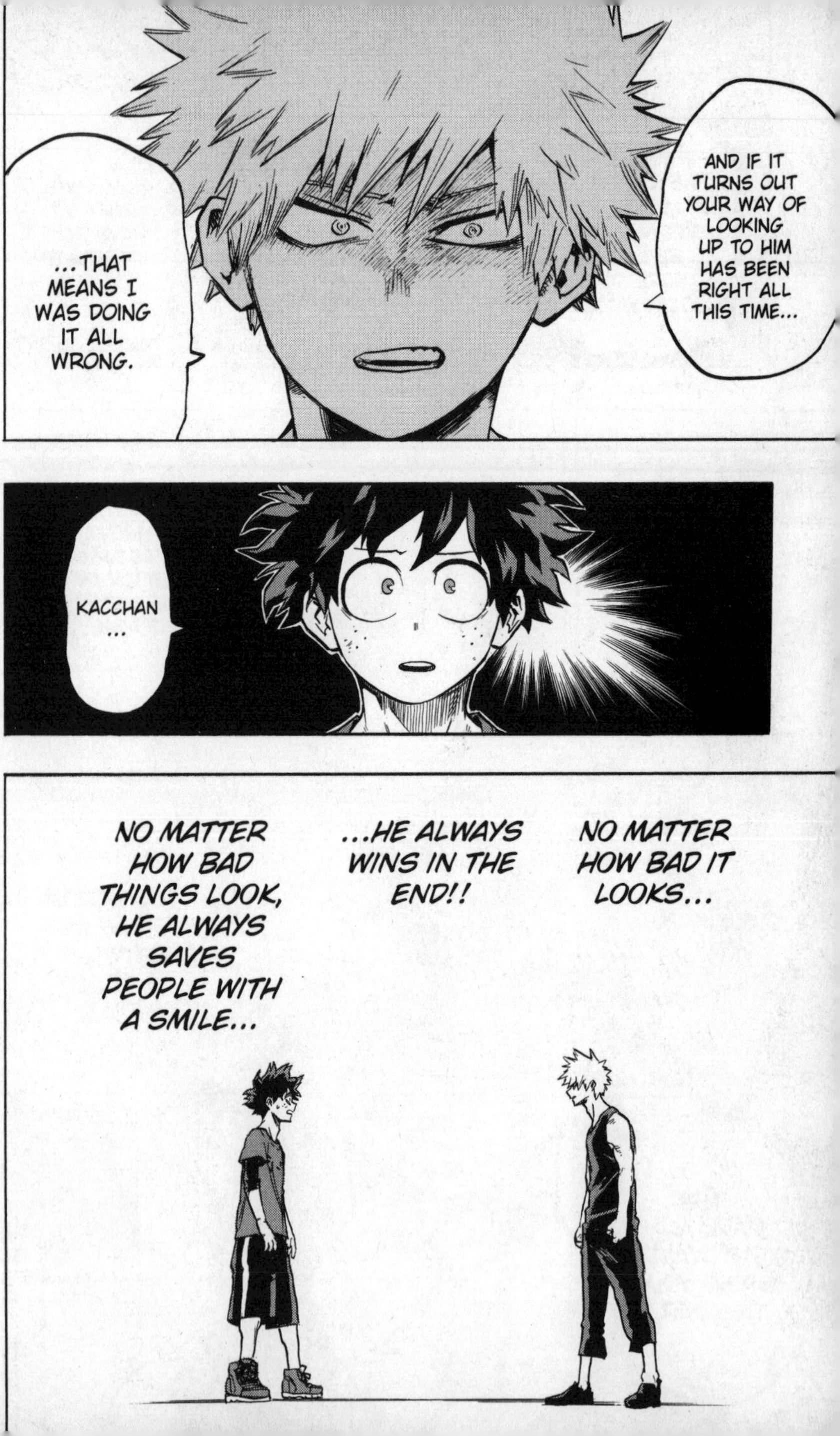
AND IF IT TURNS OUT YOUR WAY OF LOOKING UP TO HIM HAS BEEN RIGHT ALL THIS TIME...
...THAT MEANS I WAS DOING IT ALL WRONG.
KACCHAN ...
NO MATTER HOW BAD IT LOOKS...
...HE ALWAYS WINS IN THE END!!
NO MATTER HOW BAD THINGS LOOK, HE ALWAYS SAVES PEOPLE WITH A SMILE...

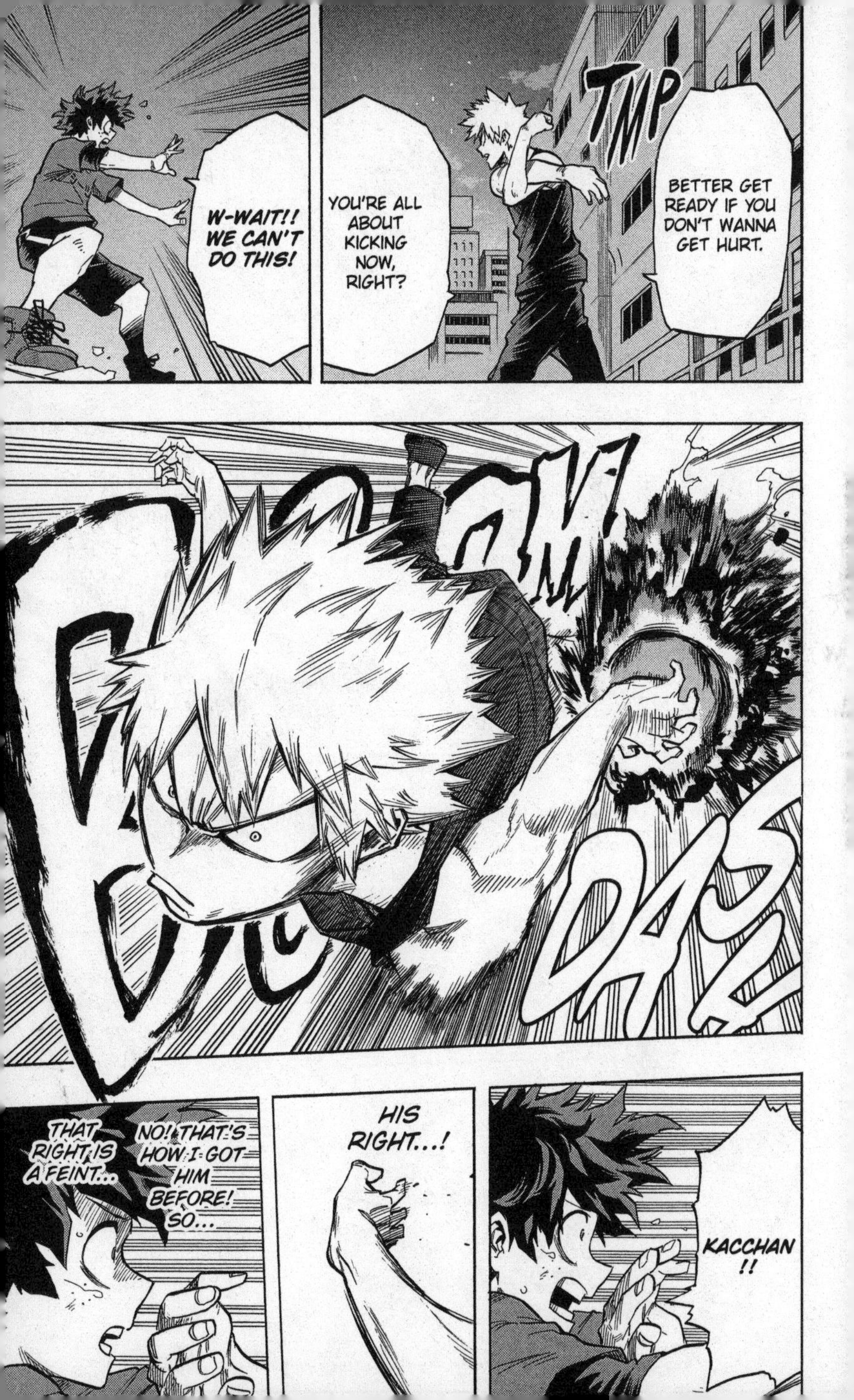
TMP
BETTER GET READY IF YOU DON'T WANNA GET HURT.
YOU'RE ALL ABOUT KICKING NOW, RIGHT?
W-WAIT!! WE CAN'T DO THIS!
KACCHAN!!
HIS RIGHT...!
THAT RIGHT IS A FEINT...
NO! THAT'S HOW I GOT HIM BEFORE! SO...

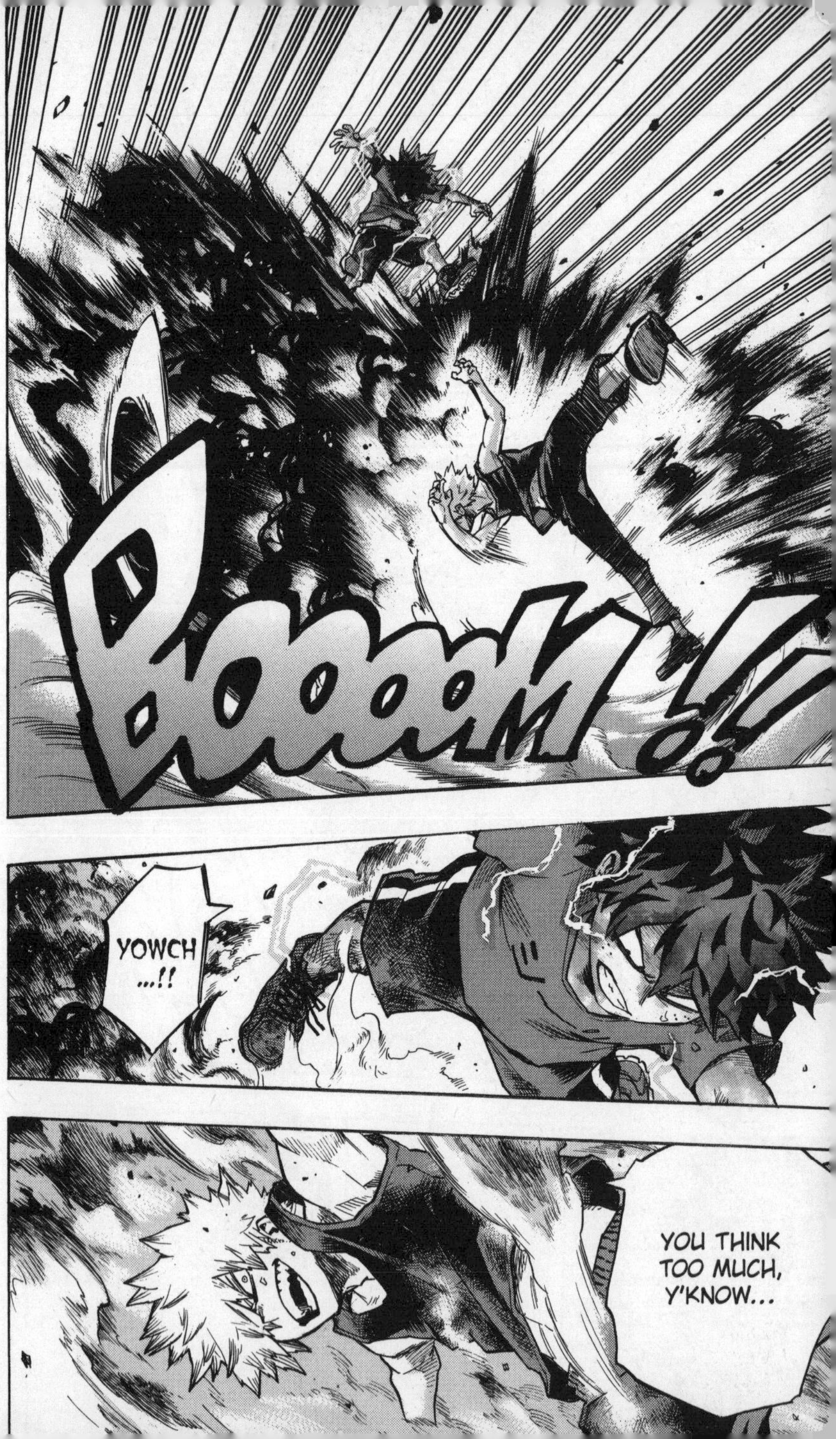
BOOOOOM!!
YOWCH ...!!
YOU THINK TOO MUCH, Y'KNOW...

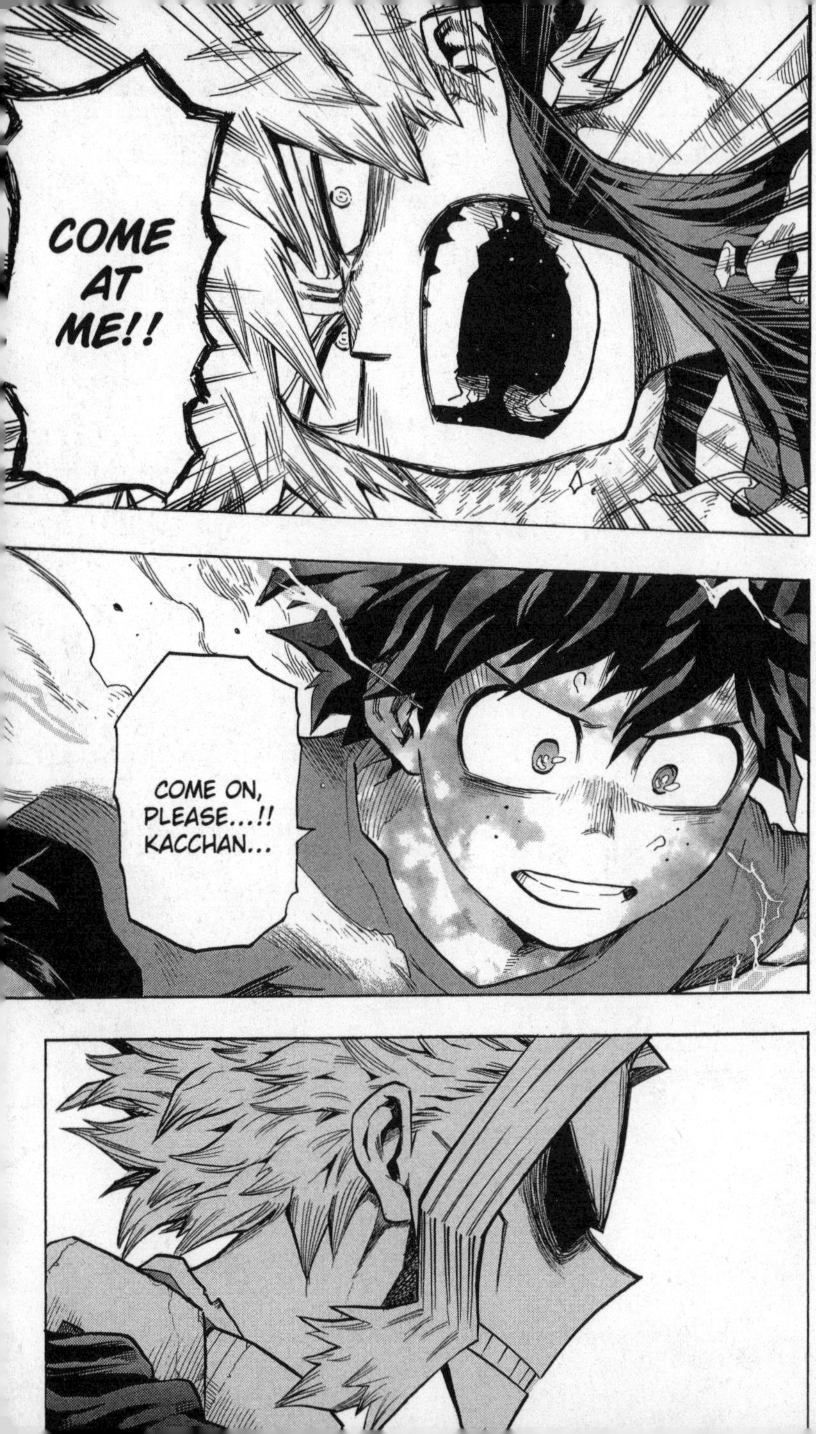
COME AT ME!!
COME ON, PLEASE...!! KACCHAN...

THE "ONLY ONE" PRINCIPLE

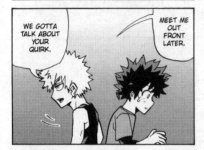

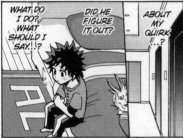

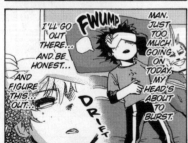

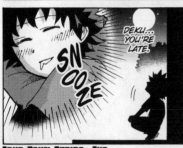

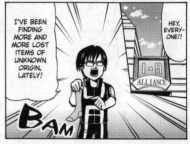

HEY, EVERYONE!!
I'VE BEEN FINDING MORE AND MORE LOST ITEMS OF UNKNOWN ORIGIN, LATELY!
1-A
ALLIANCE
BAM
LET'S WRITE OUR NAMES ON OUR PERSONAL BELONGINGS SO THEY CAN BE RETURNED TO THEIR OWNERS!!
OKAAAAAY!
RUB RUB
IDA
IDA...
NO NEED, SERIOUSLY. WE ALL KNOW THOSE ARE YOURS...

KACCHAN'S MELACHOLY

MEET ME OUT FRONT LATER.
WE GOTTA TALK ABOUT YOUR QUIRK.
ABOUT MY QUIRK...?
DID HE FIGURE IT OUT?
WHAT DO I DO? WHAT SHOULD I SAY!!?
AL
MAN. JUST TOO MUCH GOING ON TODAY. MY HEAD'S ABOUT TO BURST.
FWUMP
I'LL GO OUT THERE... AND BE HONEST... AND FIGURE THIS... OUT...
DRIFT
DEKU... YOU'RE LATE.
SNOOZE

FOUR-PANEL STRIPS - END

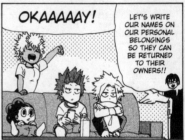

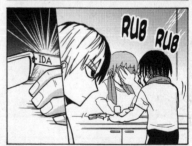

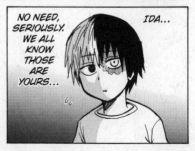

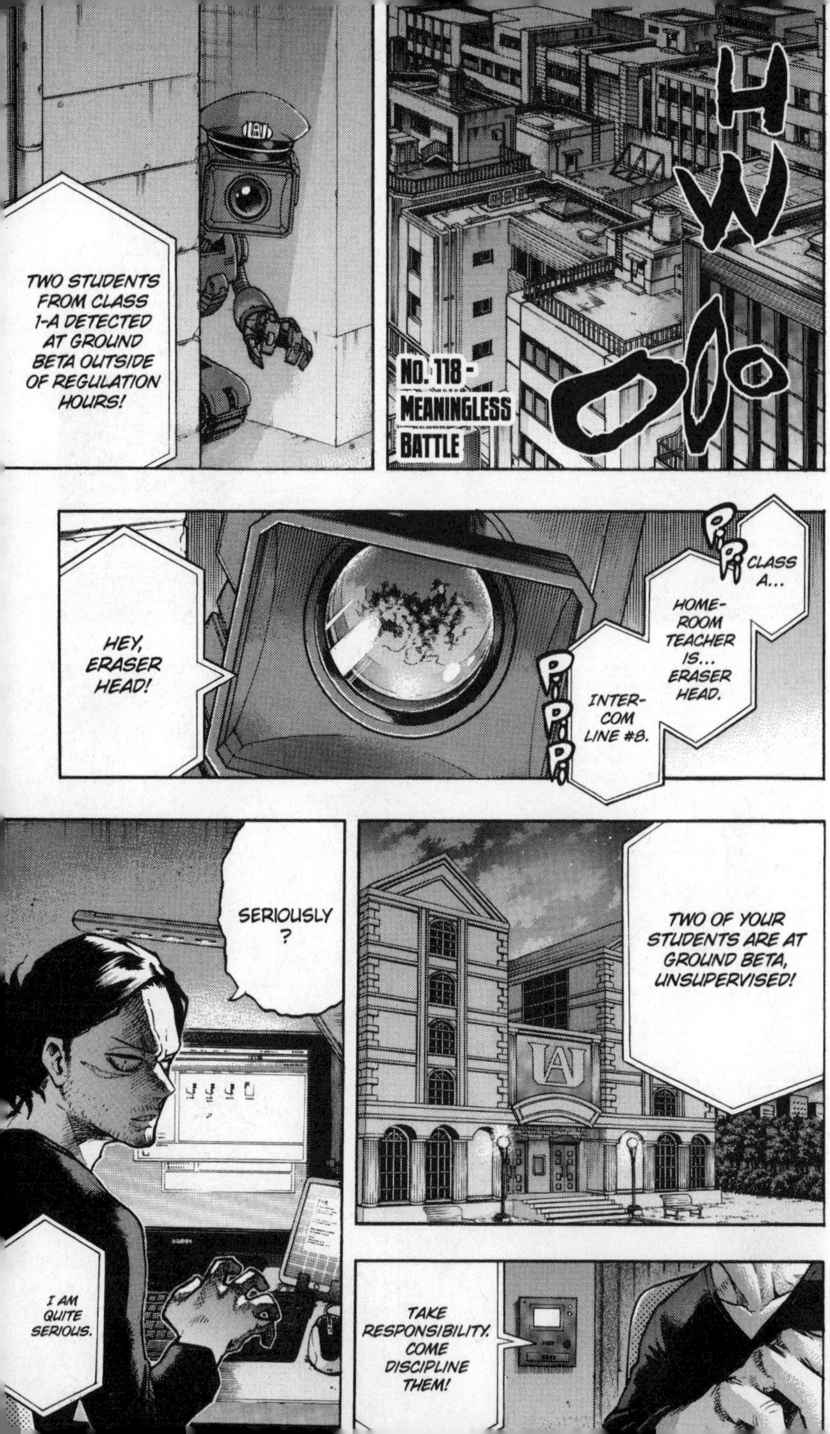
HWOO
No. 118 - Meaningless Battle
TWO STUDENTS FROM CLASS 1-A DETECTED AT GROUND BETA OUTSIDE OF REGULATION HOURS!
PIPI
CLASS A...
HOME-ROOM TEACHER IS... ERASER HEAD.
PIPIPI
INTER-COM LINE #8.
HEY, ERASER HEAD!
TWO OF YOUR STUDENTS ARE AT GROUND BETA, UNSUPERVISED!
TAKE RESPONSIBILITY. COME DISCIPLINE THEM!
SERIOUSLY?
I AM QUITE SERIOUS.

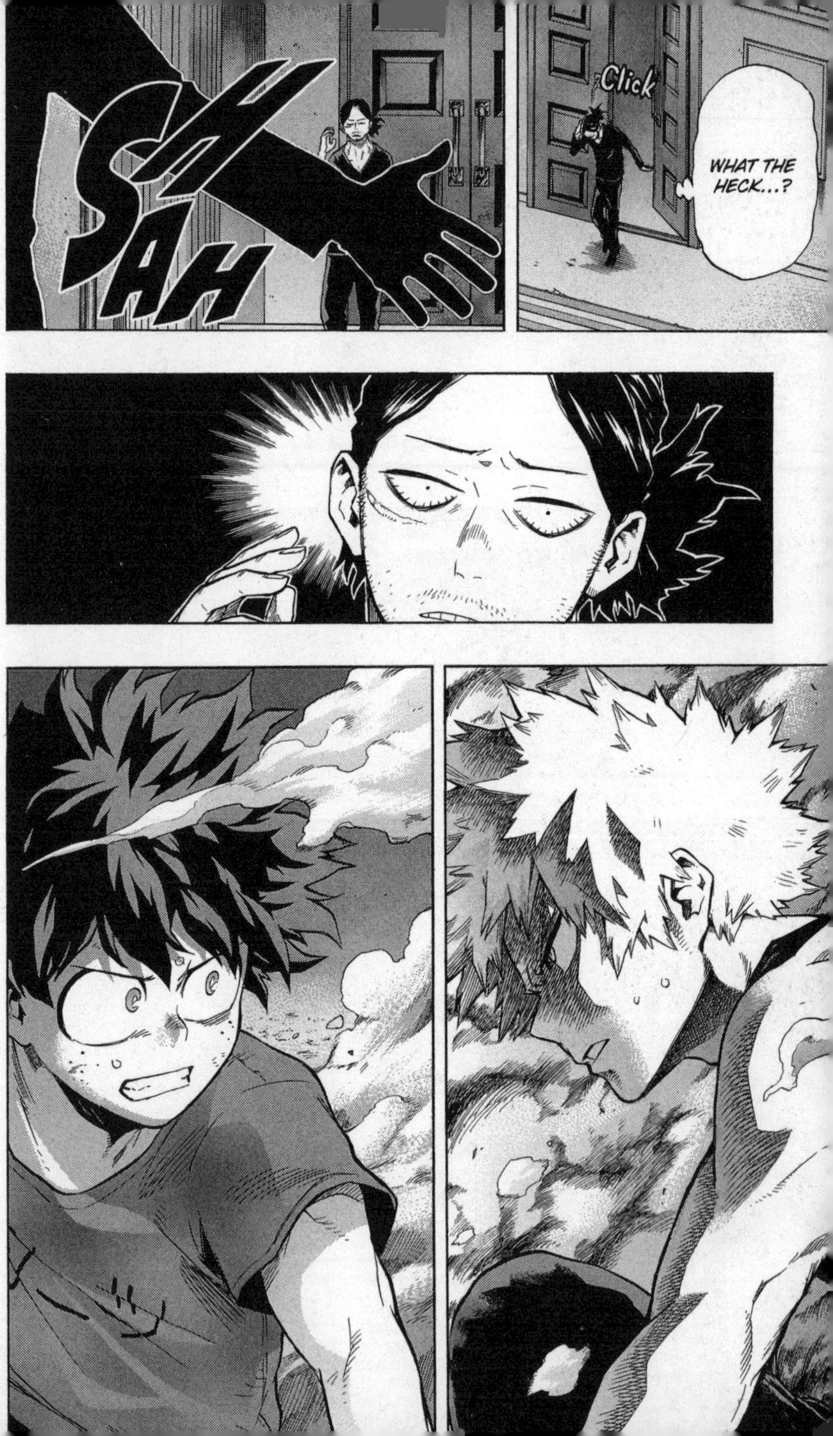
Click
WHAT THE HECK...?
SHAH

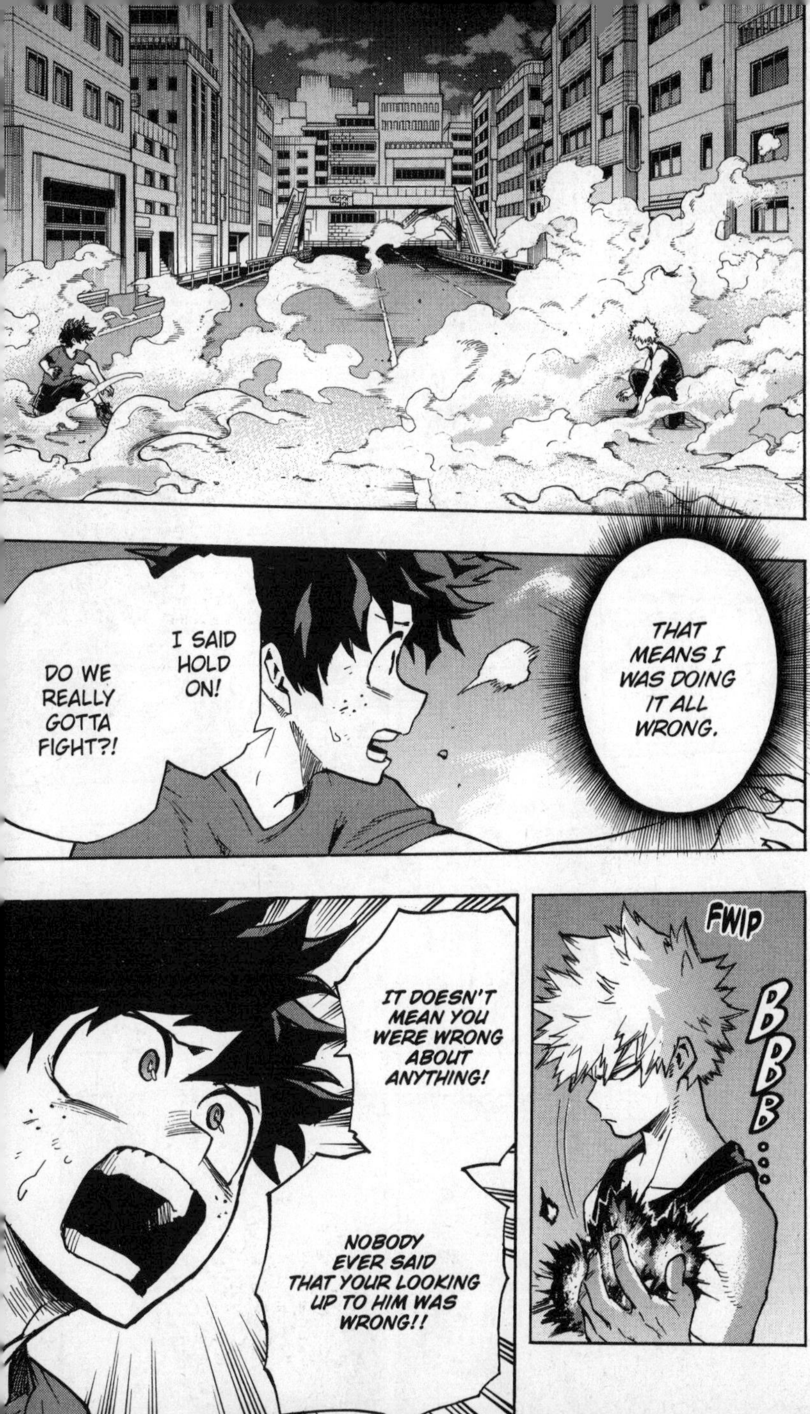
THAT MEANS I WAS DOING IT ALL WRONG.
I SAID HOLD ON!
DO WE REALLY GOTTA FIGHT?!
FWIP
BBB...
IT DOESN'T MEAN YOU WERE WRONG ABOUT ANYTHING!
NOBODY EVER SAID THAT YOUR LOOKING UP TO HIM WAS WRONG!!

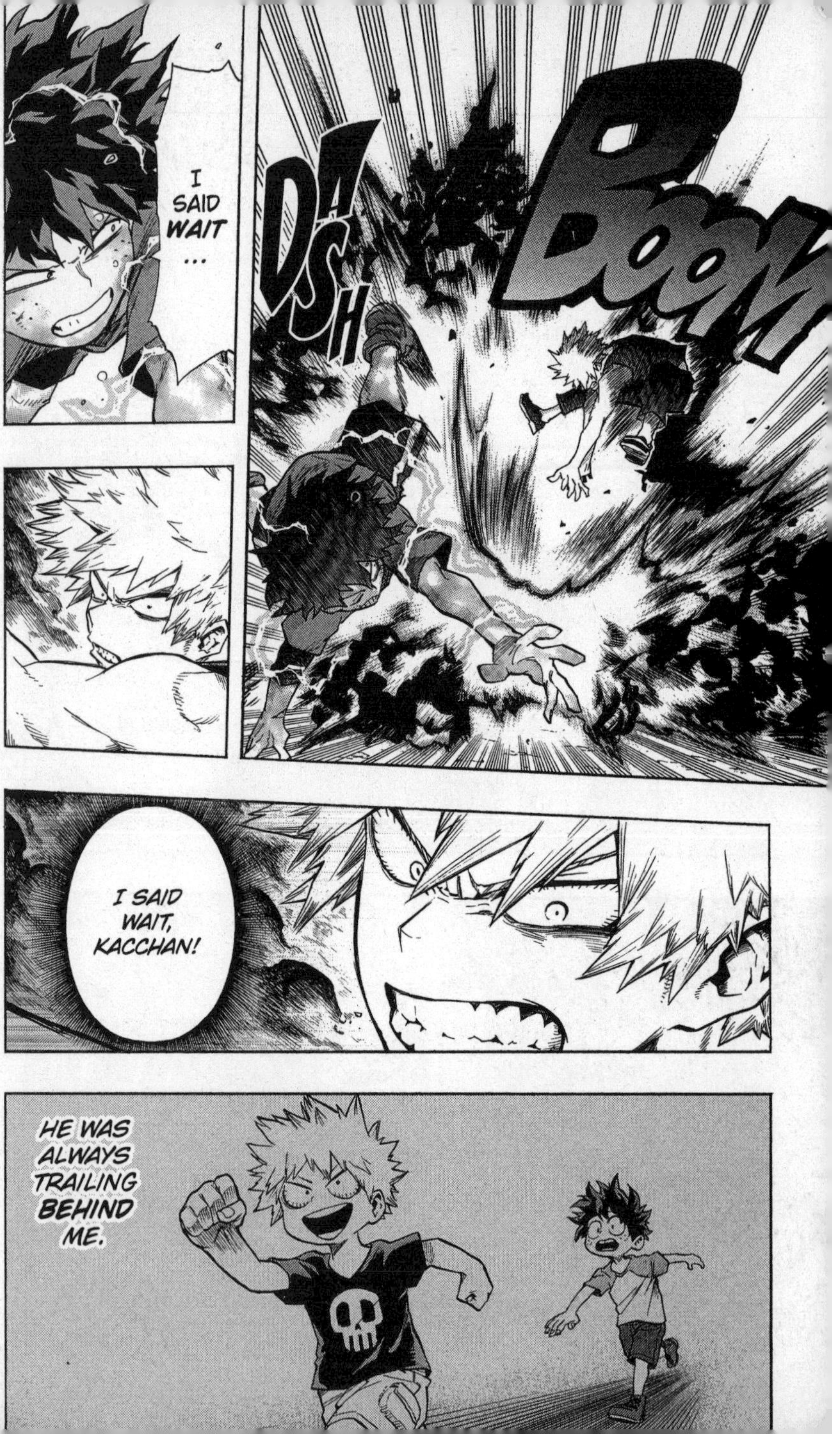
BOOM
DASH
I SAID WAIT ...
I SAID WAIT, KACCHAN!
HE WAS ALWAYS TRAILING BEHIND ME.

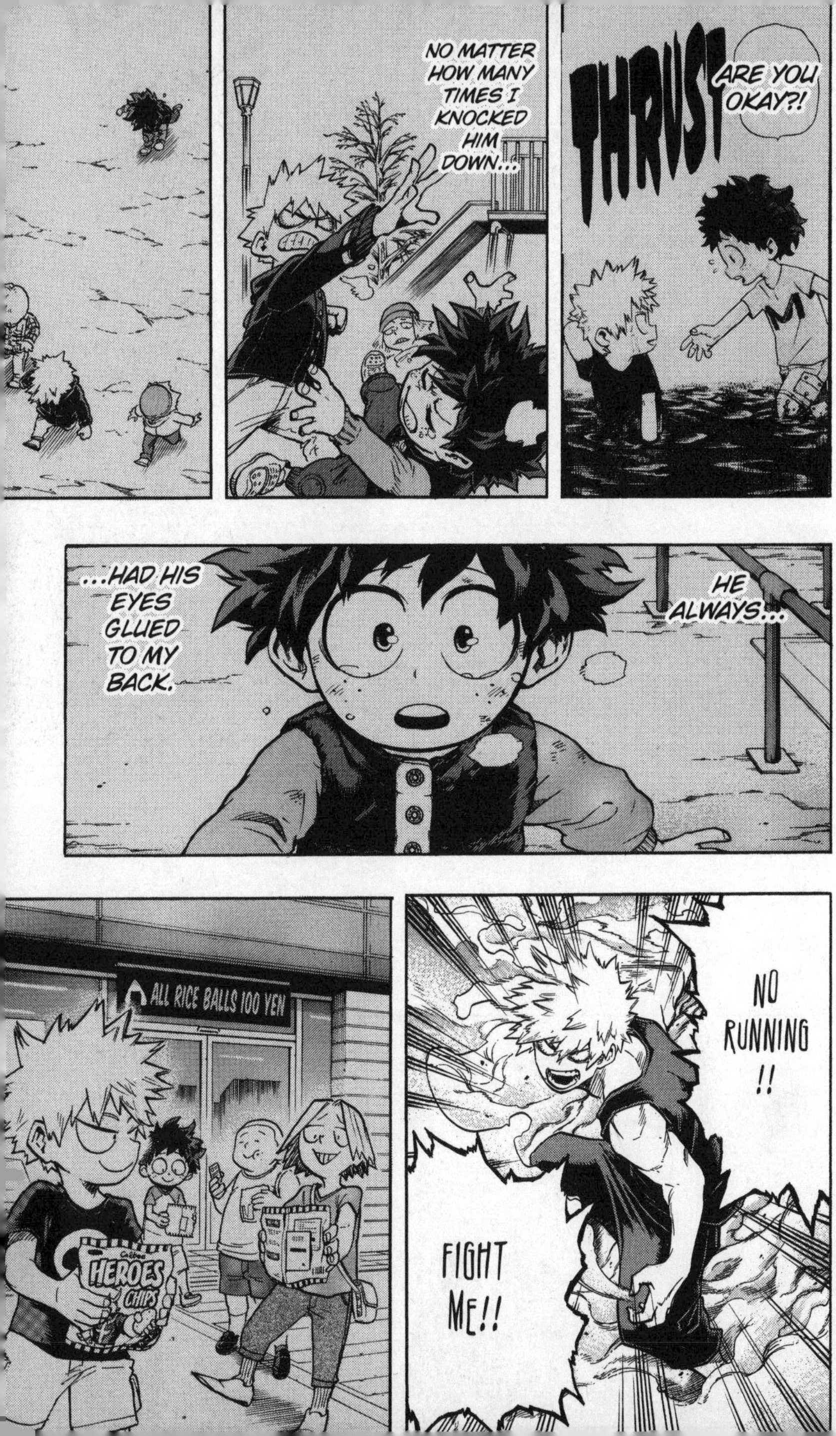
THRUST
ARE YOU OKAY?!
NO MATTER HOW MANY TIMES I KNOCKED HIM DOWN...
HE ALWAYS...
...HAD HIS EYES GLUED TO MY BACK.
NO RUNNING!!
FIGHT ME!!
ALL RICE BALLS 100 YEN
HEROES CHIPS

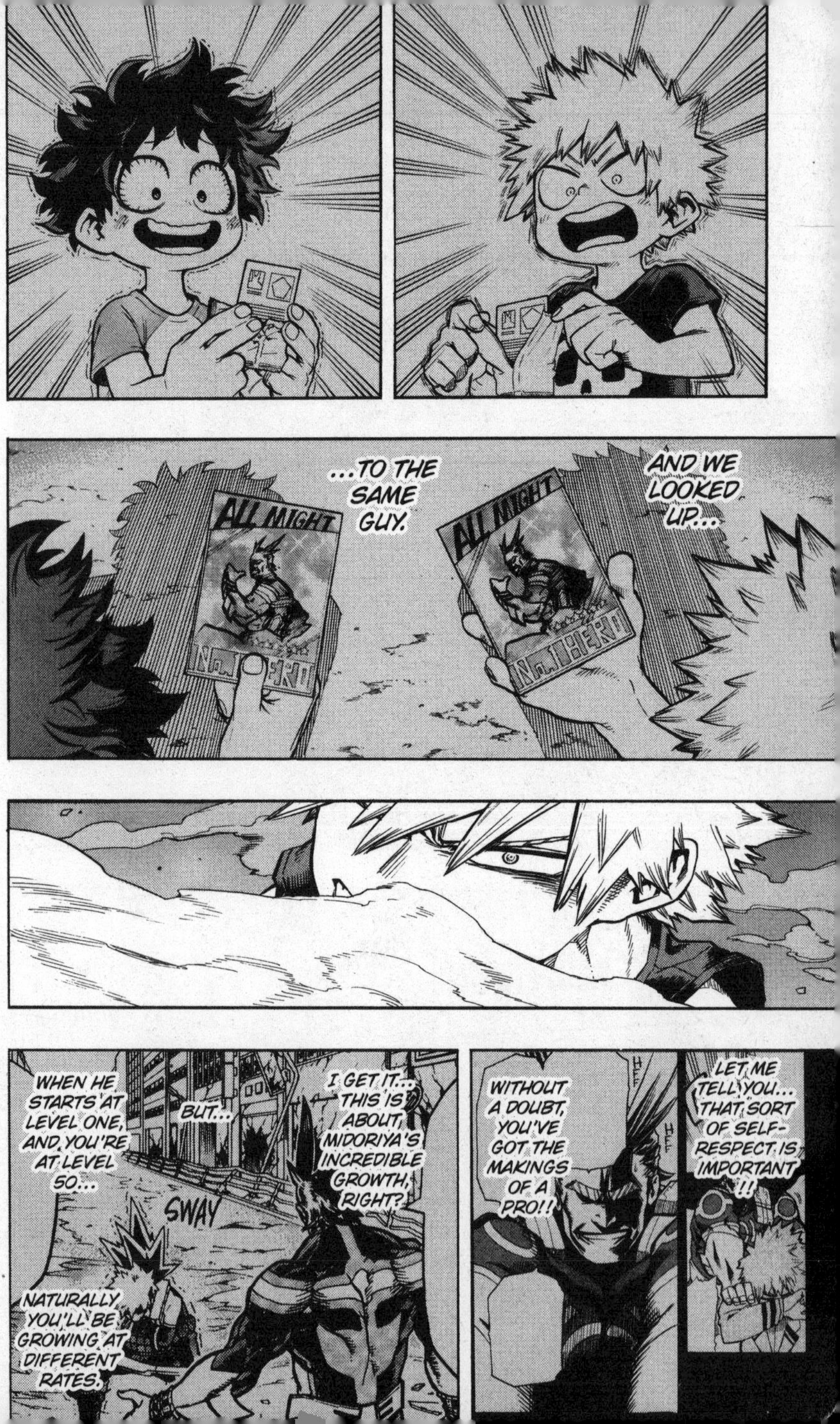
AND WE LOOKED UP...
...TO THE SAME GUY.
LET ME TELL YOU... THAT SORT OF SELF-RESPECT IS IMPORTANT!!
WITHOUT A DOUBT, YOU'VE GOT THE MAKINGS OF A PRO!!
I GET IT... THIS IS ABOUT MIDORIYA'S INCREDIBLE GROWTH, RIGHT?
BUT...
WHEN HE STARTS AT LEVEL ONE, AND YOU'RE AT LEVEL 50...
SWAY
NATURALLY YOU'LL BE GROWING AT DIFFERENT RATES.

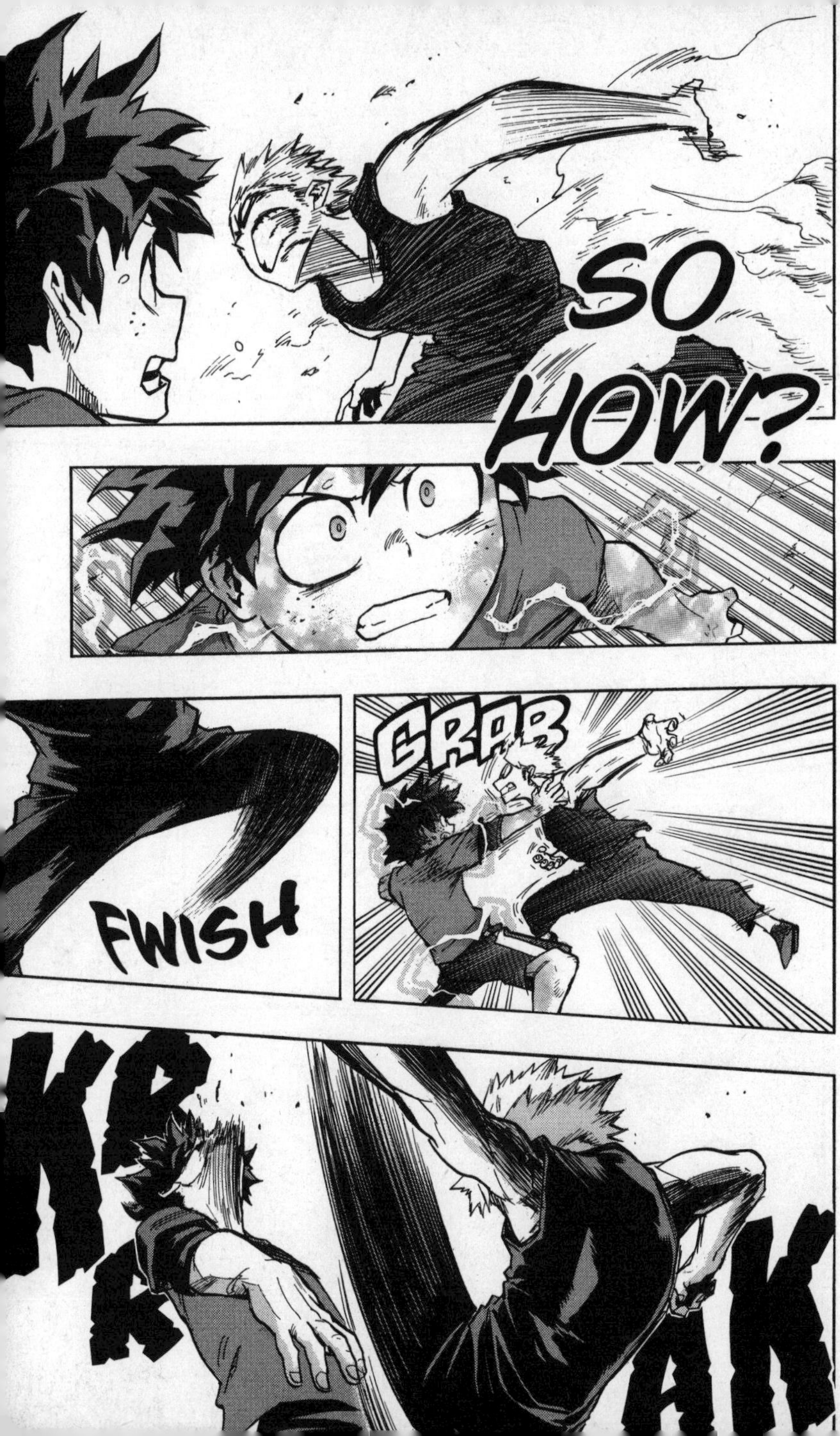
SO HOW?
GRAB
FWISH
KRRAK

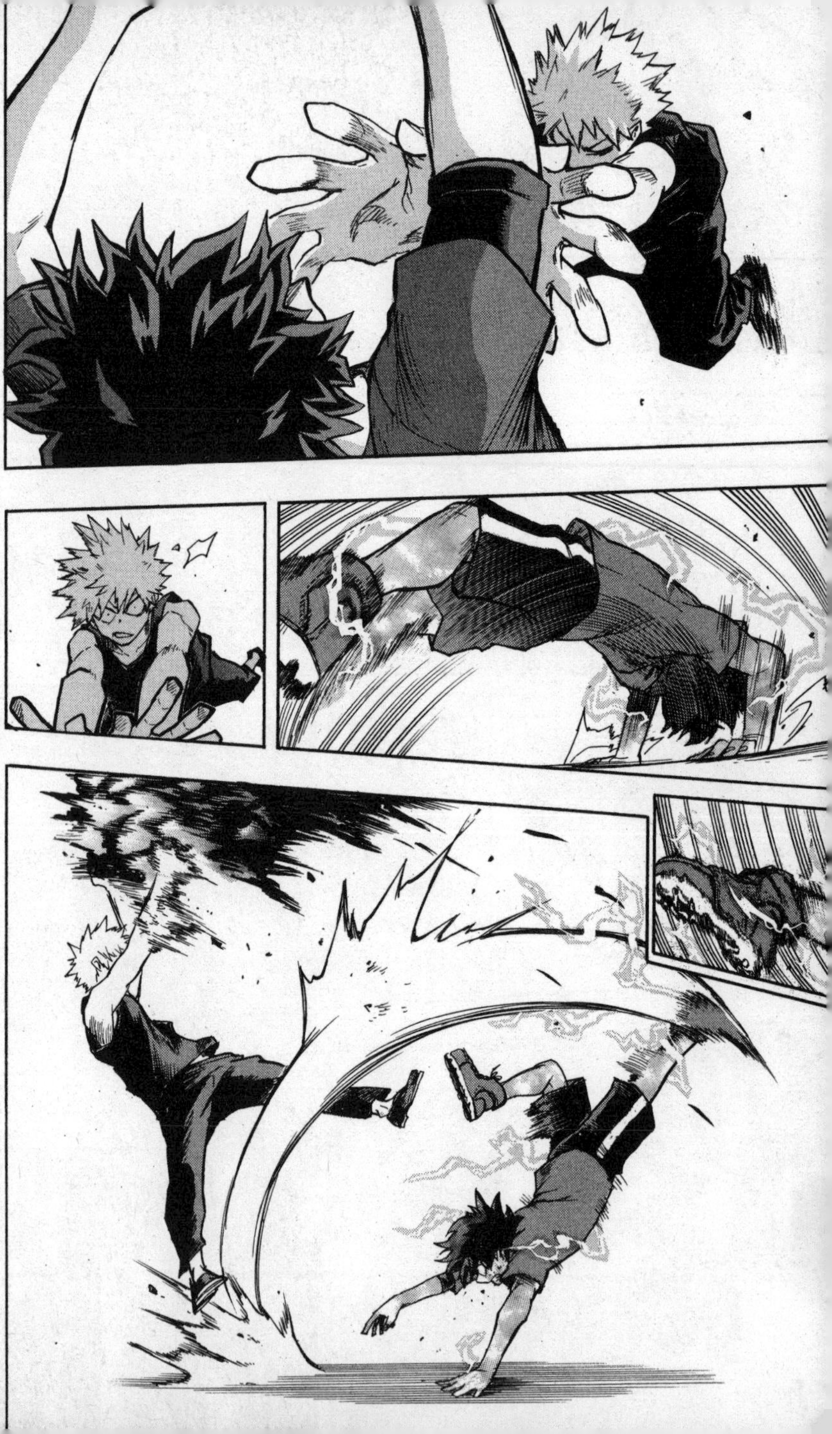

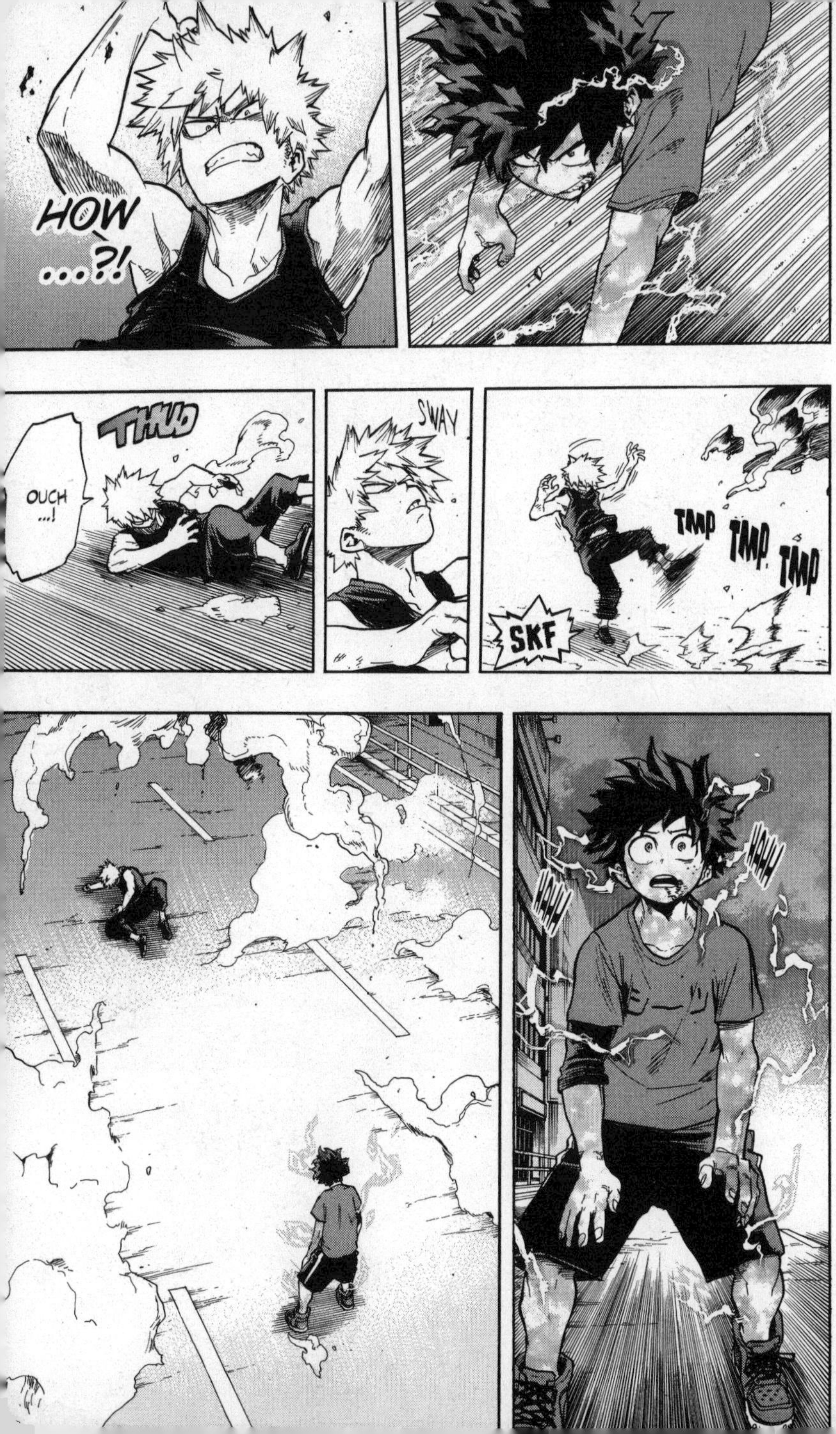
HOW ...?!
TMP TMP TMP
SKF
SWAY
THUD
OUCH ...!
HAH
HAH

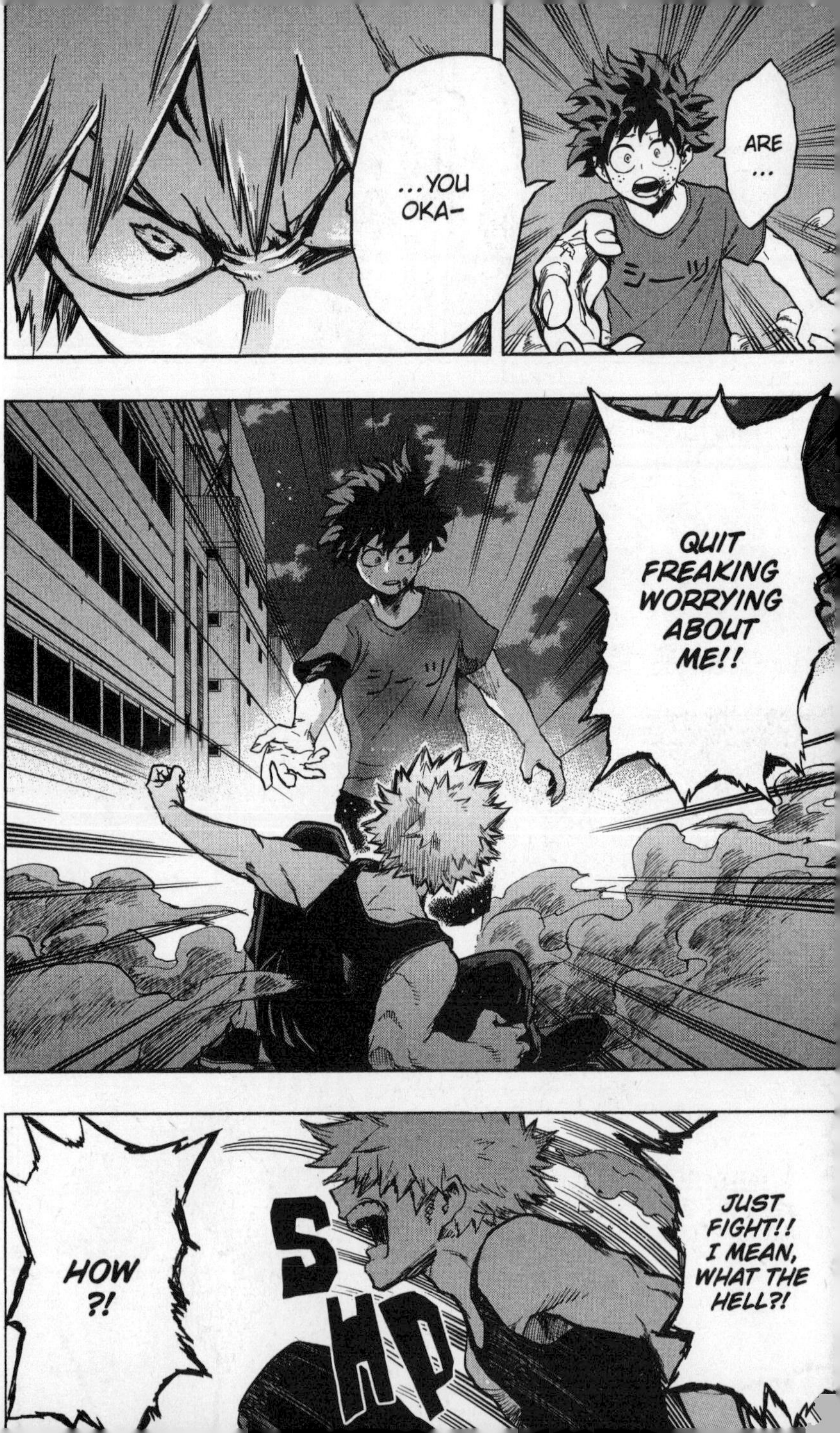
ARE ...
...YOU OKA-
QUIT FREAKING WORRYING ABOUT ME!!
JUST FIGHT!! I MEAN, WHAT THE HELL?!
SHP
HOW ?!

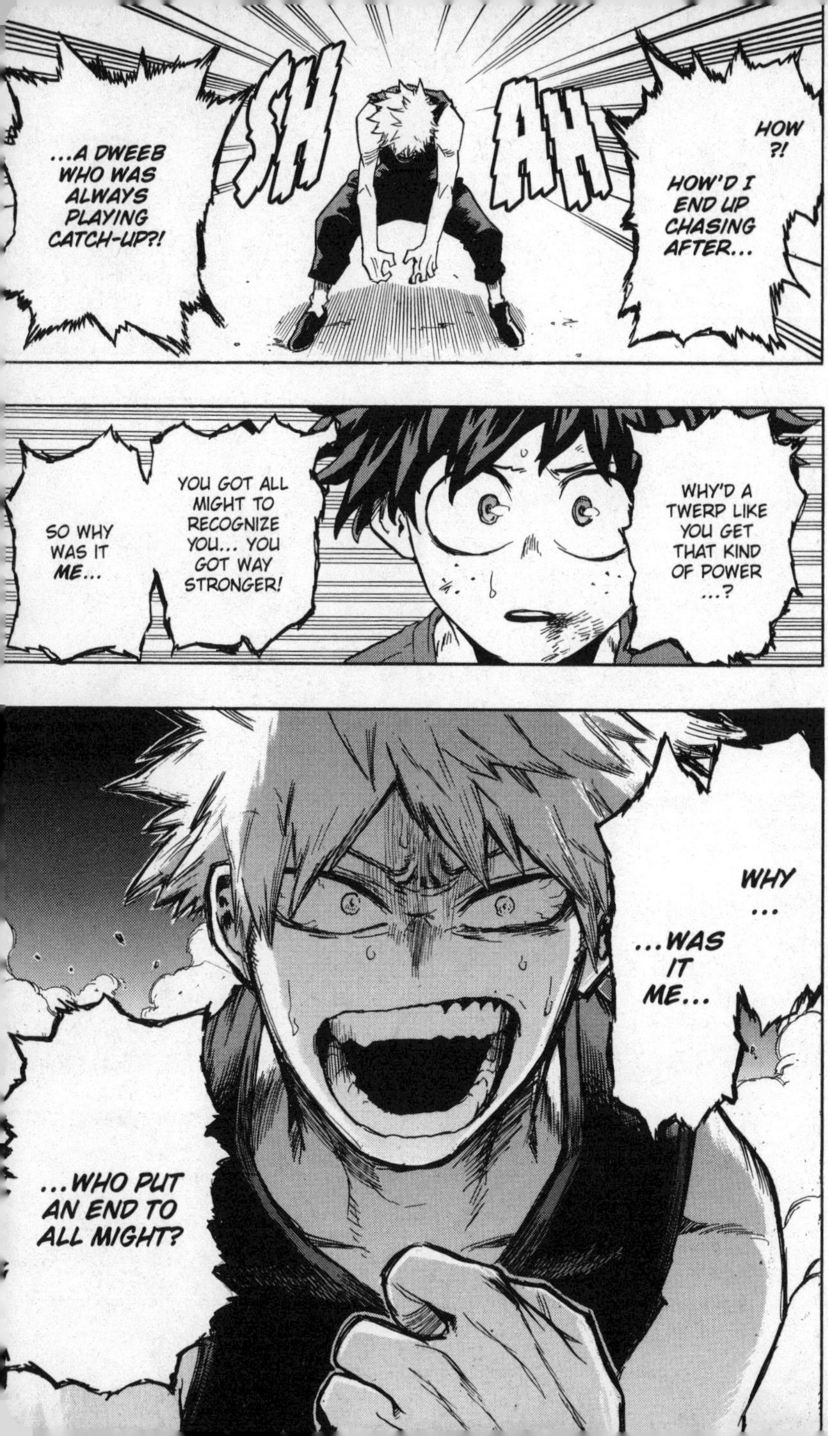
HOW ?! HOW'D I END UP CHASING AFTER...
SH AH
...A DWEEB WHO WAS ALWAYS PLAYING CATCH-UP?!
WHY'D A TWERP LIKE YOU GET THAT KIND OF POWER ...?
YOU GOT ALL MIGHT TO RECOGNIZE YOU... YOU GOT WAY STRONGER!
SO WHY WAS IT *ME*...
WHY ...
...WAS IT ME...
...WHO PUT AN END TO ALL MIGHT?

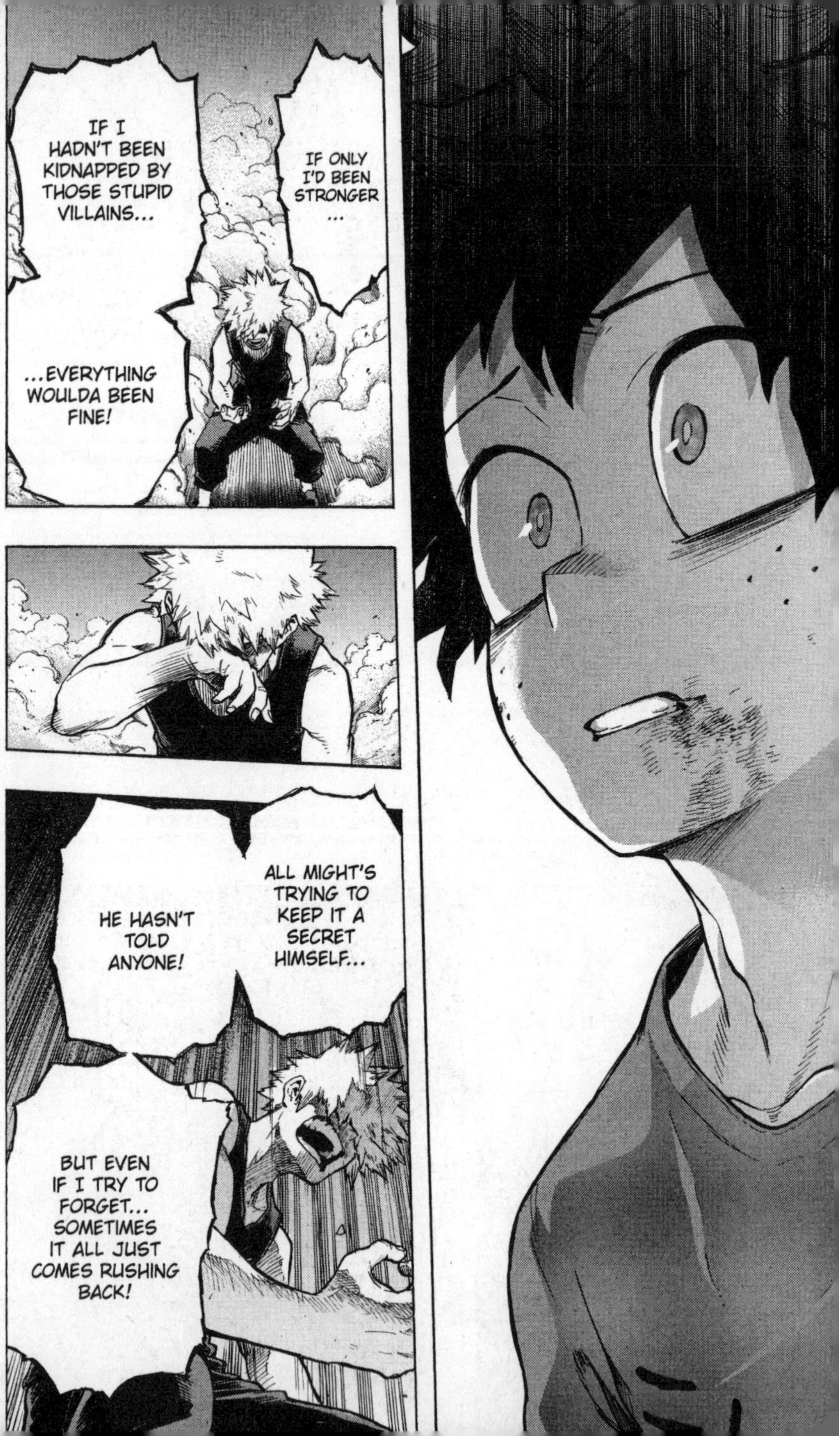
IF ONLY I'D BEEN STRONGER ...
IF I HADN'T BEEN KIDNAPPED BY THOSE STUPID VILLAINS...
...EVERYTHING WOULDA BEEN FINE!
ALL MIGHT'S TRYING TO KEEP IT A SECRET HIMSELF...
HE HASN'T TOLD ANYONE!
BUT EVEN IF I TRY TO FORGET... SOMETIMES IT ALL JUST COMES RUSHING BACK!

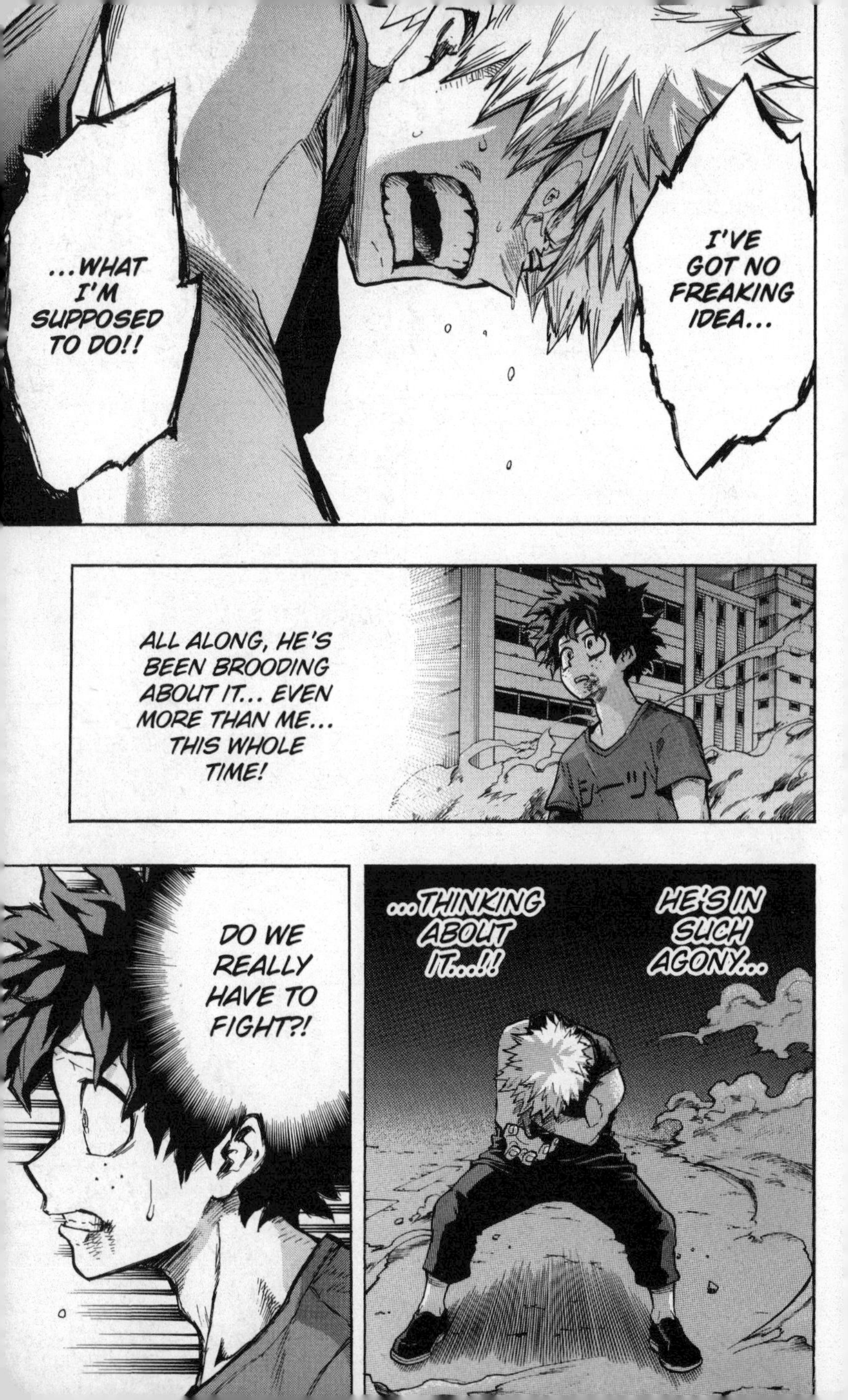
I'VE GOT NO FREAKING IDEA...
...WHAT I'M SUPPOSED TO DO!!
ALL ALONG, HE'S BEEN BROODING ABOUT IT... EVEN MORE THAN ME... THIS WHOLE TIME!
HE'S IN SUCH AGONY...
...THINKING ABOUT IT...!!
DO WE REALLY HAVE TO FIGHT?!

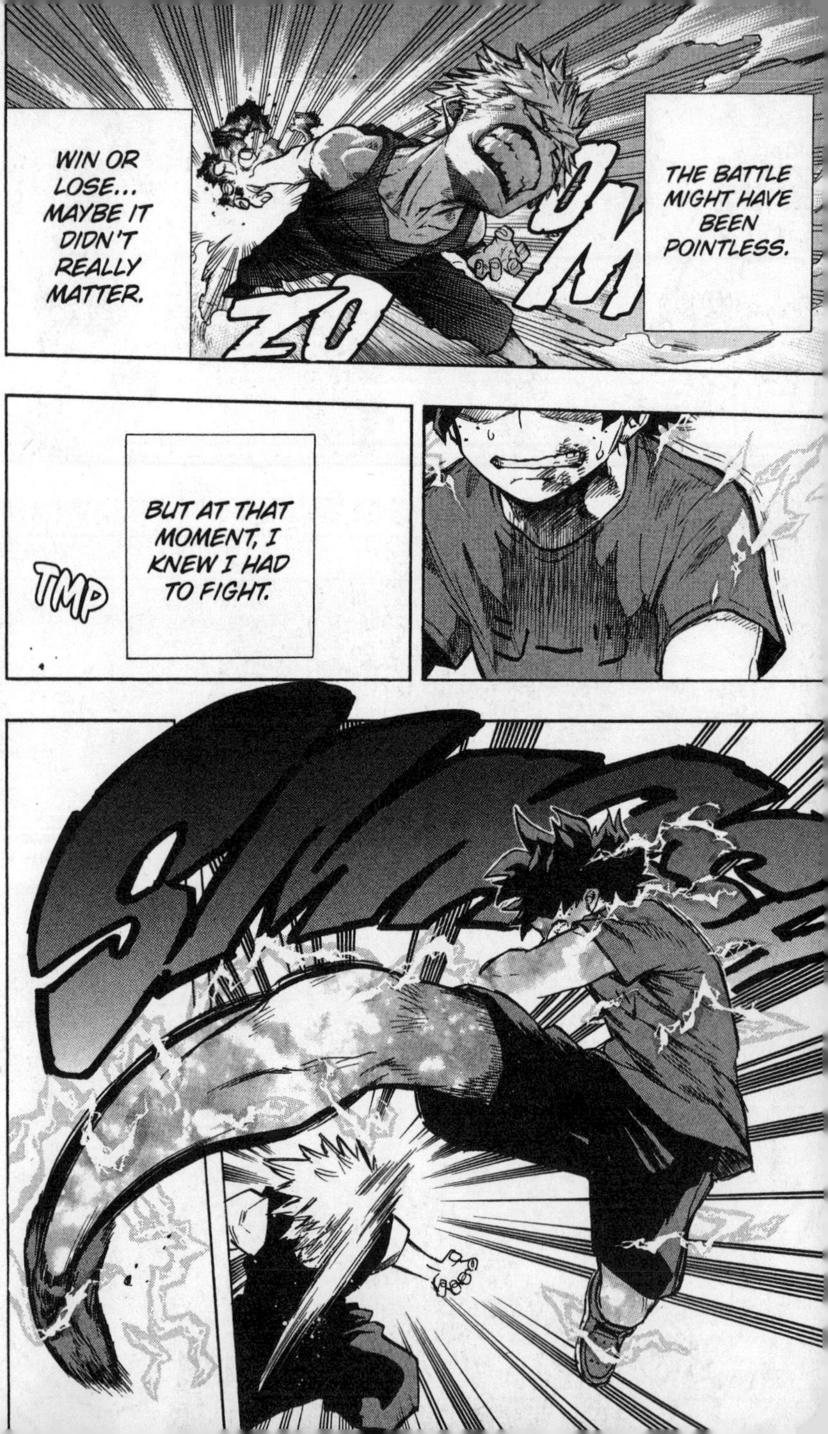
THE BATTLE MIGHT HAVE BEEN POINTLESS.
WIN OR LOSE... MAYBE IT DIDN'T REALLY MATTER.
ZOOM
BUT AT THAT MOMENT, I KNEW I HAD TO FIGHT.
TMP

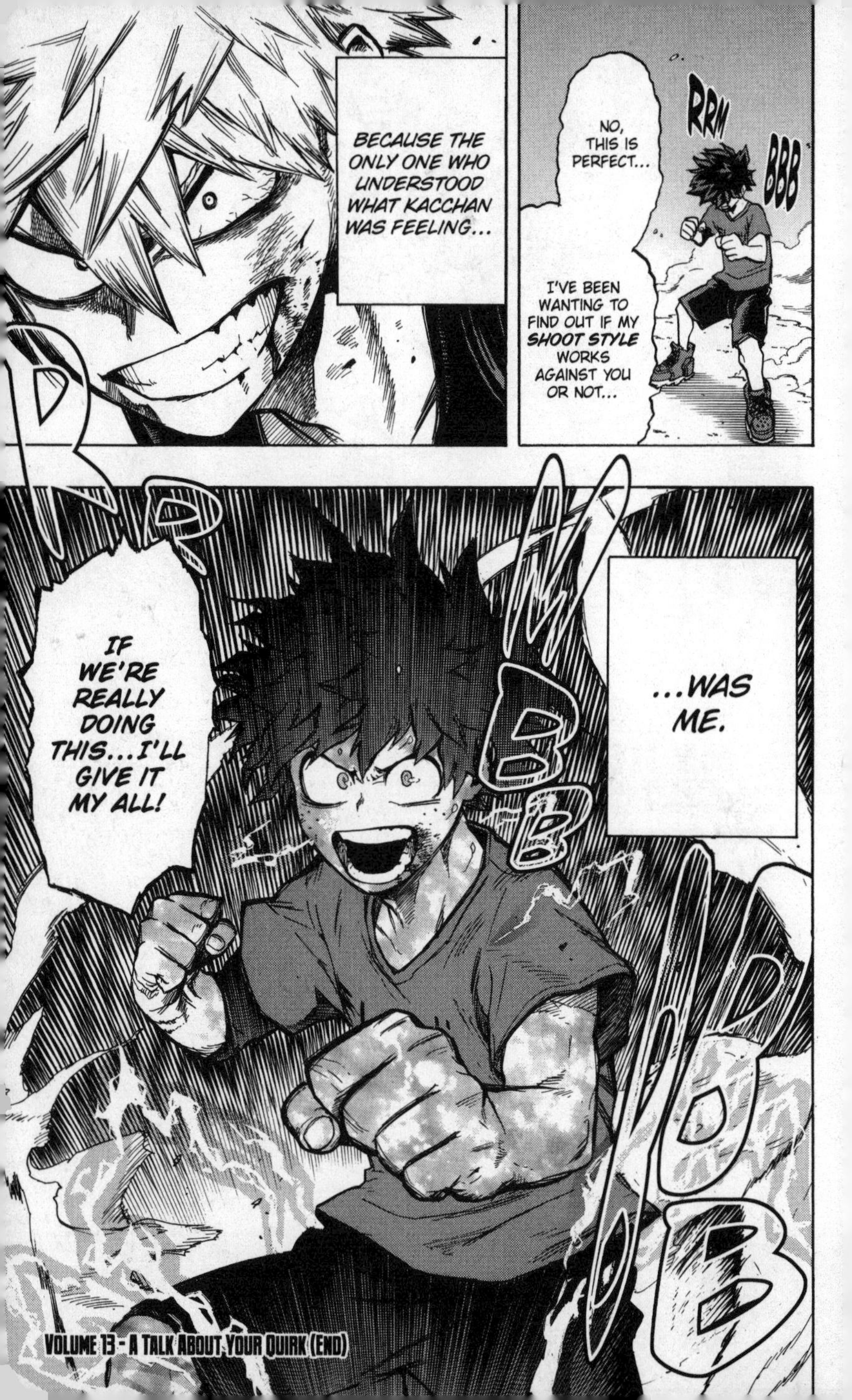
NO, THIS IS PERFECT...
RRM BBB
I'VE BEEN WANTING TO FIND OUT IF MY SHOOT STYLE WORKS AGAINST YOU OR NOT...
BECAUSE THE ONLY ONE WHO UNDERSTOOD WHAT KACCHAN WAS FEELING...
...WAS ME.
IF WE'RE REALLY DOING THIS...I'LL GIVE IT MY ALL!

VOLUME 13 - A TALK ABOUT YOUR QUIRK (END)

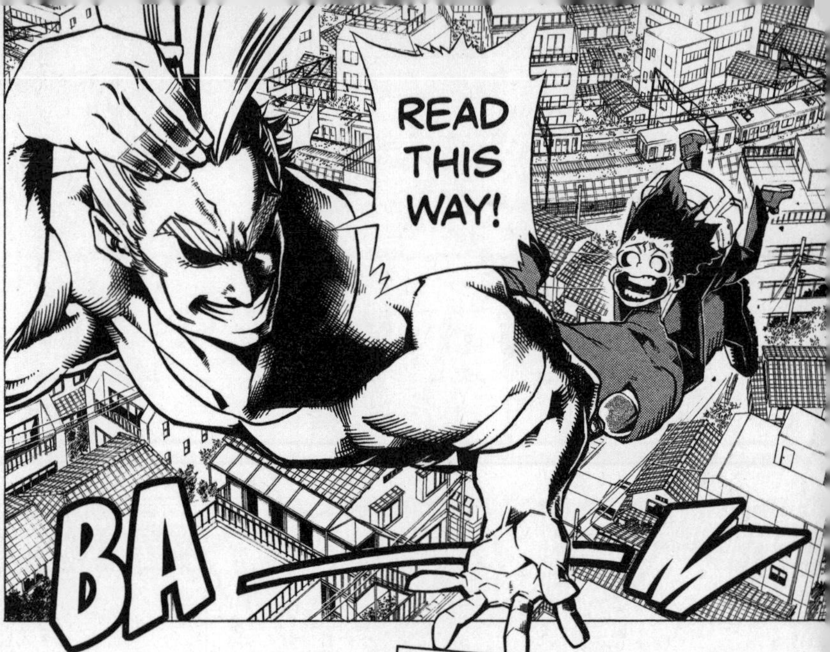
READ THIS WAY!
BA-M

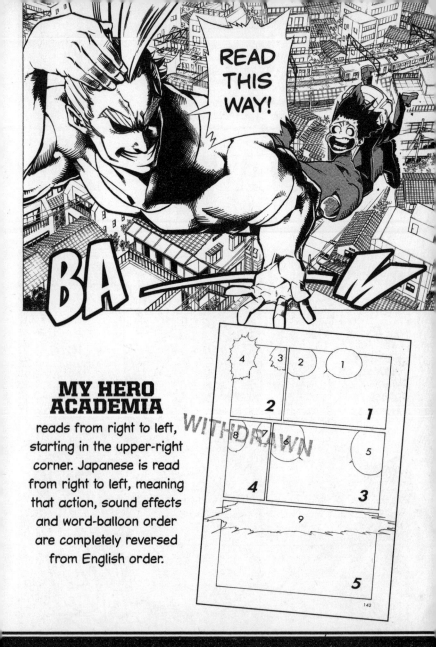

MY HERO ACADEMIA

reads from right to left, starting in the upper-right corner. Japanese is read from right to left, meaning that action, sound effects and word-balloon order are completely reversed from English order.

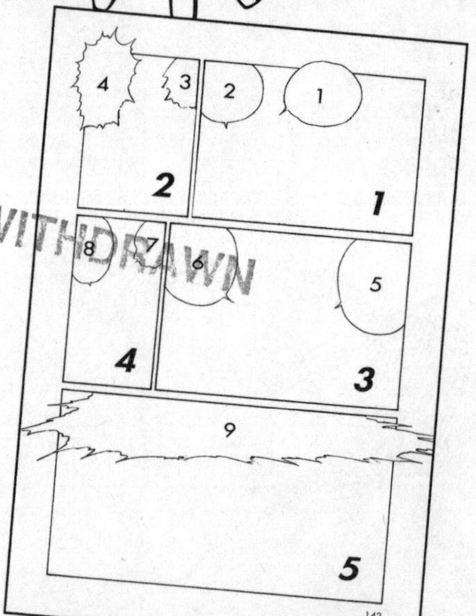